WANTED™

Wesley Gibson leads the life of quiet desperation. His dead-end job numbs him, his girlfriend cheats on him and his hypochondria convinces him he has every disease from cancer to the common cold. His world is the depth of dismay.

But there is another world, one buried just inches below what Wesley thinks is his life. What happens when the scales fall from your eyes and the real clockwork of the world is laid bare? What happens when you're Wesley Gibson, one minute the most downtrodden wretch the world has ever seen, and the next... you're Wanted?

WANTED created by **Mark Millar and J.G. Jones**

WANTED issues #1-#6
Written by **Mark Millar**
Pencils and Inks by **J.G. Jones**
Colors by **Bongotone's Paul Mounts**
Flashback sequences pgs. 6-10 of **WANTED #6** Penciled and Inked by **Dick Giordano**
For the original editions: **WANTED issues #1-6** lettering by
Dreamer Design's Robin Spehar, Dennis Heisler and Mark Roslan

For this edition
    Book Design by **Jason Medley**
    Cover Art by **J. G. Jones**

ISBN: 9781845769086
Published by Titan Books, a division of Titan Publishing Group Ltd., 144 Southwark Street, London SE1 0UP. Originally published as WANTED issues #1-6 and WANTED: Dossier. WANTED is ™
and © 2008 Mark Millar and J.G. Jones. "WANTED", its logos, all related characters and their likenesses are registered trademarks of Mark Millar and J.G. Jones. The entire contents of this
book are © 2008 Top Cow Productions, Inc. The characters, events and stories in this publication are entirely fictional. With the exception of art used for review purposes, none of the contents
of this book may be reprinted in any form without the express written consent of the license holder. A CIP catalogue record for this book is available from the British Library.
Printed in Italy. First printing: May 2008.
10 9 8 7 6 5 4 3 2 1

Special Thanks to Wizard for permission to reprint Materials from the **WANTED #1 Wizard Ace Edition**™ variant.

What did you think of this book? We love to hear from our readers. Please e-mail us at: **readerfeedback@titanemail.com**

for **Top Cow Productions, Inc.:**
Marc Silvestri_Chief Executive Officer
Matt Hawkins_President and Chief Operating Officer
Filip Sablik_Publisher
Rob Levin_Vice President - Editorial
Mel Caylo_Vice President - Marketing and Sales
Chaz Riggs_ Graphic Design
Phil Smith_Managing Editor
Joshua Cozine_Assistant Editor
Alyssa Phung_Controller
Adrian Nicita_Webmaster
Scott Newman_Production Assistant

for Image Comics
Erik Larsen
publisher
Eric Stephenson
creative director

visit us on the web at **www.titanbooks.com**

and for more on Mark Millar go to **www.millarworld.tv**

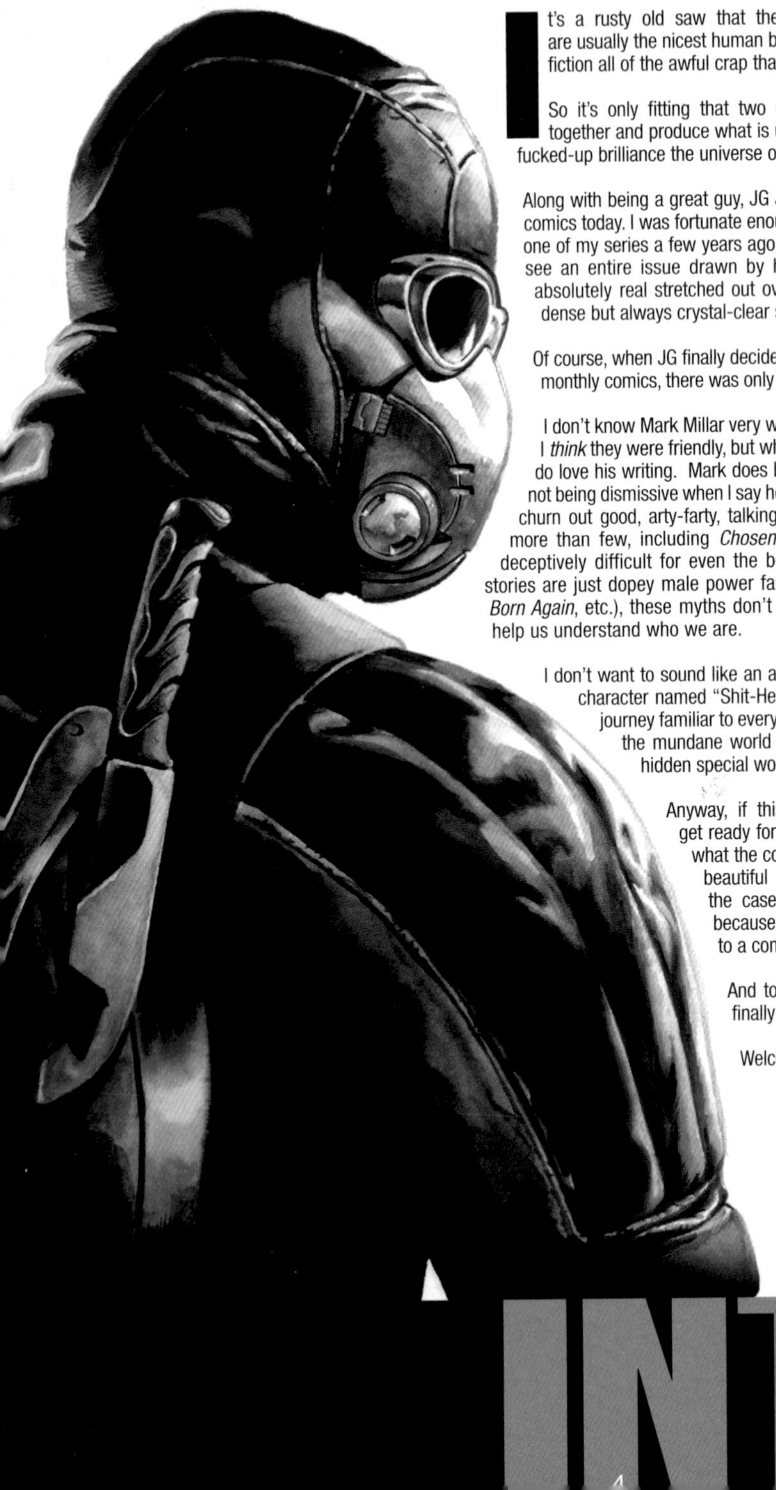

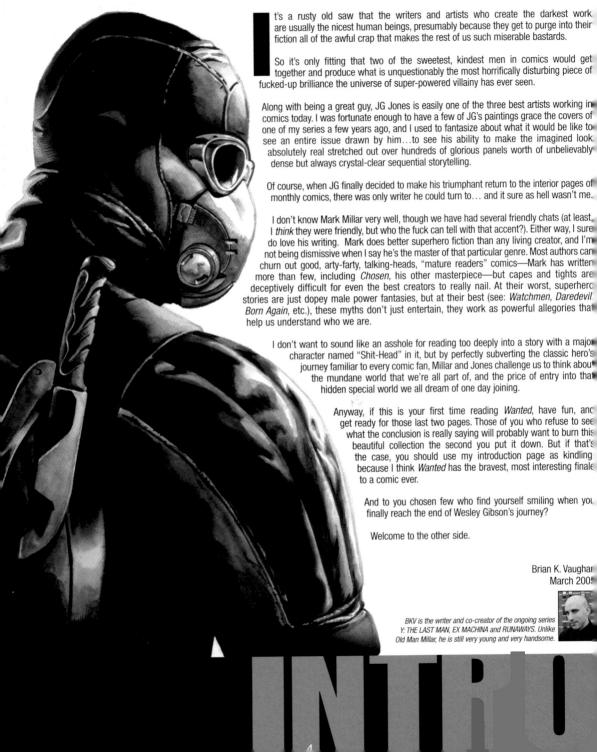

It's a rusty old saw that the writers and artists who create the darkest work are usually the nicest human beings, presumably because they get to purge into their fiction all of the awful crap that makes the rest of us such miserable bastards.

So it's only fitting that two of the sweetest, kindest men in comics would get together and produce what is unquestionably the most horrifically disturbing piece of fucked-up brilliance the universe of super-powered villainy has ever seen.

Along with being a great guy, JG Jones is easily one of the three best artists working in comics today. I was fortunate enough to have a few of JG's paintings grace the covers of one of my series a few years ago, and I used to fantasize about what it would be like to see an entire issue drawn by him...to see his ability to make the imagined look absolutely real stretched out over hundreds of glorious panels worth of unbelievably dense but always crystal-clear sequential storytelling.

Of course, when JG finally decided to make his triumphant return to the interior pages of monthly comics, there was only writer he could turn to... and it sure as hell wasn't me.

I don't know Mark Millar very well, though we have had several friendly chats (at least, I *think* they were friendly, but who the fuck can tell with that accent?). Either way, I sure do love his writing. Mark does better superhero fiction than any living creator, and I'm not being dismissive when I say he's the master of that particular genre. Most authors can churn out good, arty-farty, talking-heads, "mature readers" comics—Mark has written more than few, including *Chosen*, his other masterpiece—but capes and tights are deceptively difficult for even the best creators to really nail. At their worst, superhero stories are just dopey male power fantasies, but at their best (see: *Watchmen, Daredevil: Born Again*, etc.), these myths don't just entertain, they work as powerful allegories that help us understand who we are.

I don't want to sound like an asshole for reading too deeply into a story with a major character named "Shit-Head" in it, but by perfectly subverting the classic hero's journey familiar to every comic fan, Millar and Jones challenge us to think about the mundane world that we're all part of, and the price of entry into that hidden special world we all dream of one day joining.

Anyway, if this is your first time reading *Wanted*, have fun, and get ready for those last two pages. Those of you who refuse to see what the conclusion is really saying will probably want to burn this beautiful collection the second you put it down. But if that's the case, you should use my introduction page as kindling because I think *Wanted* has the bravest, most interesting finale to a comic ever.

And to you chosen few who find yourself smiling when you finally reach the end of Wesley Gibson's journey?

Welcome to the other side.

Brian K. Vaughan
March 2005

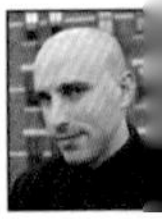

BKV is the writer and co-creator of the ongoing series Y: THE LAST MAN, EX MACHINA and RUNAWAYS. Unlike Old Man Millar, he is still very young and very handsome.

INTRO

THIS IS MY BEST FRIEND HAVING SEX WITH MY GIRLFRIEND OVER AN IKEA TABLE I PICKED UP FOR A REALLY GOOD PRICE.

BRING ON THE BAD GUYS

Written by: Mark Millar

Penciled and Inked by: J.G. Jones

Colored by: Paul Mounts

Lettered by: Dreamer Design's
Robin Spehar
Dennis Heisler
Mark Roslan

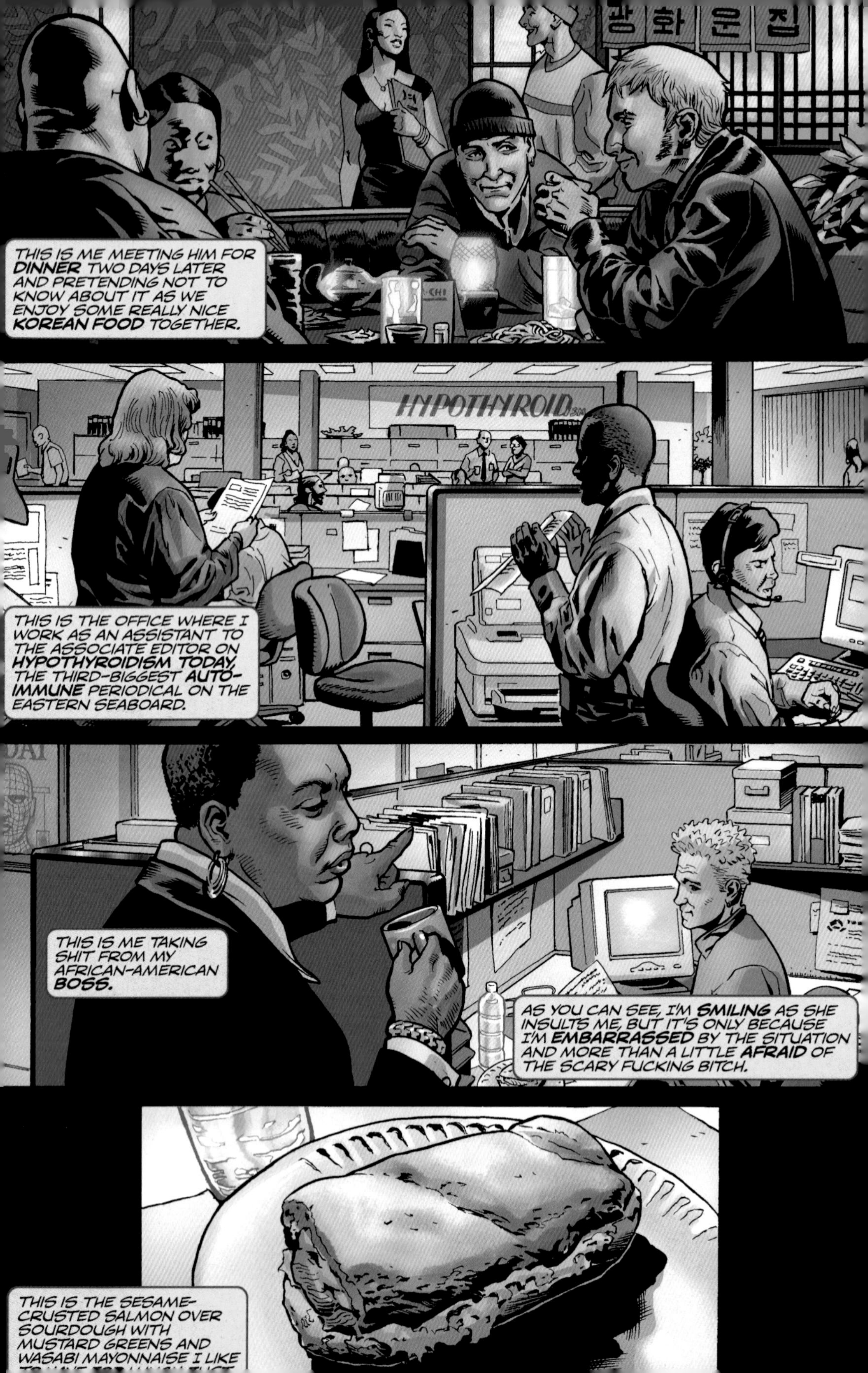

광화문집
THIS IS ME MEETING HIM FOR DINNER TWO DAYS LATER AND PRETENDING NOT TO KNOW ABOUT IT AS WE ENJOY SOME REALLY NICE KOREAN FOOD TOGETHER.
HYPOTHYROID
THIS IS THE OFFICE WHERE I WORK AS AN ASSISTANT TO THE ASSOCIATE EDITOR ON HYPOTHYROIDISM TODAY, THE THIRD-BIGGEST AUTO-IMMUNE PERIODICAL ON THE EASTERN SEABOARD.
THIS IS ME TAKING SHIT FROM MY AFRICAN-AMERICAN BOSS.
AS YOU CAN SEE, I'M SMILING AS SHE INSULTS ME, BUT IT'S ONLY BECAUSE I'M EMBARRASSED BY THE SITUATION AND MORE THAN A LITTLE AFRAID OF THE SCARY FUCKING BITCH.
THIS IS THE SESAME-CRUSTED SALMON OVER SOURDOUGH WITH MUSTARD GREENS AND WASABI MAYONNAISE I LIKE

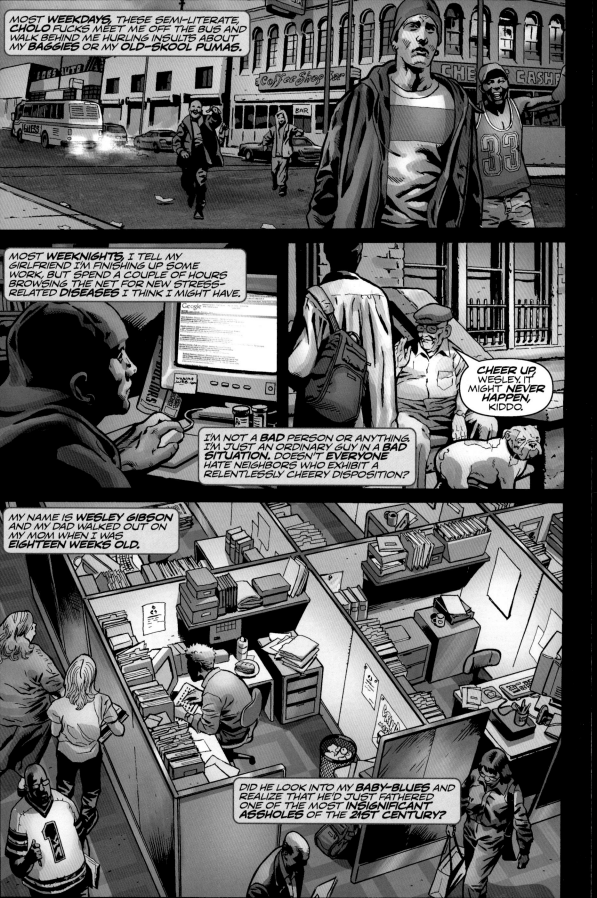

MOST **WEEKDAYS**, THESE SEMI-LITERATE, **CHOLO** FUCKS MEET ME OFF THE BUS AND WALK BEHIND ME HURLING INSULTS ABOUT MY **BAGGIES** OR MY **OLD-SKOOL PUMAS**.

MOST **WEEKNIGHTS**, I TELL MY GIRLFRIEND I'M FINISHING UP SOME WORK, BUT SPEND A COUPLE OF HOURS BROWSING THE NET FOR NEW STRESS-RELATED **DISEASES** I THINK I MIGHT HAVE.

CHEER UP, WESLEY. IT MIGHT **NEVER** HAPPEN, KIDDO.

I'M NOT A **BAD** PERSON OR ANYTHING. I'M JUST AN ORDINARY GUY IN A **BAD SITUATION**. DOESN'T **EVERYONE** HATE NEIGHBORS WHO EXHIBIT A RELENTLESSLY CHEERY DISPOSITION?

MY NAME IS **WESLEY GIBSON** AND MY DAD WALKED OUT ON MY MOM WHEN I WAS **EIGHTEEN WEEKS OLD**.

DID HE LOOK INTO MY **BABY-BLUES** AND REALIZE THAT HE'D JUST FATHERED ONE OF THE MOST **INSIGNIFICANT ASSHOLES** OF THE 21ST CENTURY?

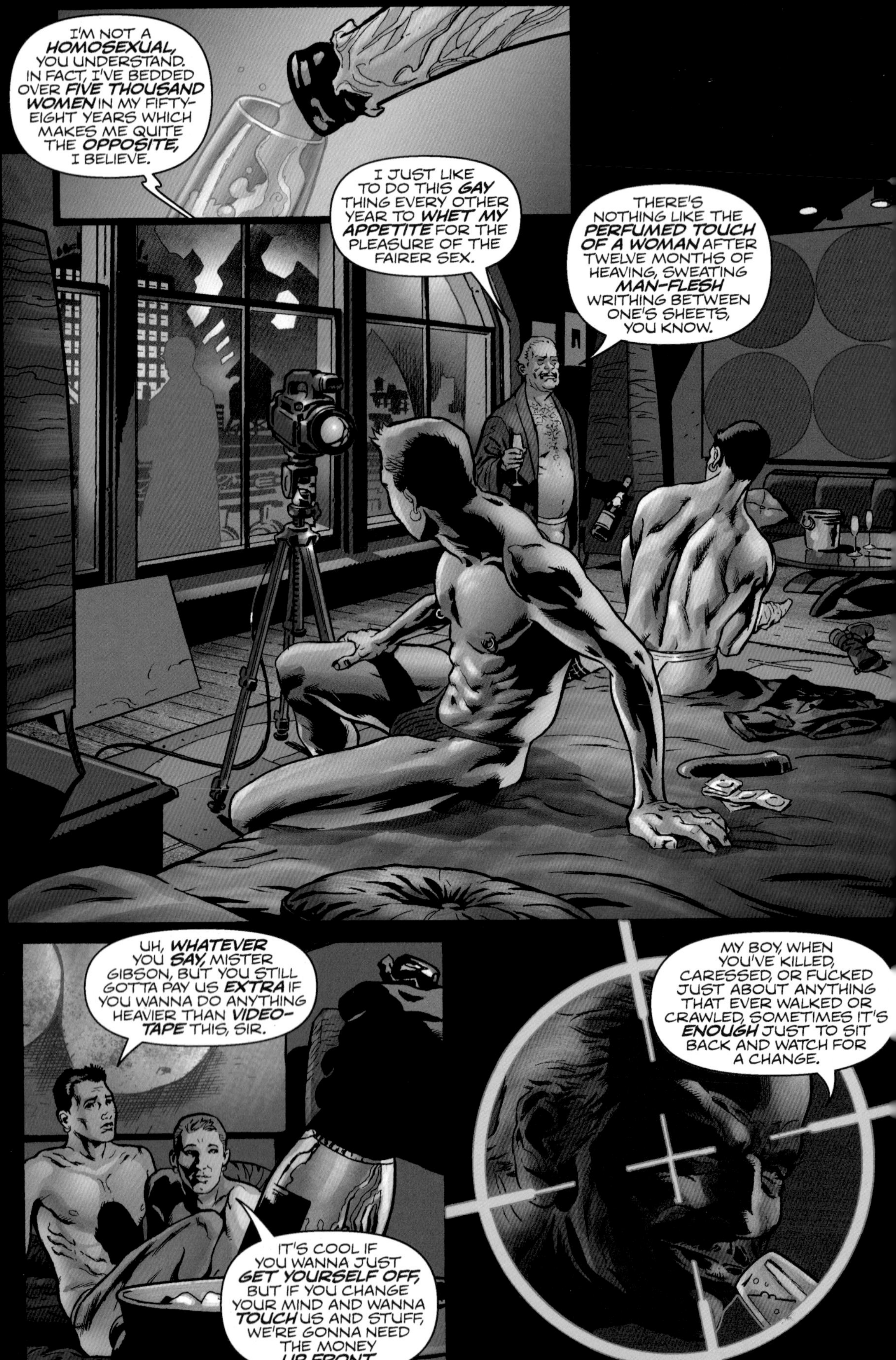
I'M NOT A HOMOSEXUAL, YOU UNDERSTAND. IN FACT, I'VE BEDDED OVER FIVE THOUSAND WOMEN IN MY FIFTY-EIGHT YEARS WHICH MAKES ME QUITE THE OPPOSITE, I BELIEVE.
I JUST LIKE TO DO THIS GAY THING EVERY OTHER YEAR TO WHET MY APPETITE FOR THE PLEASURE OF THE FAIRER SEX.
THERE'S NOTHING LIKE THE PERFUMED TOUCH OF A WOMAN AFTER TWELVE MONTHS OF HEAVING, SWEATING MAN-FLESH WRITHING BETWEEN ONE'S SHEETS, YOU KNOW.
UH, WHATEVER YOU SAY, MISTER GIBSON, BUT YOU STILL GOTTA PAY US EXTRA IF YOU WANNA DO ANYTHING HEAVIER THAN VIDEO-TAPE THIS, SIR.
IT'S COOL IF YOU WANNA JUST GET YOURSELF OFF, BUT IF YOU CHANGE YOUR MIND AND WANNA TOUCH US AND STUFF, WE'RE GONNA NEED THE MONEY UP FRONT.
MY BOY, WHEN YOU'VE KILLED, CARESSED, OR FUCKED JUST ABOUT ANYTHING THAT EVER WALKED OR CRAWLED, SOMETIMES IT'S ENOUGH JUST TO SIT BACK AND WATCH FOR A CHANGE.

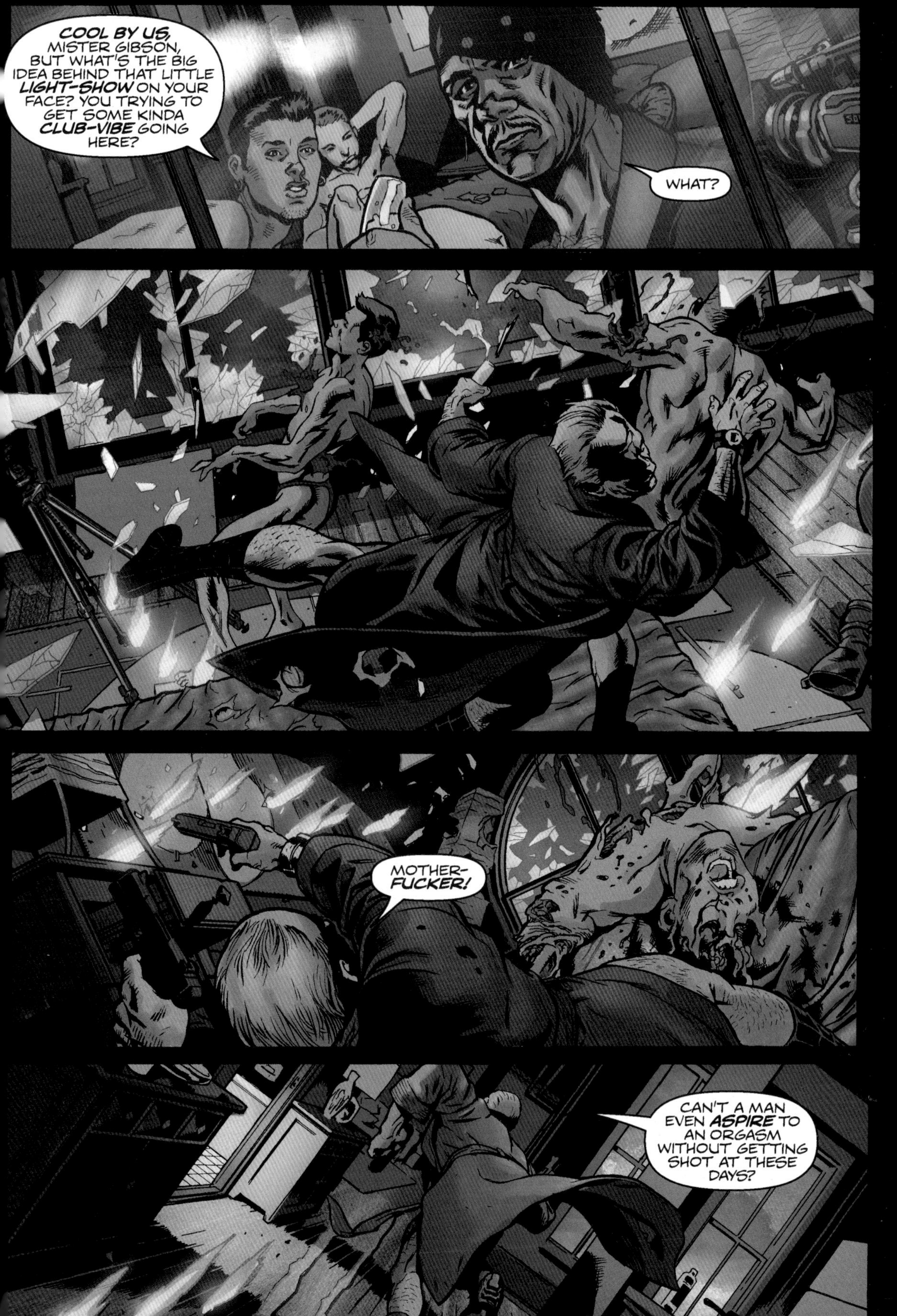
COOL BY US, MISTER GIBSON, BUT WHAT'S THE BIG IDEA BEHIND THAT LITTLE LIGHT-SHOW ON YOUR FACE? YOU TRYING TO GET SOME KINDA CLUB-VIBE GOING HERE?
WHAT?
MOTHER-FUCKER!
CAN'T A MAN EVEN ASPIRE TO AN ORGASM WITHOUT GETTING SHOT AT THESE DAYS?

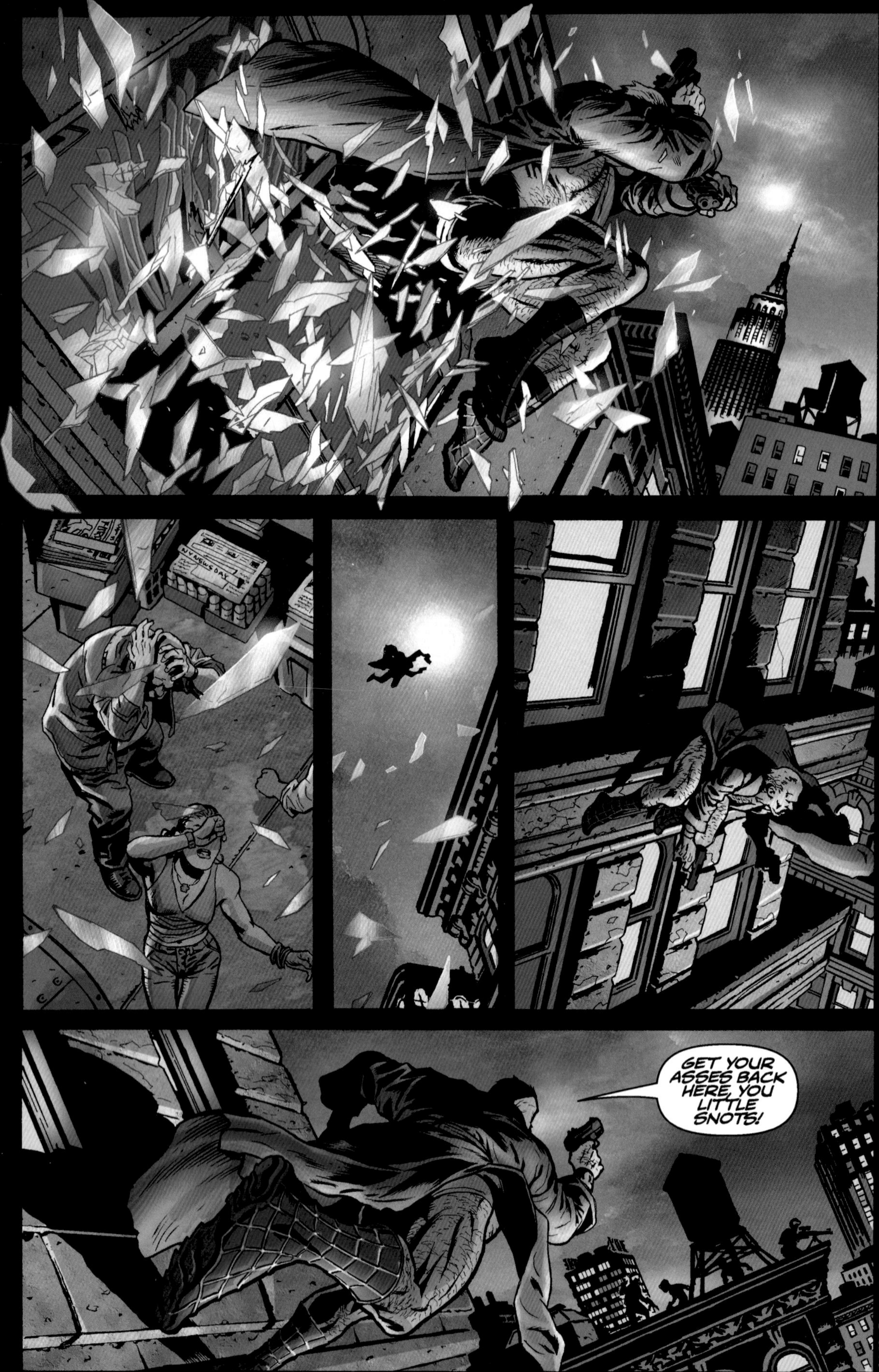
NY NEWSDAY
GET YOUR ASSES BACK HERE, YOU LITTLE SNOTS!

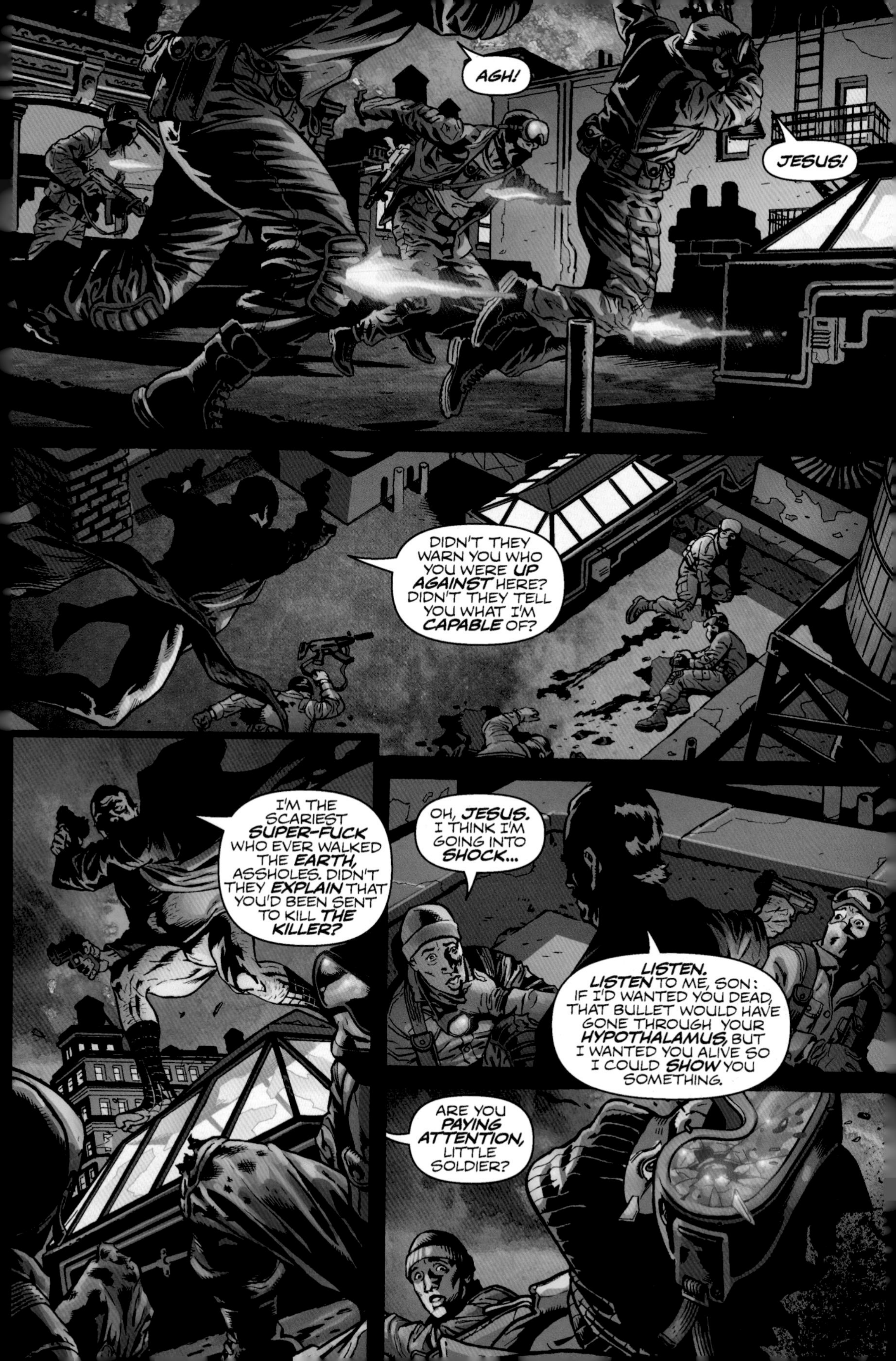
AGH!
JESUS!
DIDN'T THEY WARN YOU WHO YOU WERE UP AGAINST HERE? DIDN'T THEY TELL YOU WHAT I'M CAPABLE OF?
I'M THE SCARIEST SUPER-FUCK WHO EVER WALKED THE EARTH, ASSHOLES. DIDN'T THEY EXPLAIN THAT YOU'D BEEN SENT TO KILL THE KILLER?
OH, JESUS. I THINK I'M GOING INTO SHOCK...
LISTEN. LISTEN TO ME, SON: IF I'D WANTED YOU DEAD, THAT BULLET WOULD HAVE GONE THROUGH YOUR HYPOTHALAMUS, BUT I WANTED YOU ALIVE SO I COULD SHOW YOU SOMETHING.
ARE YOU PAYING ATTENTION, LITTLE SOLDIER?

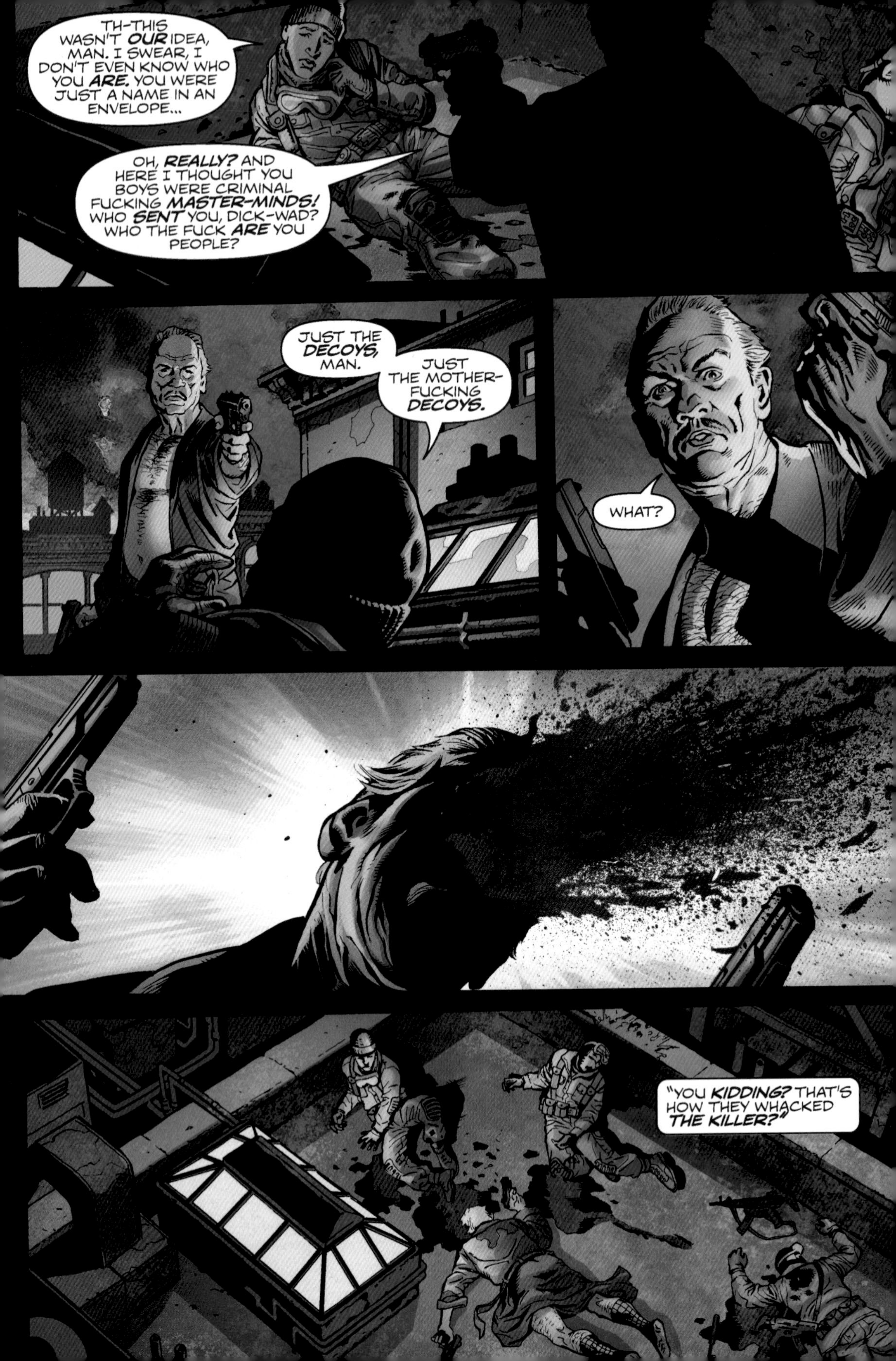
TH-THIS WASN'T OUR IDEA, MAN. I SWEAR, I DON'T EVEN KNOW WHO YOU ARE. YOU WERE JUST A NAME IN AN ENVELOPE...
OH, REALLY? AND HERE I THOUGHT YOU BOYS WERE CRIMINAL FUCKING MASTER-MINDS! WHO SENT YOU, DICK-WAD? WHO THE FUCK ARE YOU PEOPLE?
JUST THE DECOYS, MAN.
JUST THE MOTHER-FUCKING DECOYS.
WHAT?
"YOU KIDDING? THAT'S HOW THEY WHACKED THE KILLER?"

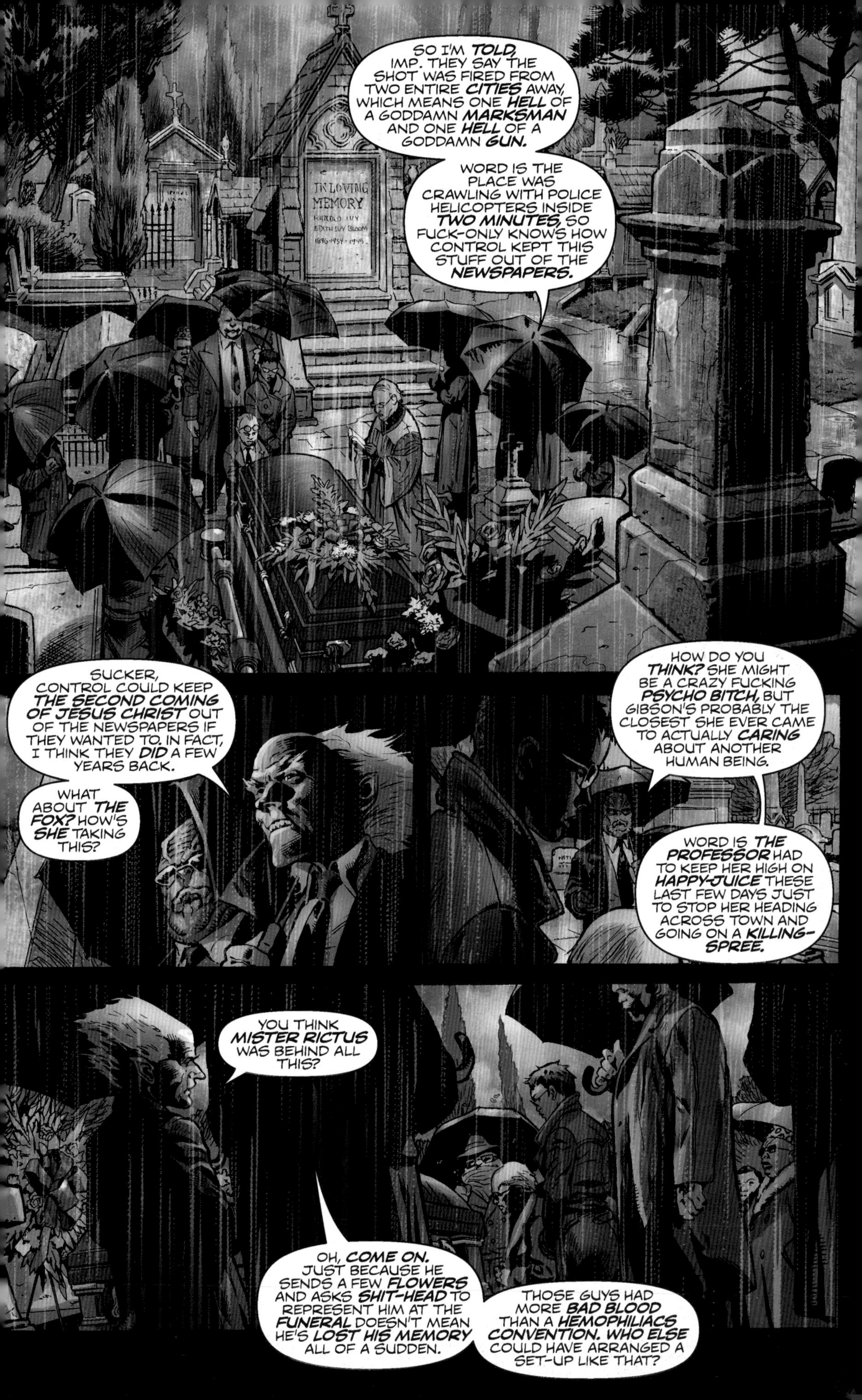
SO I'M TOLD, IMP. THEY SAY THE SHOT WAS FIRED FROM TWO ENTIRE CITIES AWAY, WHICH MEANS ONE HELL OF A GODDAMN MARKSMAN AND ONE HELL OF A GODDAMN GUN.
WORD IS THE PLACE WAS CRAWLING WITH POLICE HELICOPTERS INSIDE TWO MINUTES, SO FUCK-ONLY KNOWS HOW CONTROL KEPT THIS STUFF OUT OF THE NEWSPAPERS.
IN LOVING MEMORY
SUCKER, CONTROL COULD KEEP THE SECOND COMING OF JESUS CHRIST OUT OF THE NEWSPAPERS IF THEY WANTED TO. IN FACT, I THINK THEY DID A FEW YEARS BACK.
WHAT ABOUT THE FOX? HOW'S SHE TAKING THIS?
HOW DO YOU THINK? SHE MIGHT BE A CRAZY FUCKING PSYCHO BITCH, BUT GIBSON'S PROBABLY THE CLOSEST SHE EVER CAME TO ACTUALLY CARING ABOUT ANOTHER HUMAN BEING.
WORD IS THE PROFESSOR HAD TO KEEP HER HIGH ON HAPPY-JUICE THESE LAST FEW DAYS JUST TO STOP HER HEADING ACROSS TOWN AND GOING ON A KILLING-SPREE.
YOU THINK MISTER RICTUS WAS BEHIND ALL THIS?
OH, COME ON. JUST BECAUSE HE SENDS A FEW FLOWERS AND ASKS SHIT-HEAD TO REPRESENT HIM AT THE FUNERAL DOESN'T MEAN HE'S LOST HIS MEMORY ALL OF A SUDDEN.
THOSE GUYS HAD MORE BAD BLOOD THAN A HEMOPHILIACS CONVENTION. WHO ELSE COULD HAVE ARRANGED A SET-UP LIKE THAT?

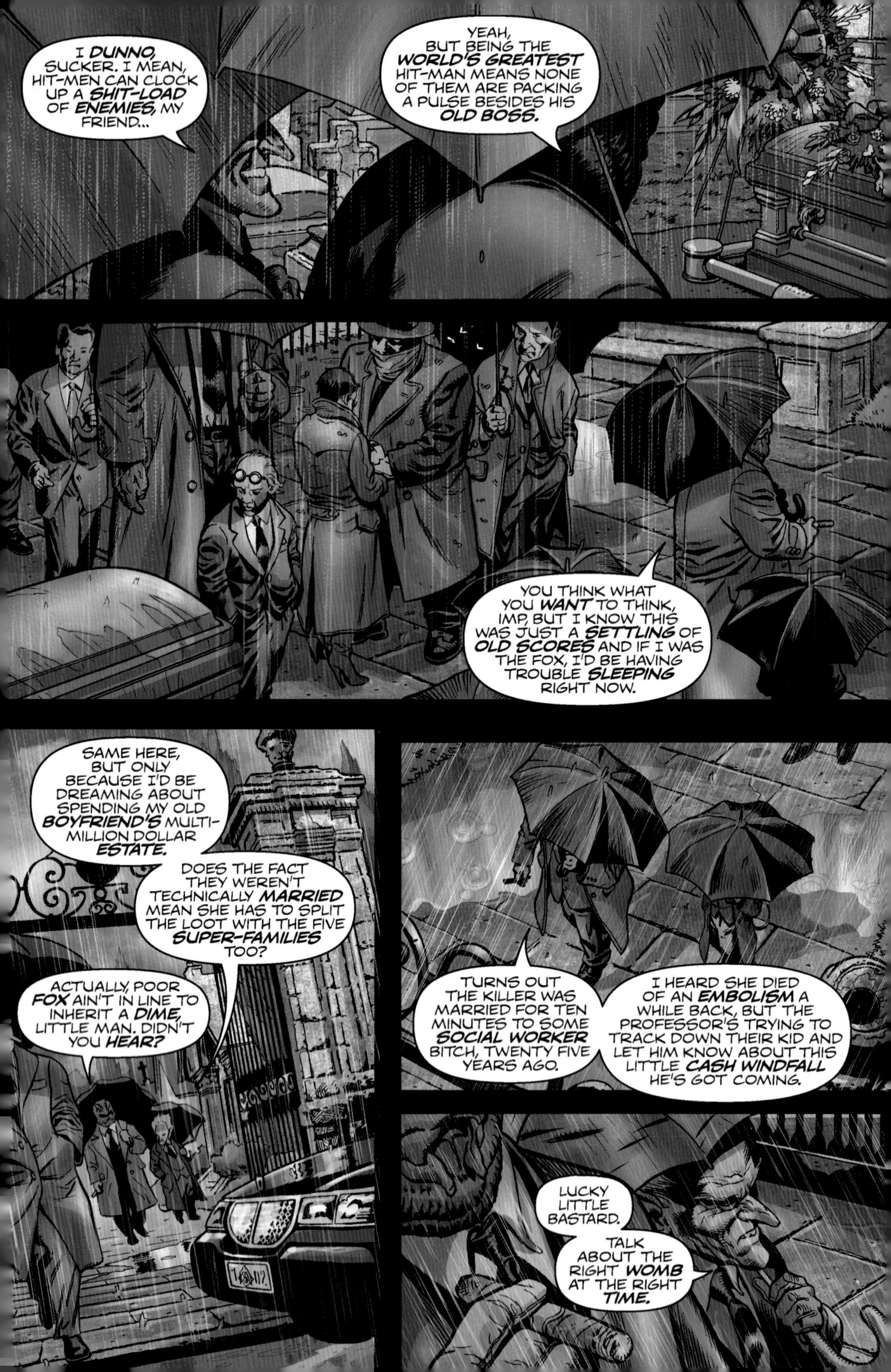
I DUNNO, SUCKER. I MEAN, HIT-MEN CAN CLOCK UP A SHIT-LOAD OF ENEMIES, MY FRIEND...
YEAH, BUT BEING THE WORLD'S GREATEST HIT-MAN MEANS NONE OF THEM ARE PACKING A PULSE BESIDES HIS OLD BOSS.
YOU THINK WHAT YOU WANT TO THINK, IMP, BUT I KNOW THIS WAS JUST A SETTLING OF OLD SCORES AND IF I WAS THE FOX, I'D BE HAVING TROUBLE SLEEPING RIGHT NOW.
SAME HERE, BUT ONLY BECAUSE I'D BE DREAMING ABOUT SPENDING MY OLD BOYFRIEND'S MULTI-MILLION DOLLAR ESTATE.
DOES THE FACT THEY WEREN'T TECHNICALLY MARRIED MEAN SHE HAS TO SPLIT THE LOOT WITH THE FIVE SUPER-FAMILIES TOO?
ACTUALLY, POOR FOX AIN'T IN LINE TO INHERIT A DIME, LITTLE MAN. DIDN'T YOU HEAR?
TURNS OUT THE KILLER WAS MARRIED FOR TEN MINUTES TO SOME SOCIAL WORKER BITCH, TWENTY FIVE YEARS AGO.
I HEARD SHE DIED OF AN EMBOLISM A WHILE BACK, BUT THE PROFESSOR'S TRYING TO TRACK DOWN THEIR KID AND LET HIM KNOW ABOUT THIS LITTLE CASH WINDFALL HE'S GOT COMING.
LUCKY LITTLE BASTARD.
TALK ABOUT THE RIGHT WOMB AT THE RIGHT TIME.

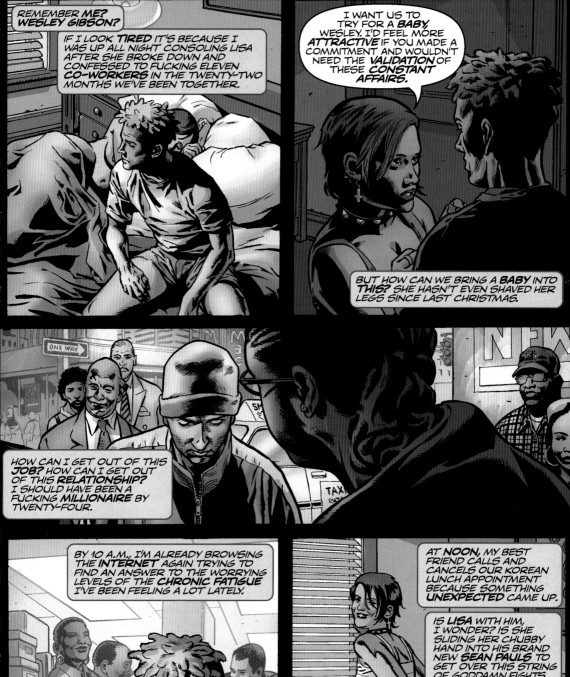

REMEMBER ME? WESLEY GIBSON?

IF I LOOK **TIRED** IT'S BECAUSE I WAS UP ALL NIGHT CONSOLING LISA AFTER SHE BROKE DOWN AND CONFESSED TO FUCKING ELEVEN **CO-WORKERS** IN THE TWENTY-TWO MONTHS WE'VE BEEN TOGETHER.

I WANT US TO TRY FOR A **BABY,** WESLEY. I'D FEEL MORE **ATTRACTIVE** IF YOU MADE A COMMITMENT AND WOULDN'T NEED THE **VALIDATION** OF THESE **CONSTANT AFFAIRS.**

BUT HOW CAN WE BRING A **BABY** INTO **THIS?** SHE HASN'T EVEN SHAVED HER LEGS SINCE LAST CHRISTMAS.

ONE WAY

TAXI

HOW CAN I GET OUT OF THIS **JOB?** HOW CAN I GET OUT OF THIS **RELATIONSHIP?** I SHOULD HAVE BEEN A FUCKING **MILLIONAIRE** BY TWENTY-FOUR.

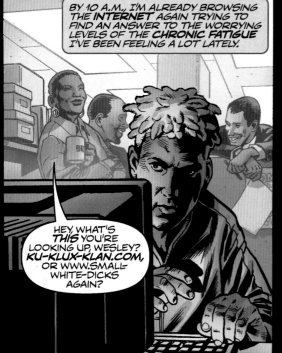

BY 10 A.M., I'M ALREADY BROWSING THE **INTERNET** AGAIN TRYING TO FIND AN ANSWER TO THE WORRYING LEVELS OF THE **CHRONIC FATIGUE** I'VE BEEN FEELING A LOT LATELY.

HEY, WHAT'S **THIS** YOU'RE LOOKING UP, WESLEY? KU-KLUX-KLAN.COM, OR WWW.SMALL-WHITE-DICKS AGAIN?

AT **NOON,** MY BEST FRIEND CALLS AND CANCELS OUR KOREAN LUNCH APPOINTMENT BECAUSE SOMETHING **UNEXPECTED** CAME UP.

IS **LISA** WITH HIM, I WONDER? IS SHE SLIDING HER CHUBBY HAND INTO HIS BRAND NEW **SEAN PAULS** TO GET OVER THIS STRING OF GODDAMN FIGHTS WE JOKINGLY CALL A **RELATIONSHIP?**

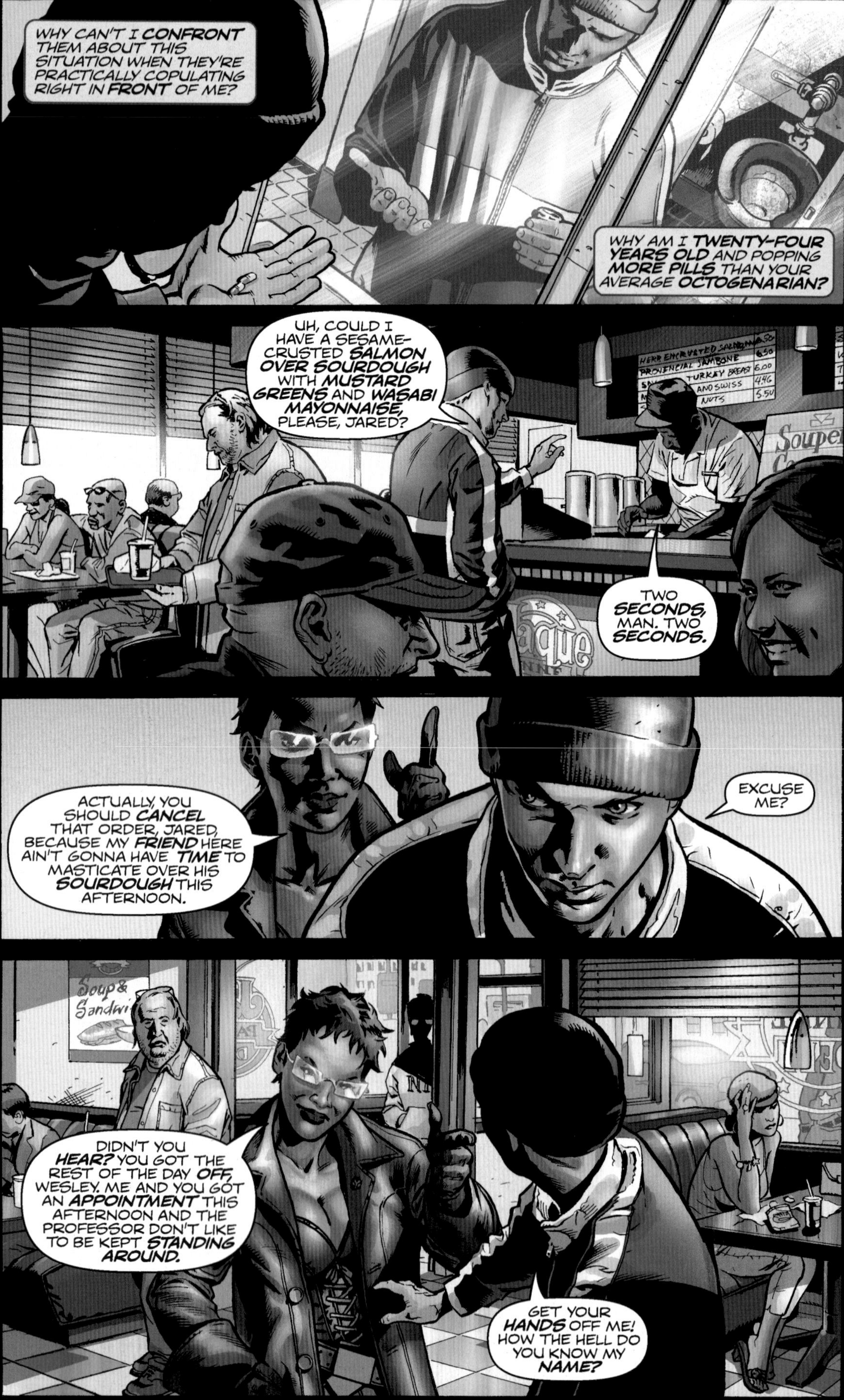
WHY CAN'T I CONFRONT THEM ABOUT THIS SITUATION WHEN THEY'RE PRACTICALLY COPULATING RIGHT IN FRONT OF ME?
WHY AM I TWENTY-FOUR YEARS OLD AND POPPING MORE PILLS THAN YOUR AVERAGE OCTOGENARIAN?
UH, COULD I HAVE A SESAME-CRUSTED SALMON OVER SOURDOUGH WITH MUSTARD GREENS AND WASABI MAYONNAISE, PLEASE, JARED?
TWO SECONDS, MAN. TWO SECONDS.
ACTUALLY, YOU SHOULD CANCEL THAT ORDER, JARED, BECAUSE MY FRIEND HERE AIN'T GONNA HAVE TIME TO MASTICATE OVER HIS SOURDOUGH THIS AFTERNOON.
EXCUSE ME?
DIDN'T YOU HEAR? YOU GOT THE REST OF THE DAY OFF, WESLEY. ME AND YOU GOT AN APPOINTMENT THIS AFTERNOON AND THE PROFESSOR DON'T LIKE TO BE KEPT STANDING AROUND.
GET YOUR HANDS OFF ME! HOW THE HELL DO YOU KNOW MY NAME?

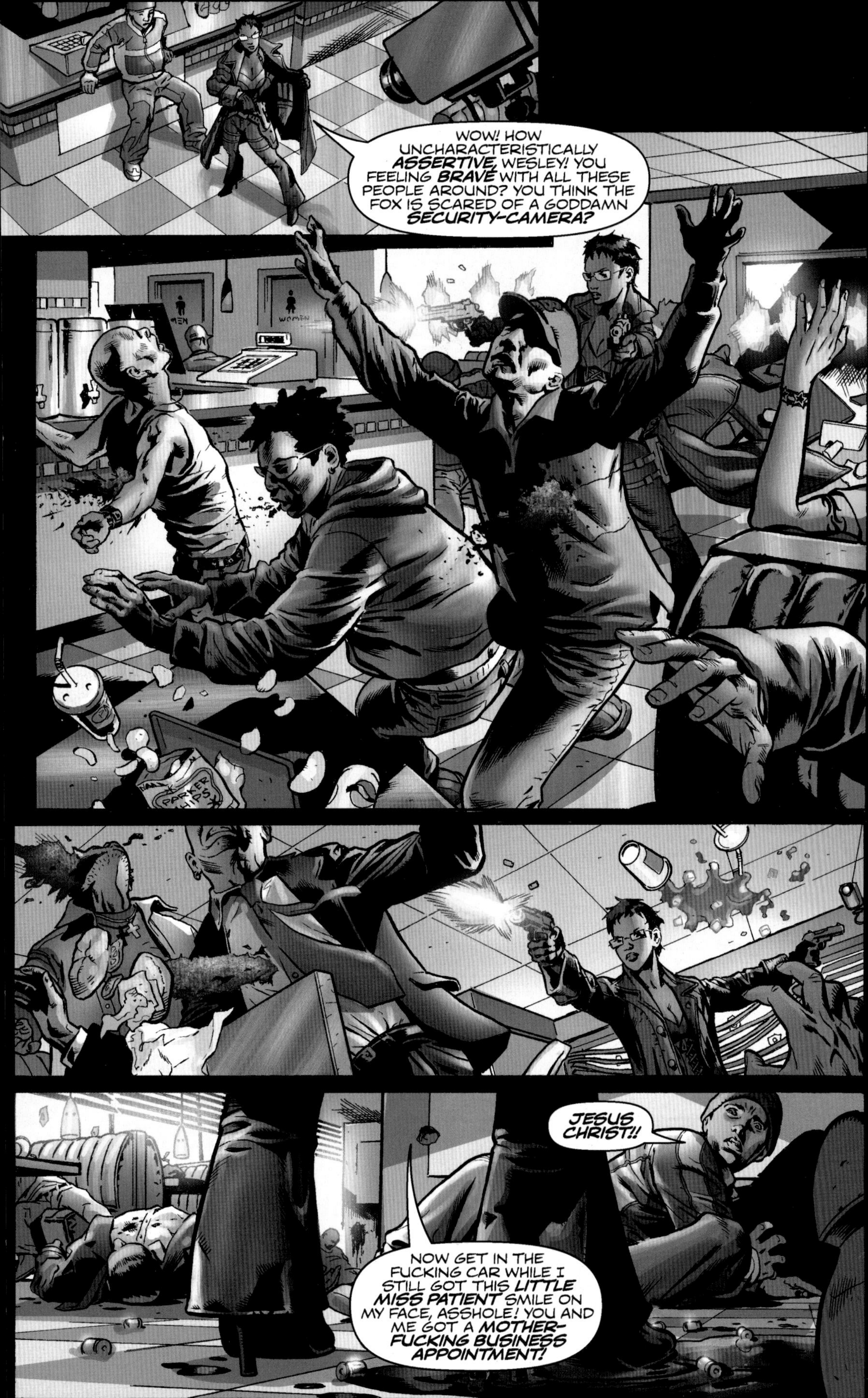
WOW! HOW UNCHARACTERISTICALLY ASSERTIVE, WESLEY! YOU FEELING BRAVE WITH ALL THESE PEOPLE AROUND? YOU THINK THE FOX IS SCARED OF A GODDAMN SECURITY-CAMERA?
MEN
WOMEN
PARKER CHIPS
JESUS CHRIST!!
NOW GET IN THE FUCKING CAR WHILE I STILL GOT THIS LITTLE MISS PATIENT SMILE ON MY FACE, ASSHOLE! YOU AND ME GOT A MOTHER-FUCKING BUSINESS APPOINTMENT!

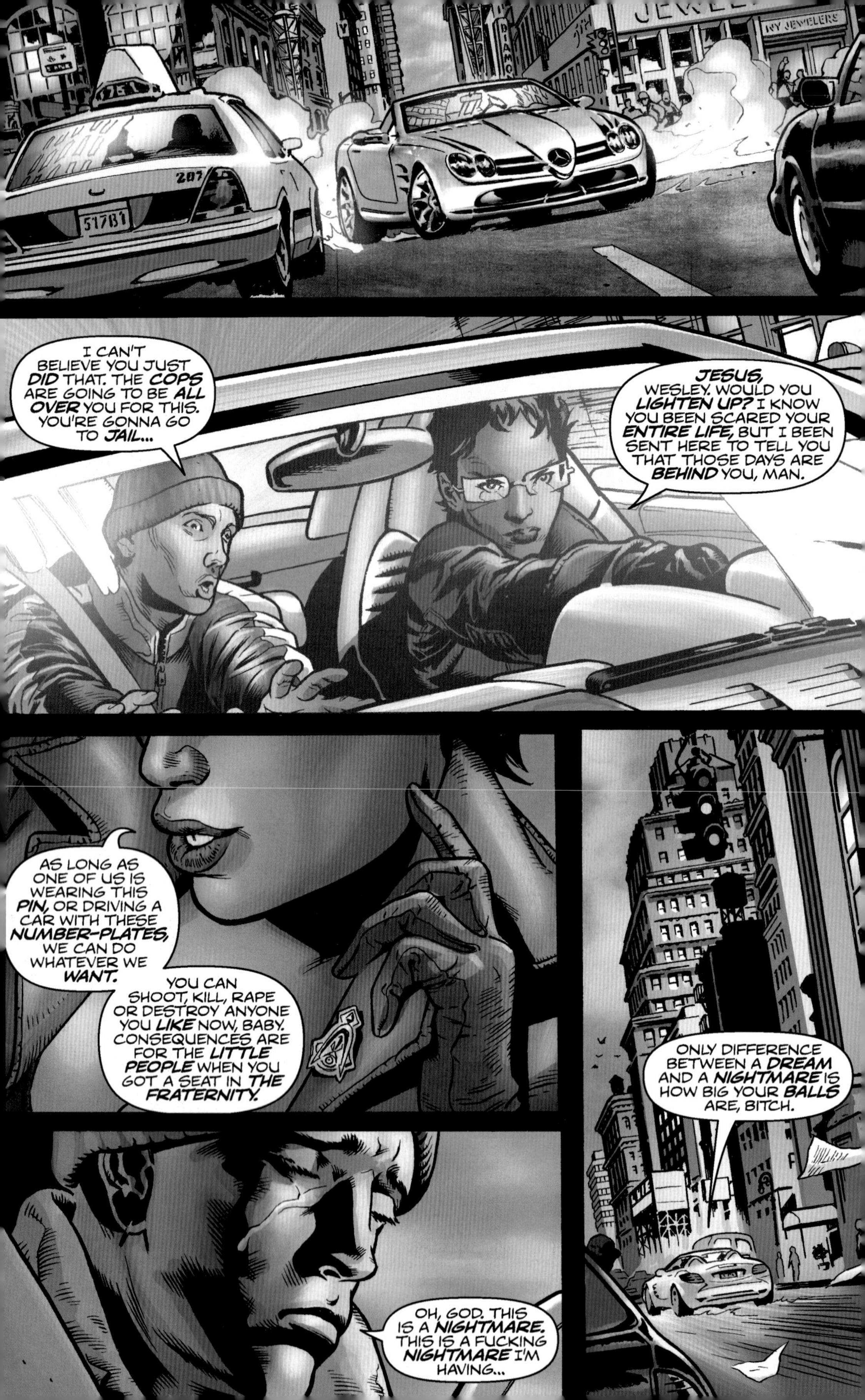

I CAN'T BELIEVE YOU JUST DID THAT. THE COPS ARE GOING TO BE ALL OVER YOU FOR THIS. YOU'RE GONNA GO TO JAIL...
JESUS, WESLEY. WOULD YOU LIGHTEN UP? I KNOW YOU BEEN SCARED YOUR ENTIRE LIFE, BUT I BEEN SENT HERE TO TELL YOU THAT THOSE DAYS ARE BEHIND YOU, MAN.
AS LONG AS ONE OF US IS WEARING THIS PIN, OR DRIVING A CAR WITH THESE NUMBER-PLATES, WE CAN DO WHATEVER WE WANT.
YOU CAN SHOOT, KILL, RAPE OR DESTROY ANYONE YOU LIKE NOW, BABY. CONSEQUENCES ARE FOR THE LITTLE PEOPLE WHEN YOU GOT A SEAT IN THE FRATERNITY.
OH, GOD. THIS IS A NIGHTMARE. THIS IS A FUCKING NIGHTMARE I'M HAVING...
ONLY DIFFERENCE BETWEEN A DREAM AND A NIGHTMARE IS HOW BIG YOUR BALLS ARE, BITCH.

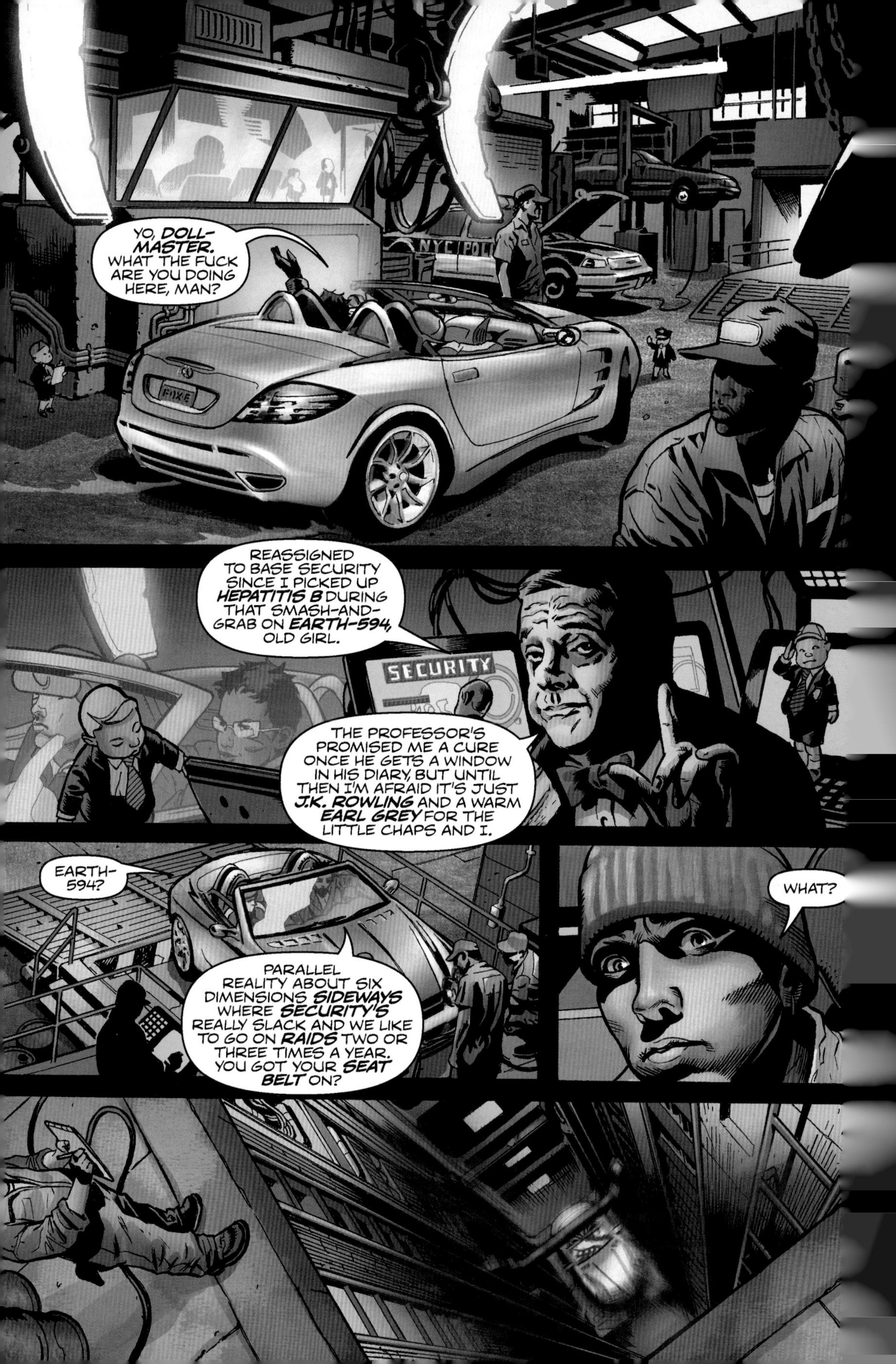
YO, DOLL-MASTER. WHAT THE FUCK ARE YOU DOING HERE, MAN?
REASSIGNED TO BASE SECURITY SINCE I PICKED UP HEPATITIS B DURING THAT SMASH-AND-GRAB ON EARTH-594, OLD GIRL.
SECURITY
THE PROFESSOR'S PROMISED ME A CURE ONCE HE GETS A WINDOW IN HIS DIARY, BUT UNTIL THEN I'M AFRAID IT'S JUST J.K. ROWLING AND A WARM EARL GREY FOR THE LITTLE CHAPS AND I.
EARTH-594?
PARALLEL REALITY ABOUT SIX DIMENSIONS SIDEWAYS WHERE SECURITY'S REALLY SLACK AND WE LIKE TO GO ON RAIDS TWO OR THREE TIMES A YEAR. YOU GOT YOUR SEAT BELT ON?
WHAT?

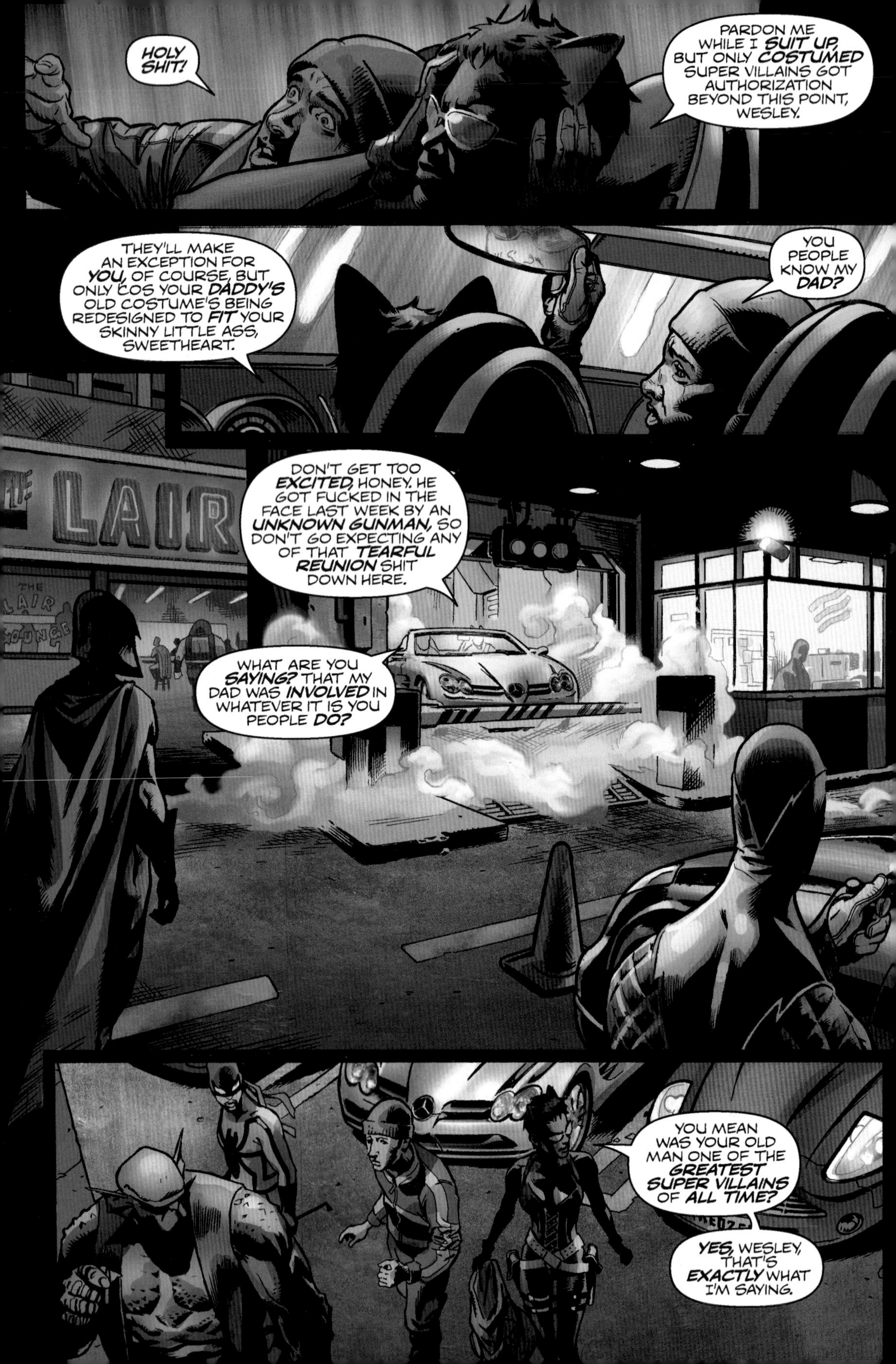
HOLY SHIT!
PARDON ME WHILE I SUIT UP, BUT ONLY COSTUMED SUPER VILLAINS GOT AUTHORIZATION BEYOND THIS POINT, WESLEY.
THEY'LL MAKE AN EXCEPTION FOR YOU, OF COURSE, BUT ONLY COS YOUR DADDY'S OLD COSTUME'S BEING REDESIGNED TO FIT YOUR SKINNY LITTLE ASS, SWEETHEART.
YOU PEOPLE KNOW MY DAD?
THE LAIR
DON'T GET TOO EXCITED, HONEY. HE GOT FUCKED IN THE FACE LAST WEEK BY AN UNKNOWN GUNMAN, SO DON'T GO EXPECTING ANY OF THAT TEARFUL REUNION SHIT DOWN HERE.
WHAT ARE YOU SAYING? THAT MY DAD WAS INVOLVED IN WHATEVER IT IS YOU PEOPLE DO?
YOU MEAN WAS YOUR OLD MAN ONE OF THE GREATEST SUPER VILLAINS OF ALL TIME?
YES, WESLEY, THAT'S EXACTLY WHAT I'M SAYING.

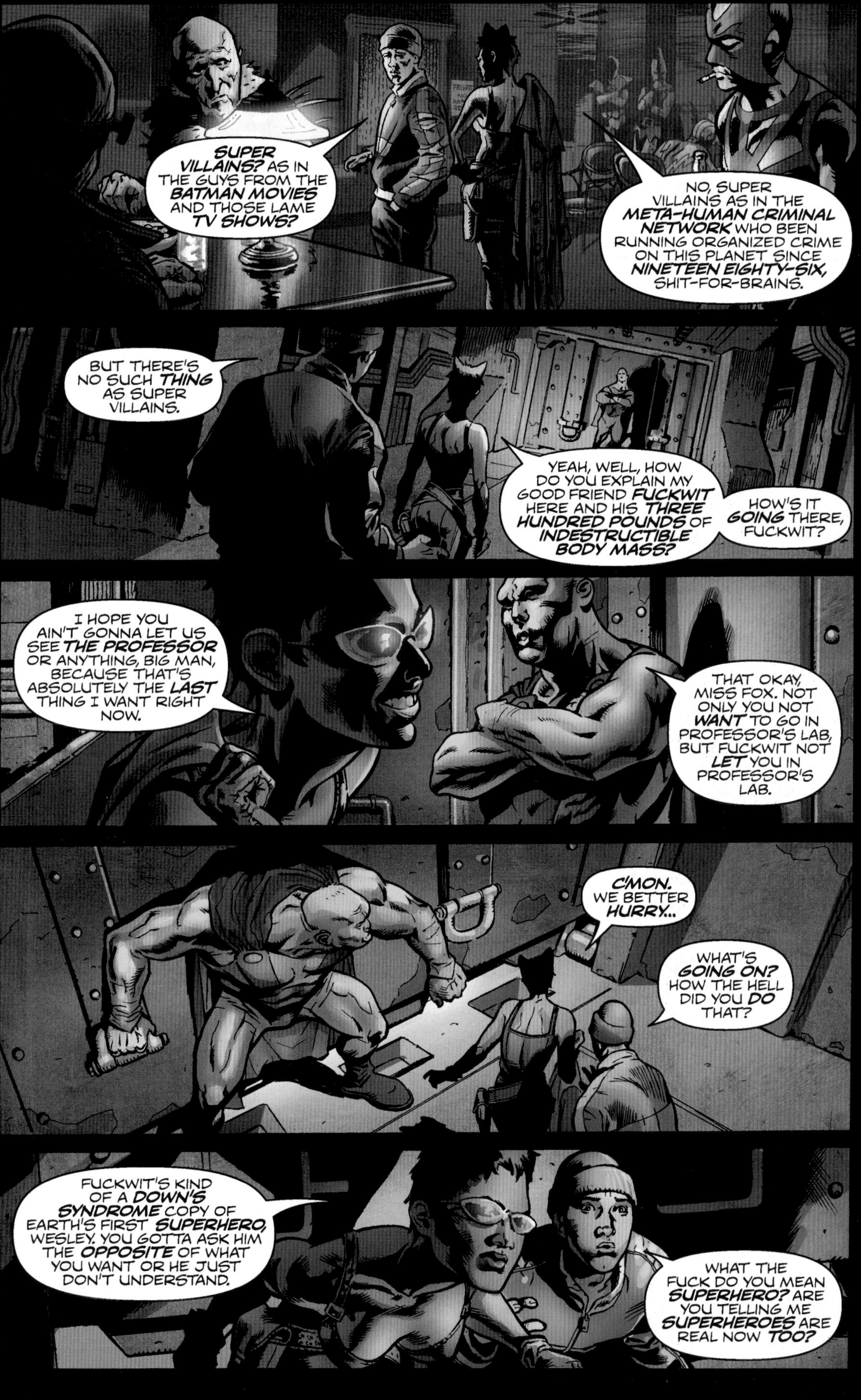
SUPER VILLAINS? AS IN THE GUYS FROM THE BATMAN MOVIES AND THOSE LAME TV SHOWS?
NO, SUPER VILLAINS AS IN THE META-HUMAN CRIMINAL NETWORK WHO BEEN RUNNING ORGANIZED CRIME ON THIS PLANET SINCE NINETEEN EIGHTY-SIX, SHIT-FOR-BRAINS.
BUT THERE'S NO SUCH THING AS SUPER VILLAINS.
YEAH, WELL, HOW DO YOU EXPLAIN MY GOOD FRIEND FUCKWIT HERE AND HIS THREE HUNDRED POUNDS OF INDESTRUCTIBLE BODY MASS?
HOW'S IT GOING THERE, FUCKWIT?
I HOPE YOU AIN'T GONNA LET US SEE THE PROFESSOR OR ANYTHING, BIG MAN, BECAUSE THAT'S ABSOLUTELY THE LAST THING I WANT RIGHT NOW.
THAT OKAY, MISS FOX. NOT ONLY YOU NOT WANT TO GO IN PROFESSOR'S LAB, BUT FUCKWIT NOT LET YOU IN PROFESSOR'S LAB.
C'MON. WE BETTER HURRY...
WHAT'S GOING ON? HOW THE HELL DID YOU DO THAT?
FUCKWIT'S KIND OF A DOWN'S SYNDROME COPY OF EARTH'S FIRST SUPERHERO, WESLEY. YOU GOTTA ASK HIM THE OPPOSITE OF WHAT YOU WANT OR HE JUST DON'T UNDERSTAND.
WHAT THE FUCK DO YOU MEAN SUPERHERO? ARE YOU TELLING ME SUPERHEROES ARE REAL NOW TOO?

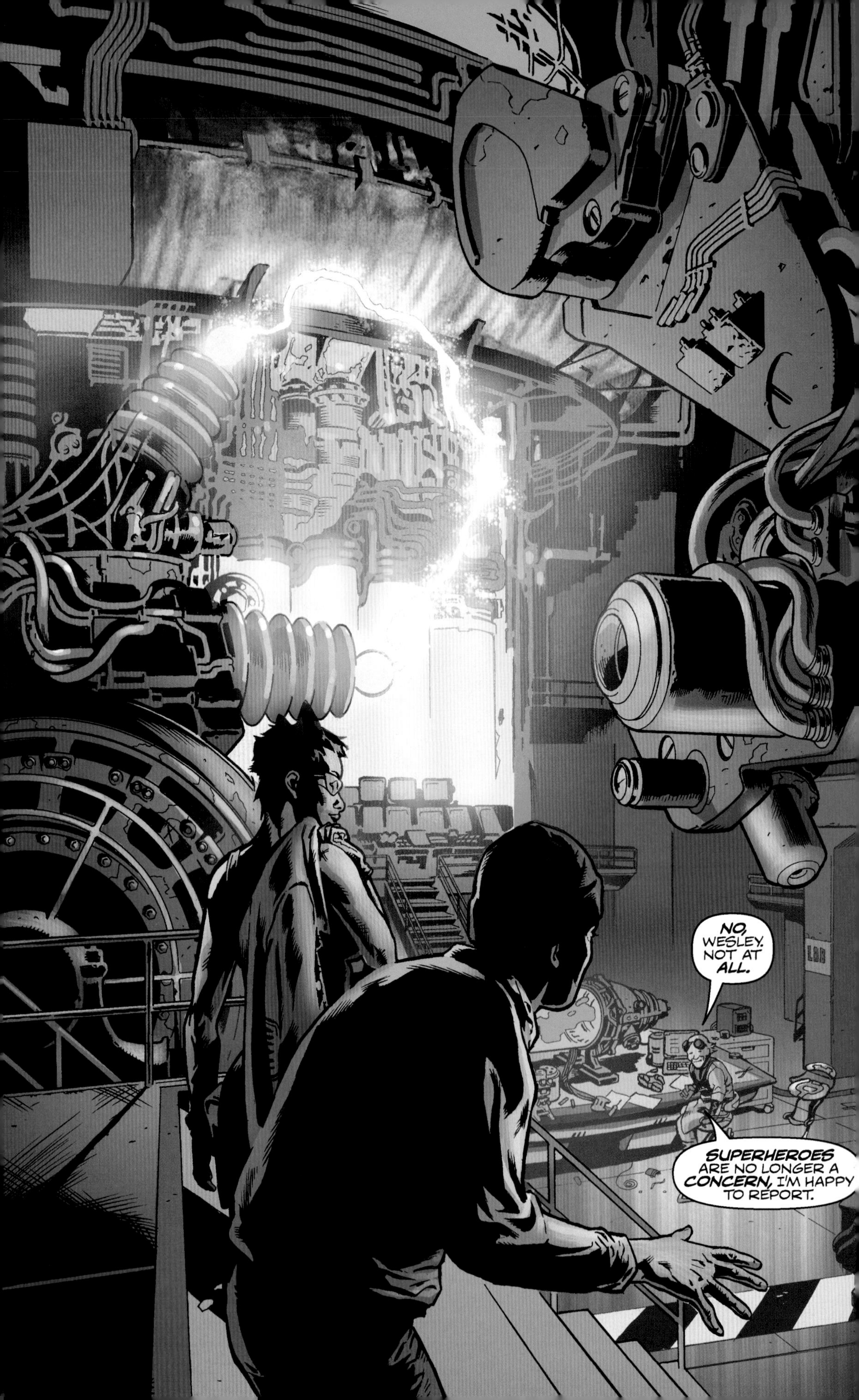
NO, WESLEY. NOT AT ALL.
SUPERHEROES ARE NO LONGER A CONCERN, I'M HAPPY TO REPORT.
LAB

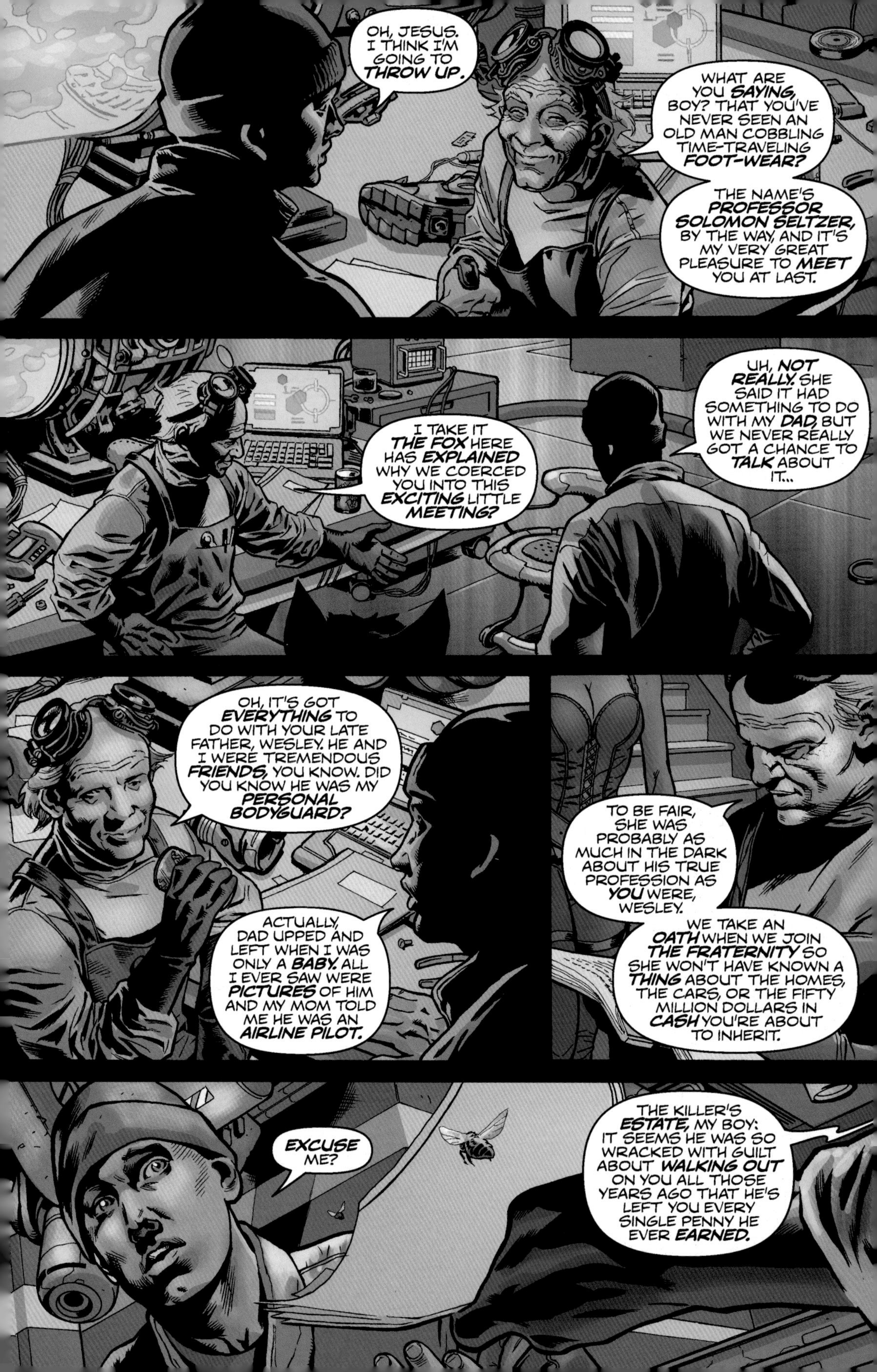
OH, JESUS. I THINK I'M GOING TO THROW UP.
WHAT ARE YOU SAYING, BOY? THAT YOU'VE NEVER SEEN AN OLD MAN COBBLING TIME-TRAVELING FOOT-WEAR?
THE NAME'S PROFESSOR SOLOMON SELTZER, BY THE WAY, AND IT'S MY VERY GREAT PLEASURE TO MEET YOU AT LAST.
I TAKE IT THE FOX HERE HAS EXPLAINED WHY WE COERCED YOU INTO THIS EXCITING LITTLE MEETING?
UH, NOT REALLY. SHE SAID IT HAD SOMETHING TO DO WITH MY DAD, BUT WE NEVER REALLY GOT A CHANCE TO TALK ABOUT IT...
OH, IT'S GOT EVERYTHING TO DO WITH YOUR LATE FATHER, WESLEY. HE AND I WERE TREMENDOUS FRIENDS, YOU KNOW. DID YOU KNOW HE WAS MY PERSONAL BODYGUARD?
ACTUALLY, DAD UPPED AND LEFT WHEN I WAS ONLY A BABY. ALL I EVER SAW WERE PICTURES OF HIM AND MY MOM TOLD ME HE WAS AN AIRLINE PILOT.
TO BE FAIR, SHE WAS PROBABLY AS MUCH IN THE DARK ABOUT HIS TRUE PROFESSION AS YOU WERE, WESLEY.
WE TAKE AN OATH WHEN WE JOIN THE FRATERNITY SO SHE WON'T HAVE KNOWN A THING ABOUT THE HOMES, THE CARS, OR THE FIFTY MILLION DOLLARS IN CASH YOU'RE ABOUT TO INHERIT.
EXCUSE ME?
THE KILLER'S ESTATE, MY BOY: IT SEEMS HE WAS SO WRACKED WITH GUILT ABOUT WALKING OUT ON YOU ALL THOSE YEARS AGO THAT HE'S LEFT YOU EVERY SINGLE PENNY HE EVER EARNED.

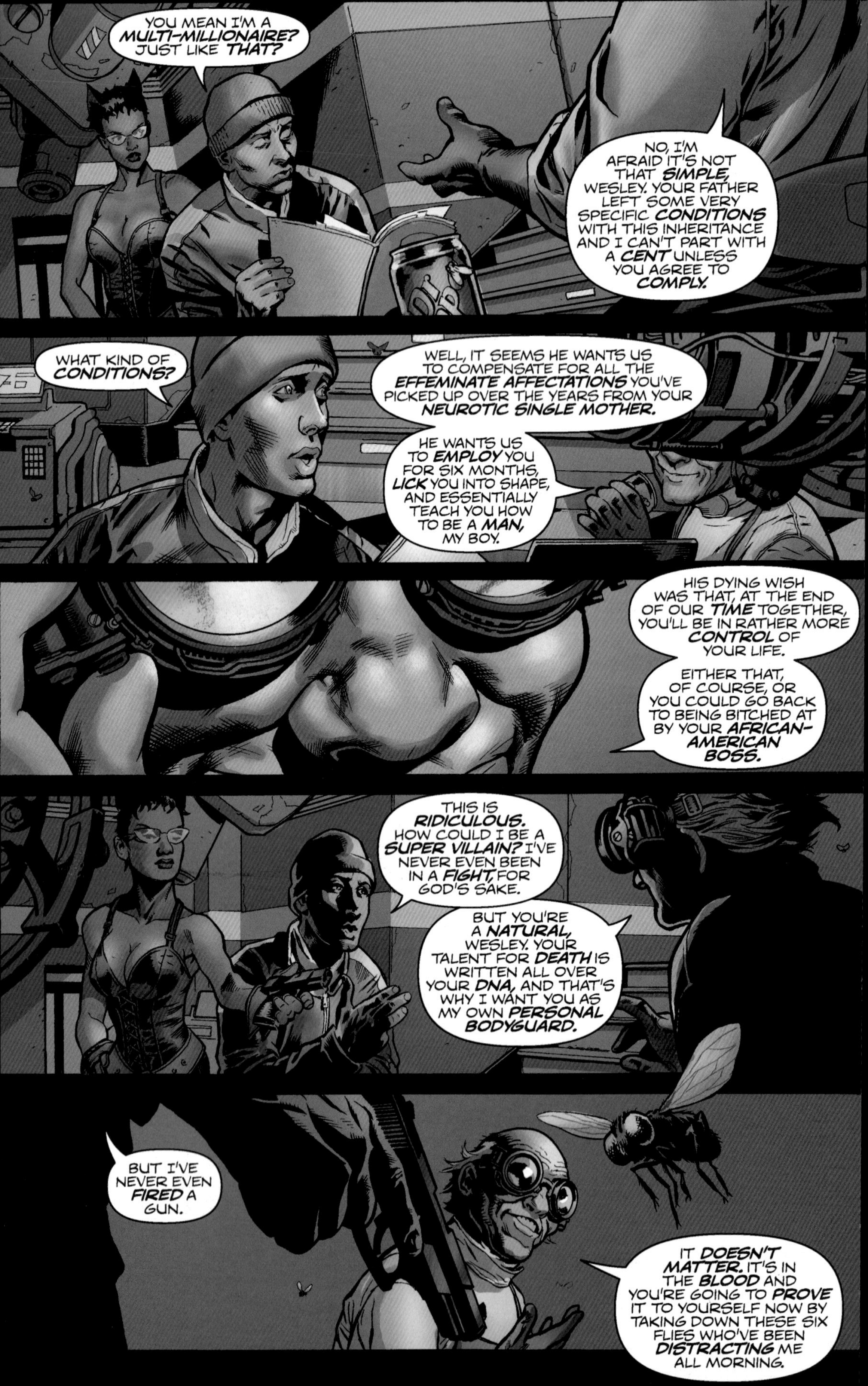
YOU MEAN I'M A MULTI-MILLIONAIRE? JUST LIKE THAT?
NO, I'M AFRAID IT'S NOT THAT SIMPLE, WESLEY. YOUR FATHER LEFT SOME VERY SPECIFIC CONDITIONS WITH THIS INHERITANCE AND I CAN'T PART WITH A CENT UNLESS YOU AGREE TO COMPLY.
WHAT KIND OF CONDITIONS?
WELL, IT SEEMS HE WANTS US TO COMPENSATE FOR ALL THE EFFEMINATE AFFECTATIONS YOU'VE PICKED UP OVER THE YEARS FROM YOUR NEUROTIC SINGLE MOTHER.
HE WANTS US TO EMPLOY YOU FOR SIX MONTHS, LICK YOU INTO SHAPE, AND ESSENTIALLY TEACH YOU HOW TO BE A MAN, MY BOY.
HIS DYING WISH WAS THAT, AT THE END OF OUR TIME TOGETHER, YOU'LL BE IN RATHER MORE CONTROL OF YOUR LIFE.
EITHER THAT, OF COURSE, OR YOU COULD GO BACK TO BEING BITCHED AT BY YOUR AFRICAN-AMERICAN BOSS.
THIS IS RIDICULOUS. HOW COULD I BE A SUPER VILLAIN? I'VE NEVER EVEN BEEN IN A FIGHT, FOR GOD'S SAKE.
BUT YOU'RE A NATURAL, WESLEY. YOUR TALENT FOR DEATH IS WRITTEN ALL OVER YOUR DNA, AND THAT'S WHY I WANT YOU AS MY OWN PERSONAL BODYGUARD.
BUT I'VE NEVER EVEN FIRED A GUN.
IT DOESN'T MATTER. IT'S IN THE BLOOD AND YOU'RE GOING TO PROVE IT TO YOURSELF NOW BY TAKING DOWN THESE SIX FLIES WHO'VE BEEN DISTRACTING ME ALL MORNING.

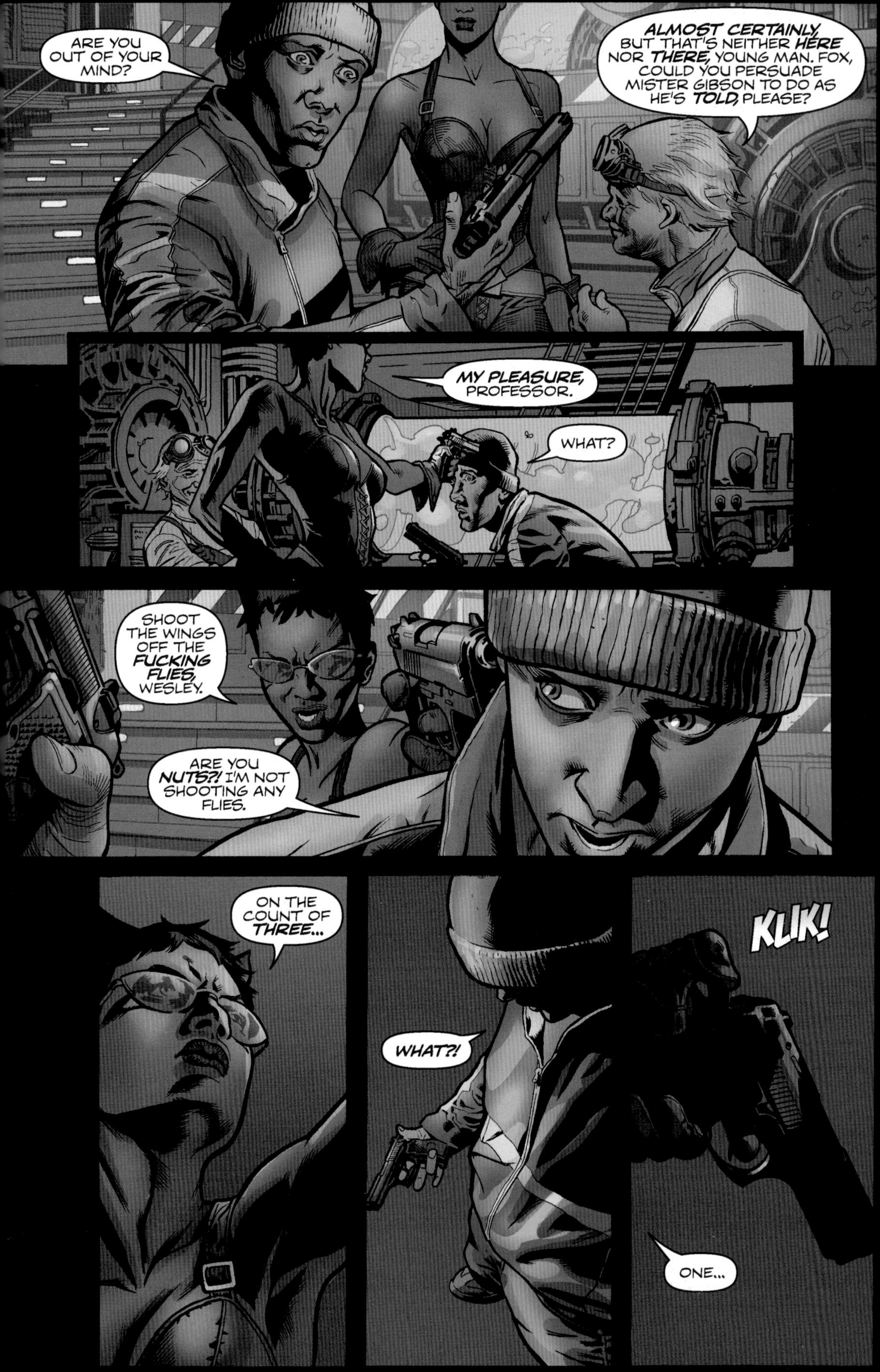
ARE YOU OUT OF YOUR MIND?
ALMOST CERTAINLY, BUT THAT'S NEITHER HERE NOR THERE, YOUNG MAN. FOX, COULD YOU PERSUADE MISTER GIBSON TO DO AS HE'S TOLD, PLEASE?
MY PLEASURE, PROFESSOR.
WHAT?
SHOOT THE WINGS OFF THE FUCKING FLIES, WESLEY.
ARE YOU NUTS?! I'M NOT SHOOTING ANY FLIES.
ON THE COUNT OF THREE...
WHAT?!
KLIK!
ONE...

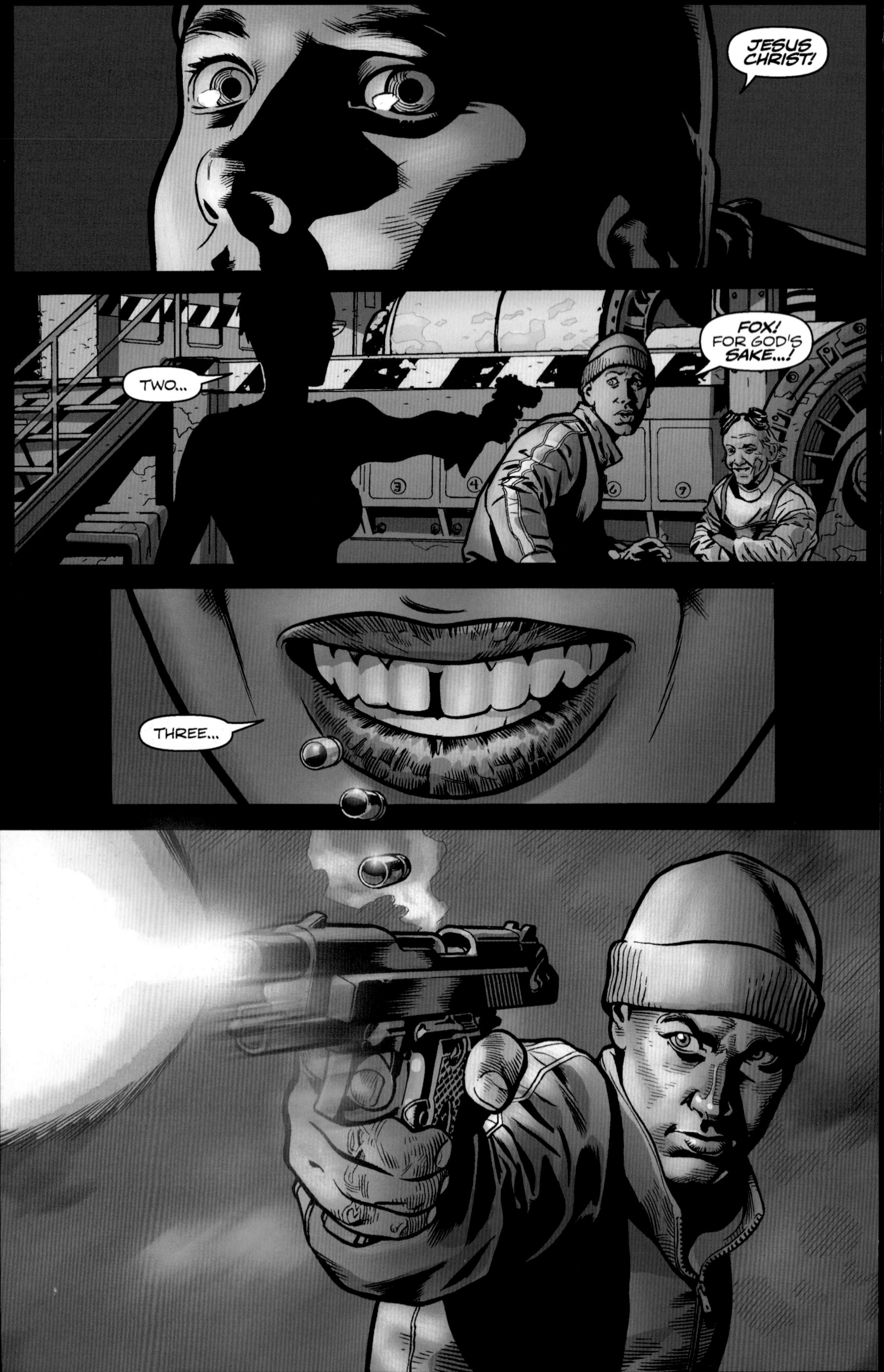
JESUS CHRIST!
TWO...
FOX! FOR GOD'S SAKE...!
THREE...

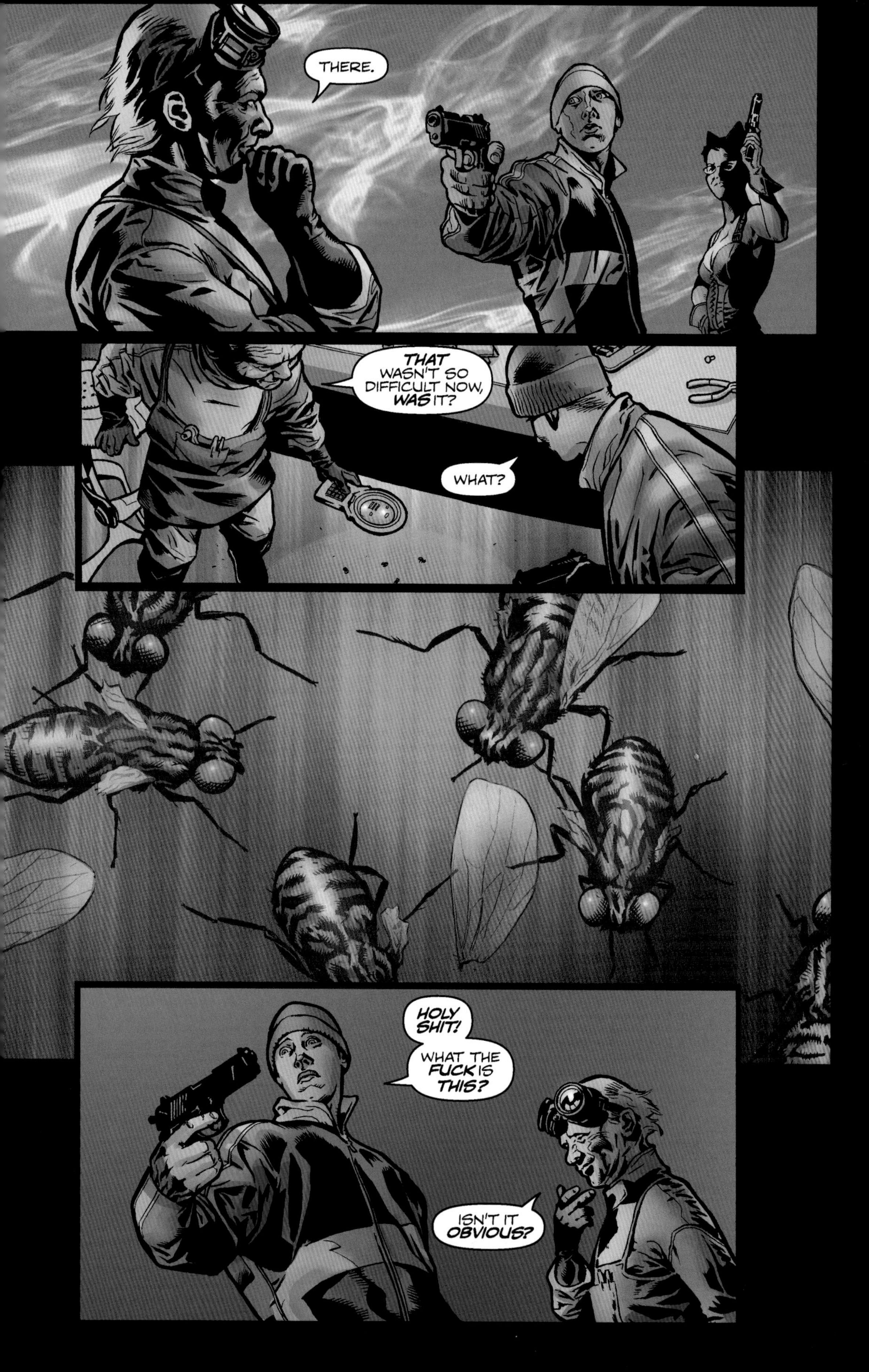
THERE.
THAT WASN'T SO DIFFICULT NOW, WAS IT?
WHAT?
HOLY SHIT!
WHAT THE FUCK IS THIS?
ISN'T IT OBVIOUS?

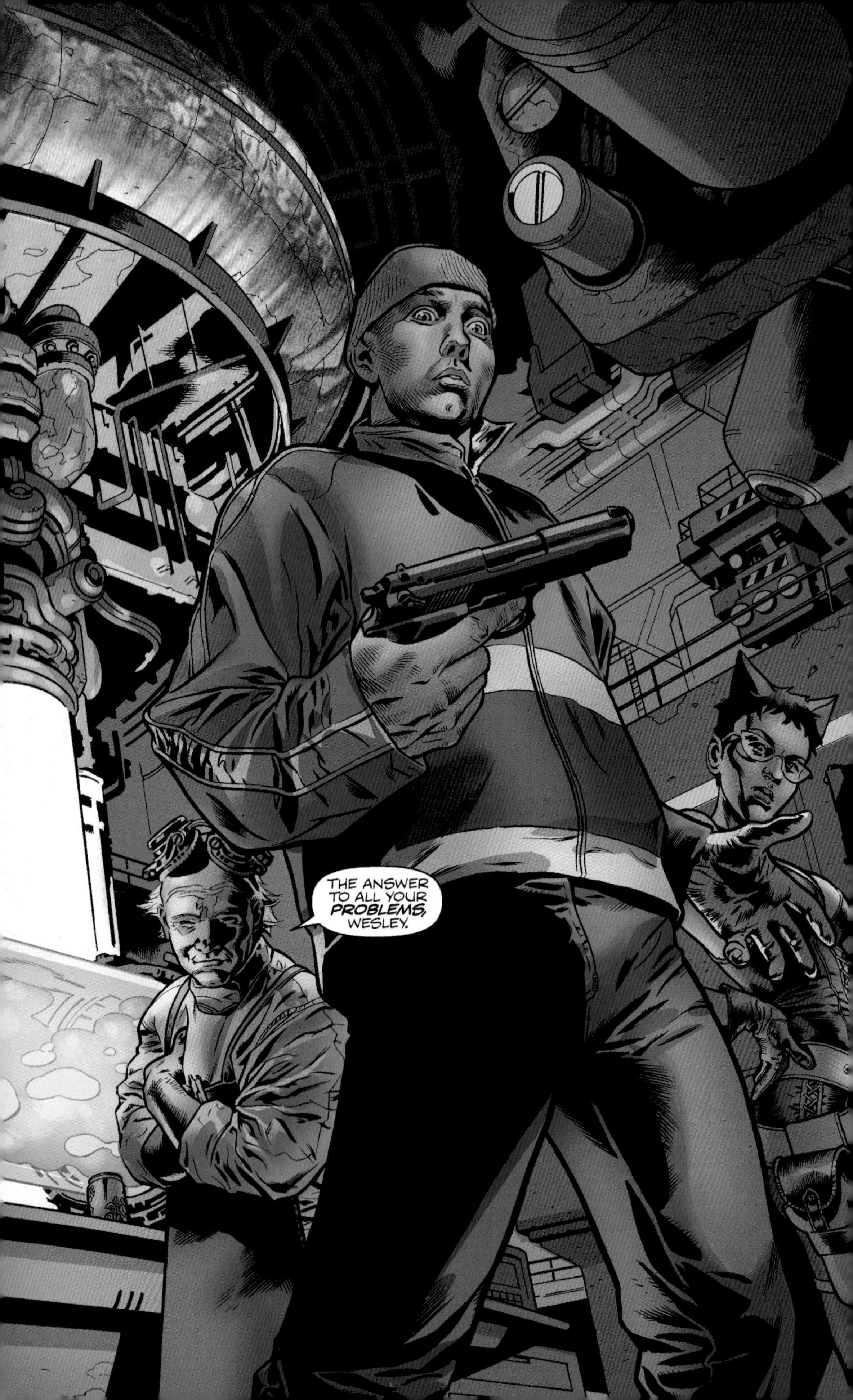
THE ANSWER TO ALL YOUR PROBLEMS, WESLEY.

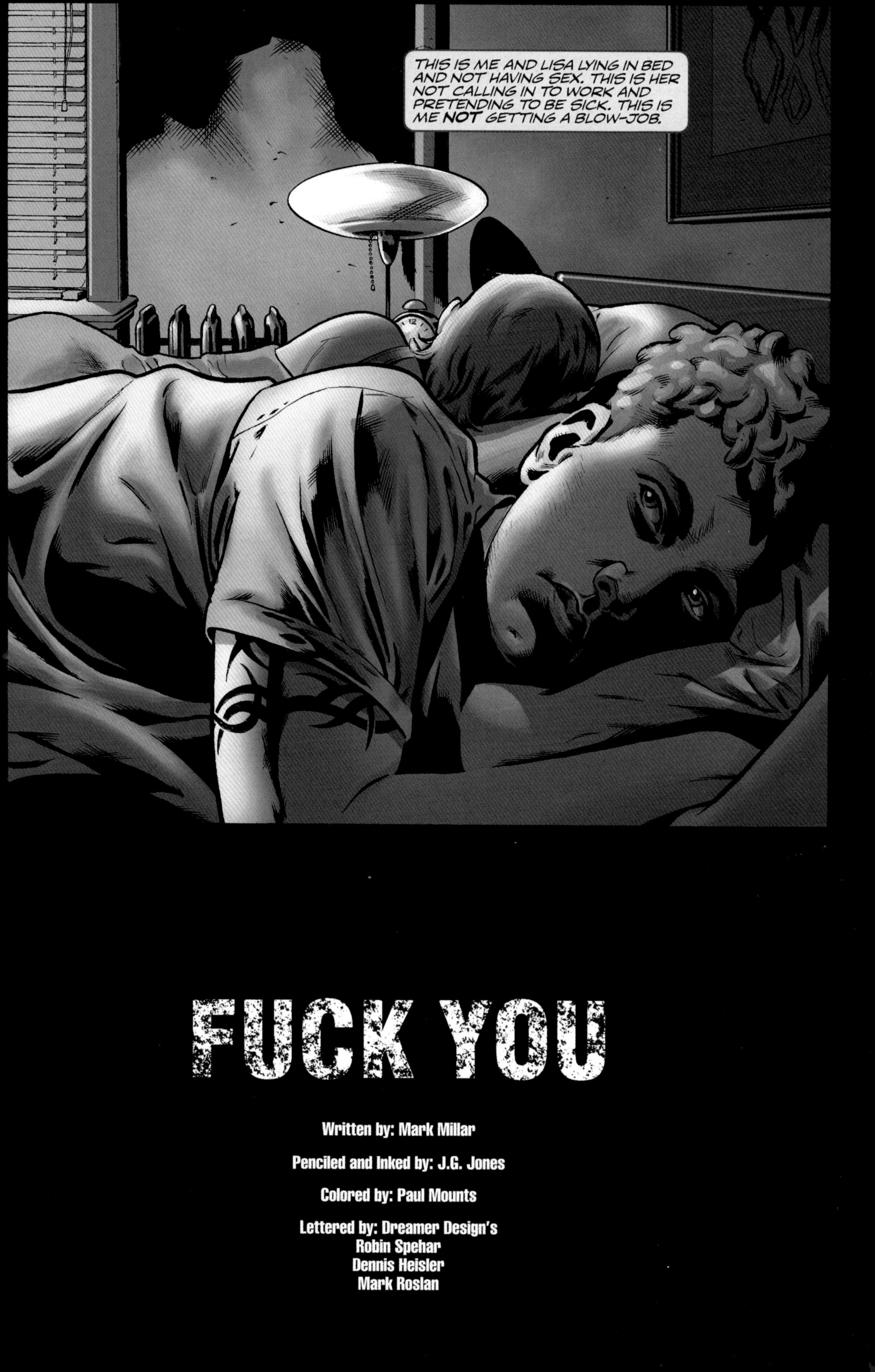
THIS IS ME AND LISA LYING IN BED AND NOT HAVING SEX. THIS IS HER NOT CALLING IN TO WORK AND PRETENDING TO BE SICK. THIS IS ME **NOT** GETTING A BLOW-JOB.

FUCK YOU

Written by: Mark Millar

Penciled and Inked by: J.G. Jones

Colored by: Paul Mounts

Lettered by: Dreamer Design's
Robin Spehar
Dennis Heisler
Mark Roslan

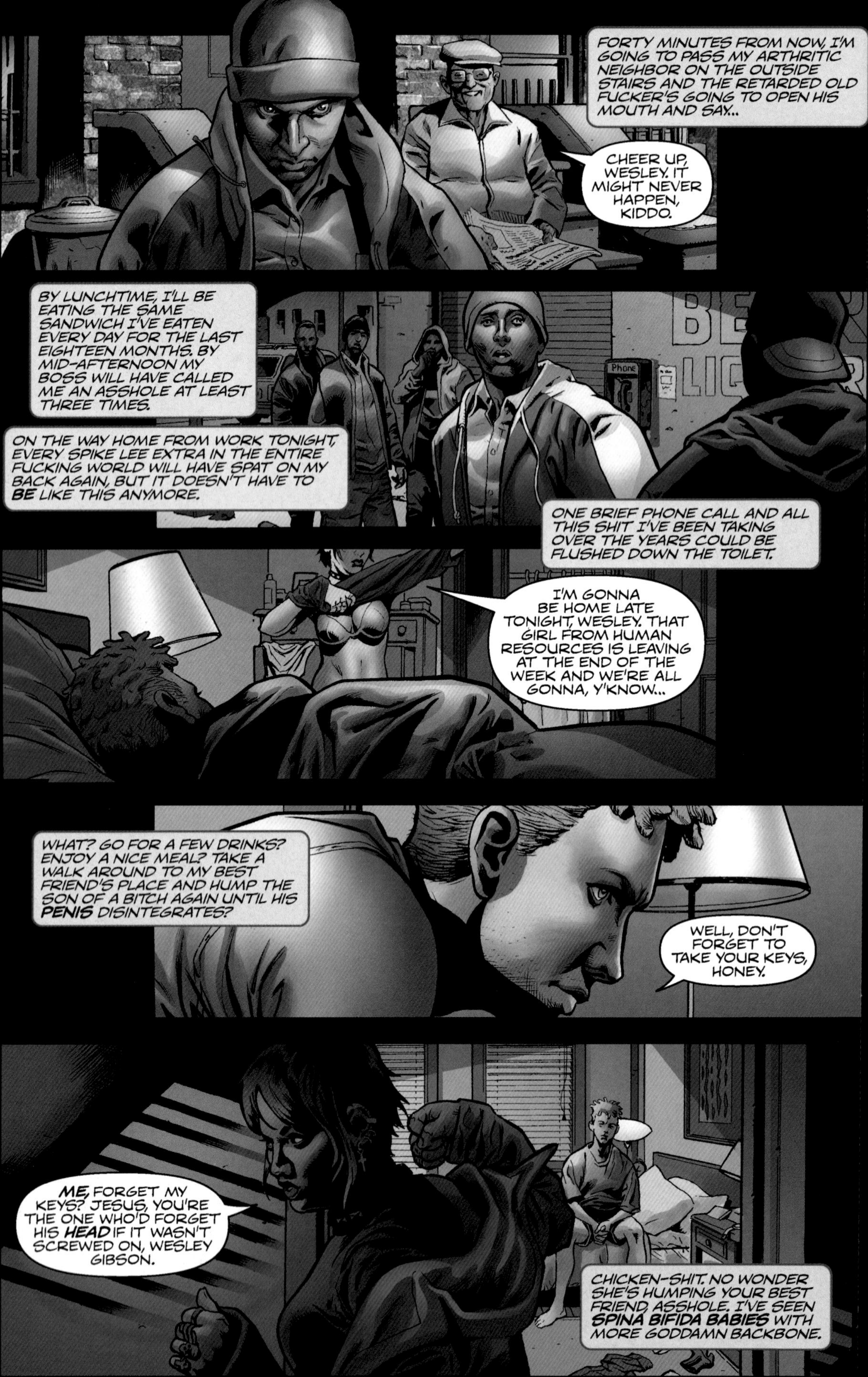
FORTY MINUTES FROM NOW, I'M GOING TO PASS MY ARTHRITIC NEIGHBOR ON THE OUTSIDE STAIRS AND THE RETARDED OLD FUCKER'S GOING TO OPEN HIS MOUTH AND SAY...
CHEER UP, WESLEY. IT MIGHT NEVER HAPPEN, KIDDO.
BY LUNCHTIME, I'LL BE EATING THE SAME SANDWICH I'VE EATEN EVERY DAY FOR THE LAST EIGHTEEN MONTHS. BY MID-AFTERNOON MY BOSS WILL HAVE CALLED ME AN ASSHOLE AT LEAST THREE TIMES.
ON THE WAY HOME FROM WORK TONIGHT, EVERY SPIKE LEE EXTRA IN THE ENTIRE FUCKING WORLD WILL HAVE SPAT ON MY BACK AGAIN, BUT IT DOESN'T HAVE TO BE LIKE THIS ANYMORE.
Phone
ONE BRIEF PHONE CALL AND ALL THIS SHIT I'VE BEEN TAKING OVER THE YEARS COULD BE FLUSHED DOWN THE TOILET.
I'M GONNA BE HOME LATE TONIGHT, WESLEY. THAT GIRL FROM HUMAN RESOURCES IS LEAVING AT THE END OF THE WEEK AND WE'RE ALL GONNA, Y'KNOW...
WHAT? GO FOR A FEW DRINKS? ENJOY A NICE MEAL? TAKE A WALK AROUND TO MY BEST FRIEND'S PLACE AND HUMP THE SON OF A BITCH AGAIN UNTIL HIS PENIS DISINTEGRATES?
WELL, DON'T FORGET TO TAKE YOUR KEYS, HONEY.
ME, FORGET MY KEYS? JESUS, YOU'RE THE ONE WHO'D FORGET HIS HEAD IF IT WASN'T SCREWED ON, WESLEY GIBSON.
CHICKEN-SHIT. NO WONDER SHE'S HUMPING YOUR BEST FRIEND, ASSHOLE. I'VE SEEN SPINA BIFIDA BABIES WITH MORE GODDAMN BACKBONE.

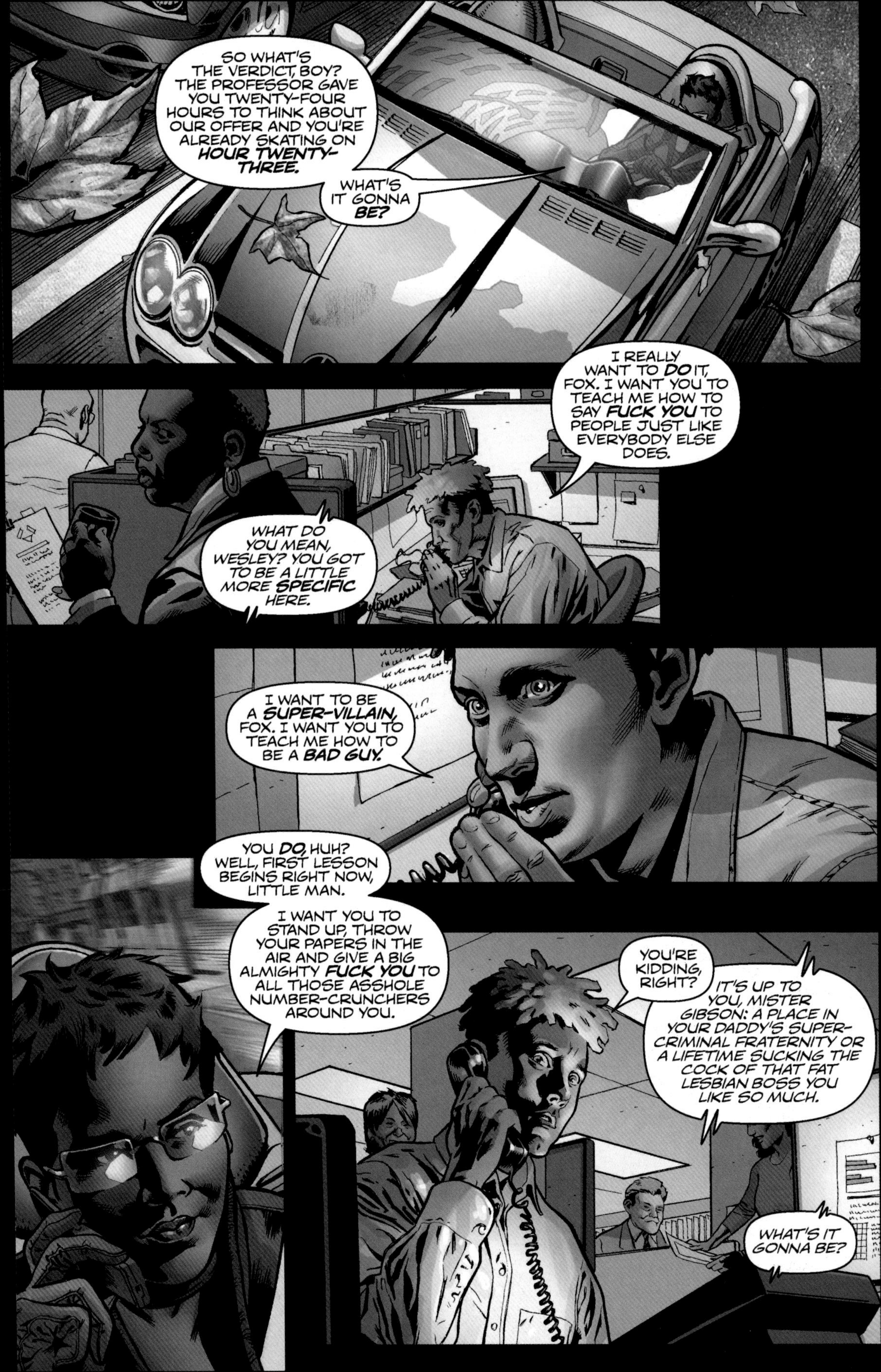
SO WHAT'S THE VERDICT, BOY? THE PROFESSOR GAVE YOU TWENTY-FOUR HOURS TO THINK ABOUT OUR OFFER AND YOU'RE ALREADY SKATING ON HOUR TWENTY-THREE.
WHAT'S IT GONNA BE?
I REALLY WANT TO DO IT, FOX. I WANT YOU TO TEACH ME HOW TO SAY FUCK YOU TO PEOPLE JUST LIKE EVERYBODY ELSE DOES.
WHAT DO YOU MEAN, WESLEY? YOU GOT TO BE A LITTLE MORE SPECIFIC HERE.
I WANT TO BE A SUPER-VILLAIN, FOX. I WANT YOU TO TEACH ME HOW TO BE A BAD GUY.
YOU DO, HUH? WELL, FIRST LESSON BEGINS RIGHT NOW, LITTLE MAN.
I WANT YOU TO STAND UP, THROW YOUR PAPERS IN THE AIR AND GIVE A BIG ALMIGHTY FUCK YOU TO ALL THOSE ASSHOLE NUMBER-CRUNCHERS AROUND YOU.
YOU'RE KIDDING, RIGHT?
IT'S UP TO YOU, MISTER GIBSON: A PLACE IN YOUR DADDY'S SUPER-CRIMINAL FRATERNITY OR A LIFETIME SUCKING THE COCK OF THAT FAT LESBIAN BOSS YOU LIKE SO MUCH.
WHAT'S IT GONNA BE?

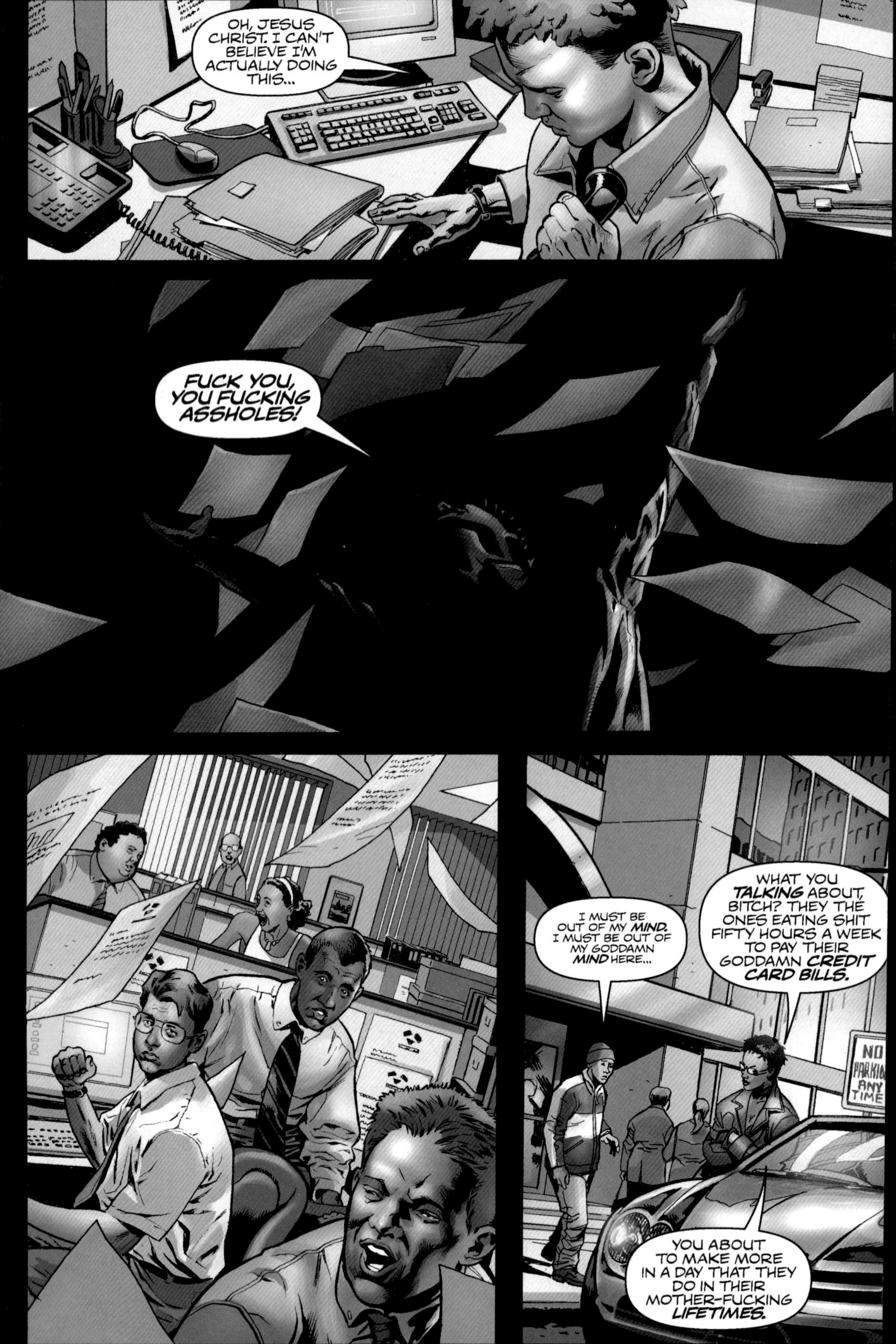
OH, JESUS CHRIST. I CAN'T BELIEVE I'M ACTUALLY DOING THIS...
FUCK YOU, YOU FUCKING ASSHOLES!
I MUST BE OUT OF MY MIND. I MUST BE OUT OF MY GODDAMN MIND HERE...
WHAT YOU TALKING ABOUT, BITCH? THEY THE ONES EATING SHIT FIFTY HOURS A WEEK TO PAY THEIR GODDAMN CREDIT CARD BILLS.
NO PARKING ANY TIME
YOU ABOUT TO MAKE MORE IN A DAY THAT THEY DO IN THEIR MOTHER-FUCKING LIFETIMES.

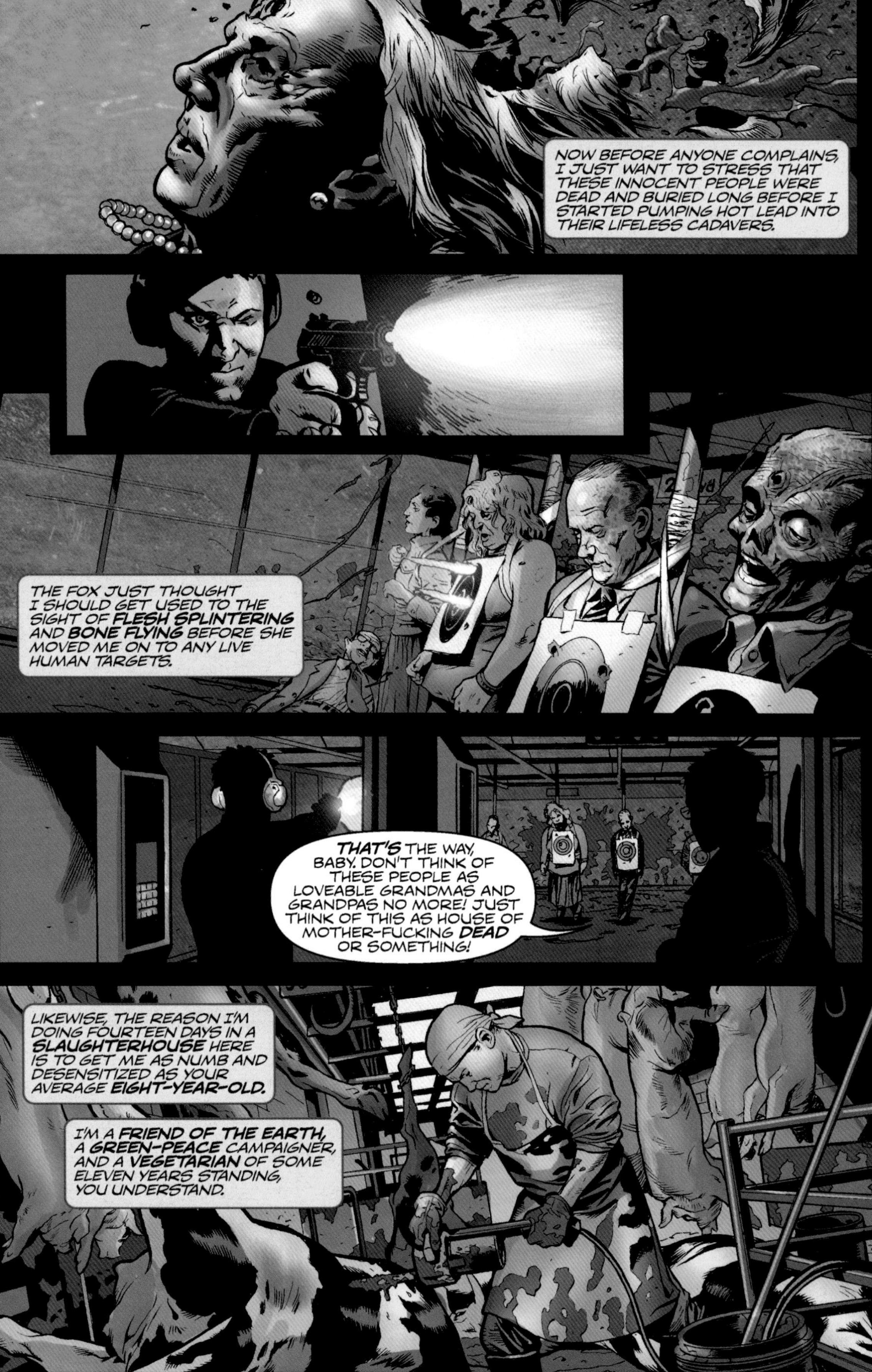
NOW BEFORE ANYONE COMPLAINS, I JUST WANT TO STRESS THAT THESE INNOCENT PEOPLE WERE DEAD AND BURIED LONG BEFORE I STARTED PUMPING HOT LEAD INTO THEIR LIFELESS CADAVERS.
THE FOX JUST THOUGHT I SHOULD GET USED TO THE SIGHT OF **FLESH SPLINTERING** AND **BONE FLYING** BEFORE SHE MOVED ME ON TO ANY LIVE HUMAN TARGETS.
THAT'S THE WAY, BABY. DON'T THINK OF THESE PEOPLE AS LOVEABLE GRANDMAS AND GRANDPAS NO MORE! JUST THINK OF THIS AS HOUSE OF MOTHER-FUCKING **DEAD** OR SOMETHING!
LIKEWISE, THE REASON I'M DOING FOURTEEN DAYS IN A **SLAUGHTERHOUSE** HERE IS TO GET ME AS NUMB AND DESENSITIZED AS YOUR AVERAGE **EIGHT-YEAR-OLD.**
I'M A **FRIEND OF THE EARTH,** A **GREEN-PEACE** CAMPAIGNER, AND A **VEGETARIAN** OF SOME ELEVEN YEARS STANDING, YOU UNDERSTAND.

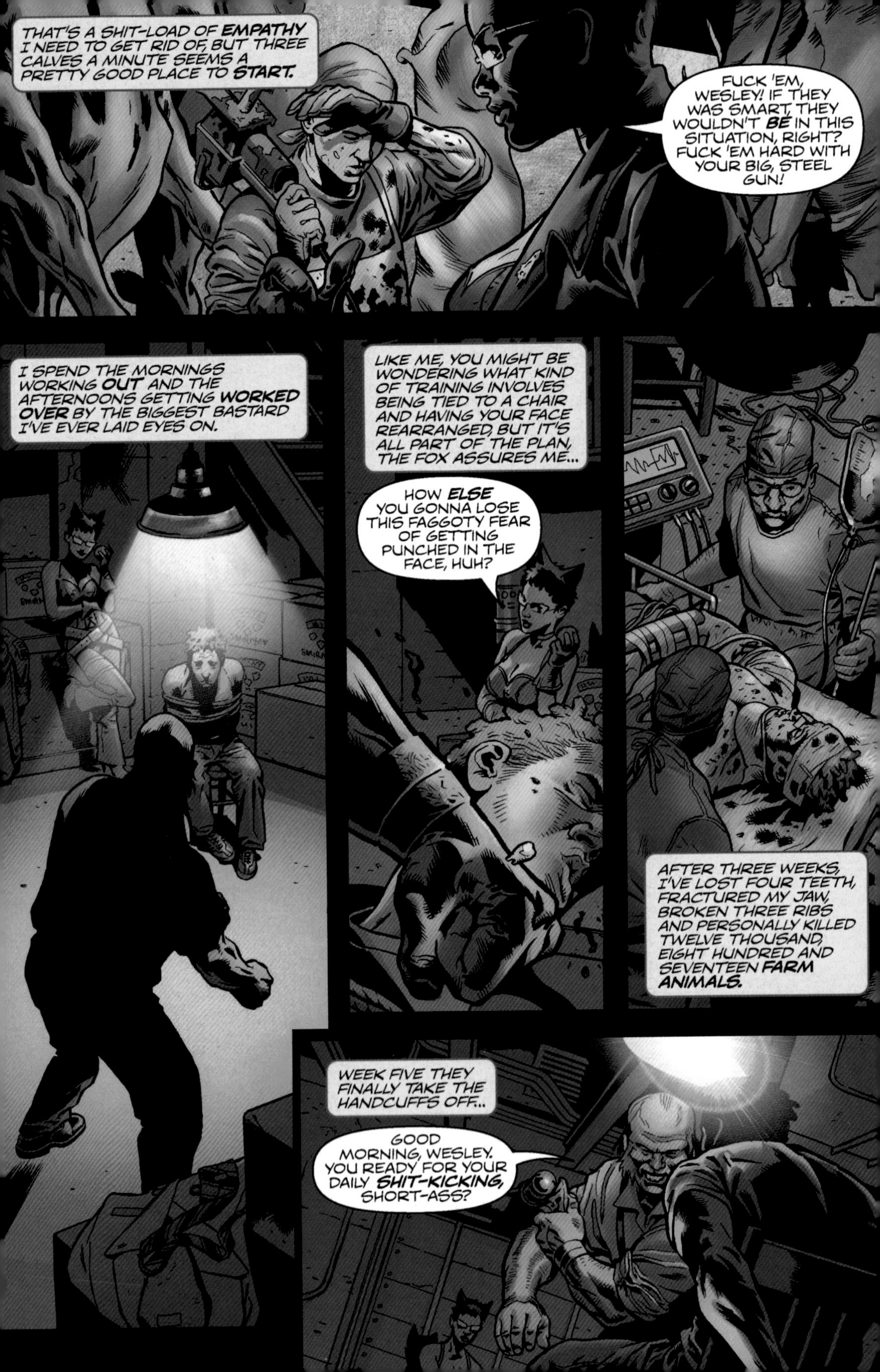
THAT'S A SHIT-LOAD OF EMPATHY I NEED TO GET RID OF, BUT THREE CALVES A MINUTE SEEMS A PRETTY GOOD PLACE TO START.
FUCK 'EM, WESLEY! IF THEY WAS SMART, THEY WOULDN'T BE IN THIS SITUATION, RIGHT? FUCK 'EM HARD WITH YOUR BIG, STEEL GUN!
I SPEND THE MORNINGS WORKING OUT AND THE AFTERNOONS GETTING WORKED OVER BY THE BIGGEST BASTARD I'VE EVER LAID EYES ON.
LIKE ME, YOU MIGHT BE WONDERING WHAT KIND OF TRAINING INVOLVES BEING TIED TO A CHAIR AND HAVING YOUR FACE REARRANGED, BUT IT'S ALL PART OF THE PLAN, THE FOX ASSURES ME...
HOW ELSE YOU GONNA LOSE THIS FAGGOTY FEAR OF GETTING PUNCHED IN THE FACE, HUH?
AFTER THREE WEEKS, I'VE LOST FOUR TEETH, FRACTURED MY JAW, BROKEN THREE RIBS AND PERSONALLY KILLED TWELVE THOUSAND, EIGHT HUNDRED AND SEVENTEEN FARM ANIMALS.
WEEK FIVE THEY FINALLY TAKE THE HANDCUFFS OFF...
GOOD MORNING, WESLEY. YOU READY FOR YOUR DAILY SHIT-KICKING, SHORT-ASS?

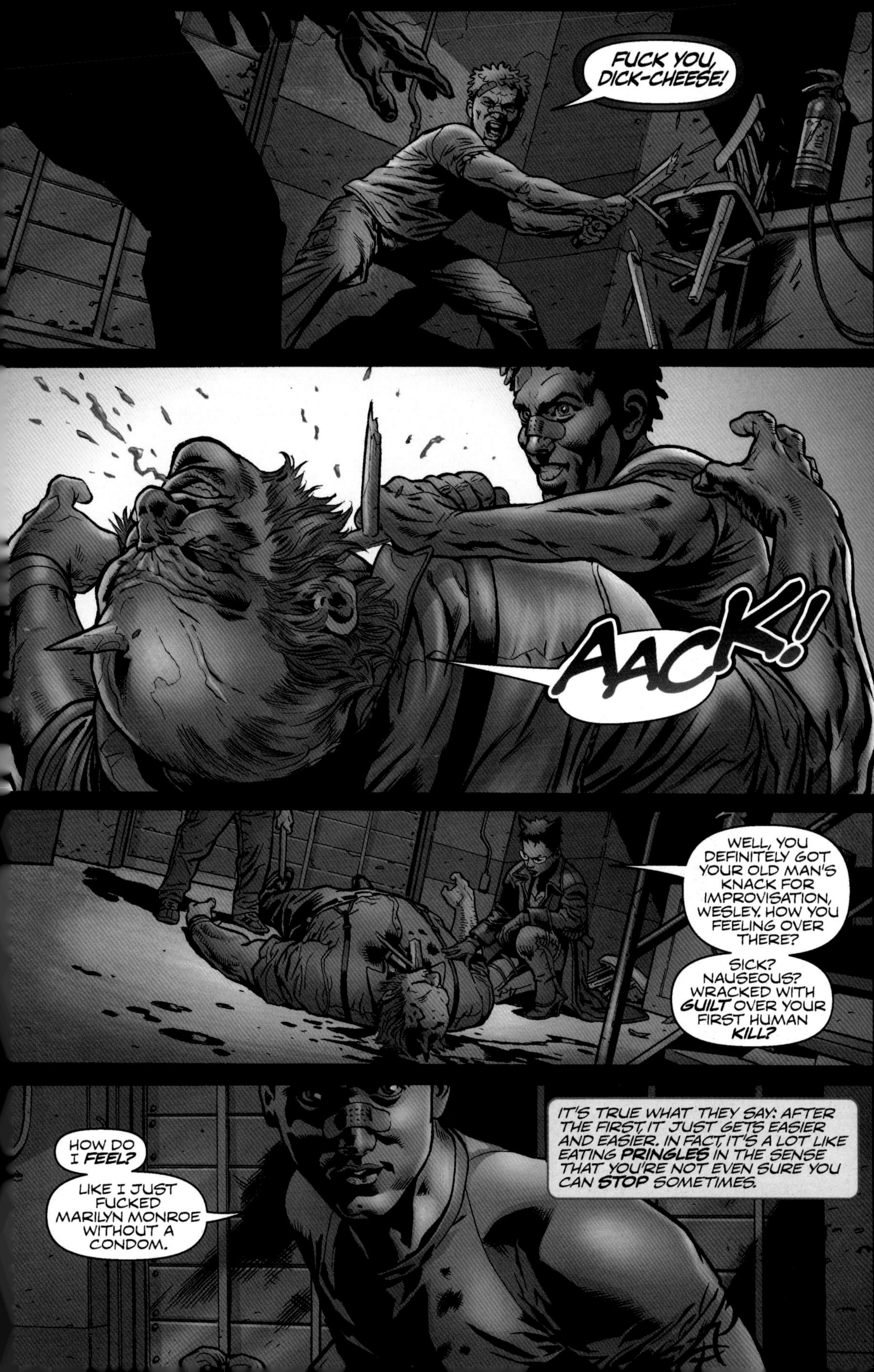
FUCK YOU, DICK-CHEESE!
AACK!!
WELL, YOU DEFINITELY GOT YOUR OLD MAN'S KNACK FOR IMPROVISATION, WESLEY. HOW YOU FEELING OVER THERE?
SICK? NAUSEOUS? WRACKED WITH GUILT OVER YOUR FIRST HUMAN KILL?
HOW DO I FEEL?
LIKE I JUST FUCKED MARILYN MONROE WITHOUT A CONDOM.
IT'S TRUE WHAT THEY SAY: AFTER THE FIRST, IT JUST GETS EASIER AND EASIER. IN FACT, IT'S A LOT LIKE EATING PRINGLES IN THE SENSE THAT YOU'RE NOT EVEN SURE YOU CAN STOP SOMETIMES.

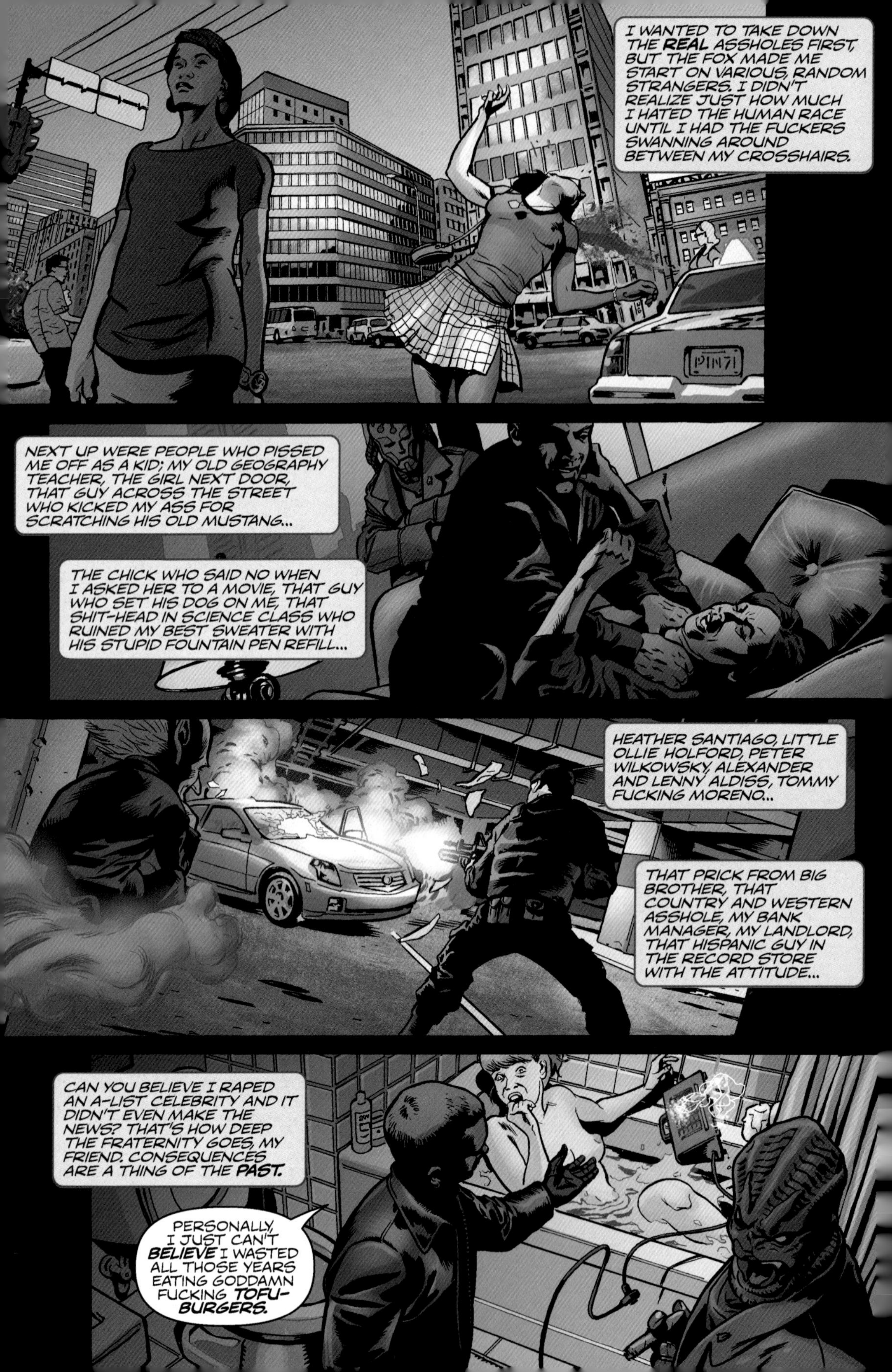
I WANTED TO TAKE DOWN THE **REAL** ASSHOLES FIRST, BUT THE FOX MADE ME START ON VARIOUS, RANDOM STRANGERS. I DIDN'T REALIZE JUST HOW MUCH I HATED THE HUMAN RACE UNTIL I HAD THE FUCKERS SWANNING AROUND BETWEEN MY CROSSHAIRS.
NEXT UP WERE PEOPLE WHO PISSED ME OFF AS A KID; MY OLD GEOGRAPHY TEACHER, THE GIRL NEXT DOOR, THAT GUY ACROSS THE STREET WHO KICKED MY ASS FOR SCRATCHING HIS OLD MUSTANG...
THE CHICK WHO SAID NO WHEN I ASKED HER TO A MOVIE, THAT GUY WHO SET HIS DOG ON ME, THAT SHIT-HEAD IN SCIENCE CLASS WHO RUINED MY BEST SWEATER WITH HIS STUPID FOUNTAIN PEN REFILL...
HEATHER SANTIAGO, LITTLE OLLIE HOLFORD, PETER WILKOWSKY, ALEXANDER AND LENNY ALDISS, TOMMY FUCKING MORENO...
THAT PRICK FROM BIG BROTHER, THAT COUNTRY AND WESTERN ASSHOLE, MY BANK MANAGER, MY LANDLORD, THAT HISPANIC GUY IN THE RECORD STORE WITH THE ATTITUDE...
CAN YOU BELIEVE I RAPED AN A-LIST CELEBRITY AND IT DIDN'T EVEN MAKE THE NEWS? THAT'S HOW DEEP THE FRATERNITY GOES, MY FRIEND. CONSEQUENCES ARE A THING OF THE **PAST.**
PERSONALLY, I JUST CAN'T **BELIEVE** I WASTED ALL THOSE YEARS EATING GODDAMN FUCKING **TOFU-BURGERS.**

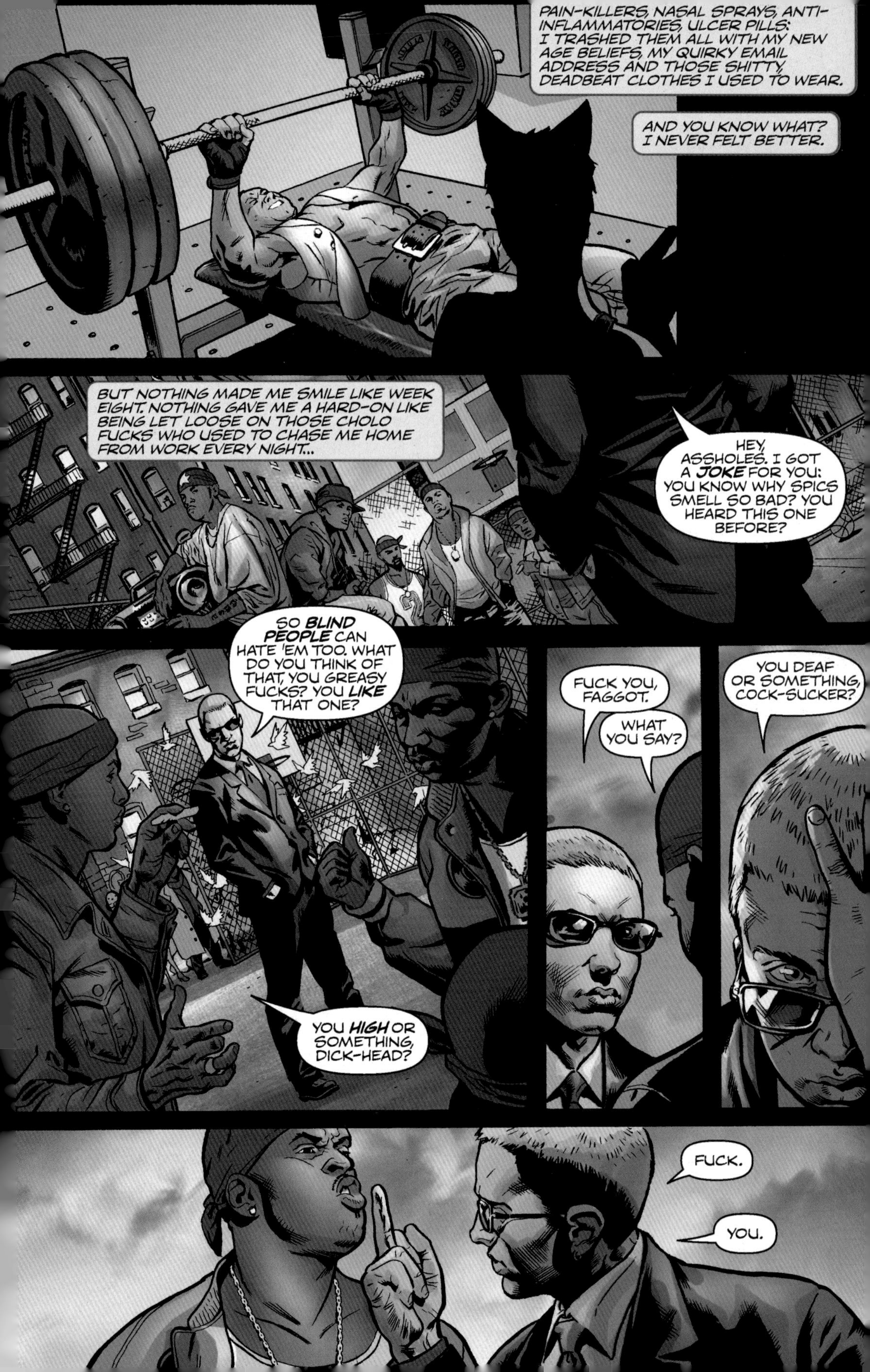
PAIN-KILLERS, NASAL SPRAYS, ANTI-INFLAMMATORIES, ULCER PILLS: I TRASHED THEM ALL WITH MY NEW AGE BELIEFS, MY QUIRKY EMAIL ADDRESS AND THOSE SHITTY, DEADBEAT CLOTHES I USED TO WEAR.
AND YOU KNOW WHAT? I NEVER FELT BETTER.
BUT NOTHING MADE ME SMILE LIKE WEEK EIGHT. NOTHING GAVE ME A HARD-ON LIKE BEING LET LOOSE ON THOSE CHOLO FUCKS WHO USED TO CHASE ME HOME FROM WORK EVERY NIGHT...
HEY, ASSHOLES. I GOT A JOKE FOR YOU: YOU KNOW WHY SPICS SMELL SO BAD? YOU HEARD THIS ONE BEFORE?
SO BLIND PEOPLE CAN HATE 'EM TOO. WHAT DO YOU THINK OF THAT, YOU GREASY FUCKS? YOU LIKE THAT ONE?
YOU HIGH OR SOMETHING, DICK-HEAD?
FUCK YOU, FAGGOT.
WHAT YOU SAY?
YOU DEAF OR SOMETHING, COCK-SUCKER?
FUCK.
YOU.

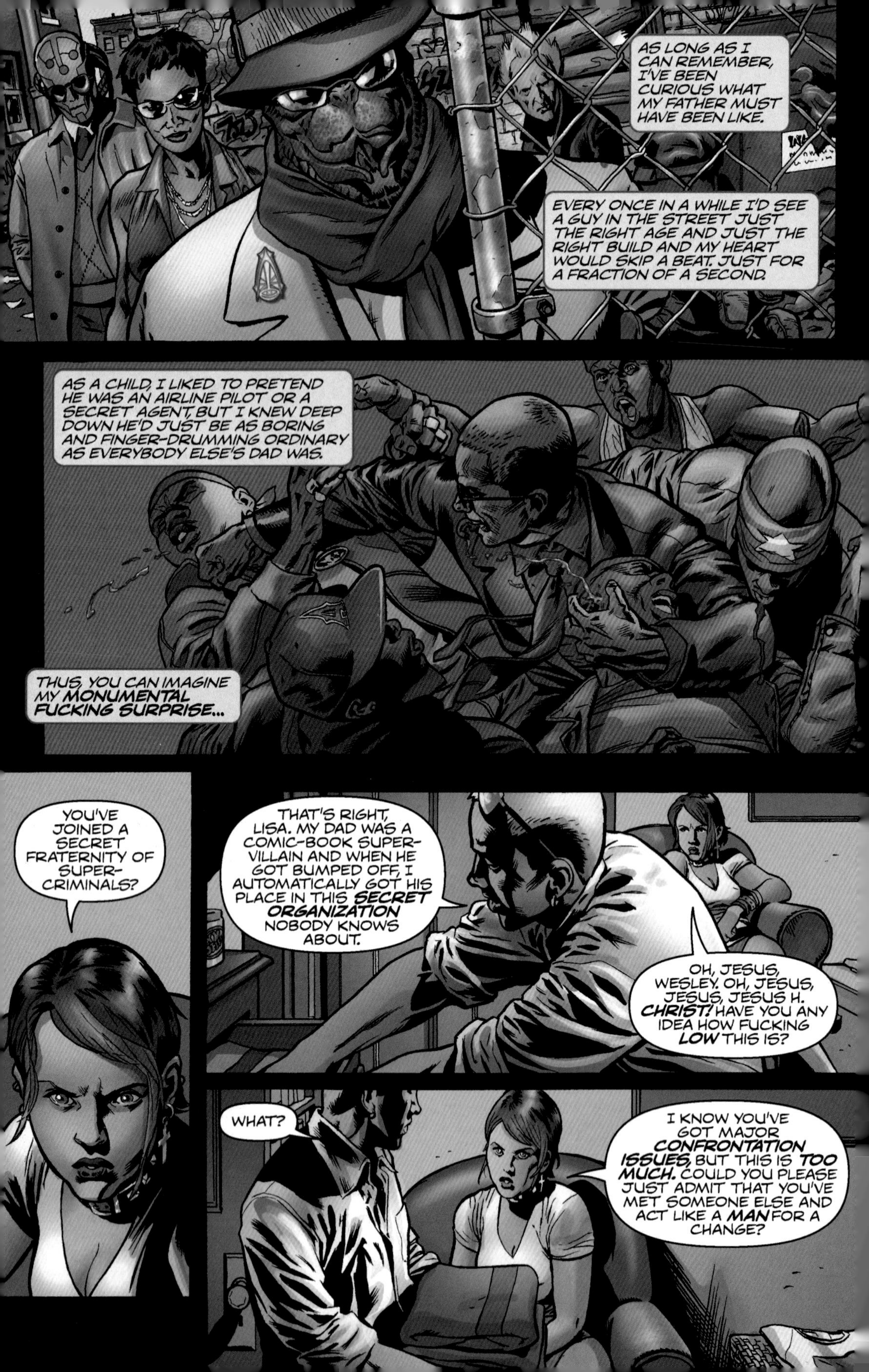
AS LONG AS I CAN REMEMBER, I'VE BEEN CURIOUS WHAT MY FATHER MUST HAVE BEEN LIKE.
EVERY ONCE IN A WHILE I'D SEE A GUY IN THE STREET JUST THE RIGHT AGE AND JUST THE RIGHT BUILD AND MY HEART WOULD SKIP A BEAT. JUST FOR A FRACTION OF A SECOND.
AS A CHILD, I LIKED TO PRETEND HE WAS AN AIRLINE PILOT OR A SECRET AGENT, BUT I KNEW DEEP DOWN HE'D JUST BE AS BORING AND FINGER-DRUMMING ORDINARY AS EVERYBODY ELSE'S DAD WAS.
THUS, YOU CAN IMAGINE MY **MONUMENTAL FUCKING SURPRISE...**
YOU'VE JOINED A SECRET FRATERNITY OF SUPER-CRIMINALS?
THAT'S RIGHT, LISA. MY DAD WAS A COMIC-BOOK SUPER-VILLAIN AND WHEN HE GOT BUMPED OFF, I AUTOMATICALLY GOT HIS PLACE IN THIS ***SECRET ORGANIZATION*** NOBODY KNOWS ABOUT.
OH, JESUS, WESLEY. OH, JESUS, JESUS, JESUS H. ***CHRIST!*** HAVE YOU ANY IDEA HOW FUCKING ***LOW*** THIS IS?
WHAT?
I KNOW YOU'VE GOT MAJOR ***CONFRONTATION ISSUES,*** BUT THIS IS ***TOO MUCH.*** COULD YOU PLEASE JUST ADMIT THAT YOU'VE MET SOMEONE ELSE AND ACT LIKE A ***MAN*** FOR A CHANGE?

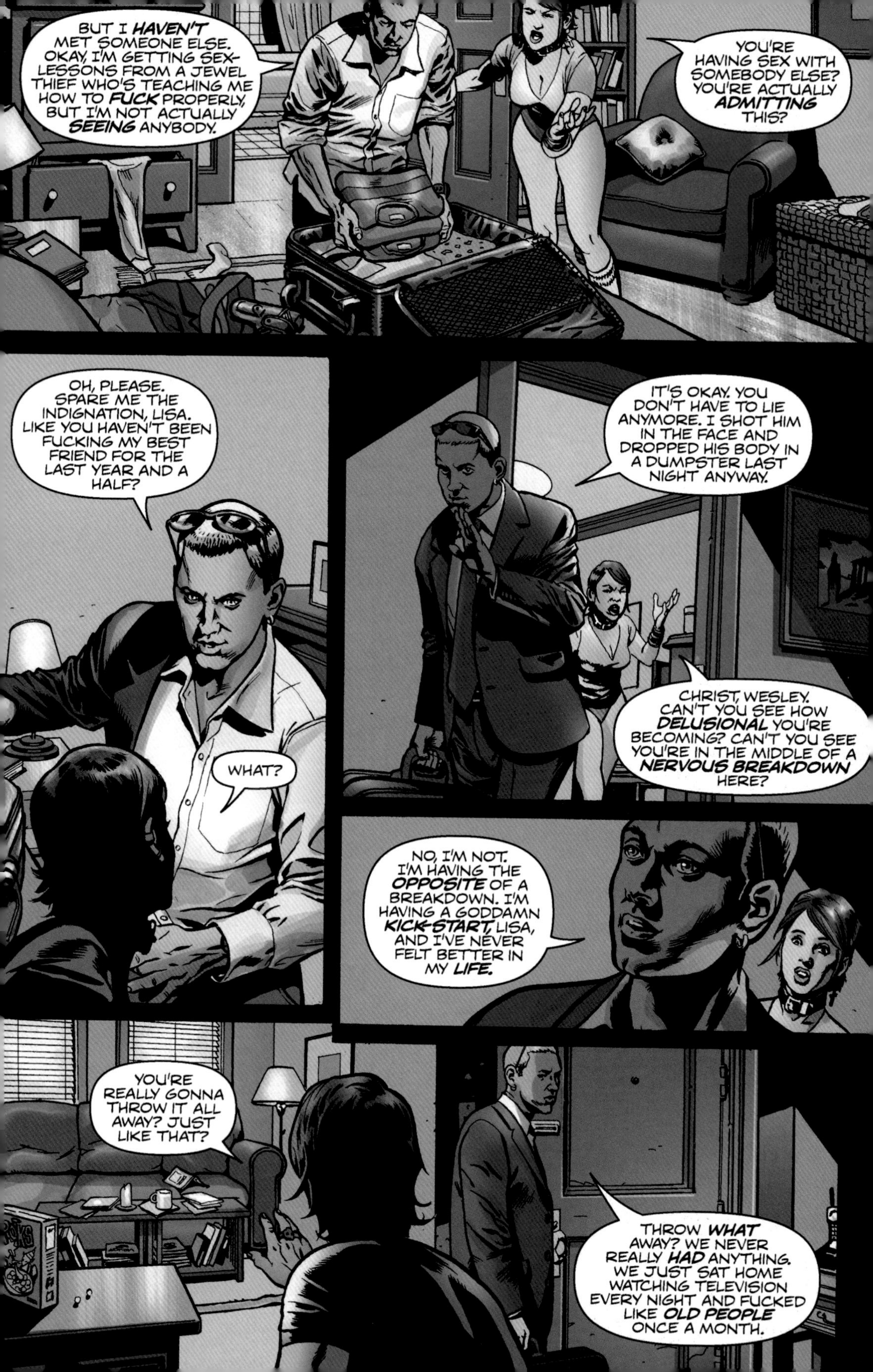
BUT I HAVEN'T MET SOMEONE ELSE. OKAY, I'M GETTING SEX-LESSONS FROM A JEWEL THIEF WHO'S TEACHING ME HOW TO FUCK PROPERLY, BUT I'M NOT ACTUALLY SEEING ANYBODY.
YOU'RE HAVING SEX WITH SOMEBODY ELSE? YOU'RE ACTUALLY ADMITTING THIS?
OH, PLEASE. SPARE ME THE INDIGNATION, LISA. LIKE YOU HAVEN'T BEEN FUCKING MY BEST FRIEND FOR THE LAST YEAR AND A HALF?
WHAT?
IT'S OKAY. YOU DON'T HAVE TO LIE ANYMORE. I SHOT HIM IN THE FACE AND DROPPED HIS BODY IN A DUMPSTER LAST NIGHT ANYWAY.
CHRIST, WESLEY. CAN'T YOU SEE HOW DELUSIONAL YOU'RE BECOMING? CAN'T YOU SEE YOU'RE IN THE MIDDLE OF A NERVOUS BREAKDOWN HERE?
NO, I'M NOT. I'M HAVING THE OPPOSITE OF A BREAKDOWN. I'M HAVING A GODDAMN KICK-START, LISA, AND I'VE NEVER FELT BETTER IN MY LIFE.
YOU'RE REALLY GONNA THROW IT ALL AWAY? JUST LIKE THAT?
THROW WHAT AWAY? WE NEVER REALLY HAD ANYTHING. WE JUST SAT HOME WATCHING TELEVISION EVERY NIGHT AND FUCKED LIKE OLD PEOPLE ONCE A MONTH.

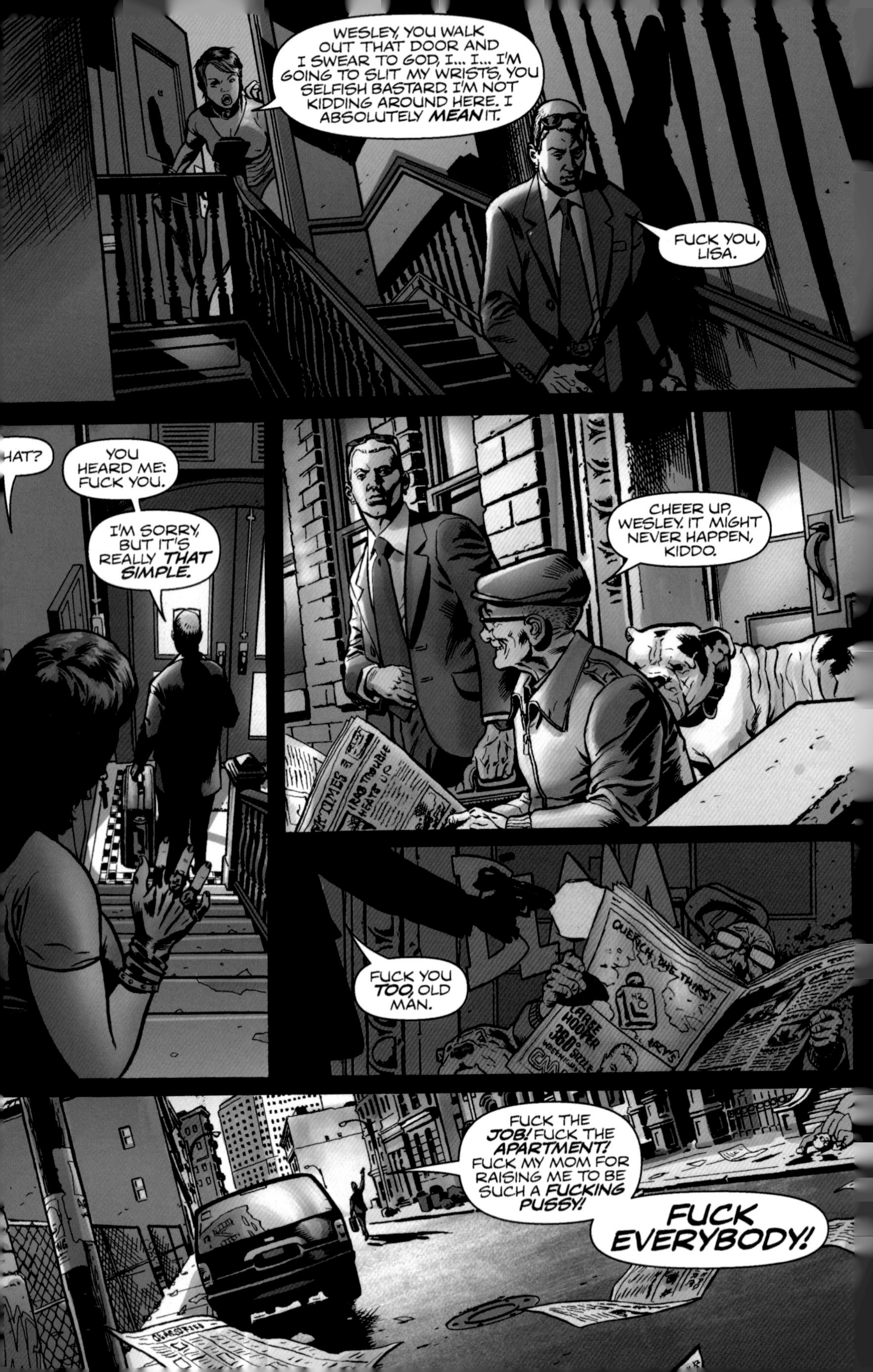

WESLEY, YOU WALK OUT THAT DOOR AND I SWEAR TO GOD, I... I... I'M GOING TO SLIT MY WRISTS, YOU SELFISH BASTARD. I'M NOT KIDDING AROUND HERE. I ABSOLUTELY MEAN IT.
FUCK YOU, LISA.
HAT?
YOU HEARD ME: FUCK YOU.
I'M SORRY, BUT IT'S REALLY THAT SIMPLE.
CHEER UP, WESLEY. IT MIGHT NEVER HAPPEN, KIDDO.
IRAQ TROUBLE HEATS UP
FUCK YOU TOO, OLD MAN.
QUENCH THE THIRST
LARRE HOOPER 360°
FUCK THE JOB! FUCK THE APARTMENT! FUCK MY MOM FOR RAISING ME TO BE SUCH A FUCKING PUSSY!
FUCK EVERYBODY!

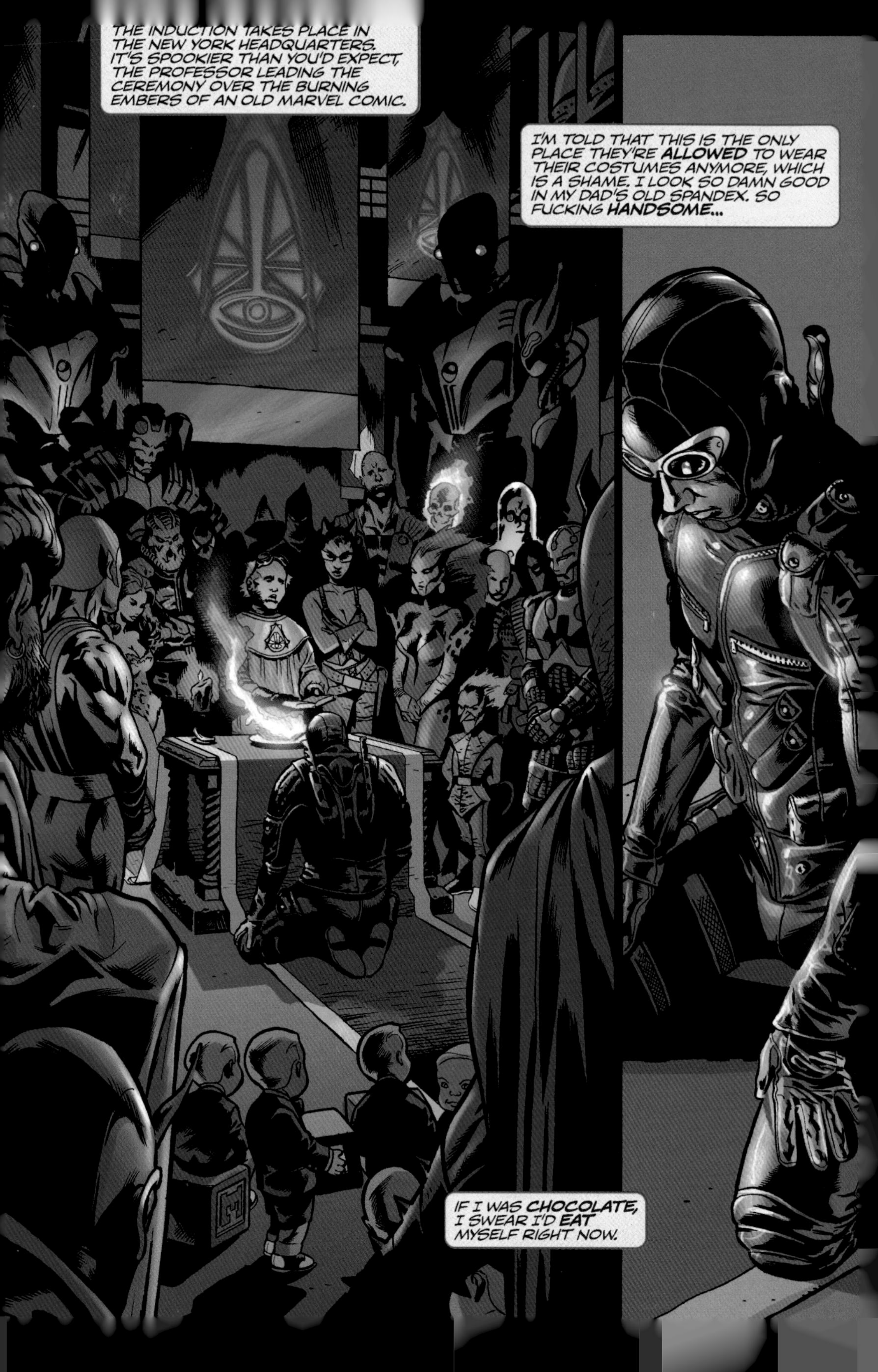
THE INDUCTION TAKES PLACE IN THE NEW YORK HEADQUARTERS. IT'S SPOOKIER THAN YOU'D EXPECT, THE PROFESSOR LEADING THE CEREMONY OVER THE BURNING EMBERS OF AN OLD MARVEL COMIC.
I'M TOLD THAT THIS IS THE ONLY PLACE THEY'RE ALLOWED TO WEAR THEIR COSTUMES ANYMORE, WHICH IS A SHAME. I LOOK SO DAMN GOOD IN MY DAD'S OLD SPANDEX. SO FUCKING HANDSOME...
IF I WAS CHOCOLATE, I SWEAR I'D EAT MYSELF RIGHT NOW.

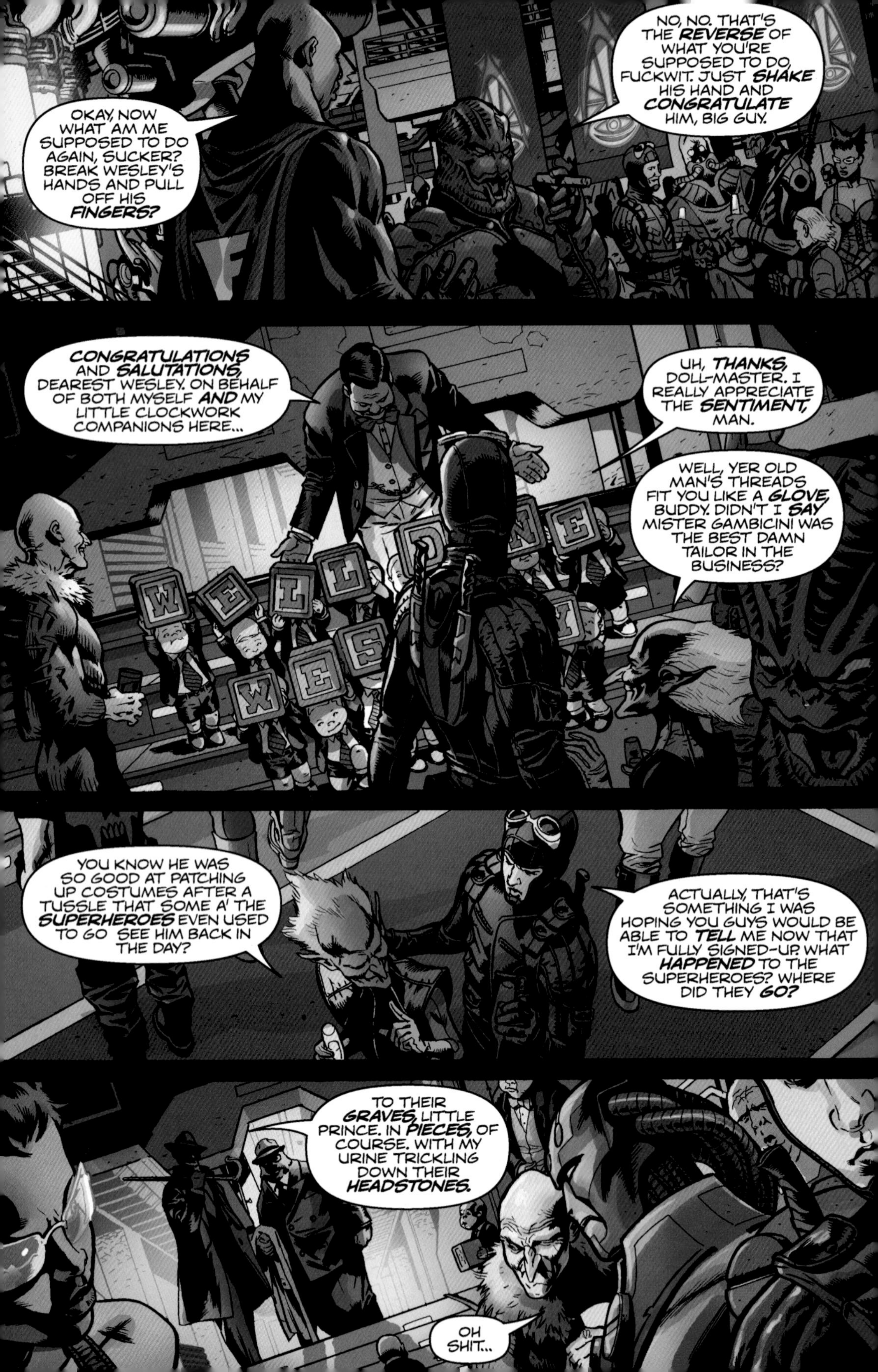
OKAY, NOW WHAT AM ME SUPPOSED TO DO AGAIN, SUCKER? BREAK WESLEY'S HANDS AND PULL OFF HIS FINGERS?
NO, NO. THAT'S THE REVERSE OF WHAT YOU'RE SUPPOSED TO DO, FUCKWIT. JUST SHAKE HIS HAND AND CONGRATULATE HIM, BIG GUY.
CONGRATULATIONS AND SALUTATIONS, DEAREST WESLEY. ON BEHALF OF BOTH MYSELF AND MY LITTLE CLOCKWORK COMPANIONS HERE...
UH, THANKS, DOLL-MASTER. I REALLY APPRECIATE THE SENTIMENT, MAN.
WELL, YER OLD MAN'S THREADS FIT YOU LIKE A GLOVE, BUDDY. DIDN'T I SAY MISTER GAMBICINI WAS THE BEST DAMN TAILOR IN THE BUSINESS?
YOU KNOW HE WAS SO GOOD AT PATCHING UP COSTUMES AFTER A TUSSLE THAT SOME A' THE SUPERHEROES EVEN USED TO GO SEE HIM BACK IN THE DAY?
ACTUALLY, THAT'S SOMETHING I WAS HOPING YOU GUYS WOULD BE ABLE TO TELL ME NOW THAT I'M FULLY SIGNED-UP. WHAT HAPPENED TO THE SUPERHEROES? WHERE DID THEY GO?
TO THEIR GRAVES, LITTLE PRINCE. IN PIECES, OF COURSE. WITH MY URINE TRICKLING DOWN THEIR HEADSTONES.
OH SHIT...

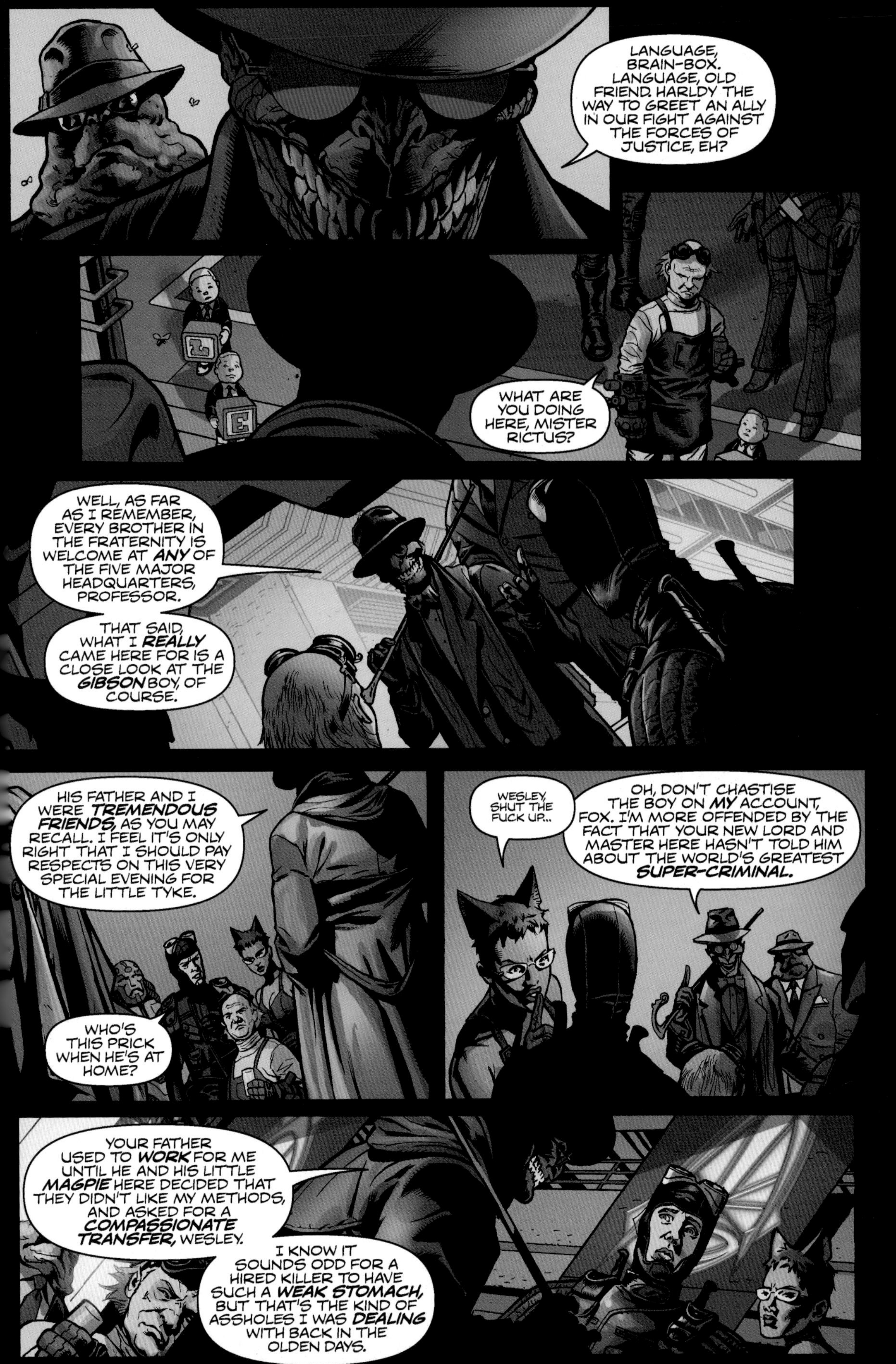
LANGUAGE, BRAIN-BOX. LANGUAGE, OLD FRIEND. HARLDY THE WAY TO GREET AN ALLY IN OUR FIGHT AGAINST THE FORCES OF JUSTICE, EH?
WHAT ARE YOU DOING HERE, MISTER RICTUS?
WELL, AS FAR AS I REMEMBER, EVERY BROTHER IN THE FRATERNITY IS WELCOME AT ANY OF THE FIVE MAJOR HEADQUARTERS, PROFESSOR.
THAT SAID, WHAT I REALLY CAME HERE FOR IS A CLOSE LOOK AT THE GIBSON BOY, OF COURSE.
HIS FATHER AND I WERE TREMENDOUS FRIENDS, AS YOU MAY RECALL. I FEEL IT'S ONLY RIGHT THAT I SHOULD PAY RESPECTS ON THIS VERY SPECIAL EVENING FOR THE LITTLE TYKE.
WHO'S THIS PRICK WHEN HE'S AT HOME?
WESLEY, SHUT THE FUCK UP...
OH, DON'T CHASTISE THE BOY ON MY ACCOUNT, FOX. I'M MORE OFFENDED BY THE FACT THAT YOUR NEW LORD AND MASTER HERE HASN'T TOLD HIM ABOUT THE WORLD'S GREATEST SUPER-CRIMINAL.
YOUR FATHER USED TO WORK FOR ME UNTIL HE AND HIS LITTLE MAGPIE HERE DECIDED THAT THEY DIDN'T LIKE MY METHODS, AND ASKED FOR A COMPASSIONATE TRANSFER, WESLEY.
I KNOW IT SOUNDS ODD FOR A HIRED KILLER TO HAVE SUCH A WEAK STOMACH, BUT THAT'S THE KIND OF ASSHOLES I WAS DEALING WITH BACK IN THE OLDEN DAYS.

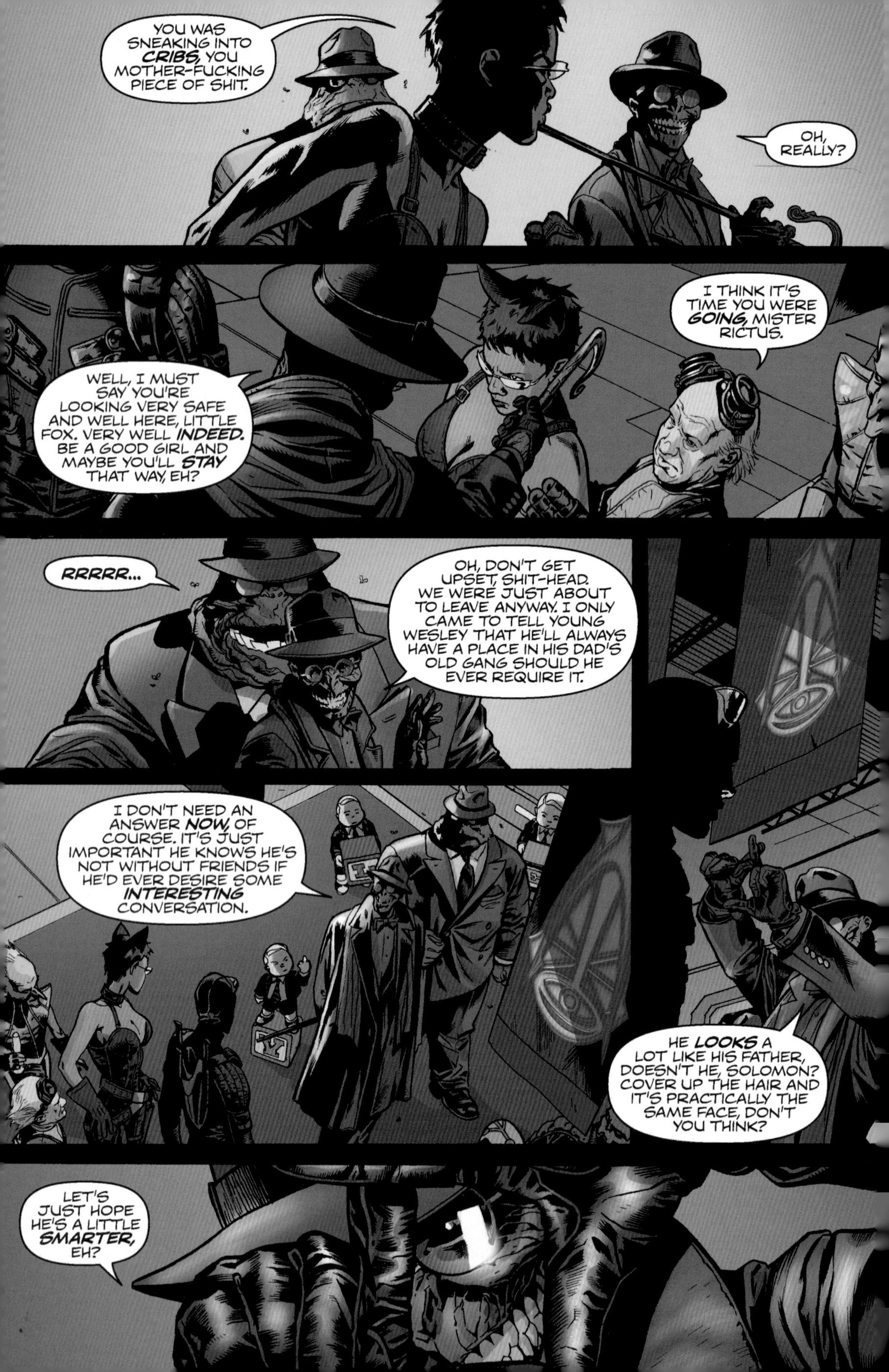
YOU WAS SNEAKING INTO CRIBS, YOU MOTHER-FUCKING PIECE OF SHIT.
OH, REALLY?
I THINK IT'S TIME YOU WERE GOING, MISTER RICTUS.
WELL, I MUST SAY YOU'RE LOOKING VERY SAFE AND WELL HERE, LITTLE FOX. VERY WELL INDEED. BE A GOOD GIRL AND MAYBE YOU'LL STAY THAT WAY, EH?
RRRRR...
OH, DON'T GET UPSET, SHIT-HEAD. WE WERE JUST ABOUT TO LEAVE ANYWAY. I ONLY CAME TO TELL YOUNG WESLEY THAT HE'LL ALWAYS HAVE A PLACE IN HIS DAD'S OLD GANG SHOULD HE EVER REQUIRE IT.
I DON'T NEED AN ANSWER NOW, OF COURSE. IT'S JUST IMPORTANT HE KNOWS HE'S NOT WITHOUT FRIENDS IF HE'D EVER DESIRE SOME INTERESTING CONVERSATION.
HE LOOKS A LOT LIKE HIS FATHER, DOESN'T HE, SOLOMON? COVER UP THE HAIR AND IT'S PRACTICALLY THE SAME FACE, DON'T YOU THINK?
LET'S JUST HOPE HE'S A LITTLE SMARTER, EH?

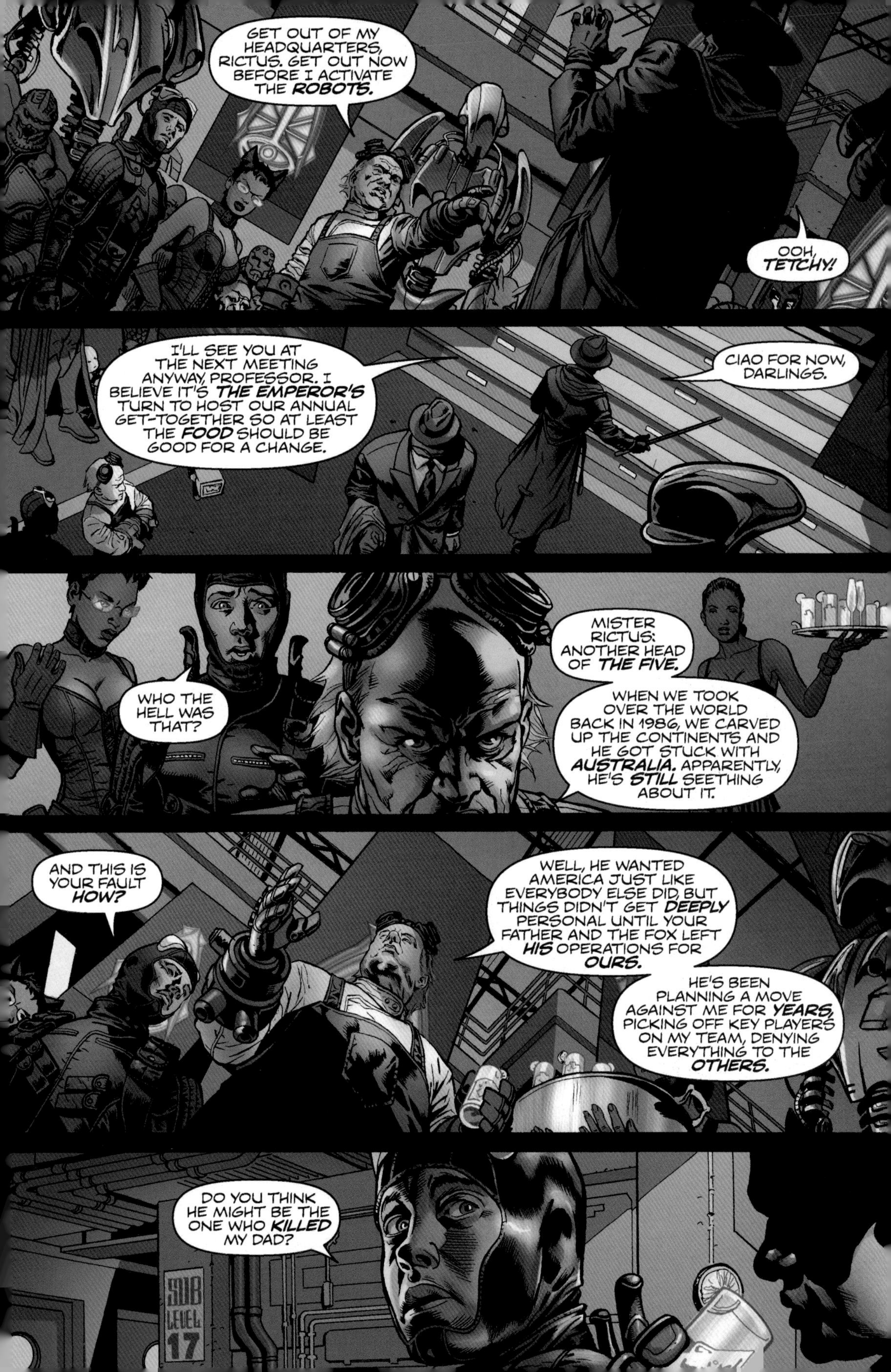
GET OUT OF MY HEADQUARTERS, RICTUS. GET OUT NOW BEFORE I ACTIVATE THE ROBOTS.
OOH, TETCHY!
I'LL SEE YOU AT THE NEXT MEETING ANYWAY, PROFESSOR. I BELIEVE IT'S THE EMPEROR'S TURN TO HOST OUR ANNUAL GET-TOGETHER SO AT LEAST THE FOOD SHOULD BE GOOD FOR A CHANGE.
CIAO FOR NOW, DARLINGS.
WHO THE HELL WAS THAT?
MISTER RICTUS: ANOTHER HEAD OF THE FIVE.
WHEN WE TOOK OVER THE WORLD BACK IN 1986, WE CARVED UP THE CONTINENTS AND HE GOT STUCK WITH AUSTRALIA. APPARENTLY, HE'S STILL SEETHING ABOUT IT.
AND THIS IS YOUR FAULT HOW?
WELL, HE WANTED AMERICA JUST LIKE EVERYBODY ELSE DID, BUT THINGS DIDN'T GET DEEPLY PERSONAL UNTIL YOUR FATHER AND THE FOX LEFT HIS OPERATIONS FOR OURS.
HE'S BEEN PLANNING A MOVE AGAINST ME FOR YEARS, PICKING OFF KEY PLAYERS ON MY TEAM, DENYING EVERYTHING TO THE OTHERS.
DO YOU THINK HE MIGHT BE THE ONE WHO KILLED MY DAD?
SUB LEVEL 17

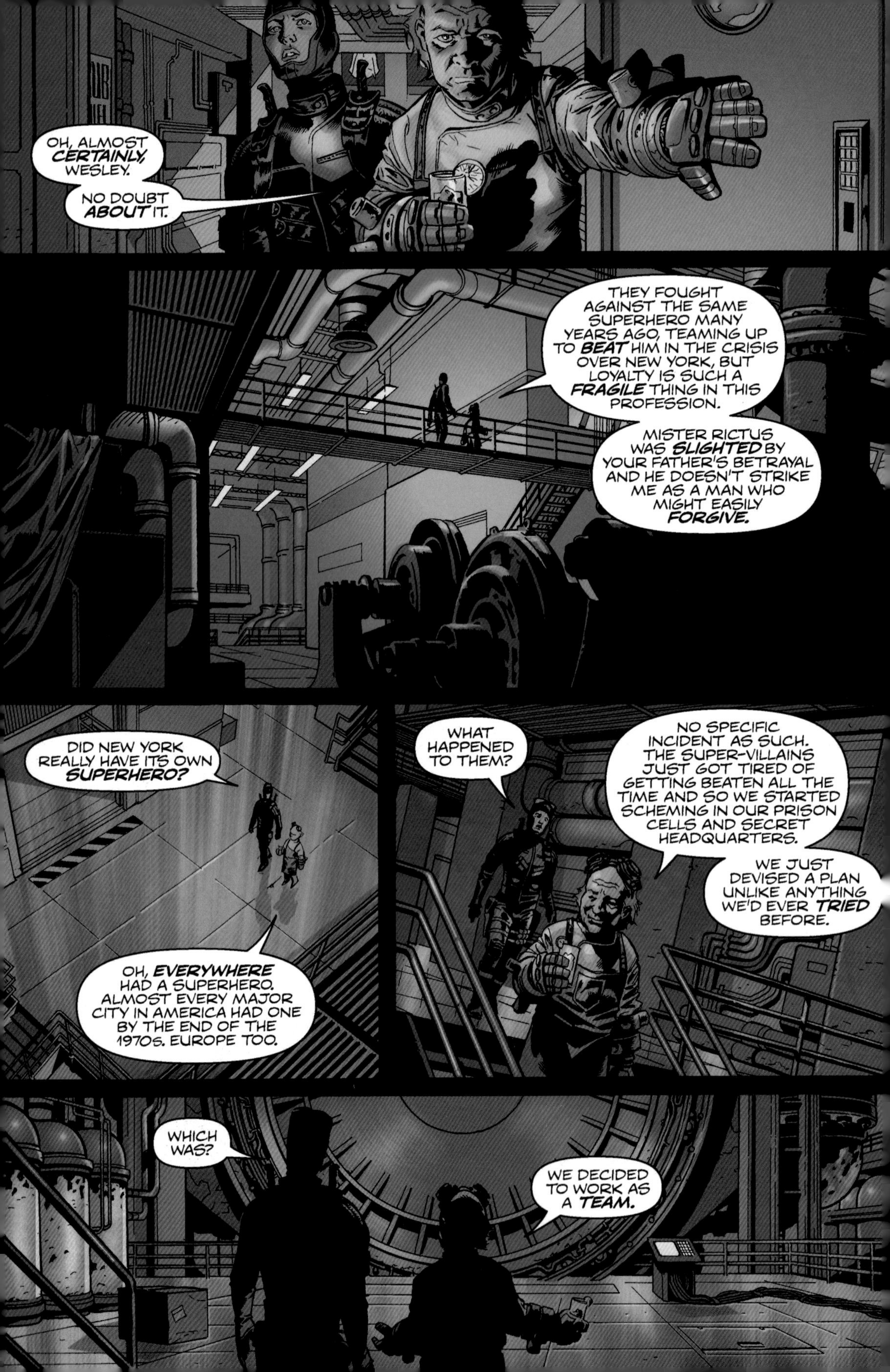

OH, ALMOST CERTAINLY, WESLEY.
NO DOUBT ABOUT IT.
THEY FOUGHT AGAINST THE SAME SUPERHERO MANY YEARS AGO, TEAMING UP TO BEAT HIM IN THE CRISIS OVER NEW YORK, BUT LOYALTY IS SUCH A FRAGILE THING IN THIS PROFESSION.
MISTER RICTUS WAS SLIGHTED BY YOUR FATHER'S BETRAYAL AND HE DOESN'T STRIKE ME AS A MAN WHO MIGHT EASILY FORGIVE.
DID NEW YORK REALLY HAVE ITS OWN SUPERHERO?
OH, EVERYWHERE HAD A SUPERHERO. ALMOST EVERY MAJOR CITY IN AMERICA HAD ONE BY THE END OF THE 1970s. EUROPE TOO.
WHAT HAPPENED TO THEM?
NO SPECIFIC INCIDENT AS SUCH. THE SUPER-VILLAINS JUST GOT TIRED OF GETTING BEATEN ALL THE TIME AND SO WE STARTED SCHEMING IN OUR PRISON CELLS AND SECRET HEADQUARTERS.
WE JUST DEVISED A PLAN UNLIKE ANYTHING WE'D EVER TRIED BEFORE.
WHICH WAS?
WE DECIDED TO WORK AS A TEAM.

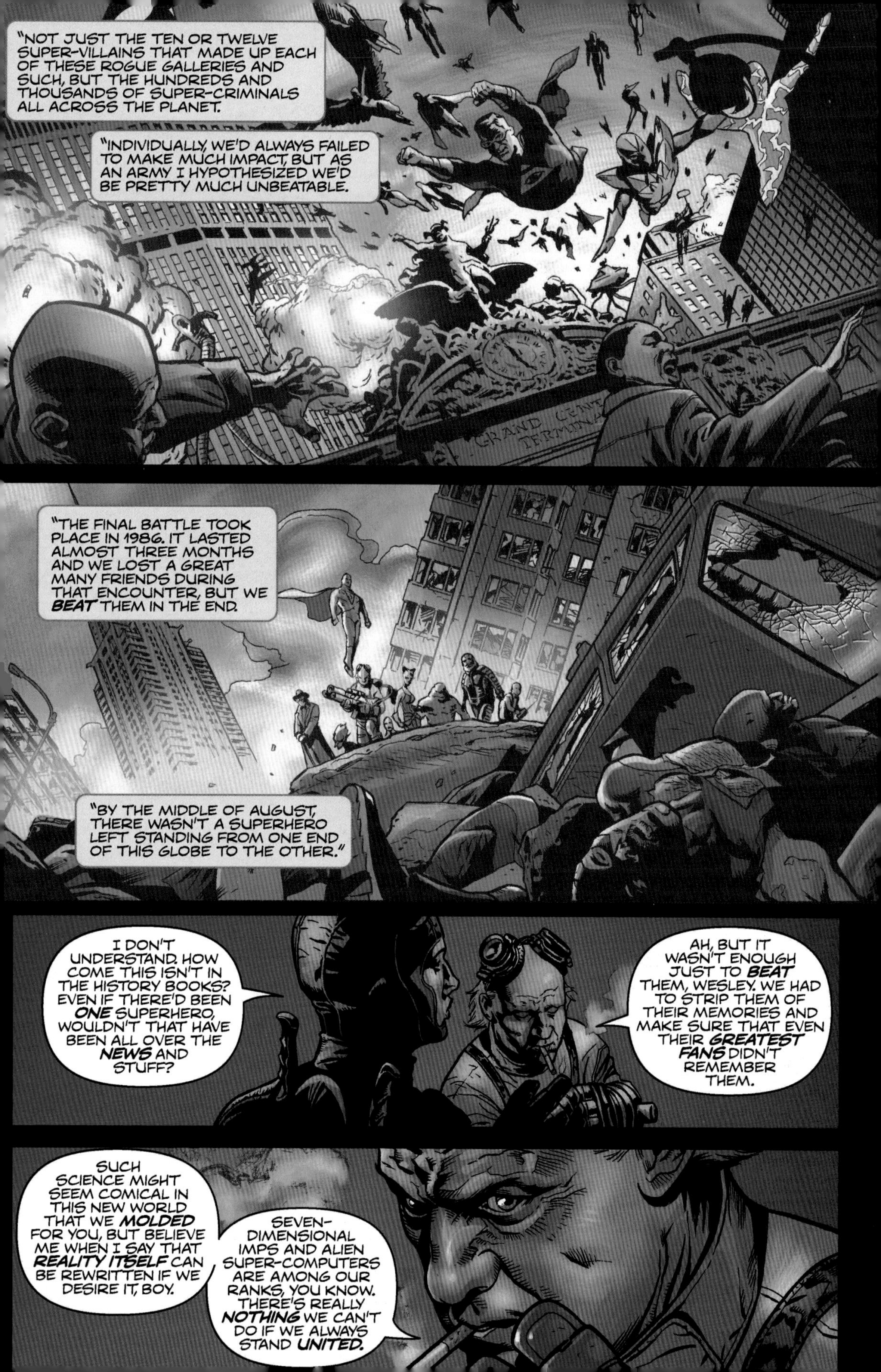
"NOT JUST THE TEN OR TWELVE SUPER-VILLAINS THAT MADE UP EACH OF THESE ROGUE GALLERIES AND SUCH, BUT THE HUNDREDS AND THOUSANDS OF SUPER-CRIMINALS ALL ACROSS THE PLANET.
"INDIVIDUALLY, WE'D ALWAYS FAILED TO MAKE MUCH IMPACT, BUT AS AN ARMY I HYPOTHESIZED WE'D BE PRETTY MUCH UNBEATABLE.
"THE FINAL BATTLE TOOK PLACE IN 1986. IT LASTED ALMOST THREE MONTHS AND WE LOST A GREAT MANY FRIENDS DURING THAT ENCOUNTER, BUT WE BEAT THEM IN THE END.
"BY THE MIDDLE OF AUGUST, THERE WASN'T A SUPERHERO LEFT STANDING FROM ONE END OF THIS GLOBE TO THE OTHER."
I DON'T UNDERSTAND. HOW COME THIS ISN'T IN THE HISTORY BOOKS? EVEN IF THERE'D BEEN ONE SUPERHERO, WOULDN'T THAT HAVE BEEN ALL OVER THE NEWS AND STUFF?
AH, BUT IT WASN'T ENOUGH JUST TO BEAT THEM, WESLEY. WE HAD TO STRIP THEM OF THEIR MEMORIES AND MAKE SURE THAT EVEN THEIR GREATEST FANS DIDN'T REMEMBER THEM.
SUCH SCIENCE MIGHT SEEM COMICAL IN THIS NEW WORLD THAT WE MOLDED FOR YOU, BUT BELIEVE ME WHEN I SAY THAT REALITY ITSELF CAN BE REWRITTEN IF WE DESIRE IT, BOY.
SEVEN-DIMENSIONAL IMPS AND ALIEN SUPER-COMPUTERS ARE AMONG OUR RANKS, YOU KNOW. THERE'S REALLY NOTHING WE CAN'T DO IF WE ALWAYS STAND UNITED.

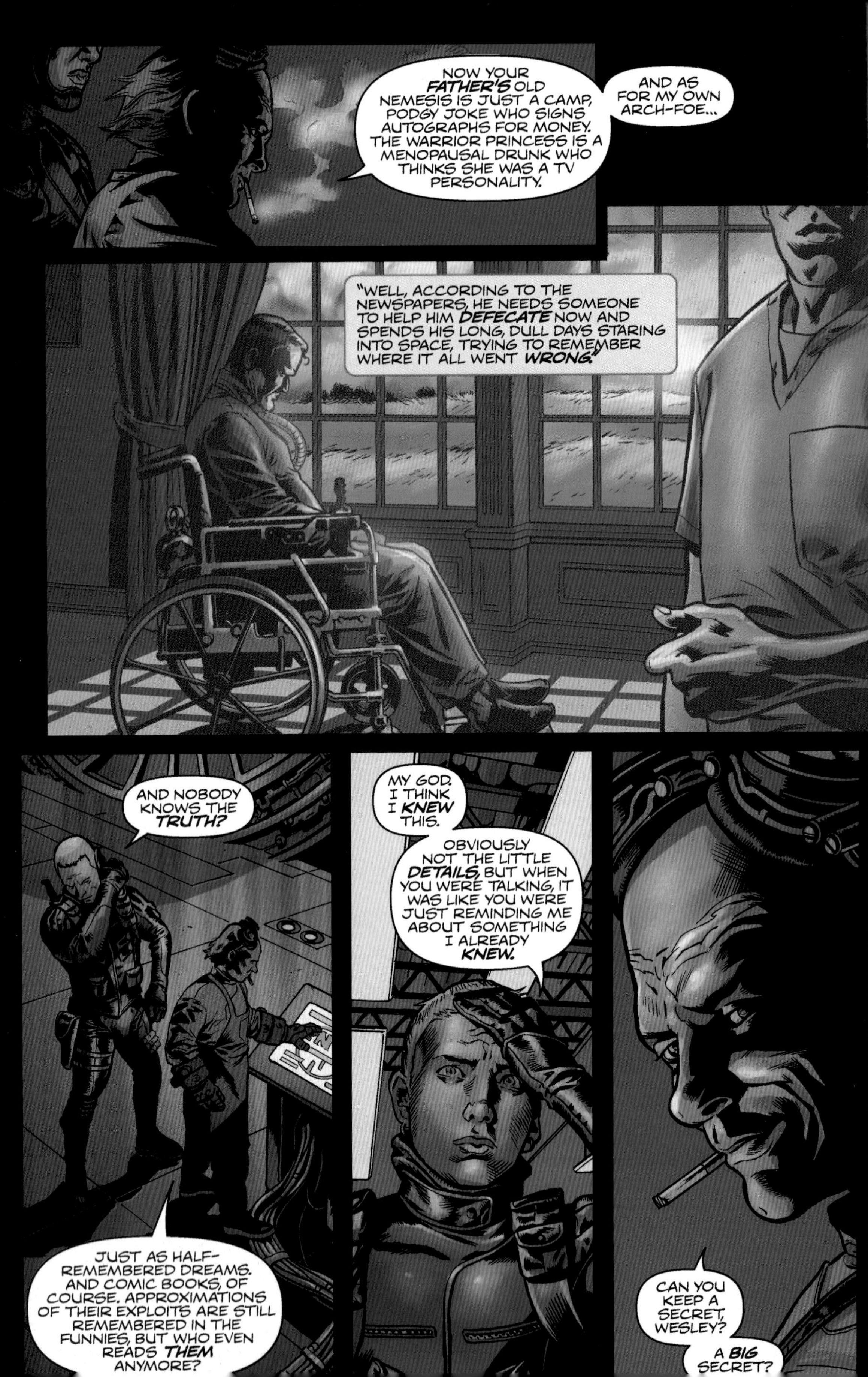
NOW YOUR FATHER'S OLD NEMESIS IS JUST A CAMP, PODGY JOKE WHO SIGNS AUTOGRAPHS FOR MONEY. THE WARRIOR PRINCESS IS A MENOPAUSAL DRUNK WHO THINKS SHE WAS A TV PERSONALITY.
AND AS FOR MY OWN ARCH-FOE...
"WELL, ACCORDING TO THE NEWSPAPERS, HE NEEDS SOMEONE TO HELP HIM DEFECATE NOW AND SPENDS HIS LONG, DULL DAYS STARING INTO SPACE, TRYING TO REMEMBER WHERE IT ALL WENT WRONG."
AND NOBODY KNOWS THE TRUTH?
JUST AS HALF-REMEMBERED DREAMS. AND COMIC BOOKS, OF COURSE. APPROXIMATIONS OF THEIR EXPLOITS ARE STILL REMEMBERED IN THE FUNNIES, BUT WHO EVEN READS THEM ANYMORE?
MY GOD. I THINK I KNEW THIS.
OBVIOUSLY NOT THE LITTLE DETAILS, BUT WHEN YOU WERE TALKING, IT WAS LIKE YOU WERE JUST REMINDING ME ABOUT SOMETHING I ALREADY KNEW.
CAN YOU KEEP A SECRET, WESLEY?
A BIG SECRET?

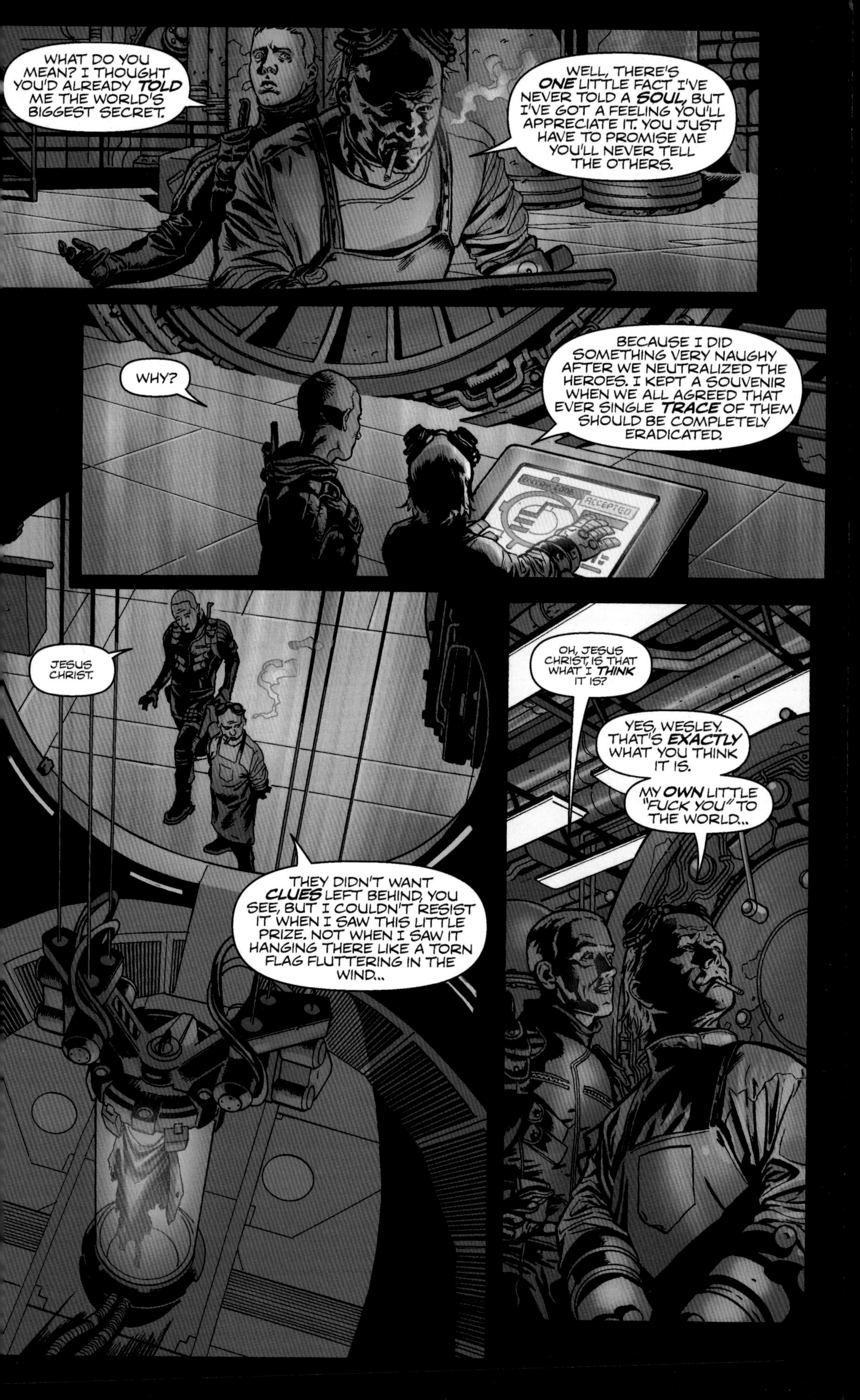
WHAT DO YOU MEAN? I THOUGHT YOU'D ALREADY TOLD ME THE WORLD'S BIGGEST SECRET.
WELL, THERE'S ONE LITTLE FACT I'VE NEVER TOLD A SOUL, BUT I'VE GOT A FEELING YOU'LL APPRECIATE IT. YOU JUST HAVE TO PROMISE ME YOU'LL NEVER TELL THE OTHERS.
WHY?
BECAUSE I DID SOMETHING VERY NAUGHY AFTER WE NEUTRALIZED THE HEROES. I KEPT A SOUVENIR WHEN WE ALL AGREED THAT EVER SINGLE TRACE OF THEM SHOULD BE COMPLETELY ERADICATED.
ACCEPTED
JESUS CHRIST.
THEY DIDN'T WANT CLUES LEFT BEHIND, YOU SEE, BUT I COULDN'T RESIST IT WHEN I SAW THIS LITTLE PRIZE. NOT WHEN I SAW IT HANGING THERE LIKE A TORN FLAG FLUTTERING IN THE WIND...
OH, JESUS CHRIST, IS THAT WHAT I THINK IT IS?
YES, WESLEY. THAT'S EXACTLY WHAT YOU THINK IT IS.
MY OWN LITTLE "FUCK YOU" TO THE WORLD...

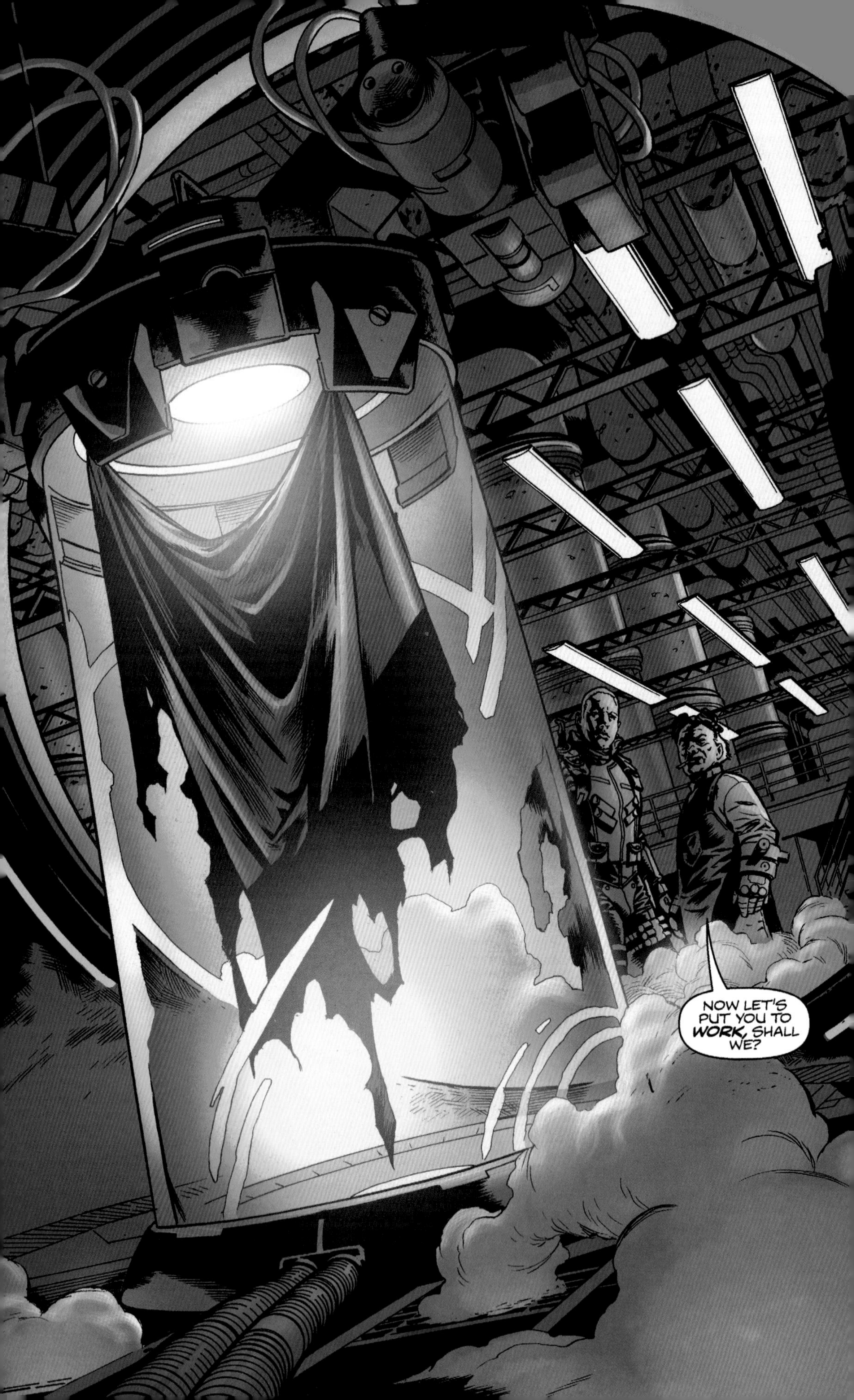
NOW LET'S PUT YOU TO **WORK,** SHALL WE?

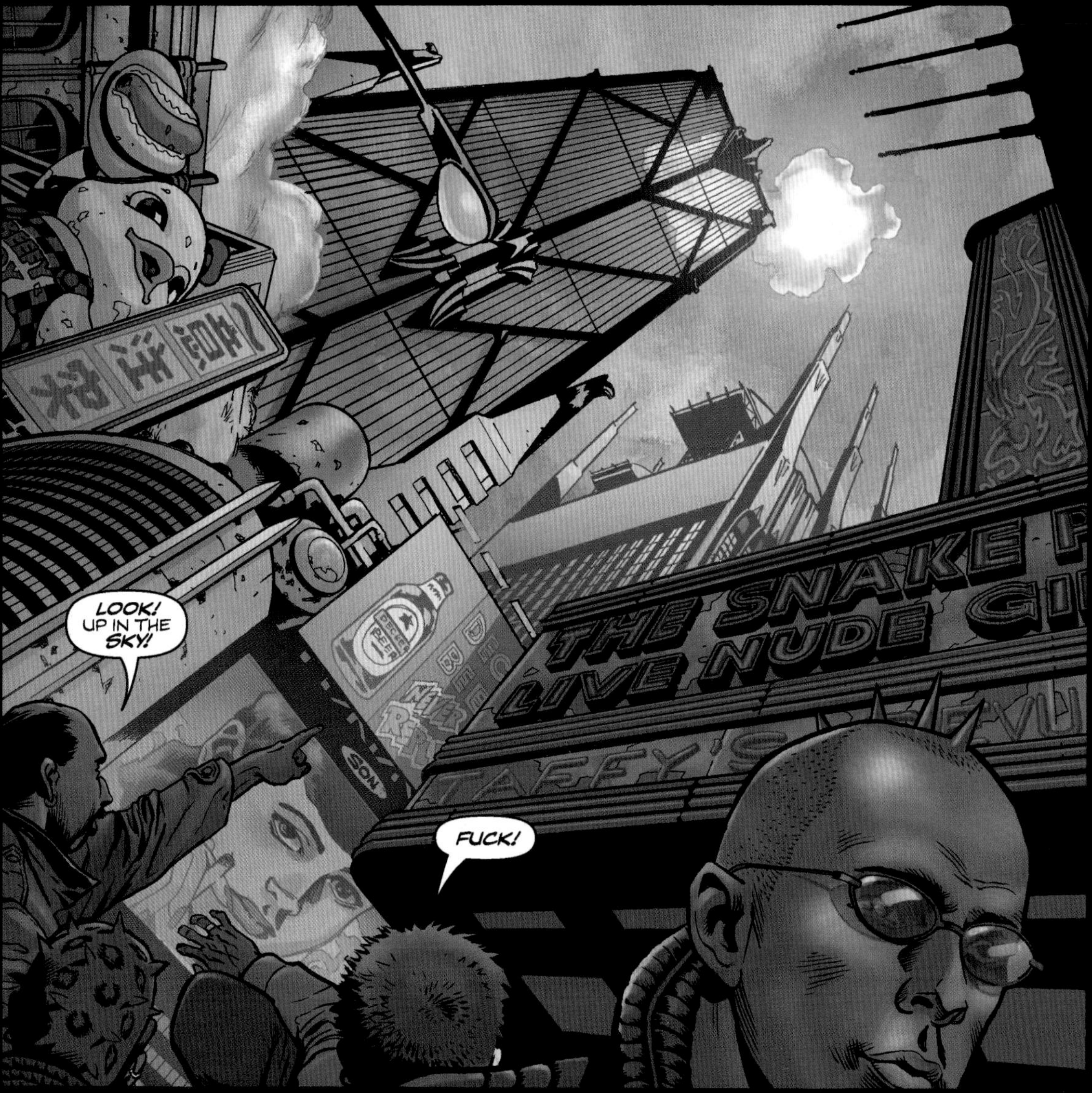
LOOK! UP IN THE SKY!
FUCK!

SUPERGANGBANG

Written by: Mark Millar

Penciled and Inked by: J.G. Jones

Colored by: Paul Mounts

Lettered by: Dreamer Design's
Robin Spehar
Dennis Heisler
Mark Roslan

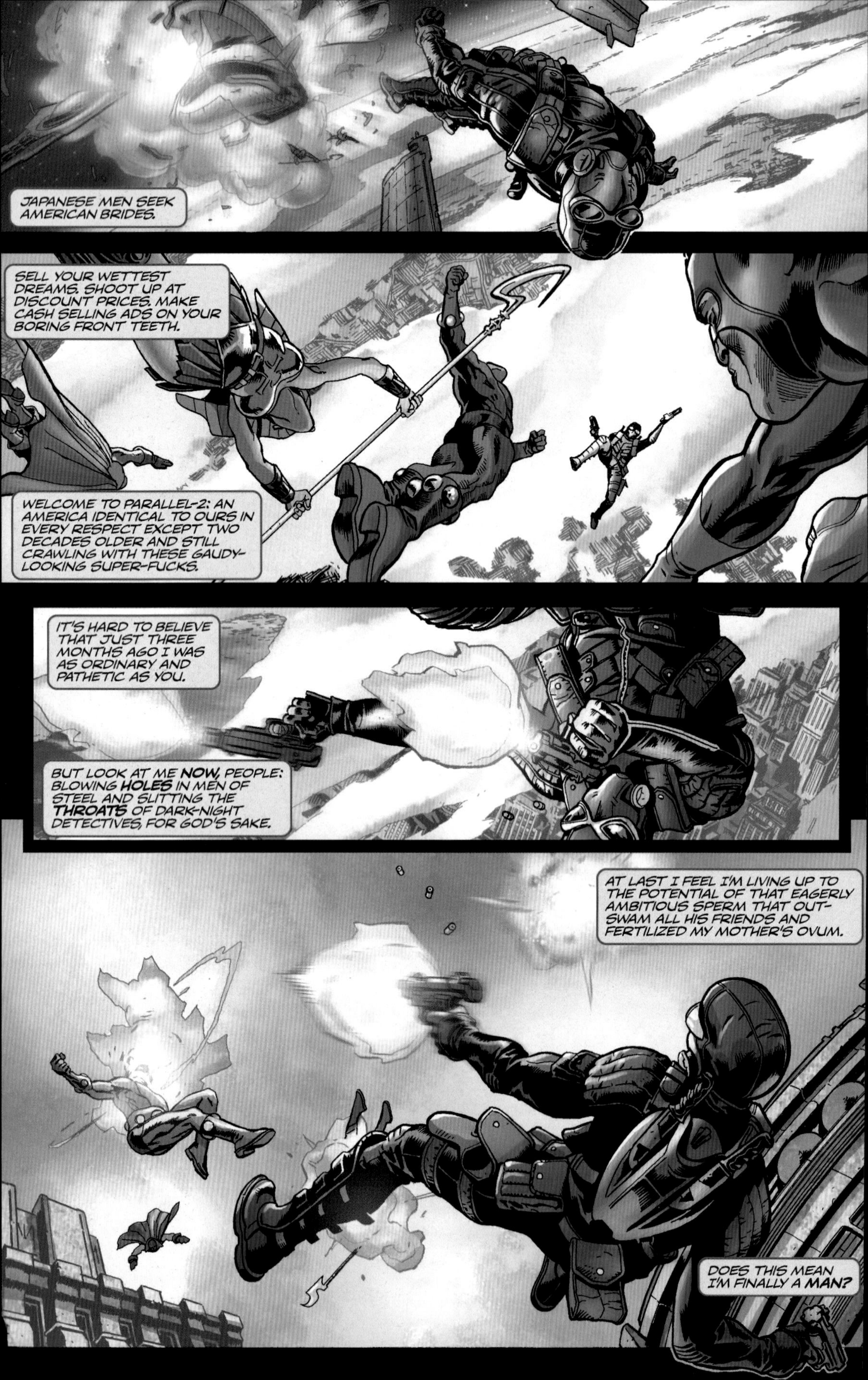

JAPANESE MEN SEEK AMERICAN BRIDES.
SELL YOUR WETTEST DREAMS. SHOOT UP AT DISCOUNT PRICES. MAKE CASH SELLING ADS ON YOUR BORING FRONT TEETH.
WELCOME TO PARALLEL-2: AN AMERICA IDENTICAL TO OURS IN EVERY RESPECT EXCEPT TWO DECADES OLDER AND STILL CRAWLING WITH THESE GAUDY-LOOKING SUPER-FUCKS.
IT'S HARD TO BELIEVE THAT JUST THREE MONTHS AGO I WAS AS ORDINARY AND PATHETIC AS YOU.
BUT LOOK AT ME NOW, PEOPLE: BLOWING HOLES IN MEN OF STEEL AND SLITTING THE THROATS OF DARK-NIGHT DETECTIVES, FOR GOD'S SAKE.
AT LAST I FEEL I'M LIVING UP TO THE POTENTIAL OF THAT EAGERLY AMBITIOUS SPERM THAT OUT-SWAM ALL HIS FRIENDS AND FERTILIZED MY MOTHER'S OVUM.
DOES THIS MEAN I'M FINALLY A MAN?

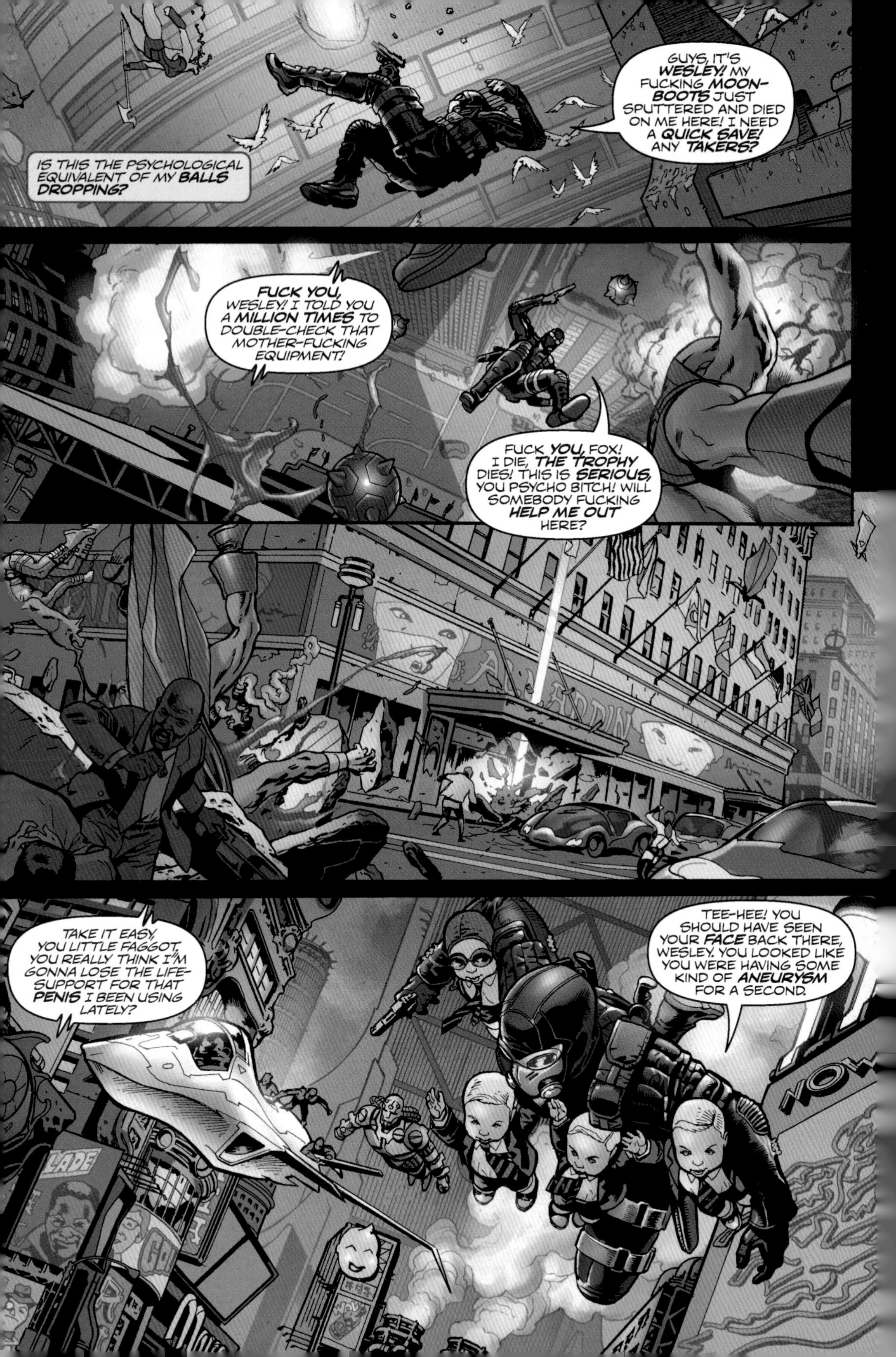
IS THIS THE PSYCHOLOGICAL EQUIVALENT OF MY BALLS DROPPING?
GUYS, IT'S WESLEY! MY FUCKING MOON-BOOTS JUST SPUTTERED AND DIED ON ME HERE! I NEED A QUICK SAVE! ANY TAKERS?
FUCK YOU, WESLEY! I TOLD YOU A MILLION TIMES TO DOUBLE-CHECK THAT MOTHER-FUCKING EQUIPMENT!
FUCK YOU, FOX! I DIE, THE TROPHY DIES! THIS IS SERIOUS, YOU PSYCHO BITCH! WILL SOMEBODY FUCKING HELP ME OUT HERE?
TAKE IT EASY, YOU LITTLE FAGGOT. YOU REALLY THINK I'M GONNA LOSE THE LIFE-SUPPORT FOR THAT PENIS I BEEN USING LATELY?
TEE-HEE! YOU SHOULD HAVE SEEN YOUR FACE BACK THERE, WESLEY. YOU LOOKED LIKE YOU WERE HAVING SOME KIND OF ANEURYSM FOR A SECOND.

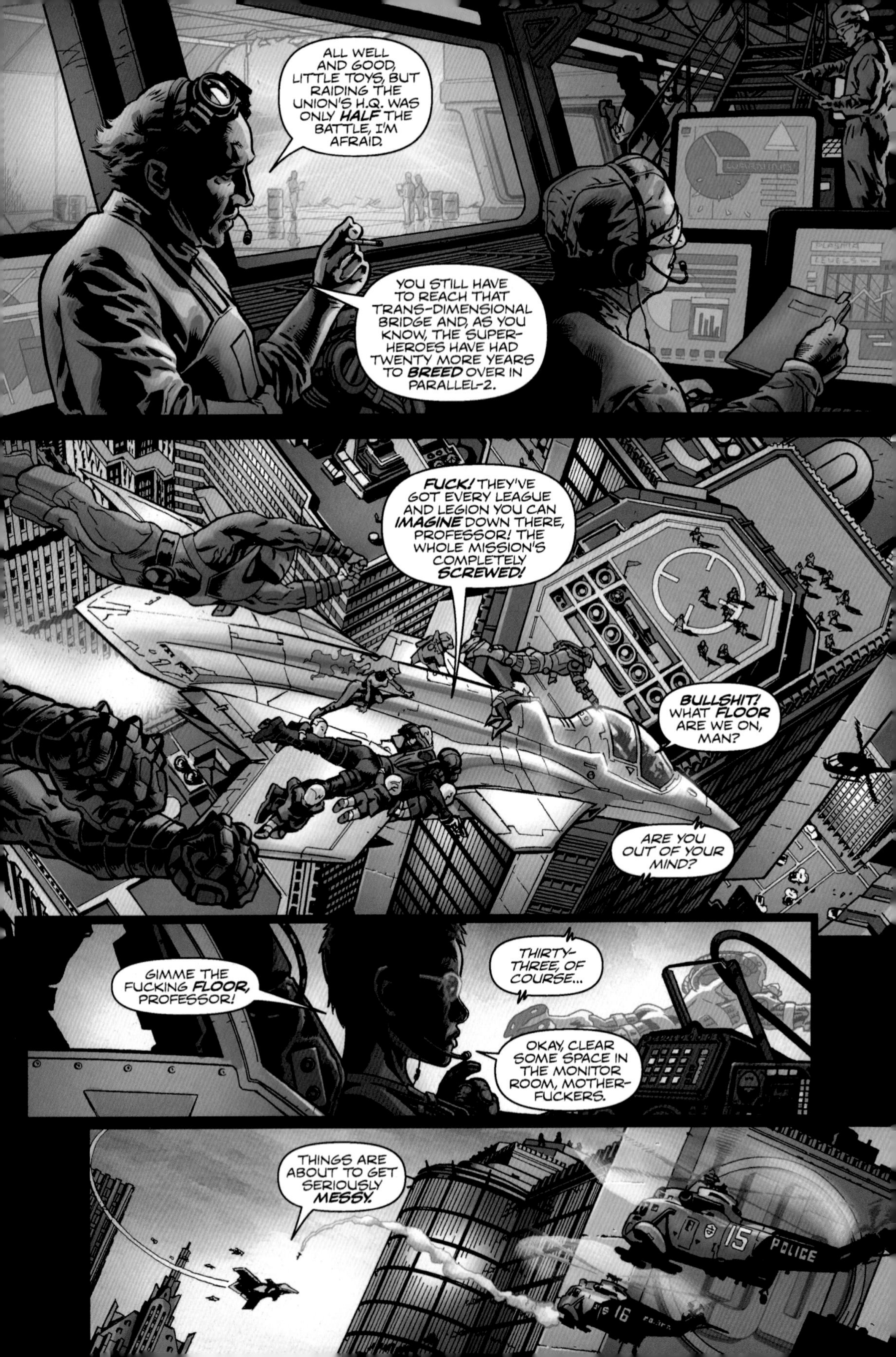
ALL WELL AND GOOD, LITTLE TOYS, BUT RAIDING THE UNION'S H.Q. WAS ONLY HALF THE BATTLE, I'M AFRAID.
YOU STILL HAVE TO REACH THAT TRANS-DIMENSIONAL BRIDGE AND, AS YOU KNOW, THE SUPER-HEROES HAVE HAD TWENTY MORE YEARS TO BREED OVER IN PARALLEL-2.
FUCK! THEY'VE GOT EVERY LEAGUE AND LEGION YOU CAN IMAGINE DOWN THERE, PROFESSOR! THE WHOLE MISSION'S COMPLETELY SCREWED!
BULLSHIT! WHAT FLOOR ARE WE ON, MAN?
ARE YOU OUT OF YOUR MIND?
GIMME THE FUCKING FLOOR, PROFESSOR!
THIRTY-THREE, OF COURSE...
OKAY, CLEAR SOME SPACE IN THE MONITOR ROOM, MOTHER-FUCKERS.
THINGS ARE ABOUT TO GET SERIOUSLY MESSY.
15
POLICE
16

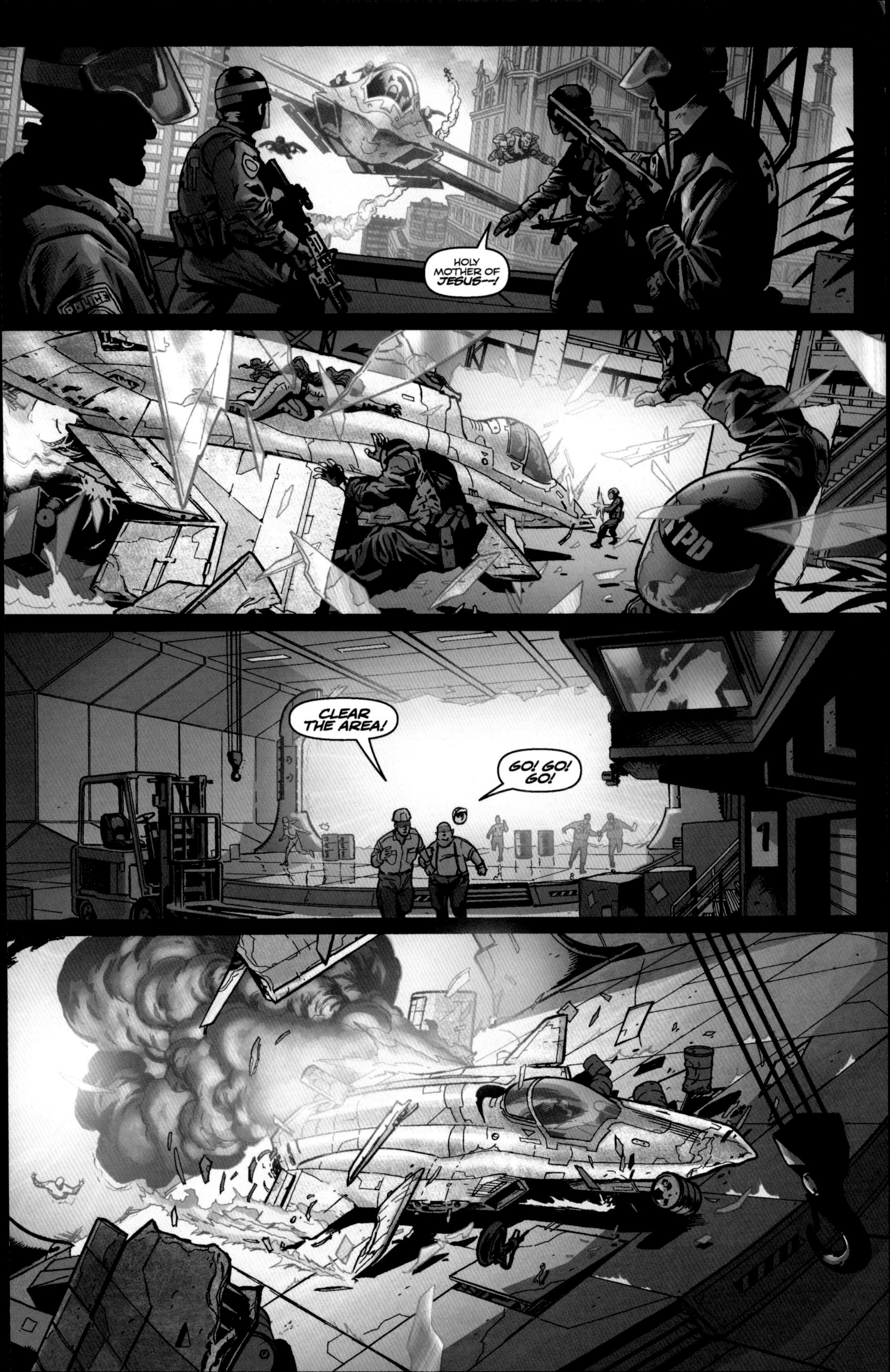
HOLY MOTHER OF JESUS---!
CLEAR THE AREA!
GO! GO! GO!

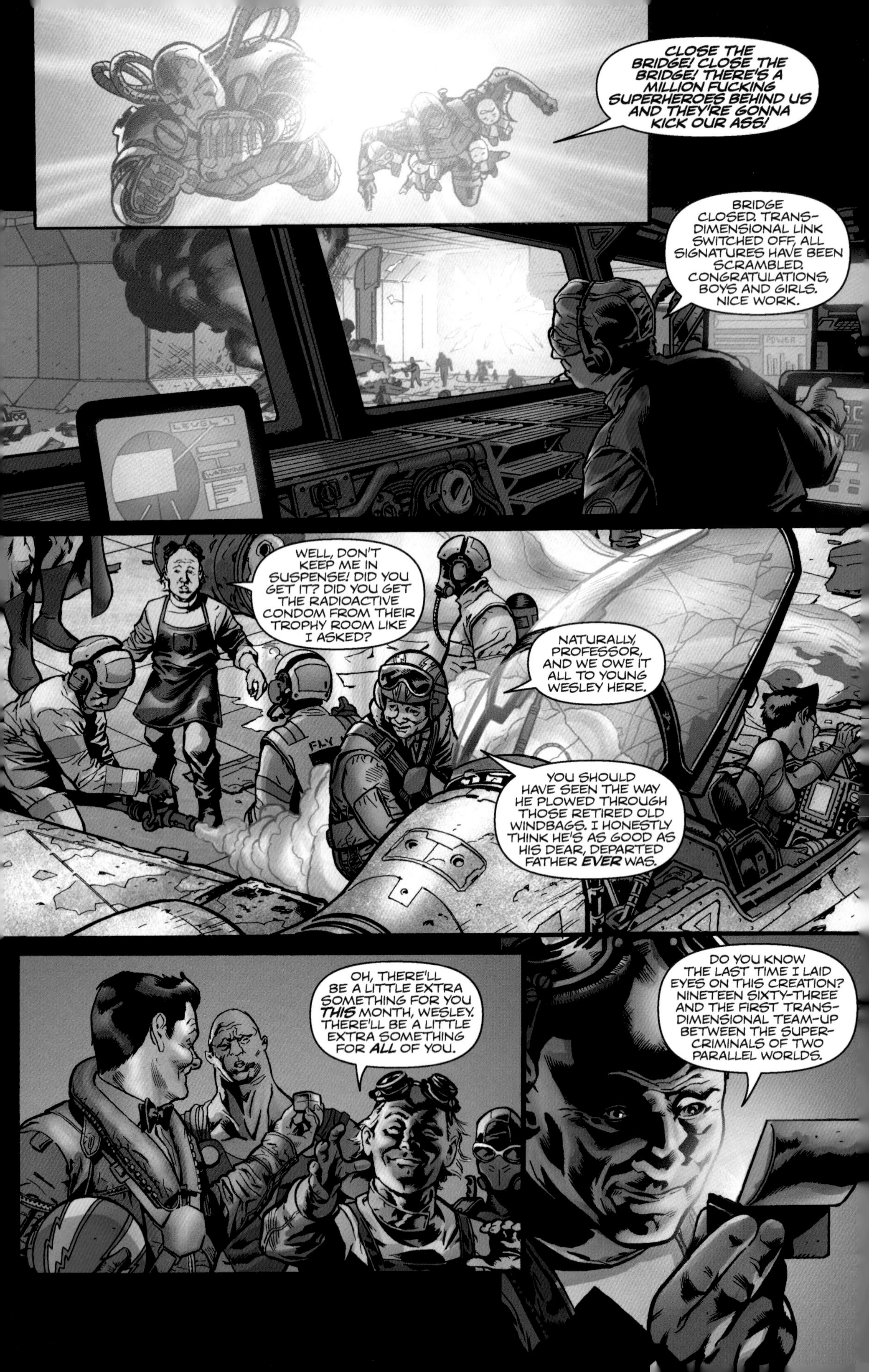
CLOSE THE BRIDGE! CLOSE THE BRIDGE! THERE'S A MILLION FUCKING SUPERHEROES BEHIND US AND THEY'RE GONNA KICK OUR ASS!
BRIDGE CLOSED. TRANS-DIMENSIONAL LINK SWITCHED OFF, ALL SIGNATURES HAVE BEEN SCRAMBLED. CONGRATULATIONS, BOYS AND GIRLS. NICE WORK.
WELL, DON'T KEEP ME IN SUSPENSE! DID YOU GET IT? DID YOU GET THE RADIOACTIVE CONDOM FROM THEIR TROPHY ROOM LIKE I ASKED?
NATURALLY, PROFESSOR, AND WE OWE IT ALL TO YOUNG WESLEY HERE.
YOU SHOULD HAVE SEEN THE WAY HE PLOWED THROUGH THOSE RETIRED OLD WINDBAGS. I HONESTLY THINK HE'S AS GOOD AS HIS DEAR, DEPARTED FATHER EVER WAS.
OH, THERE'LL BE A LITTLE EXTRA SOMETHING FOR YOU THIS MONTH, WESLEY. THERE'LL BE A LITTLE EXTRA SOMETHING FOR ALL OF YOU.
DO YOU KNOW THE LAST TIME I LAID EYES ON THIS CREATION? NINETEEN SIXTY-THREE AND THE FIRST TRANS-DIMENSIONAL TEAM-UP BETWEEN THE SUPER-CRIMINALS OF TWO PARALLEL WORLDS.

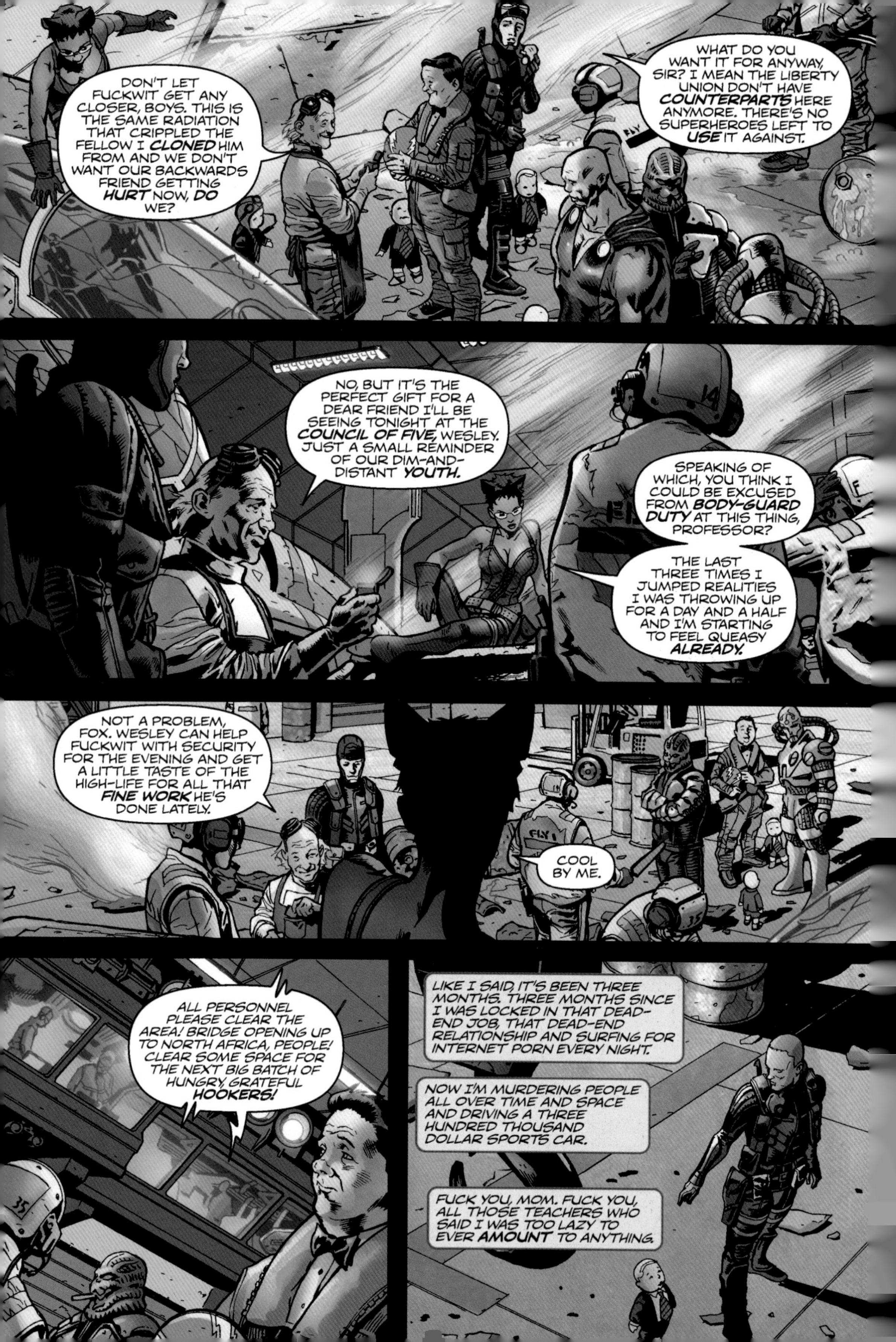
DON'T LET FUCKWIT GET ANY CLOSER, BOYS. THIS IS THE SAME RADIATION THAT CRIPPLED THE FELLOW I CLONED HIM FROM AND WE DON'T WANT OUR BACKWARDS FRIEND GETTING HURT NOW, DO WE?
WHAT DO YOU WANT IT FOR ANYWAY, SIR? I MEAN THE LIBERTY UNION DON'T HAVE COUNTERPARTS HERE ANYMORE. THERE'S NO SUPERHEROES LEFT TO USE IT AGAINST.
NO, BUT IT'S THE PERFECT GIFT FOR A DEAR FRIEND I'LL BE SEEING TONIGHT AT THE COUNCIL OF FIVE, WESLEY. JUST A SMALL REMINDER OF OUR DIM-AND-DISTANT YOUTH.
SPEAKING OF WHICH, YOU THINK I COULD BE EXCUSED FROM BODY-GUARD DUTY AT THIS THING, PROFESSOR?
THE LAST THREE TIMES I JUMPED REALITIES I WAS THROWING UP FOR A DAY AND A HALF AND I'M STARTING TO FEEL QUEASY ALREADY.
NOT A PROBLEM, FOX. WESLEY CAN HELP FUCKWIT WITH SECURITY FOR THE EVENING AND GET A LITTLE TASTE OF THE HIGH-LIFE FOR ALL THAT FINE WORK HE'S DONE LATELY.
COOL BY ME.
ALL PERSONNEL PLEASE CLEAR THE AREA! BRIDGE OPENING UP TO NORTH AFRICA, PEOPLE! CLEAR SOME SPACE FOR THE NEXT BIG BATCH OF HUNGRY, GRATEFUL HOOKERS!
LIKE I SAID, IT'S BEEN THREE MONTHS. THREE MONTHS SINCE I WAS LOCKED IN THAT DEAD-END JOB, THAT DEAD-END RELATIONSHIP AND SURFING FOR INTERNET PORN EVERY NIGHT.
NOW I'M MURDERING PEOPLE ALL OVER TIME AND SPACE AND DRIVING A THREE HUNDRED THOUSAND DOLLAR SPORTS CAR.
FUCK YOU, MOM. FUCK YOU, ALL THOSE TEACHERS WHO SAID I WAS TOO LAZY TO EVER AMOUNT TO ANYTHING.

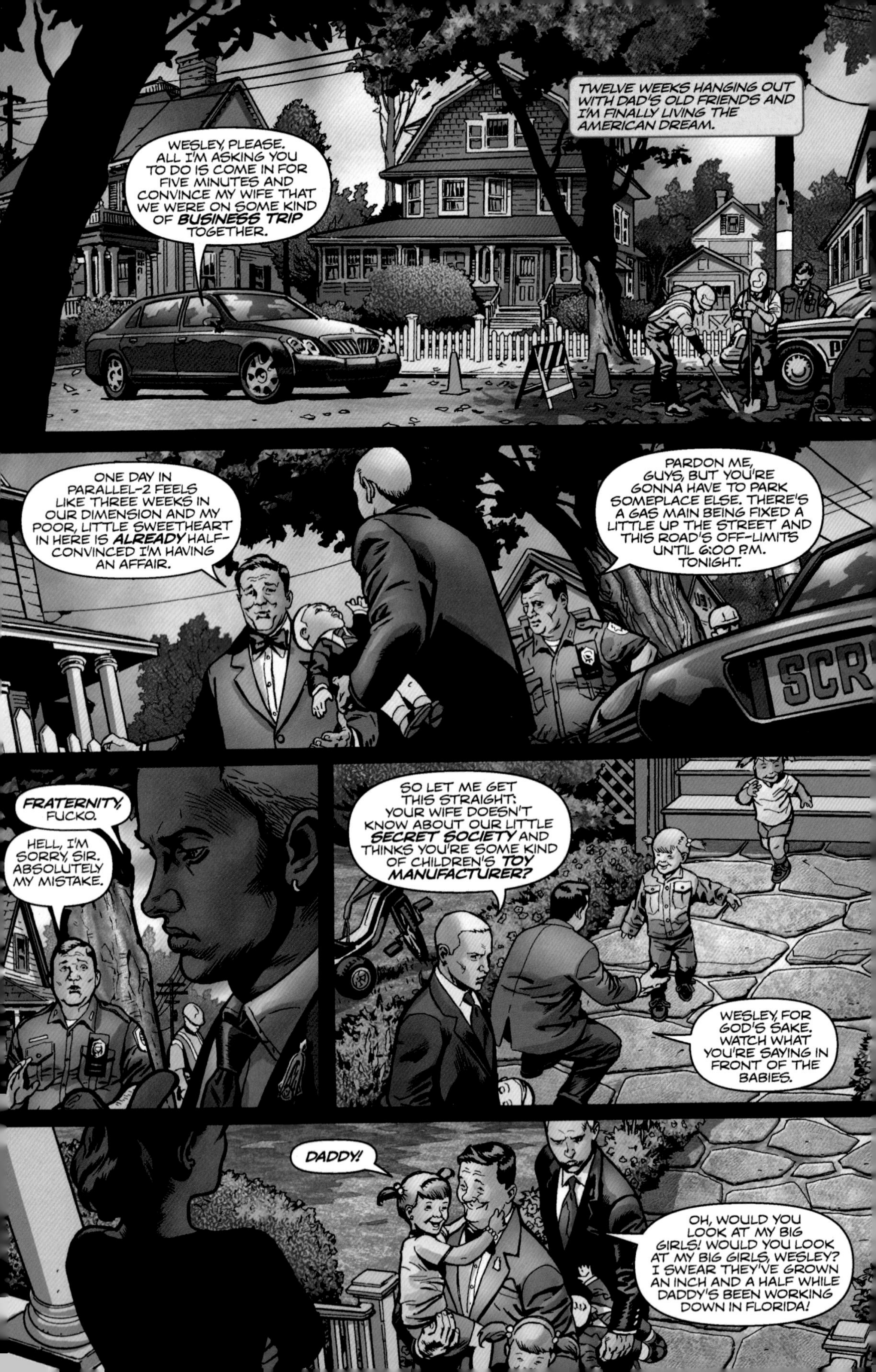

WESLEY, PLEASE. ALL I'M ASKING YOU TO DO IS COME IN FOR FIVE MINUTES AND CONVINCE MY WIFE THAT WE WERE ON SOME KIND OF BUSINESS TRIP TOGETHER.
TWELVE WEEKS HANGING OUT WITH DAD'S OLD FRIENDS AND I'M FINALLY LIVING THE AMERICAN DREAM.
ONE DAY IN PARALLEL-2 FEELS LIKE THREE WEEKS IN OUR DIMENSION AND MY POOR, LITTLE SWEETHEART IN HERE IS ALREADY HALF-CONVINCED I'M HAVING AN AFFAIR.
PARDON ME, GUYS, BUT YOU'RE GONNA HAVE TO PARK SOMEPLACE ELSE. THERE'S A GAS MAIN BEING FIXED A LITTLE UP THE STREET AND THIS ROAD'S OFF-LIMITS UNTIL 6:00 P.M. TONIGHT.
FRATERNITY, FUCKO.
HELL, I'M SORRY, SIR. ABSOLUTELY MY MISTAKE.
SO LET ME GET THIS STRAIGHT: YOUR WIFE DOESN'T KNOW ABOUT OUR LITTLE SECRET SOCIETY AND THINKS YOU'RE SOME KIND OF CHILDREN'S TOY MANUFACTURER?
WESLEY, FOR GOD'S SAKE. WATCH WHAT YOU'RE SAYING IN FRONT OF THE BABIES.
DADDY!
OH, WOULD YOU LOOK AT MY BIG GIRLS! WOULD YOU LOOK AT MY BIG GIRLS, WESLEY? I SWEAR THEY'VE GROWN AN INCH AND A HALF WHILE DADDY'S BEEN WORKING DOWN IN FLORIDA!

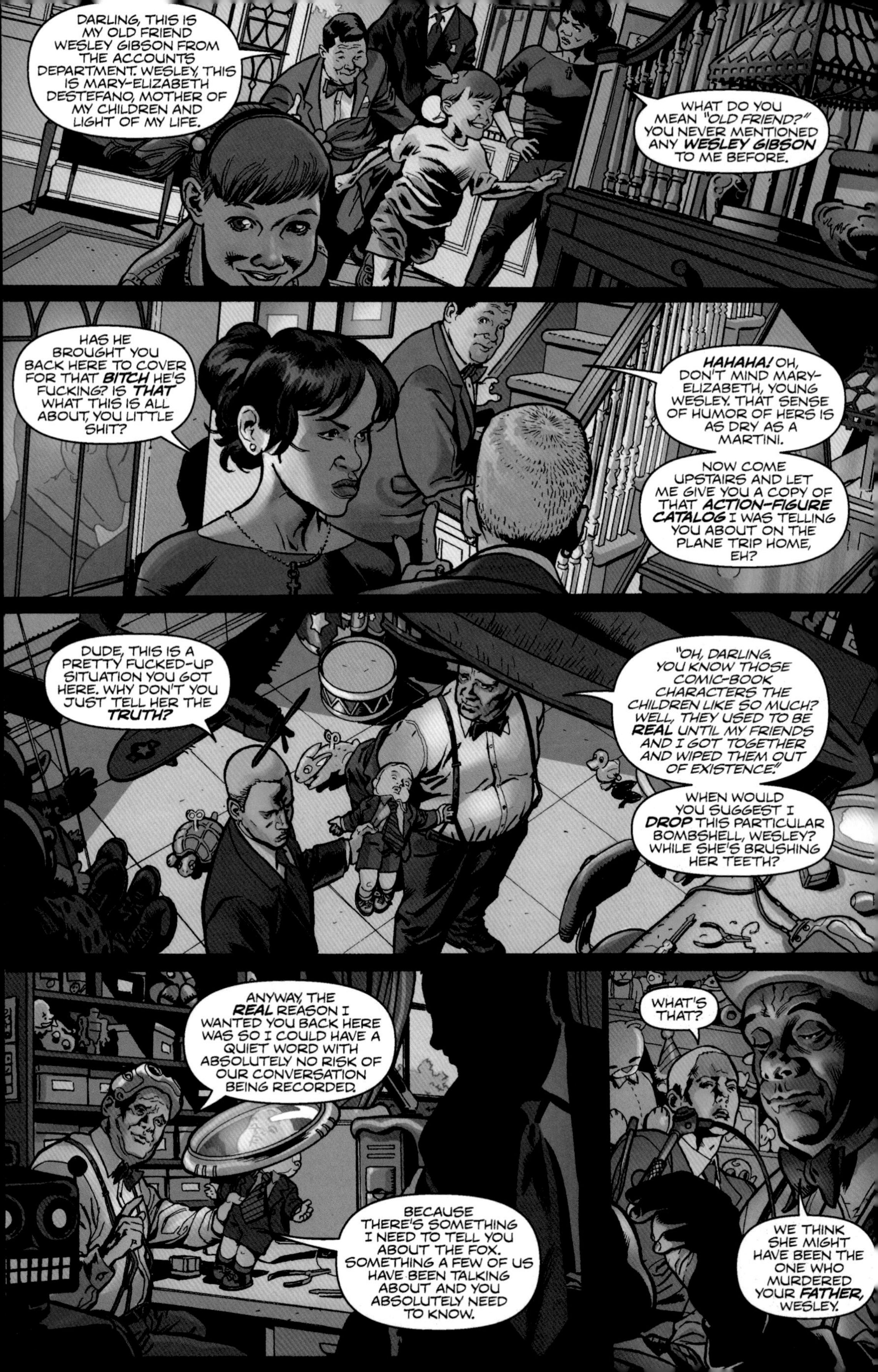
DARLING, THIS IS MY OLD FRIEND WESLEY GIBSON FROM THE ACCOUNTS DEPARTMENT. WESLEY, THIS IS MARY-ELIZABETH DESTEFANO, MOTHER OF MY CHILDREN AND LIGHT OF MY LIFE.
WHAT DO YOU MEAN "OLD FRIEND?" YOU NEVER MENTIONED ANY WESLEY GIBSON TO ME BEFORE.
HAS HE BROUGHT YOU BACK HERE TO COVER FOR THAT BITCH HE'S FUCKING? IS THAT WHAT THIS IS ALL ABOUT, YOU LITTLE SHIT?
HAHAHA! OH, DON'T MIND MARY-ELIZABETH, YOUNG WESLEY. THAT SENSE OF HUMOR OF HERS IS AS DRY AS A MARTINI.
NOW COME UPSTAIRS AND LET ME GIVE YOU A COPY OF THAT ACTION-FIGURE CATALOG I WAS TELLING YOU ABOUT ON THE PLANE TRIP HOME, EH?
DUDE, THIS IS A PRETTY FUCKED-UP SITUATION YOU GOT HERE. WHY DON'T YOU JUST TELL HER THE TRUTH?
"OH, DARLING. YOU KNOW THOSE COMIC-BOOK CHARACTERS THE CHILDREN LIKE SO MUCH? WELL, THEY USED TO BE REAL UNTIL MY FRIENDS AND I GOT TOGETHER AND WIPED THEM OUT OF EXISTENCE."
WHEN WOULD YOU SUGGEST I DROP THIS PARTICULAR BOMBSHELL, WESLEY? WHILE SHE'S BRUSHING HER TEETH?
ANYWAY, THE REAL REASON I WANTED YOU BACK HERE WAS SO I COULD HAVE A QUIET WORD WITH ABSOLUTELY NO RISK OF OUR CONVERSATION BEING RECORDED.
BECAUSE THERE'S SOMETHING I NEED TO TELL YOU ABOUT THE FOX. SOMETHING A FEW OF US HAVE BEEN TALKING ABOUT AND YOU ABSOLUTELY NEED TO KNOW.
WHAT'S THAT?
WE THINK SHE MIGHT HAVE BEEN THE ONE WHO MURDERED YOUR FATHER, WESLEY.

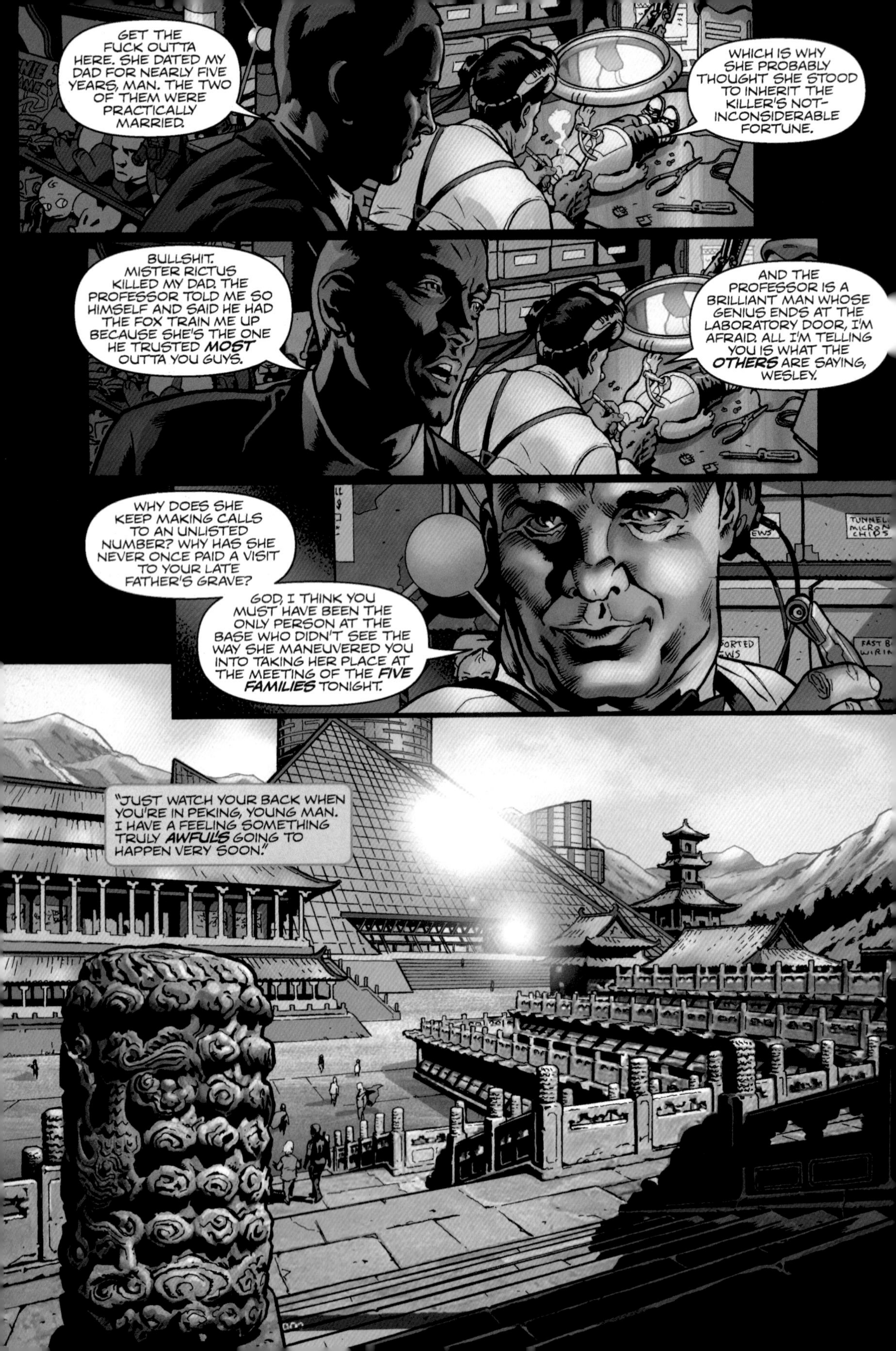
GET THE FUCK OUTTA HERE. SHE DATED MY DAD FOR NEARLY FIVE YEARS, MAN. THE TWO OF THEM WERE PRACTICALLY MARRIED.
WHICH IS WHY SHE PROBABLY THOUGHT SHE STOOD TO INHERIT THE KILLER'S NOT-INCONSIDERABLE FORTUNE.
BULLSHIT. MISTER RICTUS KILLED MY DAD. THE PROFESSOR TOLD ME SO HIMSELF AND SAID HE HAD THE FOX TRAIN ME UP BECAUSE SHE'S THE ONE HE TRUSTED MOST OUTTA YOU GUYS.
AND THE PROFESSOR IS A BRILLIANT MAN WHOSE GENIUS ENDS AT THE LABORATORY DOOR, I'M AFRAID. ALL I'M TELLING YOU IS WHAT THE OTHERS ARE SAYING, WESLEY.
WHY DOES SHE KEEP MAKING CALLS TO AN UNLISTED NUMBER? WHY HAS SHE NEVER ONCE PAID A VISIT TO YOUR LATE FATHER'S GRAVE?
GOD, I THINK YOU MUST HAVE BEEN THE ONLY PERSON AT THE BASE WHO DIDN'T SEE THE WAY SHE MANEUVERED YOU INTO TAKING HER PLACE AT THE MEETING OF THE FIVE FAMILIES TONIGHT.
"JUST WATCH YOUR BACK WHEN YOU'RE IN PEKING, YOUNG MAN. I HAVE A FEELING SOMETHING TRULY AWFUL'S GOING TO HAPPEN VERY SOON."

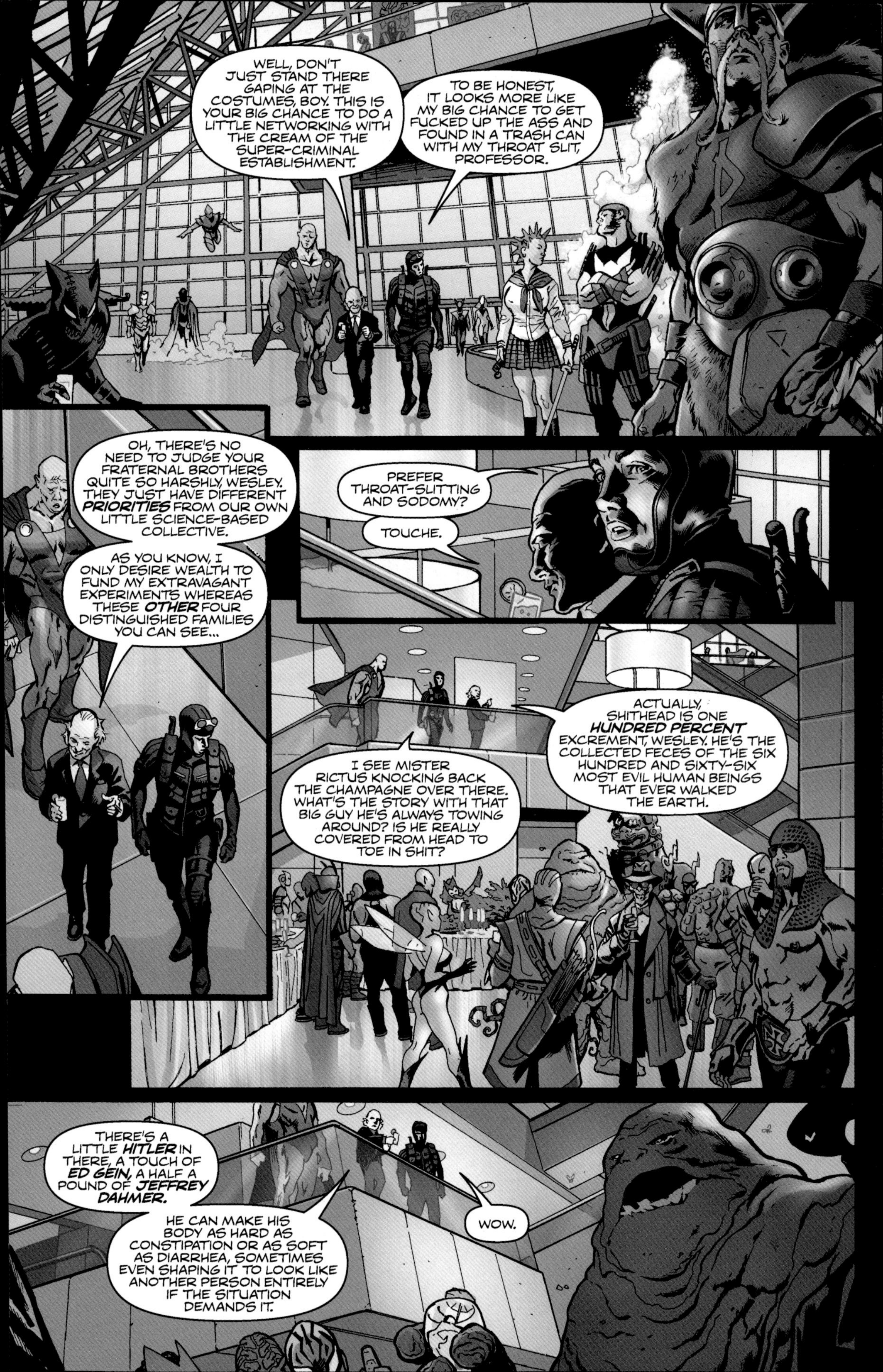
WELL, DON'T JUST STAND THERE GAPING AT THE COSTUMES, BOY. THIS IS YOUR BIG CHANCE TO DO A LITTLE NETWORKING WITH THE CREAM OF THE SUPER-CRIMINAL ESTABLISHMENT.
TO BE HONEST, IT LOOKS MORE LIKE MY BIG CHANCE TO GET FUCKED UP THE ASS AND FOUND IN A TRASH CAN WITH MY THROAT SLIT, PROFESSOR.
OH, THERE'S NO NEED TO JUDGE YOUR FRATERNAL BROTHERS QUITE SO HARSHLY, WESLEY. THEY JUST HAVE DIFFERENT **PRIORITIES** FROM OUR OWN LITTLE SCIENCE-BASED COLLECTIVE.
AS YOU KNOW, I ONLY DESIRE WEALTH TO FUND MY EXTRAVAGANT EXPERIMENTS WHEREAS THESE **OTHER** FOUR DISTINGUISHED FAMILIES YOU CAN SEE...
PREFER THROAT-SLITTING AND SODOMY?
TOUCHE.
I SEE MISTER RICTUS KNOCKING BACK THE CHAMPAGNE OVER THERE. WHAT'S THE STORY WITH THAT BIG GUY HE'S ALWAYS TOWING AROUND? IS HE REALLY COVERED FROM HEAD TO TOE IN SHIT?
ACTUALLY, SHITHEAD IS ONE **HUNDRED PERCENT** EXCREMENT, WESLEY. HE'S THE COLLECTED FECES OF THE SIX HUNDRED AND SIXTY-SIX MOST EVIL HUMAN BEINGS THAT EVER WALKED THE EARTH.
THERE'S A LITTLE **HITLER** IN THERE, A TOUCH OF **ED GEIN**, A HALF A POUND OF **JEFFREY DAHMER.**
HE CAN MAKE HIS BODY AS HARD AS CONSTIPATION OR AS SOFT AS DIARRHEA, SOMETIMES EVEN SHAPING IT TO LOOK LIKE ANOTHER PERSON ENTIRELY IF THE SITUATION DEMANDS IT.
WOW.

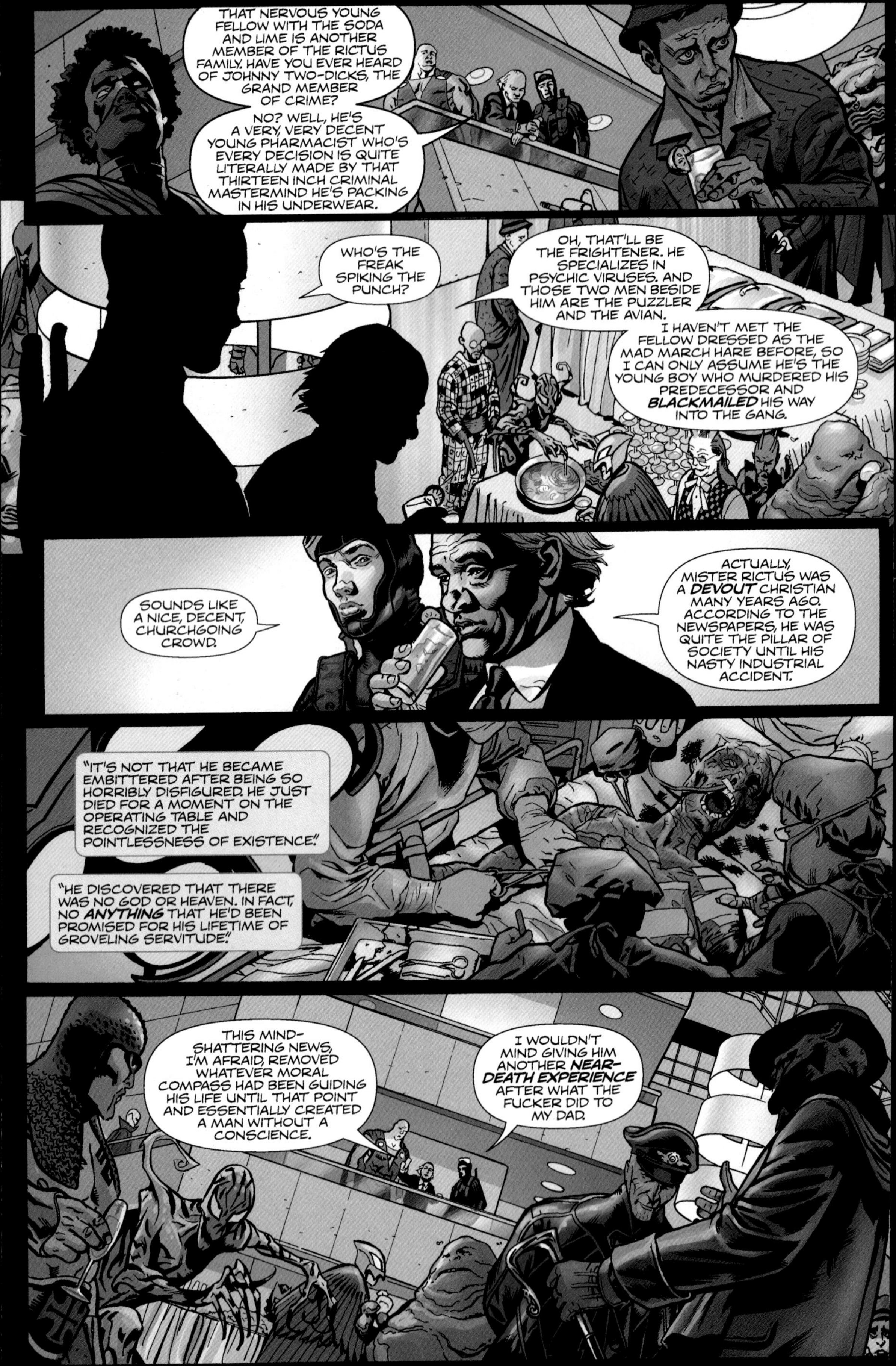
THAT NERVOUS YOUNG FELLOW WITH THE SODA AND LIME IS ANOTHER MEMBER OF THE RICTUS FAMILY. HAVE YOU EVER HEARD OF JOHNNY TWO-DICKS, THE GRAND MEMBER OF CRIME?
NO? WELL, HE'S A VERY, VERY DECENT YOUNG PHARMACIST WHO'S EVERY DECISION IS QUITE LITERALLY MADE BY THAT THIRTEEN INCH CRIMINAL MASTERMIND HE'S PACKING IN HIS UNDERWEAR.
WHO'S THE FREAK SPIKING THE PUNCH?
OH, THAT'LL BE THE FRIGHTENER. HE SPECIALIZES IN PSYCHIC VIRUSES. AND THOSE TWO MEN BESIDE HIM ARE THE PUZZLER AND THE AVIAN.
I HAVEN'T MET THE FELLOW DRESSED AS THE MAD MARCH HARE BEFORE, SO I CAN ONLY ASSUME HE'S THE YOUNG BOY WHO MURDERED HIS PREDECESSOR AND ***BLACKMAILED*** HIS WAY INTO THE GANG.
SOUNDS LIKE A NICE, DECENT, CHURCHGOING CROWD.
ACTUALLY, MISTER RICTUS WAS A ***DEVOUT*** CHRISTIAN MANY YEARS AGO. ACCORDING TO THE NEWSPAPERS, HE WAS QUITE THE PILLAR OF SOCIETY UNTIL HIS NASTY INDUSTRIAL ACCIDENT.
"IT'S NOT THAT HE BECAME EMBITTERED AFTER BEING SO HORRIBLY DISFIGURED. HE JUST DIED FOR A MOMENT ON THE OPERATING TABLE AND RECOGNIZED THE POINTLESSNESS OF EXISTENCE."
"HE DISCOVERED THAT THERE WAS NO GOD OR HEAVEN. IN FACT, NO ***ANYTHING*** THAT HE'D BEEN PROMISED FOR HIS LIFETIME OF GROVELING SERVITUDE."
THIS MIND-SHATTERING NEWS, I'M AFRAID, REMOVED WHATEVER MORAL COMPASS HAD BEEN GUIDING HIS LIFE UNTIL THAT POINT AND ESSENTIALLY CREATED A MAN WITHOUT A CONSCIENCE.
I WOULDN'T MIND GIVING HIM ANOTHER ***NEAR-DEATH EXPERIENCE*** AFTER WHAT THE FUCKER DID TO MY DAD.

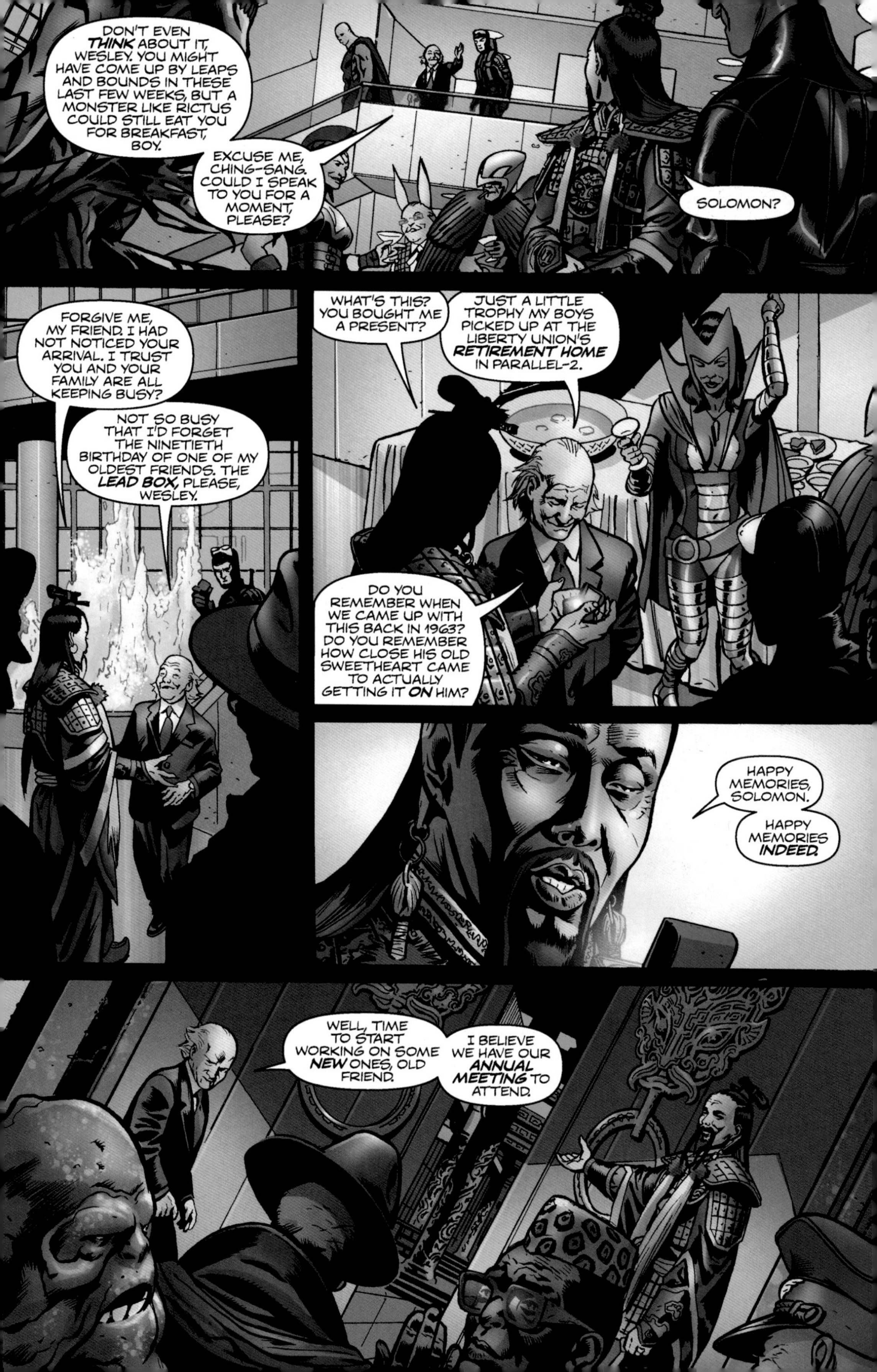
DON'T EVEN THINK ABOUT IT, WESLEY. YOU MIGHT HAVE COME UP BY LEAPS AND BOUNDS IN THESE LAST FEW WEEKS, BUT A MONSTER LIKE RICTUS COULD STILL EAT YOU FOR BREAKFAST, BOY.
EXCUSE ME, CHING-SANG. COULD I SPEAK TO YOU FOR A MOMENT, PLEASE?
SOLOMON?
FORGIVE ME, MY FRIEND. I HAD NOT NOTICED YOUR ARRIVAL. I TRUST YOU AND YOUR FAMILY ARE ALL KEEPING BUSY?
NOT SO BUSY THAT I'D FORGET THE NINETIETH BIRTHDAY OF ONE OF MY OLDEST FRIENDS. THE LEAD BOX, PLEASE, WESLEY.
WHAT'S THIS? YOU BOUGHT ME A PRESENT?
JUST A LITTLE TROPHY MY BOYS PICKED UP AT THE LIBERTY UNION'S RETIREMENT HOME IN PARALLEL-2.
DO YOU REMEMBER WHEN WE CAME UP WITH THIS BACK IN 1963? DO YOU REMEMBER HOW CLOSE HIS OLD SWEETHEART CAME TO ACTUALLY GETTING IT ON HIM?
HAPPY MEMORIES, SOLOMON.
HAPPY MEMORIES INDEED.
WELL, TIME TO START WORKING ON SOME NEW ONES, OLD FRIEND.
I BELIEVE WE HAVE OUR ANNUAL MEETING TO ATTEND.

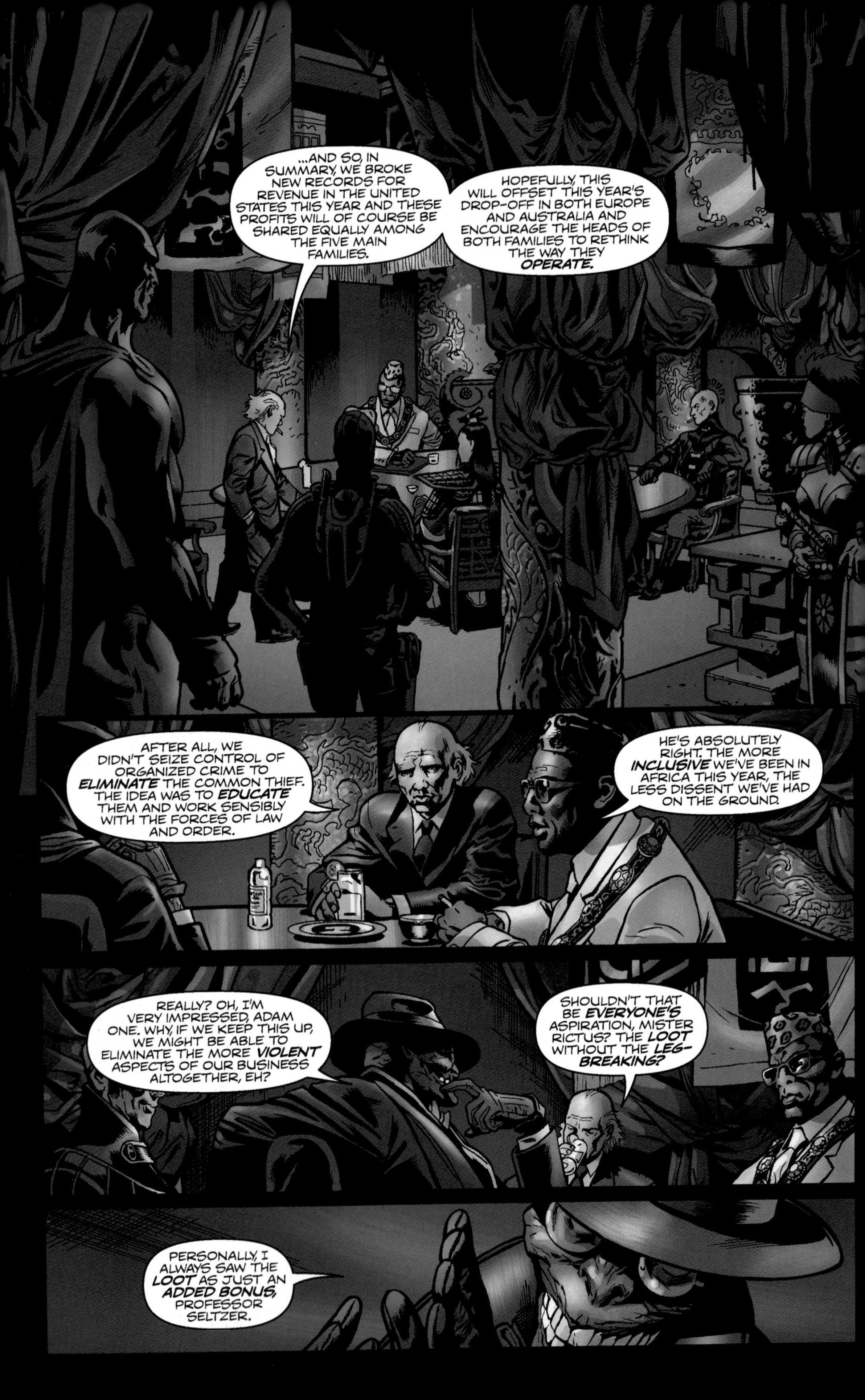
...AND SO, IN SUMMARY, WE BROKE NEW RECORDS FOR REVENUE IN THE UNITED STATES THIS YEAR AND THESE PROFITS WILL OF COURSE BE SHARED EQUALLY AMONG THE FIVE MAIN FAMILIES.
HOPEFULLY, THIS WILL OFFSET THIS YEAR'S DROP-OFF IN BOTH EUROPE AND AUSTRALIA AND ENCOURAGE THE HEADS OF BOTH FAMILIES TO RETHINK THE WAY THEY OPERATE.
AFTER ALL, WE DIDN'T SEIZE CONTROL OF ORGANIZED CRIME TO ELIMINATE THE COMMON THIEF. THE IDEA WAS TO EDUCATE THEM AND WORK SENSIBLY WITH THE FORCES OF LAW AND ORDER.
HE'S ABSOLUTELY RIGHT. THE MORE INCLUSIVE WE'VE BEEN IN AFRICA THIS YEAR, THE LESS DISSENT WE'VE HAD ON THE GROUND.
REALLY? OH, I'M VERY IMPRESSED, ADAM ONE. WHY, IF WE KEEP THIS UP, WE MIGHT BE ABLE TO ELIMINATE THE MORE VIOLENT ASPECTS OF OUR BUSINESS ALTOGETHER, EH?
SHOULDN'T THAT BE EVERYONE'S ASPIRATION, MISTER RICTUS? THE LOOT WITHOUT THE LEG-BREAKING?
PERSONALLY, I ALWAYS SAW THE LOOT AS JUST AN ADDED BONUS, PROFESSOR SELTZER.

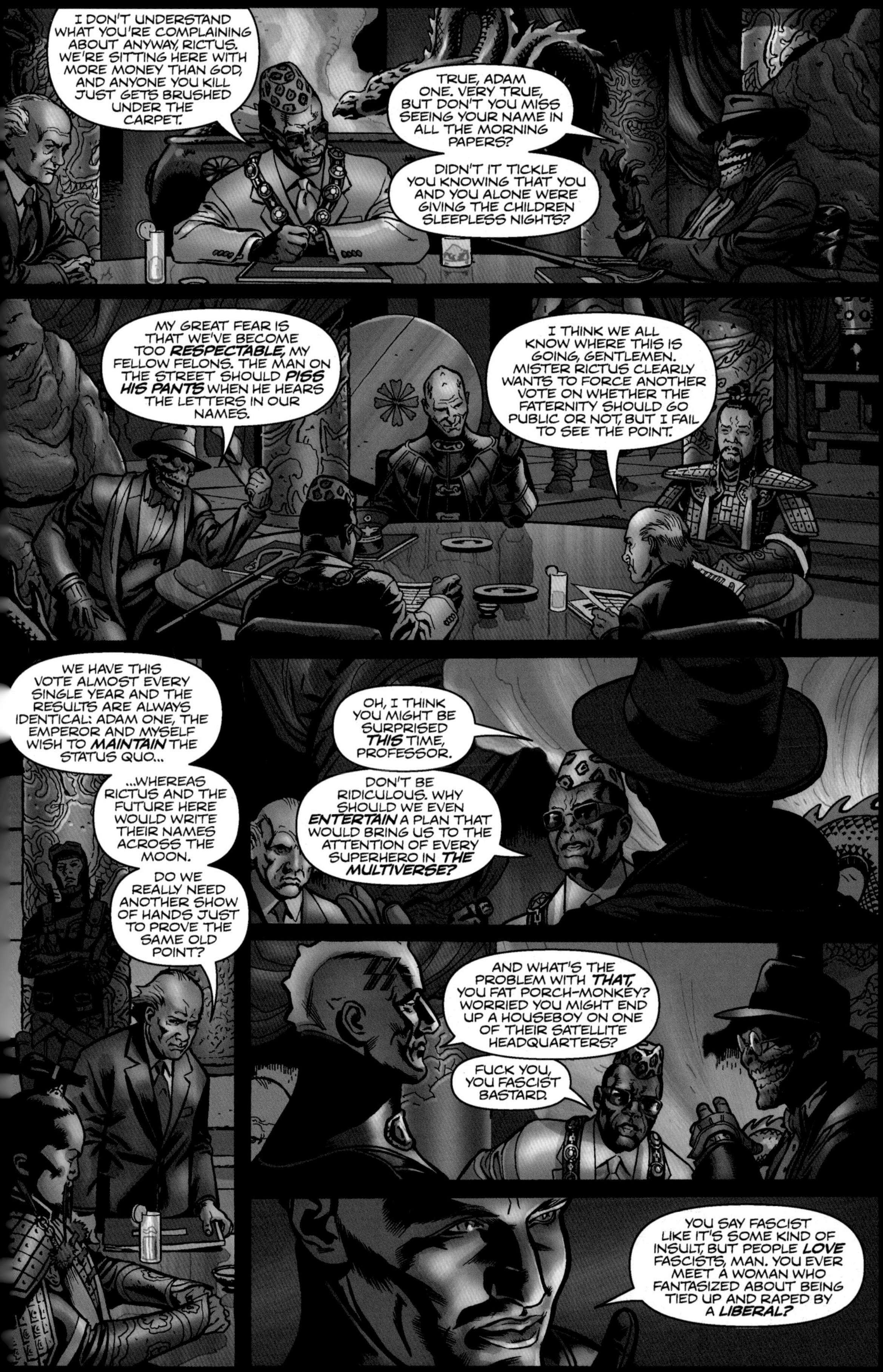
I DON'T UNDERSTAND WHAT YOU'RE COMPLAINING ABOUT ANYWAY, RICTUS. WE'RE SITTING HERE WITH MORE MONEY THAN GOD, AND ANYONE YOU KILL JUST GETS BRUSHED UNDER THE CARPET.
TRUE, ADAM ONE. VERY TRUE, BUT DON'T YOU MISS SEEING YOUR NAME IN ALL THE MORNING PAPERS?
DIDN'T IT TICKLE YOU KNOWING THAT YOU AND YOU ALONE WERE GIVING THE CHILDREN SLEEPLESS NIGHTS?
MY GREAT FEAR IS THAT WE'VE BECOME TOO RESPECTABLE, MY FELLOW FELONS. THE MAN ON THE STREET SHOULD PISS HIS PANTS WHEN HE HEARS THE LETTERS IN OUR NAMES.
I THINK WE ALL KNOW WHERE THIS IS GOING, GENTLEMEN. MISTER RICTUS CLEARLY WANTS TO FORCE ANOTHER VOTE ON WHETHER THE FATERNITY SHOULD GO PUBLIC OR NOT, BUT I FAIL TO SEE THE POINT.
WE HAVE THIS VOTE ALMOST EVERY SINGLE YEAR AND THE RESULTS ARE ALWAYS IDENTICAL: ADAM ONE, THE EMPEROR AND MYSELF WISH TO MAINTAIN THE STATUS QUO...
...WHEREAS RICTUS AND THE FUTURE HERE WOULD WRITE THEIR NAMES ACROSS THE MOON.
DO WE REALLY NEED ANOTHER SHOW OF HANDS JUST TO PROVE THE SAME OLD POINT?
OH, I THINK YOU MIGHT BE SURPRISED THIS TIME, PROFESSOR.
DON'T BE RIDICULOUS. WHY SHOULD WE EVEN ENTERTAIN A PLAN THAT WOULD BRING US TO THE ATTENTION OF EVERY SUPERHERO IN THE MULTIVERSE?
AND WHAT'S THE PROBLEM WITH THAT, YOU FAT PORCH-MONKEY? WORRIED YOU MIGHT END UP A HOUSEBOY ON ONE OF THEIR SATELLITE HEADQUARTERS?
FUCK YOU, YOU FASCIST BASTARD.
YOU SAY FASCIST LIKE IT'S SOME KIND OF INSULT, BUT PEOPLE LOVE FASCISTS, MAN. YOU EVER MEET A WOMAN WHO FANTASIZED ABOUT BEING TIED UP AND RAPED BY A LIBERAL?

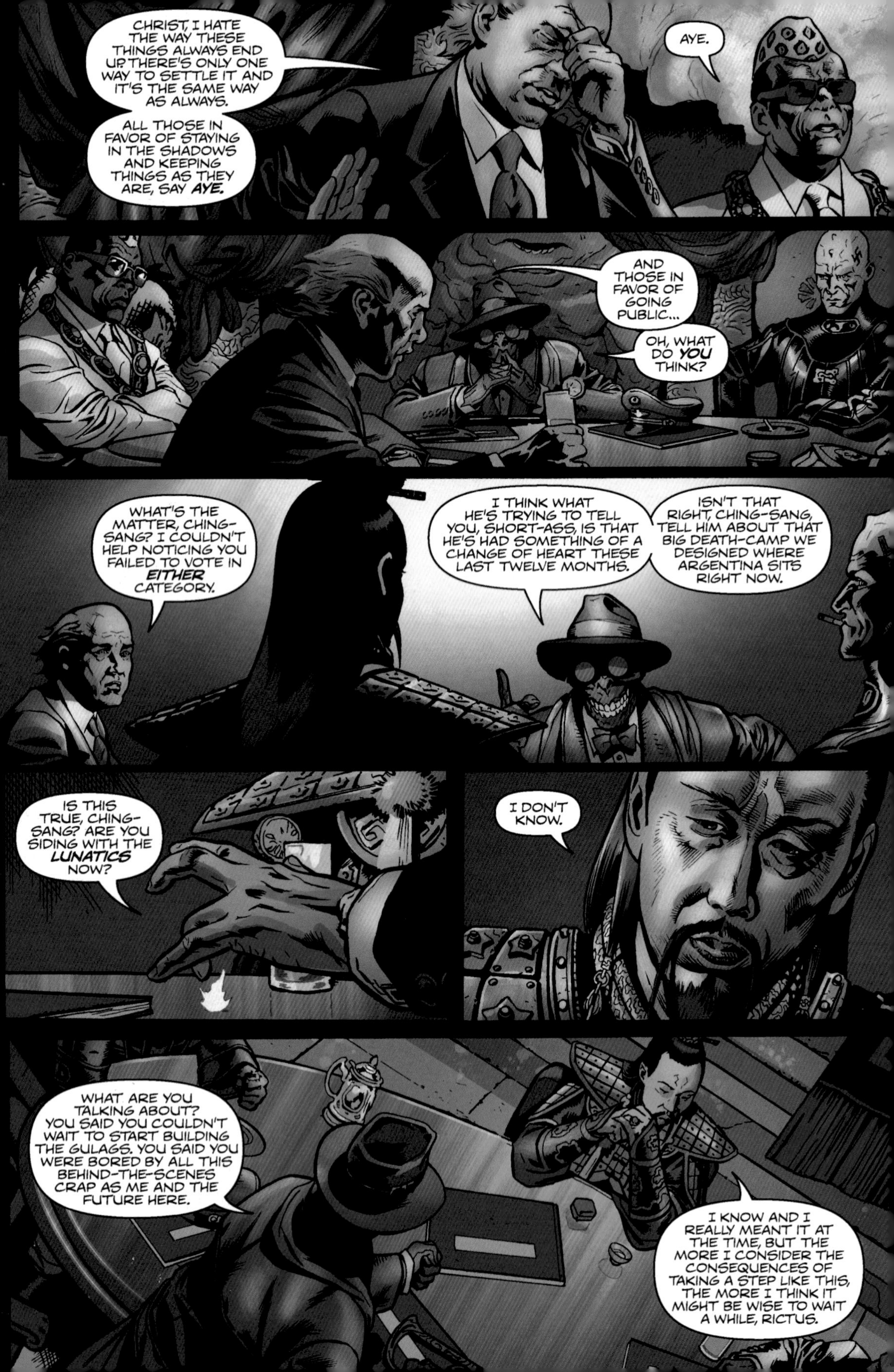
CHRIST, I HATE THE WAY THESE THINGS ALWAYS END UP. THERE'S ONLY ONE WAY TO SETTLE IT AND IT'S THE SAME WAY AS ALWAYS.
ALL THOSE IN FAVOR OF STAYING IN THE SHADOWS AND KEEPING THINGS AS THEY ARE, SAY AYE.
AYE.
AND THOSE IN FAVOR OF GOING PUBLIC...
OH, WHAT DO YOU THINK?
WHAT'S THE MATTER, CHING-SANG? I COULDN'T HELP NOTICING YOU FAILED TO VOTE IN EITHER CATEGORY.
I THINK WHAT HE'S TRYING TO TELL YOU, SHORT-ASS, IS THAT HE'S HAD SOMETHING OF A CHANGE OF HEART THESE LAST TWELVE MONTHS.
ISN'T THAT RIGHT, CHING-SANG, TELL HIM ABOUT THAT BIG DEATH-CAMP WE DESIGNED WHERE ARGENTINA SITS RIGHT NOW.
IS THIS TRUE, CHING-SANG? ARE YOU SIDING WITH THE LUNATICS NOW?
I DON'T KNOW.
WHAT ARE YOU TALKING ABOUT? YOU SAID YOU COULDN'T WAIT TO START BUILDING THE GULAGS. YOU SAID YOU WERE BORED BY ALL THIS BEHIND-THE-SCENES CRAP AS ME AND THE FUTURE HERE.
I KNOW AND I REALLY MEANT IT AT THE TIME, BUT THE MORE I CONSIDER THE CONSEQUENCES OF TAKING A STEP LIKE THIS, THE MORE I THINK IT MIGHT BE WISE TO WAIT A WHILE, RICTUS.

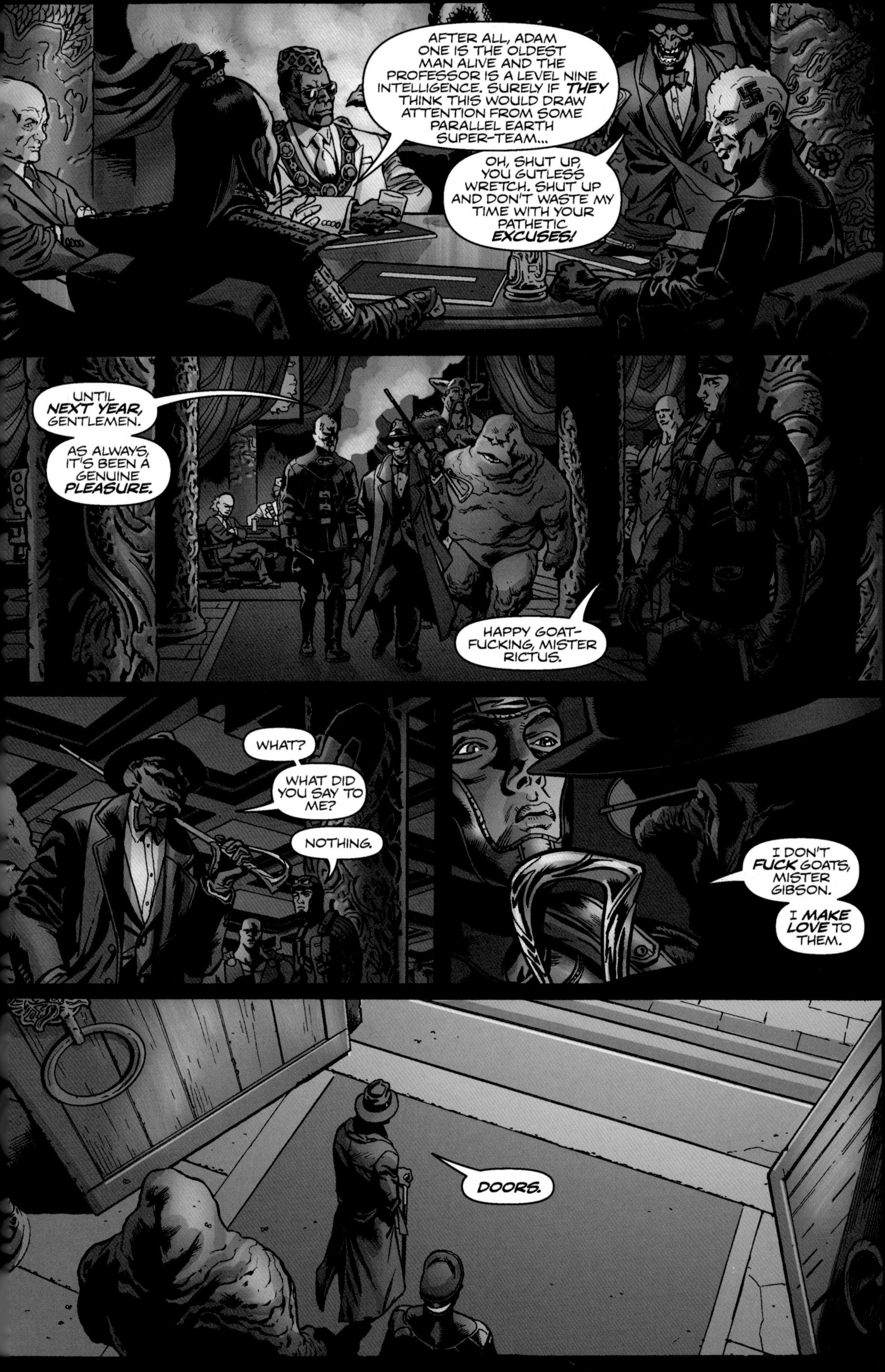
AFTER ALL, ADAM ONE IS THE OLDEST MAN ALIVE AND THE PROFESSOR IS A LEVEL NINE INTELLIGENCE. SURELY IF THEY THINK THIS WOULD DRAW ATTENTION FROM SOME PARALLEL EARTH SUPER-TEAM...
OH, SHUT UP, YOU GUTLESS WRETCH. SHUT UP AND DON'T WASTE MY TIME WITH YOUR PATHETIC EXCUSES!
UNTIL NEXT YEAR, GENTLEMEN.
AS ALWAYS, IT'S BEEN A GENUINE PLEASURE.
HAPPY GOAT-FUCKING, MISTER RICTUS.
WHAT?
WHAT DID YOU SAY TO ME?
NOTHING.
I DON'T FUCK GOATS, MISTER GIBSON.
I MAKE LOVE TO THEM.
DOORS.

IT WAS THE TROPHY I BROUGHT BACK FROM THE PARALLEL WORLD, RIGHT?

EXCUSE ME?

THAT'S WHAT YOU USED TO GET THE EMPEROR BACK ONSIDE. YOU TAPPED INTO A LITTLE SHARED HISTORY AND GOT HIM ALL MISTY-EYED ABOUT THE GOOD OLD DAYS. THAT WAS BRILLIANT.

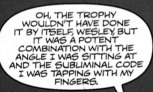

OH, THE TROPHY WOULDN'T HAVE DONE IT BY ITSELF, WESLEY, BUT IT WAS A POTENT COMBINATION WITH THE ANGLE I WAS SITTING AT AND THE SUBLIMINAL CODE I WAS TAPPING WITH MY FINGERS.

NOT TO MENTION, OF COURSE, THE COLOGNE I WAS WEARING WHICH I BELIEVE WAS A FAVORITE OF HIS LATE, BELOVED FATHER.

UNBELIEVABLE.

ACTUALLY, IT'S ALL QUITE SIMPLE WHEN YOU BREAK IT DOWN AND EXAMINE THE BASIC COMPONENTS, BUT EVEN I MUST ADMIT I'M FEELING PLEASED WITH MYSELF AFTER A SOLID NIGHT'S WORK.

I THINK I MIGHT HEAD BACK TO THE LAB AND TREAT MYSELF TO A FEW HOURS EXTRA TIME ON THIS MAP OF THE HUMAN SOUL I'VE BEEN PIECING TOGETHER IN MY RECREATION TIME.

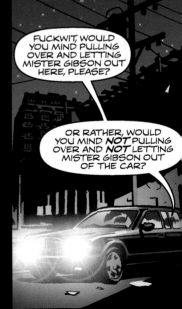

FUCKWIT, WOULD YOU MIND PULLING OVER AND LETTING MISTER GIBSON OUT HERE, PLEASE?

OR RATHER, WOULD YOU MIND *NOT* PULLING OVER AND *NOT* LETTING MISTER GIBSON OUT OF THE CAR?

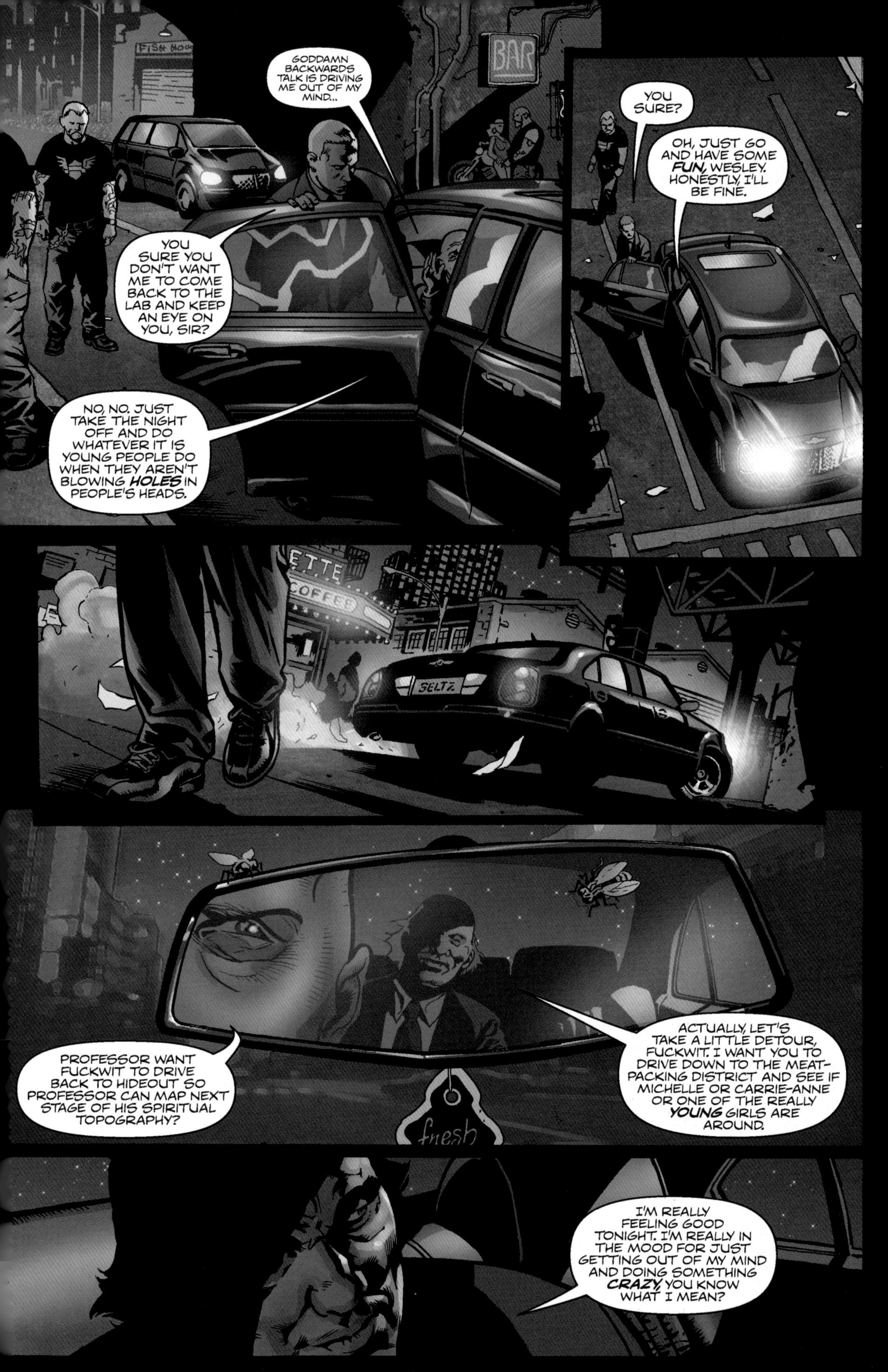
GODDAMN BACKWARDS TALK IS DRIVING ME OUT OF MY MIND...
YOU SURE YOU DON'T WANT ME TO COME BACK TO THE LAB AND KEEP AN EYE ON YOU, SIR?
NO, NO. JUST TAKE THE NIGHT OFF AND DO WHATEVER IT IS YOUNG PEOPLE DO WHEN THEY AREN'T BLOWING HOLES IN PEOPLE'S HEADS.
YOU SURE?
OH, JUST GO AND HAVE SOME FUN, WESLEY. HONESTLY, I'LL BE FINE.
PROFESSOR WANT FUCKWIT TO DRIVE BACK TO HIDEOUT SO PROFESSOR CAN MAP NEXT STAGE OF HIS SPIRITUAL TOPOGRAPHY?
ACTUALLY, LET'S TAKE A LITTLE DETOUR, FUCKWIT. I WANT YOU TO DRIVE DOWN TO THE MEAT-PACKING DISTRICT AND SEE IF MICHELLE OR CARRIE-ANNE OR ONE OF THE REALLY YOUNG GIRLS ARE AROUND.
I'M REALLY FEELING GOOD TONIGHT. I'M REALLY IN THE MOOD FOR JUST GETTING OUT OF MY MIND AND DOING SOMETHING CRAZY, YOU KNOW WHAT I MEAN?

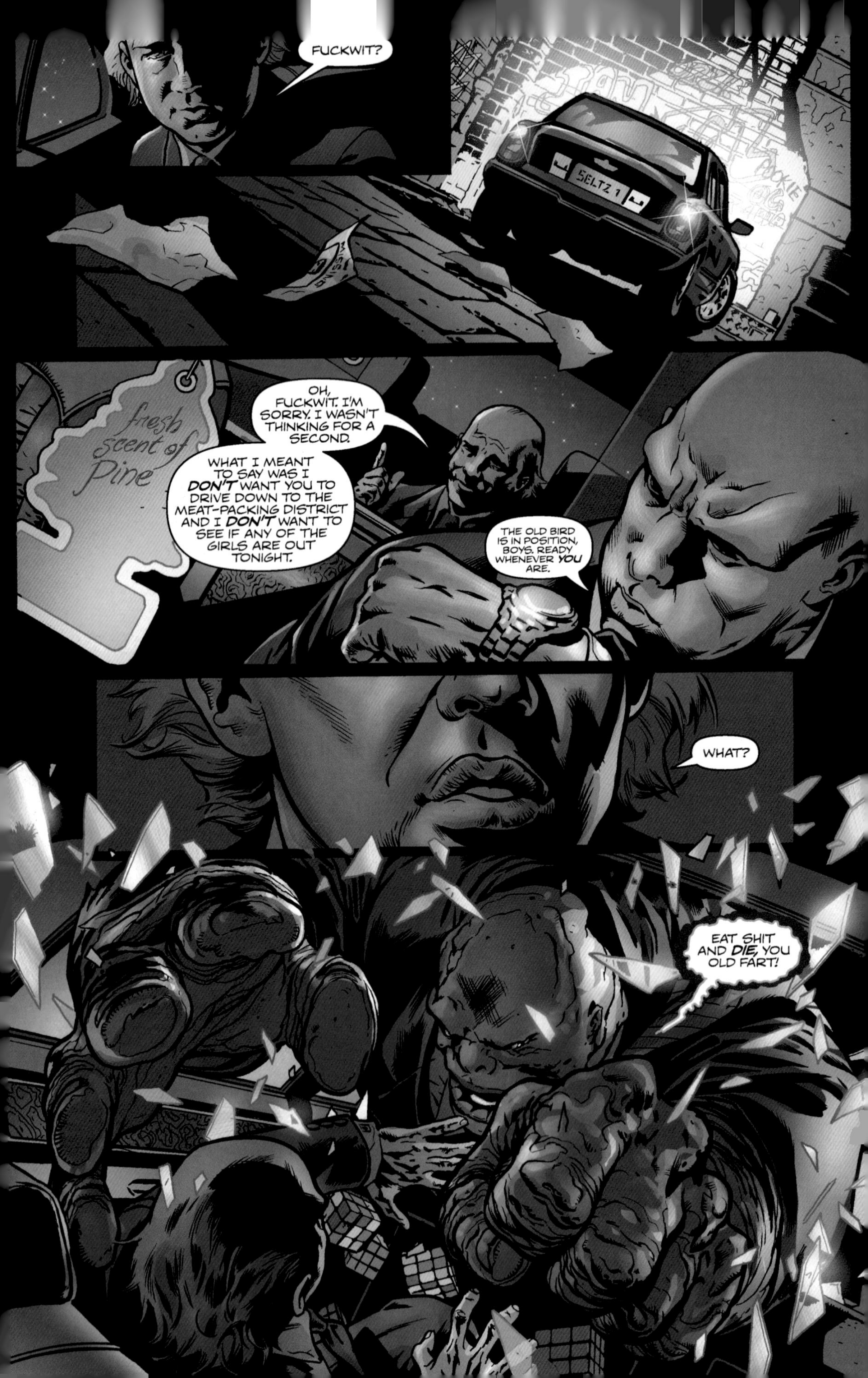
FUCKWIT?
SELTZ 1
OH, FUCKWIT. I'M SORRY. I WASN'T THINKING FOR A SECOND.
WHAT I MEANT TO SAY WAS I DON'T WANT YOU TO DRIVE DOWN TO THE MEAT-PACKING DISTRICT AND I DON'T WANT TO SEE IF ANY OF THE GIRLS ARE OUT TONIGHT.
fresh scent of Pine
THE OLD BIRD IS IN POSITION, BOYS. READY WHENEVER YOU ARE.
WHAT?
EAT SHIT AND DIE, YOU OLD FART!

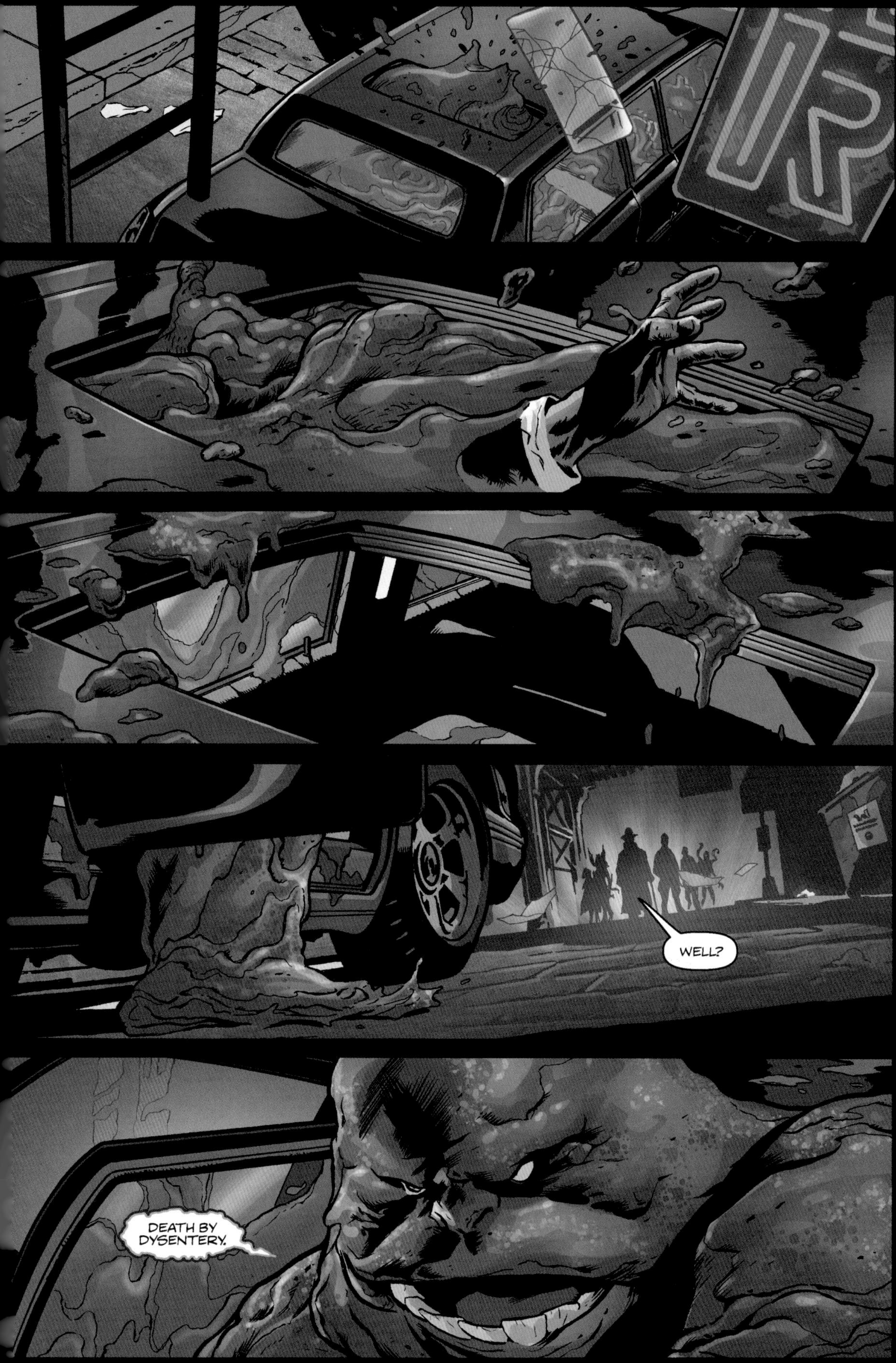
WELL?
DEATH BY DYSENTERY.

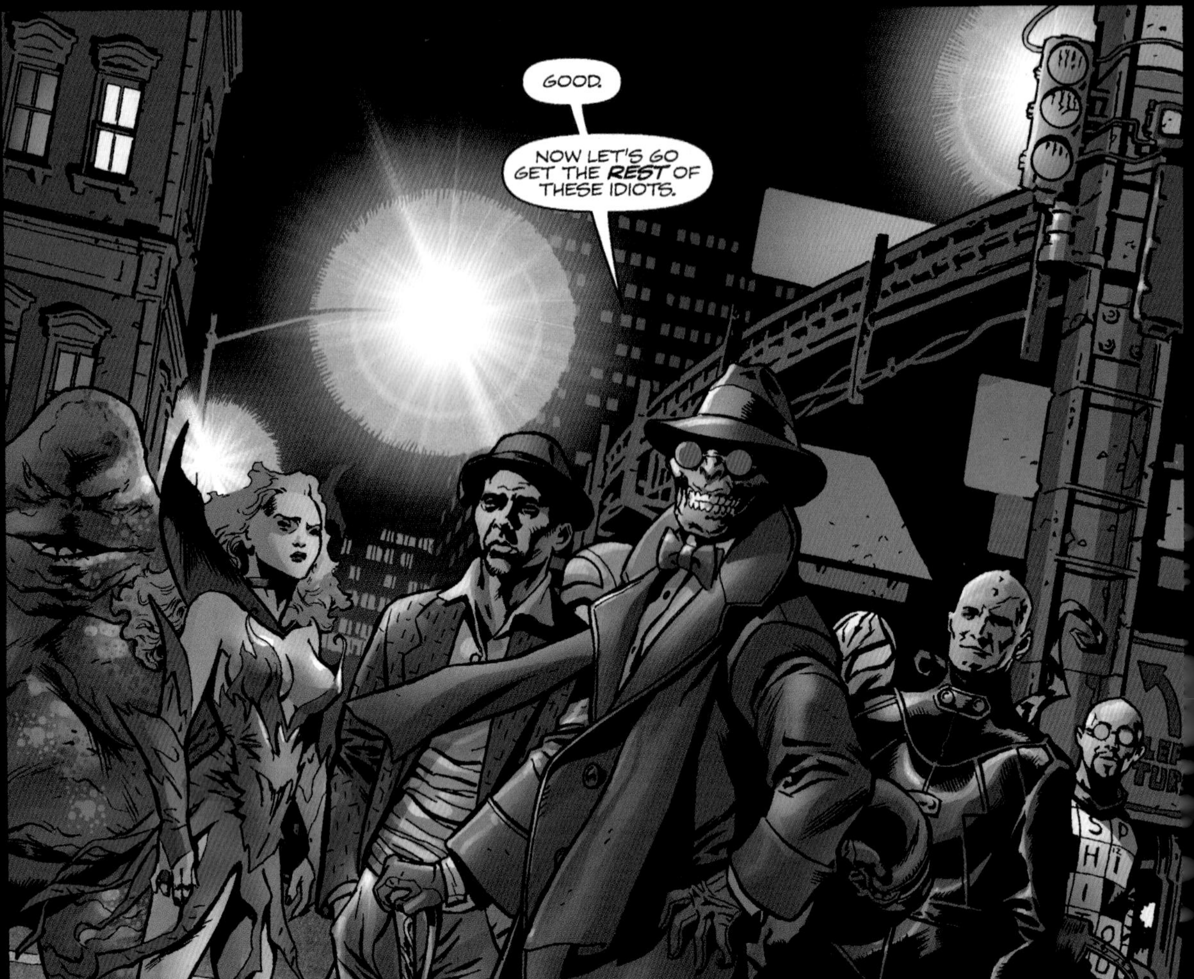
GOOD.
NOW LET'S GO GET THE **REST** OF THESE IDIOTS.

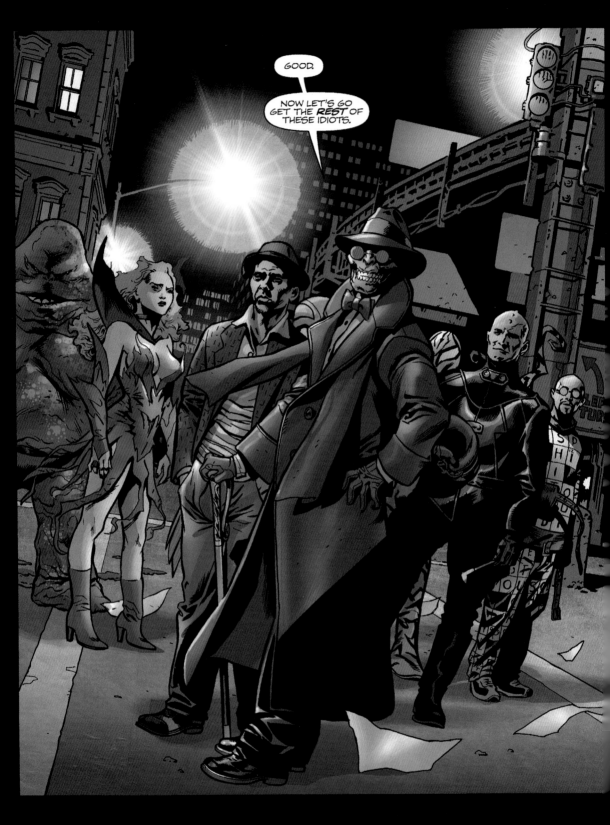

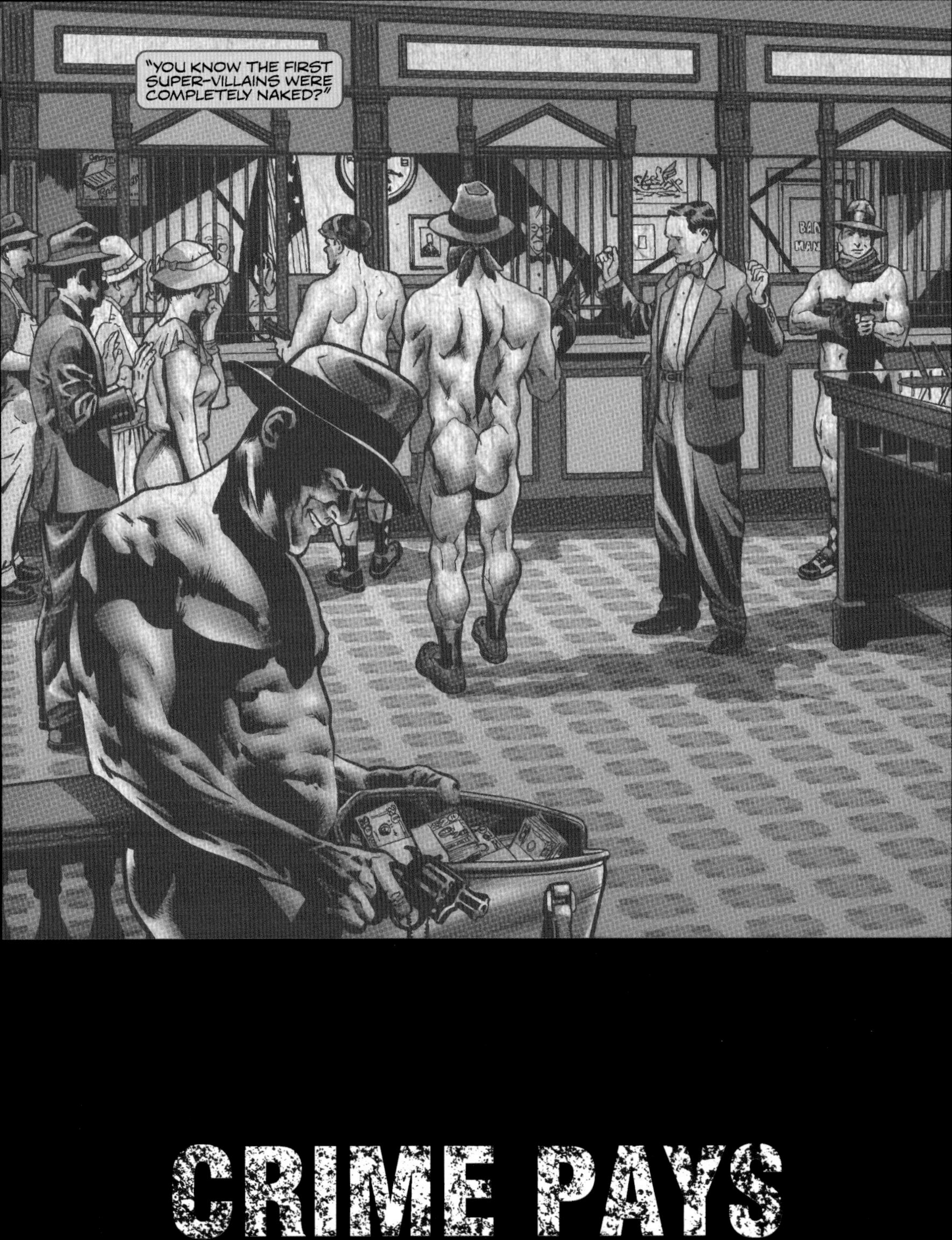
"YOU KNOW THE FIRST SUPER-VILLAINS WERE COMPLETELY NAKED?"

CRIME PAYS

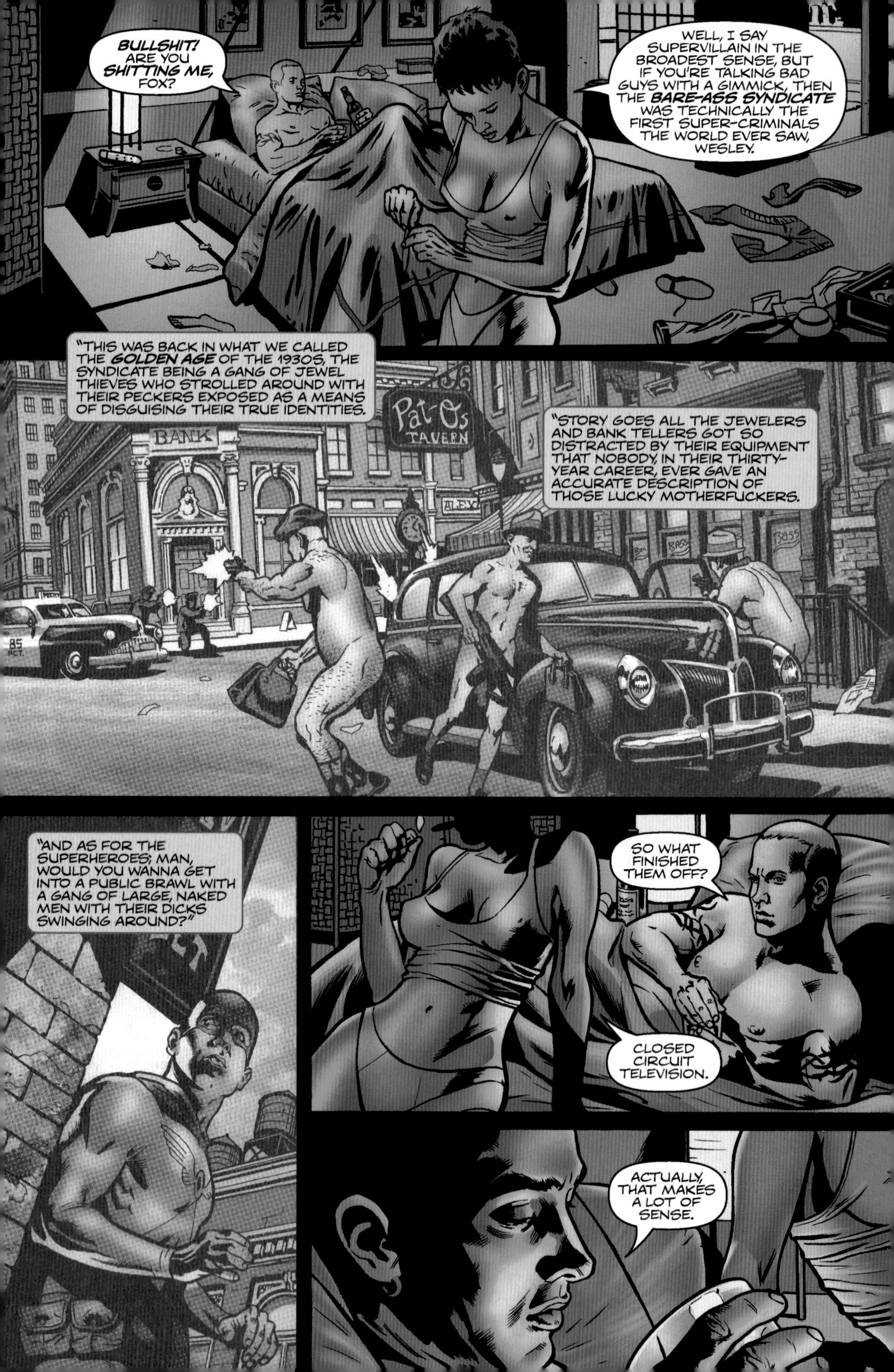
BULLSHIT! ARE YOU SHITTING ME, FOX?
WELL, I SAY SUPERVILLAIN IN THE BROADEST SENSE, BUT IF YOU'RE TALKING BAD GUYS WITH A GIMMICK, THEN THE BARE-ASS SYNDICATE WAS TECHNICALLY THE FIRST SUPER-CRIMINALS THE WORLD EVER SAW, WESLEY.
"THIS WAS BACK IN WHAT WE CALLED THE GOLDEN AGE OF THE 1930S, THE SYNDICATE BEING A GANG OF JEWEL THIEVES WHO STROLLED AROUND WITH THEIR PECKERS EXPOSED AS A MEANS OF DISGUISING THEIR TRUE IDENTITIES.
Pat-O's TAVERN
BANK
"STORY GOES ALL THE JEWELERS AND BANK TELLERS GOT SO DISTRACTED BY THEIR EQUIPMENT THAT NOBODY, IN THEIR THIRTY-YEAR CAREER, EVER GAVE AN ACCURATE DESCRIPTION OF THOSE LUCKY MOTHERFUCKERS.
"AND AS FOR THE SUPERHEROES; MAN, WOULD YOU WANNA GET INTO A PUBLIC BRAWL WITH A GANG OF LARGE, NAKED MEN WITH THEIR DICKS SWINGING AROUND?"
SO WHAT FINISHED THEM OFF?
CLOSED CIRCUIT TELEVISION.
ACTUALLY, THAT MAKES A LOT OF SENSE.

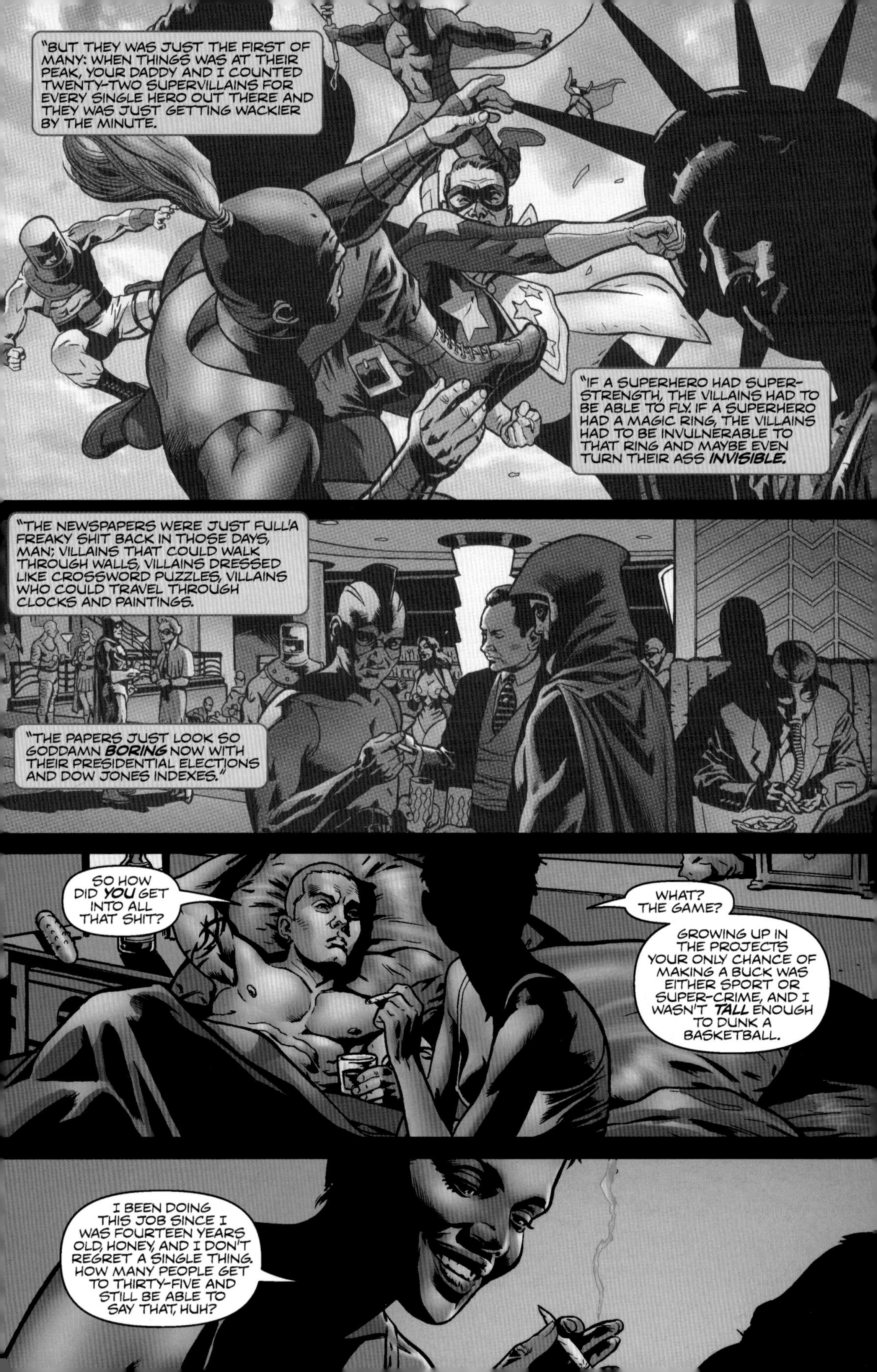
"BUT THEY WAS JUST THE FIRST OF MANY: WHEN THINGS WAS AT THEIR PEAK, YOUR DADDY AND I COUNTED TWENTY-TWO SUPERVILLAINS FOR EVERY SINGLE HERO OUT THERE AND THEY WAS JUST GETTING WACKIER BY THE MINUTE.
"IF A SUPERHERO HAD SUPER-STRENGTH, THE VILLAINS HAD TO BE ABLE TO FLY. IF A SUPERHERO HAD A MAGIC RING, THE VILLAINS HAD TO BE INVULNERABLE TO THAT RING AND MAYBE EVEN TURN THEIR ASS *INVISIBLE.*
"THE NEWSPAPERS WERE JUST FULL'A FREAKY SHIT BACK IN THOSE DAYS, MAN; VILLAINS THAT COULD WALK THROUGH WALLS, VILLAINS DRESSED LIKE CROSSWORD PUZZLES, VILLAINS WHO COULD TRAVEL THROUGH CLOCKS AND PAINTINGS.
"THE PAPERS JUST LOOK SO GODDAMN *BORING* NOW WITH THEIR PRESIDENTIAL ELECTIONS AND DOW JONES INDEXES."
SO HOW DID *YOU* GET INTO ALL THAT SHIT?
WHAT? THE GAME?
GROWING UP IN THE PROJECTS YOUR ONLY CHANCE OF MAKING A BUCK WAS EITHER SPORT OR SUPER-CRIME, AND I WASN'T *TALL* ENOUGH TO DUNK A BASKETBALL.
I BEEN DOING THIS JOB SINCE I WAS FOURTEEN YEARS OLD, HONEY, AND I DON'T REGRET A SINGLE THING. HOW MANY PEOPLE GET TO THIRTY-FIVE AND STILL BE ABLE TO SAY THAT, HUH?

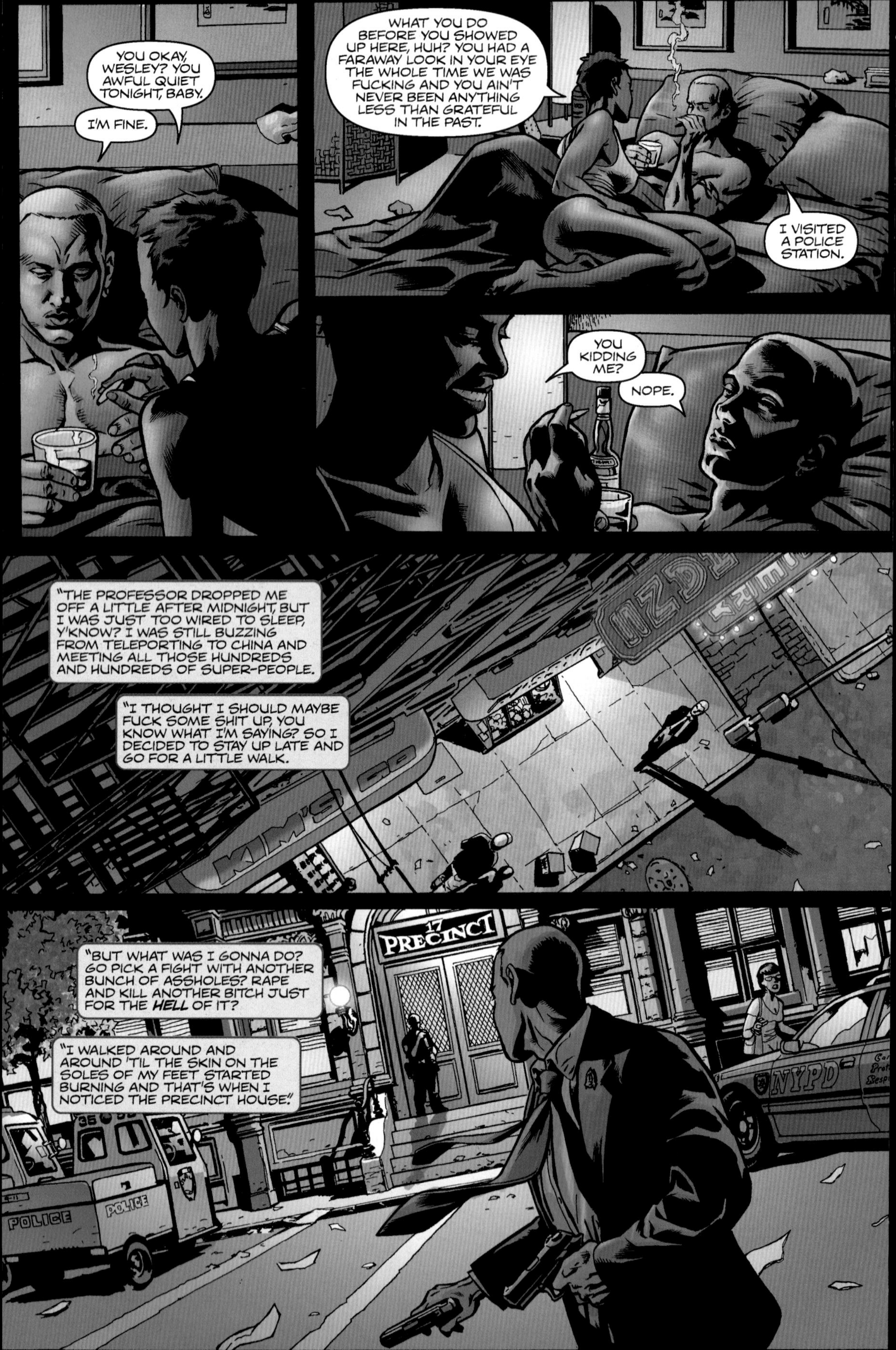
YOU OKAY, WESLEY? YOU AWFUL QUIET TONIGHT, BABY.
I'M FINE.
WHAT YOU DO BEFORE YOU SHOWED UP HERE, HUH? YOU HAD A FARAWAY LOOK IN YOUR EYE THE WHOLE TIME WE WAS FUCKING AND YOU AIN'T NEVER BEEN ANYTHING LESS THAN GRATEFUL IN THE PAST.
I VISITED A POLICE STATION.
YOU KIDDING ME?
NOPE.
"THE PROFESSOR DROPPED ME OFF A LITTLE AFTER MIDNIGHT, BUT I WAS JUST TOO WIRED TO SLEEP, Y'KNOW? I WAS STILL BUZZING FROM TELEPORTING TO CHINA AND MEETING ALL THOSE HUNDREDS AND HUNDREDS OF SUPER-PEOPLE.
"I THOUGHT I SHOULD MAYBE FUCK SOME SHIT UP, YOU KNOW WHAT I'M SAYING? SO I DECIDED TO STAY UP LATE AND GO FOR A LITTLE WALK.
KIM'S
17 PRECINCT
"BUT WHAT WAS I GONNA DO? GO PICK A FIGHT WITH ANOTHER BUNCH OF ASSHOLES? RAPE AND KILL ANOTHER BITCH JUST FOR THE HELL OF IT?
"I WALKED AROUND AND AROUND 'TIL THE SKIN ON THE SOLES OF MY FEET STARTED BURNING AND THAT'S WHEN I NOTICED THE PRECINCT HOUSE."
POLICE
POLICE
NYPD

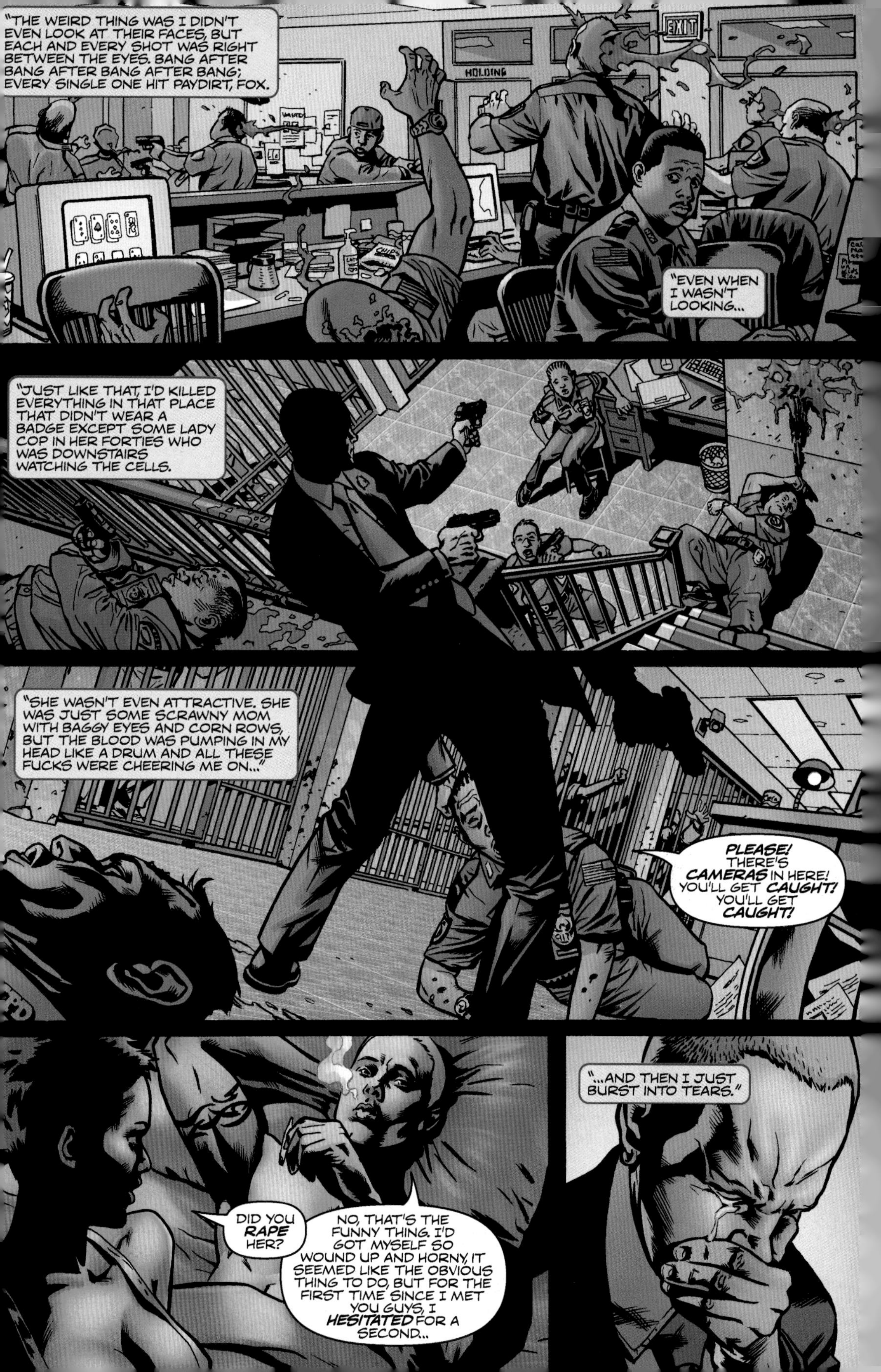
"THE WEIRD THING WAS I DIDN'T EVEN LOOK AT THEIR FACES, BUT EACH AND EVERY SHOT WAS RIGHT BETWEEN THE EYES. BANG AFTER BANG AFTER BANG AFTER BANG; EVERY SINGLE ONE HIT PAYDIRT, FOX.
EXIT
HOLDING
"EVEN WHEN I WASN'T LOOKING...
"JUST LIKE THAT, I'D KILLED EVERYTHING IN THAT PLACE THAT DIDN'T WEAR A BADGE EXCEPT SOME LADY COP IN HER FORTIES WHO WAS DOWNSTAIRS WATCHING THE CELLS.
"SHE WASN'T EVEN ATTRACTIVE. SHE WAS JUST SOME SCRAWNY MOM WITH BAGGY EYES AND CORN ROWS, BUT THE BLOOD WAS PUMPING IN MY HEAD LIKE A DRUM AND ALL THESE FUCKS WERE CHEERING ME ON..."
PLEASE! THERE'S CAMERAS IN HERE! YOU'LL GET CAUGHT! YOU'LL GET CAUGHT!
DID YOU RAPE HER?
NO, THAT'S THE FUNNY THING. I'D GOT MYSELF SO WOUND UP AND HORNY, IT SEEMED LIKE THE OBVIOUS THING TO DO, BUT FOR THE FIRST TIME SINCE I MET YOU GUYS, I HESITATED FOR A SECOND...
"...AND THEN I JUST BURST INTO TEARS."

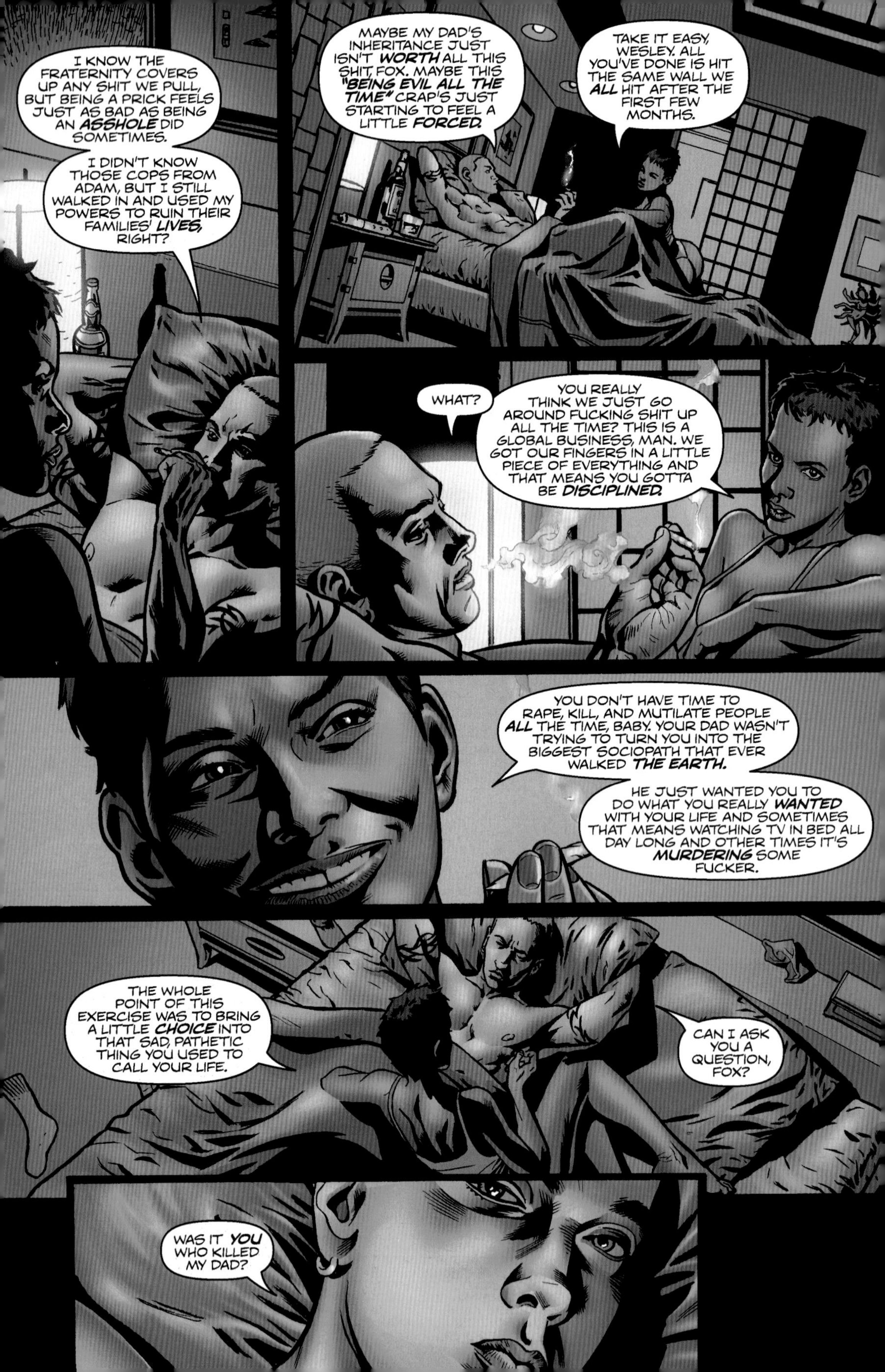
I KNOW THE FRATERNITY COVERS UP ANY SHIT WE PULL, BUT BEING A PRICK FEELS JUST AS BAD AS BEING AN ASSHOLE DID SOMETIMES.
I DIDN'T KNOW THOSE COPS FROM ADAM, BUT I STILL WALKED IN AND USED MY POWERS TO RUIN THEIR FAMILIES' LIVES, RIGHT?
MAYBE MY DAD'S INHERITANCE JUST ISN'T WORTH ALL THIS SHIT, FOX. MAYBE THIS "BEING EVIL ALL THE TIME" CRAP'S JUST STARTING TO FEEL A LITTLE FORCED.
TAKE IT EASY, WESLEY. ALL YOU'VE DONE IS HIT THE SAME WALL WE ALL HIT AFTER THE FIRST FEW MONTHS.
WHAT?
YOU REALLY THINK WE JUST GO AROUND FUCKING SHIT UP ALL THE TIME? THIS IS A GLOBAL BUSINESS, MAN. WE GOT OUR FINGERS IN A LITTLE PIECE OF EVERYTHING AND THAT MEANS YOU GOTTA BE DISCIPLINED.
YOU DON'T HAVE TIME TO RAPE, KILL, AND MUTILATE PEOPLE ALL THE TIME, BABY. YOUR DAD WASN'T TRYING TO TURN YOU INTO THE BIGGEST SOCIOPATH THAT EVER WALKED THE EARTH.
HE JUST WANTED YOU TO DO WHAT YOU REALLY WANTED WITH YOUR LIFE AND SOMETIMES THAT MEANS WATCHING TV IN BED ALL DAY LONG AND OTHER TIMES IT'S MURDERING SOME FUCKER.
THE WHOLE POINT OF THIS EXERCISE WAS TO BRING A LITTLE CHOICE INTO THAT SAD, PATHETIC THING YOU USED TO CALL YOUR LIFE.
CAN I ASK YOU A QUESTION, FOX?
WAS IT YOU WHO KILLED MY DAD?

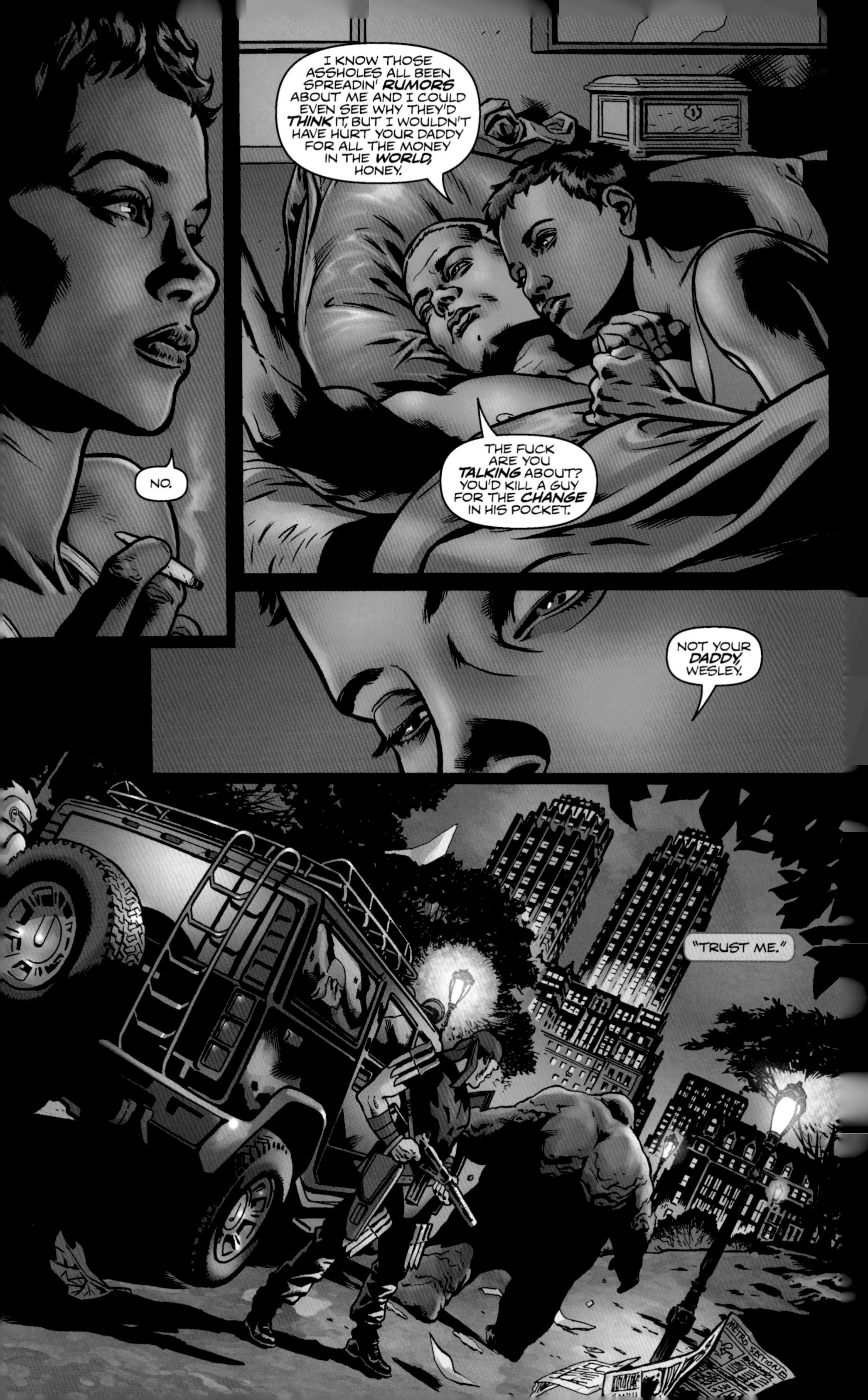

I KNOW THOSE ASSHOLES ALL BEEN SPREADIN' RUMORS ABOUT ME AND I COULD EVEN SEE WHY THEY'D THINK IT, BUT I WOULDN'T HAVE HURT YOUR DADDY FOR ALL THE MONEY IN THE WORLD, HONEY.
NO.
THE FUCK ARE YOU TALKING ABOUT? YOU'D KILL A GUY FOR THE CHANGE IN HIS POCKET.
NOT YOUR DADDY, WESLEY.
"TRUST ME."
METRO STATION

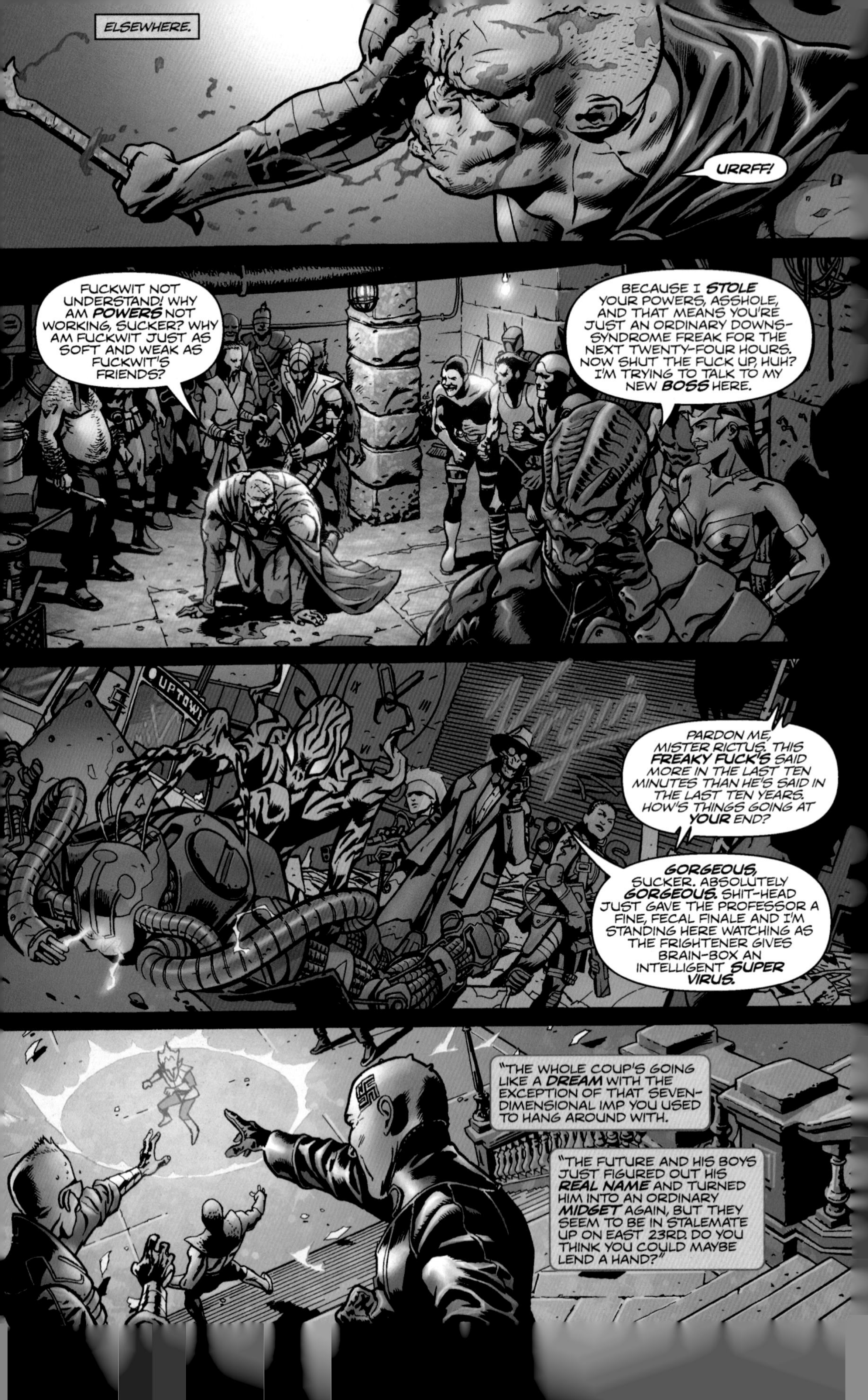
ELSEWHERE.
URRFF!
FUCKWIT NOT UNDERSTAND! WHY AM POWERS NOT WORKING, SUCKER? WHY AM FUCKWIT JUST AS SOFT AND WEAK AS FUCKWIT'S FRIENDS?
BECAUSE I STOLE YOUR POWERS, ASSHOLE, AND THAT MEANS YOU'RE JUST AN ORDINARY DOWNS-SYNDROME FREAK FOR THE NEXT TWENTY-FOUR HOURS. NOW SHUT THE FUCK UP, HUH? I'M TRYING TO TALK TO MY NEW BOSS HERE.
UPTOWN
PARDON ME, MISTER RICTUS. THIS FREAKY FUCK'S SAID MORE IN THE LAST TEN MINUTES THAN HE'S SAID IN THE LAST TEN YEARS. HOW'S THINGS GOING AT YOUR END?
GORGEOUS, SUCKER. ABSOLUTELY GORGEOUS. SHIT-HEAD JUST GAVE THE PROFESSOR A FINE, FECAL FINALE AND I'M STANDING HERE WATCHING AS THE FRIGHTENER GIVES BRAIN-BOX AN INTELLIGENT SUPER VIRUS.
"THE WHOLE COUP'S GOING LIKE A DREAM WITH THE EXCEPTION OF THAT SEVEN-DIMENSIONAL IMP YOU USED TO HANG AROUND WITH.
"THE FUTURE AND HIS BOYS JUST FIGURED OUT HIS REAL NAME AND TURNED HIM INTO AN ORDINARY MIDGET AGAIN, BUT THEY SEEM TO BE IN STALEMATE UP ON EAST 23RD. DO YOU THINK YOU COULD MAYBE LEND A HAND?"

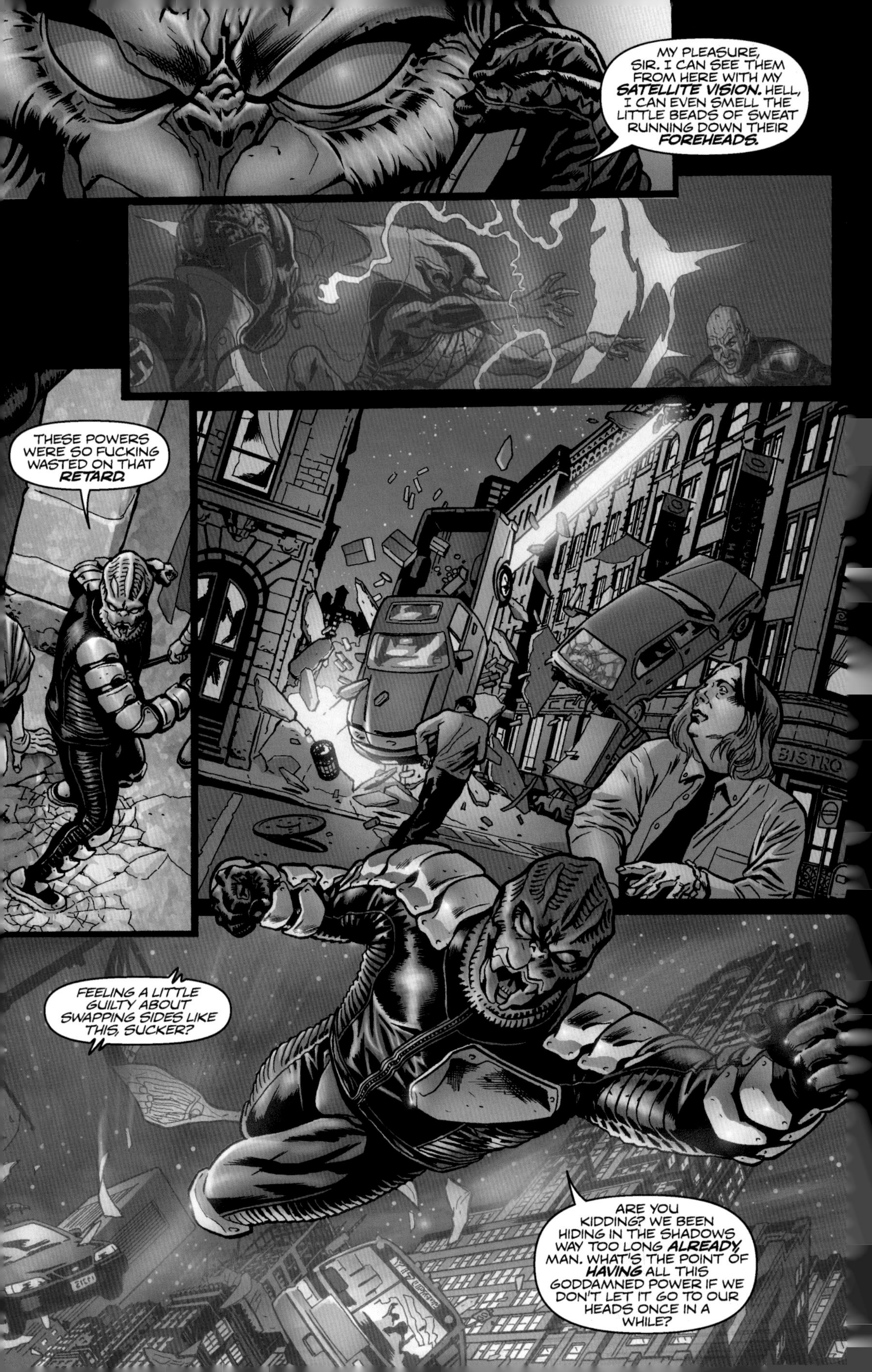
MY PLEASURE, SIR. I CAN SEE THEM FROM HERE WITH MY SATELLITE VISION. HELL, I CAN EVEN SMELL THE LITTLE BEADS OF SWEAT RUNNING DOWN THEIR FOREHEADS.
THESE POWERS WERE SO FUCKING WASTED ON THAT RETARD.
BISTRO
FEELING A LITTLE GUILTY ABOUT SWAPPING SIDES LIKE THIS, SUCKER?
ARE YOU KIDDING? WE BEEN HIDING IN THE SHADOWS WAY TOO LONG ALREADY, MAN. WHAT'S THE POINT OF HAVING ALL THIS GODDAMNED POWER IF WE DON'T LET IT GO TO OUR HEADS ONCE IN A WHILE?

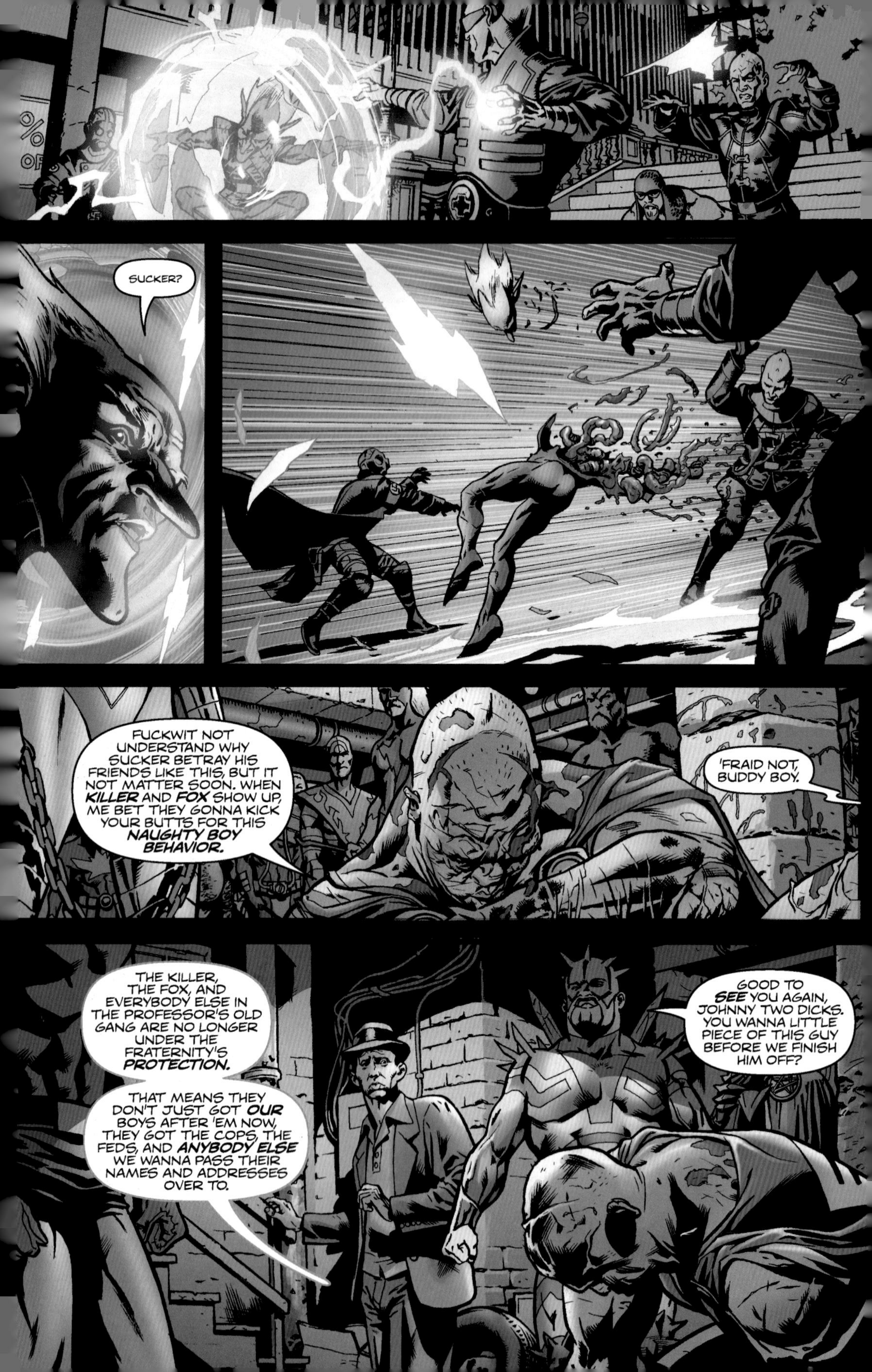
SUCKER?
FUCKWIT NOT UNDERSTAND WHY SUCKER BETRAY HIS FRIENDS LIKE THIS, BUT IT NOT MATTER SOON. WHEN KILLER AND FOX SHOW UP, ME BET THEY GONNA KICK YOUR BUTTS FOR THIS NAUGHTY BOY BEHAVIOR.
'FRAID NOT, BUDDY BOY.
THE KILLER, THE FOX, AND EVERYBODY ELSE IN THE PROFESSOR'S OLD GANG ARE NO LONGER UNDER THE FRATERNITY'S PROTECTION.
THAT MEANS THEY DON'T JUST GOT OUR BOYS AFTER 'EM NOW, THEY GOT THE COPS, THE FEDS, AND ANYBODY ELSE WE WANNA PASS THEIR NAMES AND ADDRESSES OVER TO.
GOOD TO SEE YOU AGAIN, JOHNNY TWO DICKS. YOU WANNA LITTLE PIECE OF THIS GUY BEFORE WE FINISH HIM OFF?

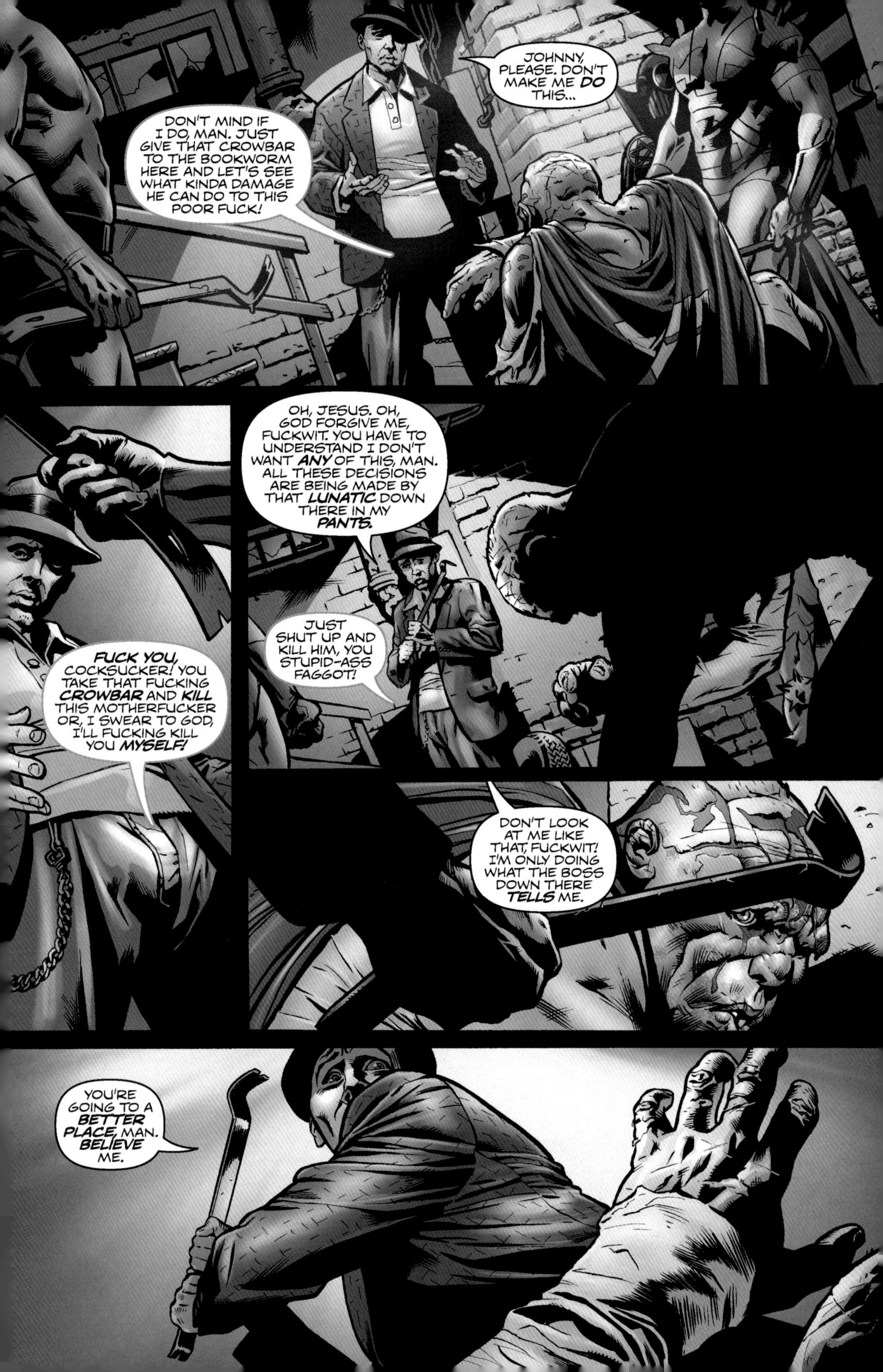
JOHNNY, PLEASE. DON'T MAKE ME DO THIS...
DON'T MIND IF I DO, MAN. JUST GIVE THAT CROWBAR TO THE BOOKWORM HERE AND LET'S SEE WHAT KINDA DAMAGE HE CAN DO TO THIS POOR FUCK!
FUCK YOU, COCKSUCKER! YOU TAKE THAT FUCKING CROWBAR AND KILL THIS MOTHERFUCKER OR, I SWEAR TO GOD, I'LL FUCKING KILL YOU MYSELF!
OH, JESUS. OH, GOD FORGIVE ME, FUCKWIT. YOU HAVE TO UNDERSTAND I DON'T WANT ANY OF THIS, MAN. ALL THESE DECISIONS ARE BEING MADE BY THAT LUNATIC DOWN THERE IN MY PANTS.
JUST SHUT UP AND KILL HIM, YOU STUPID-ASS FAGGOT!
DON'T LOOK AT ME LIKE THAT, FUCKWIT! I'M ONLY DOING WHAT THE BOSS DOWN THERE TELLS ME.
YOU'RE GOING TO A BETTER PLACE, MAN. BELIEVE ME.

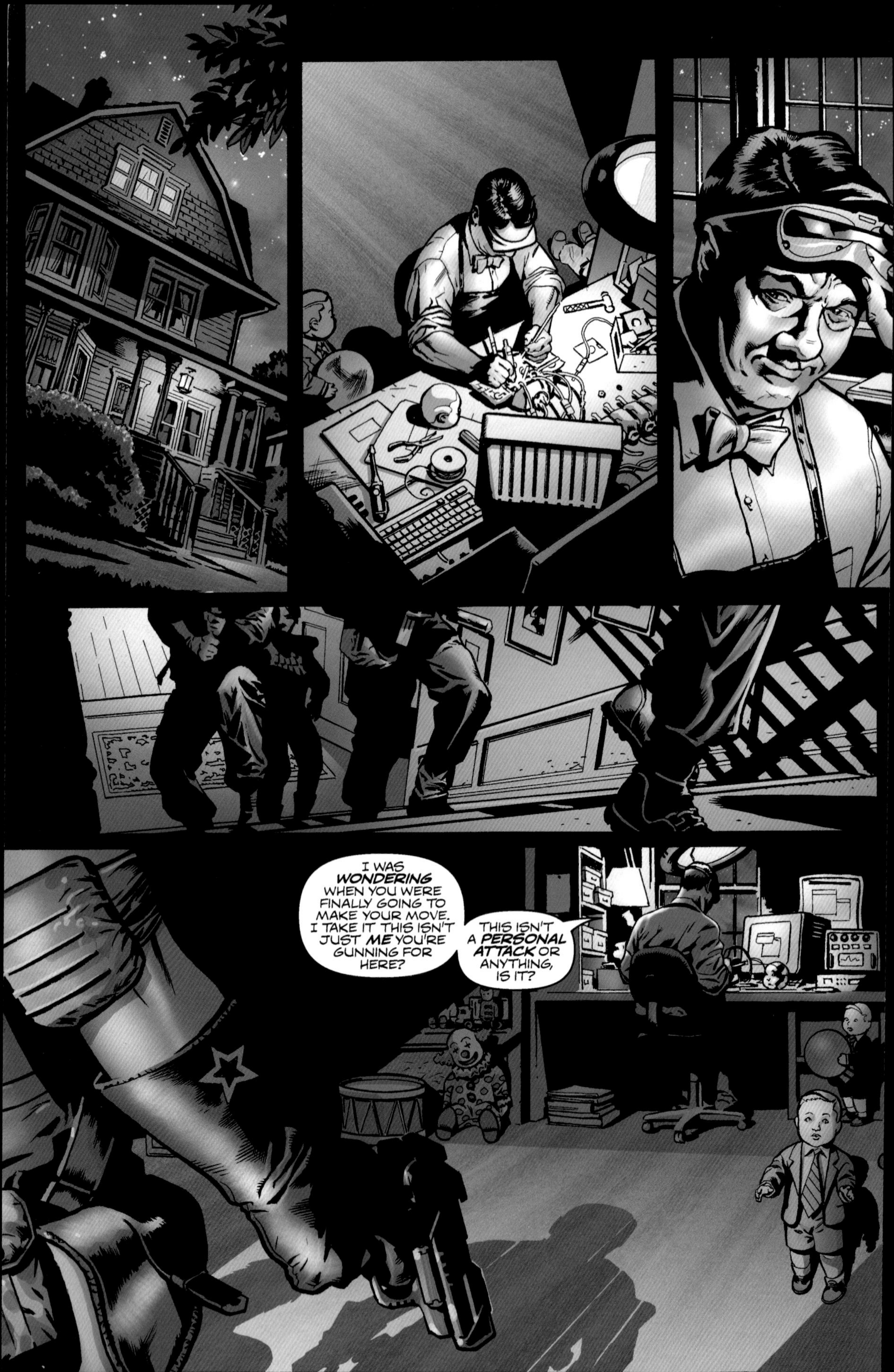
I WAS WONDERING WHEN YOU WERE FINALLY GOING TO MAKE YOUR MOVE. I TAKE IT THIS ISN'T JUST ME YOU'RE GUNNING FOR HERE?
THIS ISN'T A PERSONAL ATTACK OR ANYTHING, IS IT?

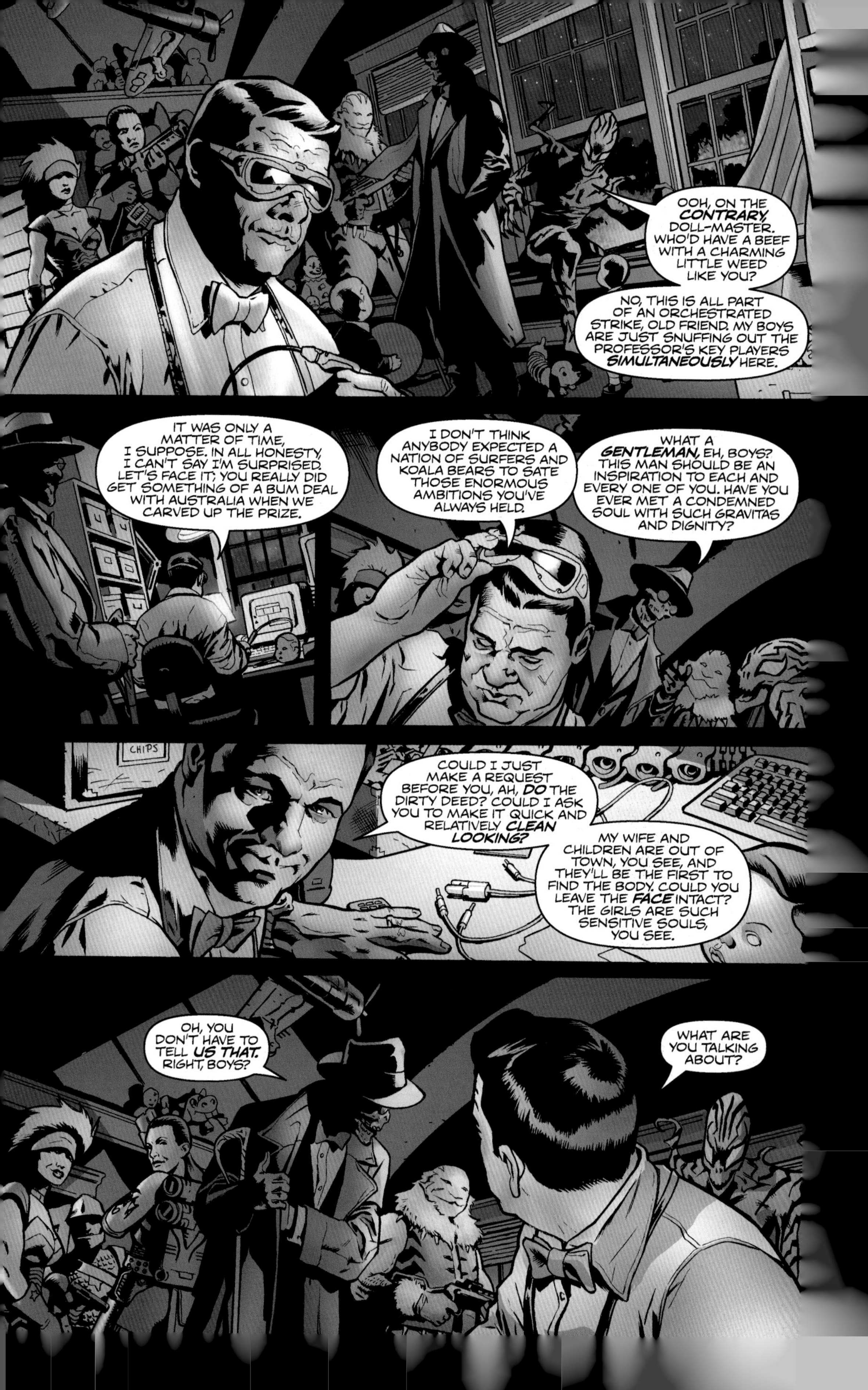

OOH, ON THE CONTRARY, DOLL-MASTER. WHO'D HAVE A BEEF WITH A CHARMING LITTLE WEED LIKE YOU?
NO, THIS IS ALL PART OF AN ORCHESTRATED STRIKE, OLD FRIEND. MY BOYS ARE JUST SNUFFING OUT THE PROFESSOR'S KEY PLAYERS SIMULTANEOUSLY HERE.
IT WAS ONLY A MATTER OF TIME, I SUPPOSE. IN ALL HONESTY, I CAN'T SAY I'M SURPRISED. LET'S FACE IT; YOU REALLY DID GET SOMETHING OF A BUM DEAL WITH AUSTRALIA WHEN WE CARVED UP THE PRIZE.
I DON'T THINK ANYBODY EXPECTED A NATION OF SURFERS AND KOALA BEARS TO SATE THOSE ENORMOUS AMBITIONS YOU'VE ALWAYS HELD.
WHAT A GENTLEMAN, EH, BOYS? THIS MAN SHOULD BE AN INSPIRATION TO EACH AND EVERY ONE OF YOU. HAVE YOU EVER MET A CONDEMNED SOUL WITH SUCH GRAVITAS AND DIGNITY?
CHIPS
COULD I JUST MAKE A REQUEST BEFORE YOU, AH, DO THE DIRTY DEED? COULD I ASK YOU TO MAKE IT QUICK AND RELATIVELY CLEAN LOOKING?
MY WIFE AND CHILDREN ARE OUT OF TOWN, YOU SEE, AND THEY'LL BE THE FIRST TO FIND THE BODY. COULD YOU LEAVE THE FACE INTACT? THE GIRLS ARE SUCH SENSITIVE SOULS, YOU SEE.
OH, YOU DON'T HAVE TO TELL US THAT. RIGHT, BOYS?
WHAT ARE YOU TALKING ABOUT?

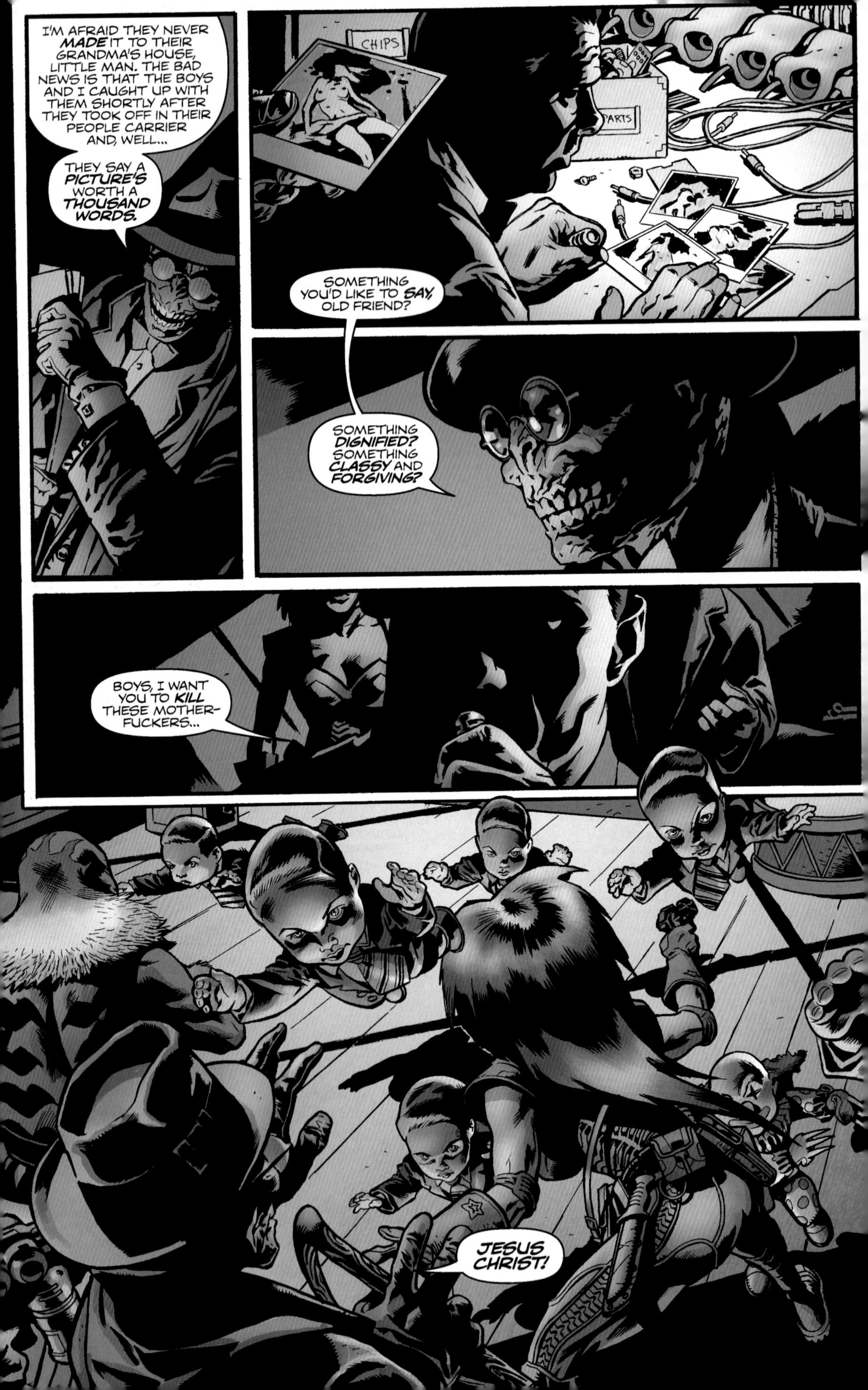
I'M AFRAID THEY NEVER MADE IT TO THEIR GRANDMA'S HOUSE, LITTLE MAN. THE BAD NEWS IS THAT THE BOYS AND I CAUGHT UP WITH THEM SHORTLY AFTER THEY TOOK OFF IN THEIR PEOPLE CARRIER AND, WELL...
THEY SAY A PICTURE'S WORTH A THOUSAND WORDS.
CHIPS
PARTS
SOMETHING YOU'D LIKE TO SAY, OLD FRIEND?
SOMETHING DIGNIFIED? SOMETHING CLASSY AND FORGIVING?
BOYS, I WANT YOU TO KILL THESE MOTHER-FUCKERS...
JESUS CHRIST!

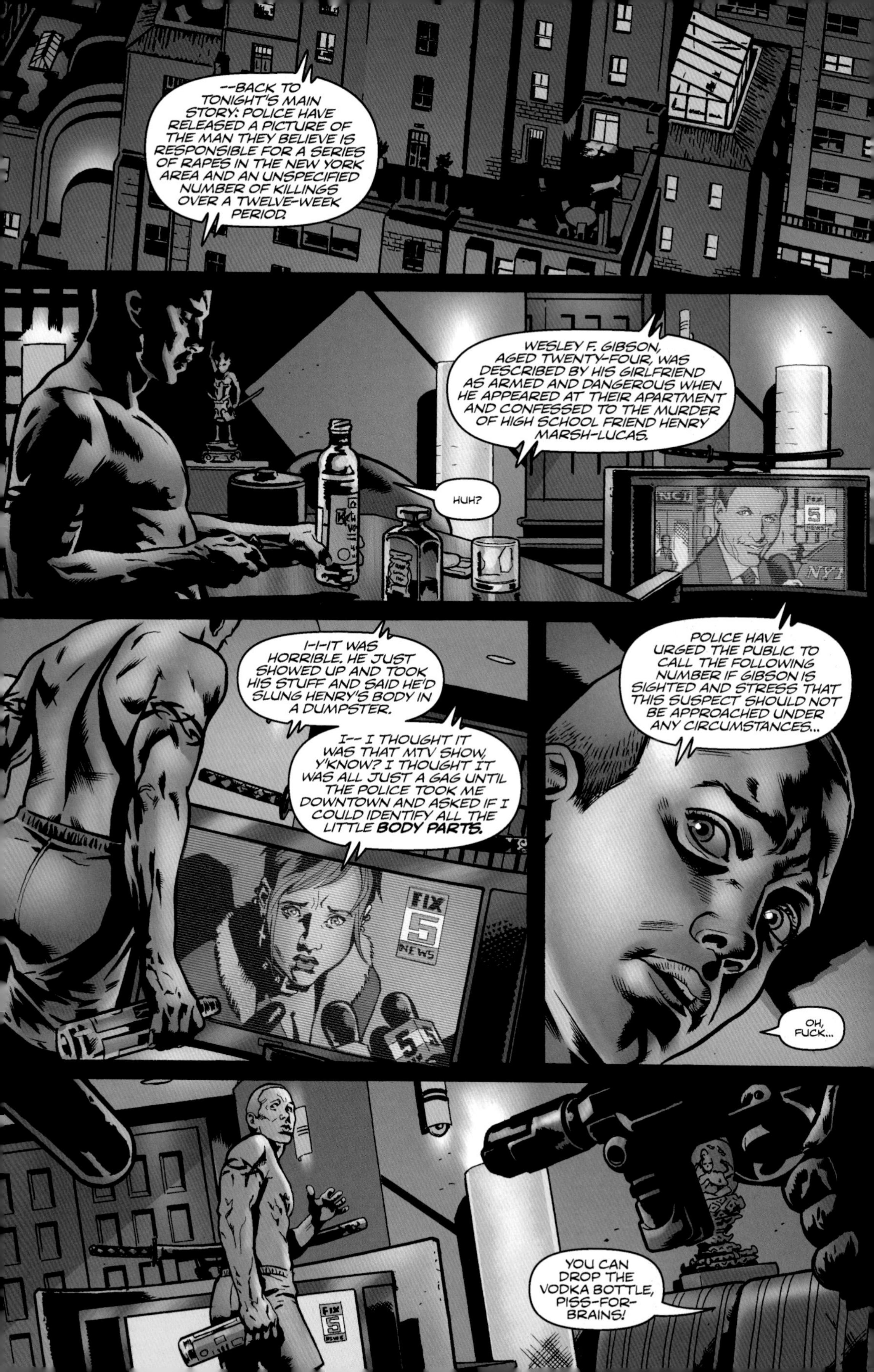
--BACK TO TONIGHT'S MAIN STORY: POLICE HAVE RELEASED A PICTURE OF THE MAN THEY BELIEVE IS RESPONSIBLE FOR A SERIES OF RAPES IN THE NEW YORK AREA AND AN UNSPECIFIED NUMBER OF KILLINGS OVER A TWELVE-WEEK PERIOD.
WESLEY F. GIBSON, AGED TWENTY-FOUR, WAS DESCRIBED BY HIS GIRLFRIEND AS ARMED AND DANGEROUS WHEN HE APPEARED AT THEIR APARTMENT AND CONFESSED TO THE MURDER OF HIGH SCHOOL FRIEND HENRY MARSH-LUCAS.
HUH?
I-I-IT WAS HORRIBLE. HE JUST SHOWED UP AND TOOK HIS STUFF AND SAID HE'D SLUNG HENRY'S BODY IN A DUMPSTER.
I-- I THOUGHT IT WAS THAT MTV SHOW, Y'KNOW? I THOUGHT IT WAS ALL JUST A GAG UNTIL THE POLICE TOOK ME DOWNTOWN AND ASKED IF I COULD IDENTIFY ALL THE LITTLE **BODY PARTS.**
FIX 5 NEWS
POLICE HAVE URGED THE PUBLIC TO CALL THE FOLLOWING NUMBER IF GIBSON IS SIGHTED AND STRESS THAT THIS SUSPECT SHOULD NOT BE APPROACHED UNDER ANY CIRCUMSTANCES...
OH, FUCK...
YOU CAN DROP THE VODKA BOTTLE, PISS-FOR-BRAINS!

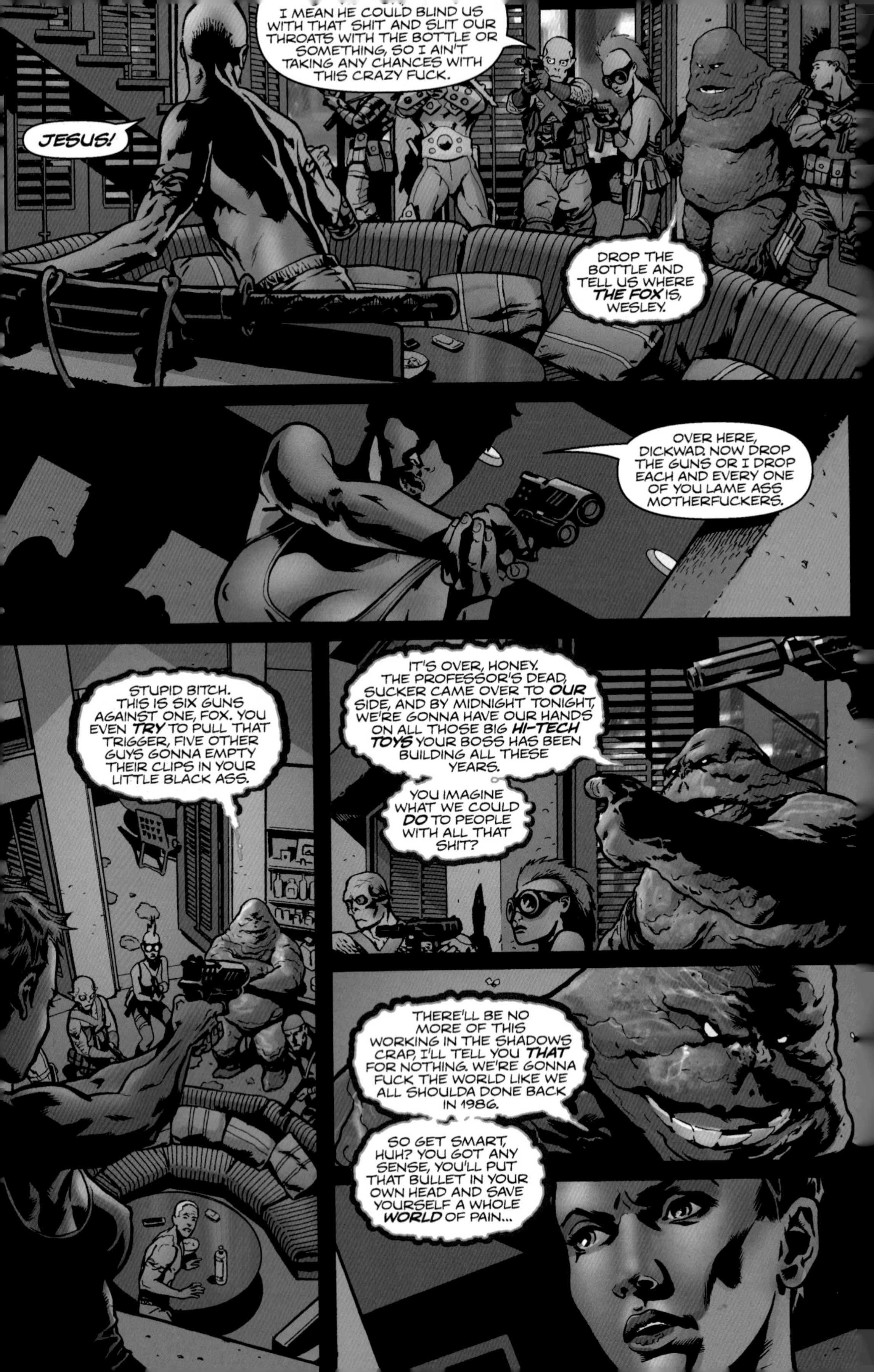
I MEAN HE COULD BLIND US WITH THAT SHIT AND SLIT OUR THROATS WITH THE BOTTLE OR SOMETHING, SO I AIN'T TAKING ANY CHANCES WITH THIS CRAZY FUCK.
JESUS!
DROP THE BOTTLE AND TELL US WHERE THE FOX IS, WESLEY.
OVER HERE, DICKWAD. NOW DROP THE GUNS OR I DROP EACH AND EVERY ONE OF YOU LAME ASS MOTHERFUCKERS.
STUPID BITCH. THIS IS SIX GUNS AGAINST ONE, FOX. YOU EVEN TRY TO PULL THAT TRIGGER, FIVE OTHER GUYS GONNA EMPTY THEIR CLIPS IN YOUR LITTLE BLACK ASS.
IT'S OVER, HONEY. THE PROFESSOR'S DEAD, SUCKER CAME OVER TO OUR SIDE, AND BY MIDNIGHT TONIGHT, WE'RE GONNA HAVE OUR HANDS ON ALL THOSE BIG HI-TECH TOYS YOUR BOSS HAS BEEN BUILDING ALL THESE YEARS.
YOU IMAGINE WHAT WE COULD DO TO PEOPLE WITH ALL THAT SHIT?
THERE'LL BE NO MORE OF THIS WORKING IN THE SHADOWS CRAP, I'LL TELL YOU THAT FOR NOTHING. WE'RE GONNA FUCK THE WORLD LIKE WE ALL SHOULDA DONE BACK IN 1986.
SO GET SMART, HUH? YOU GOT ANY SENSE, YOU'LL PUT THAT BULLET IN YOUR OWN HEAD AND SAVE YOURSELF A WHOLE WORLD OF PAIN...

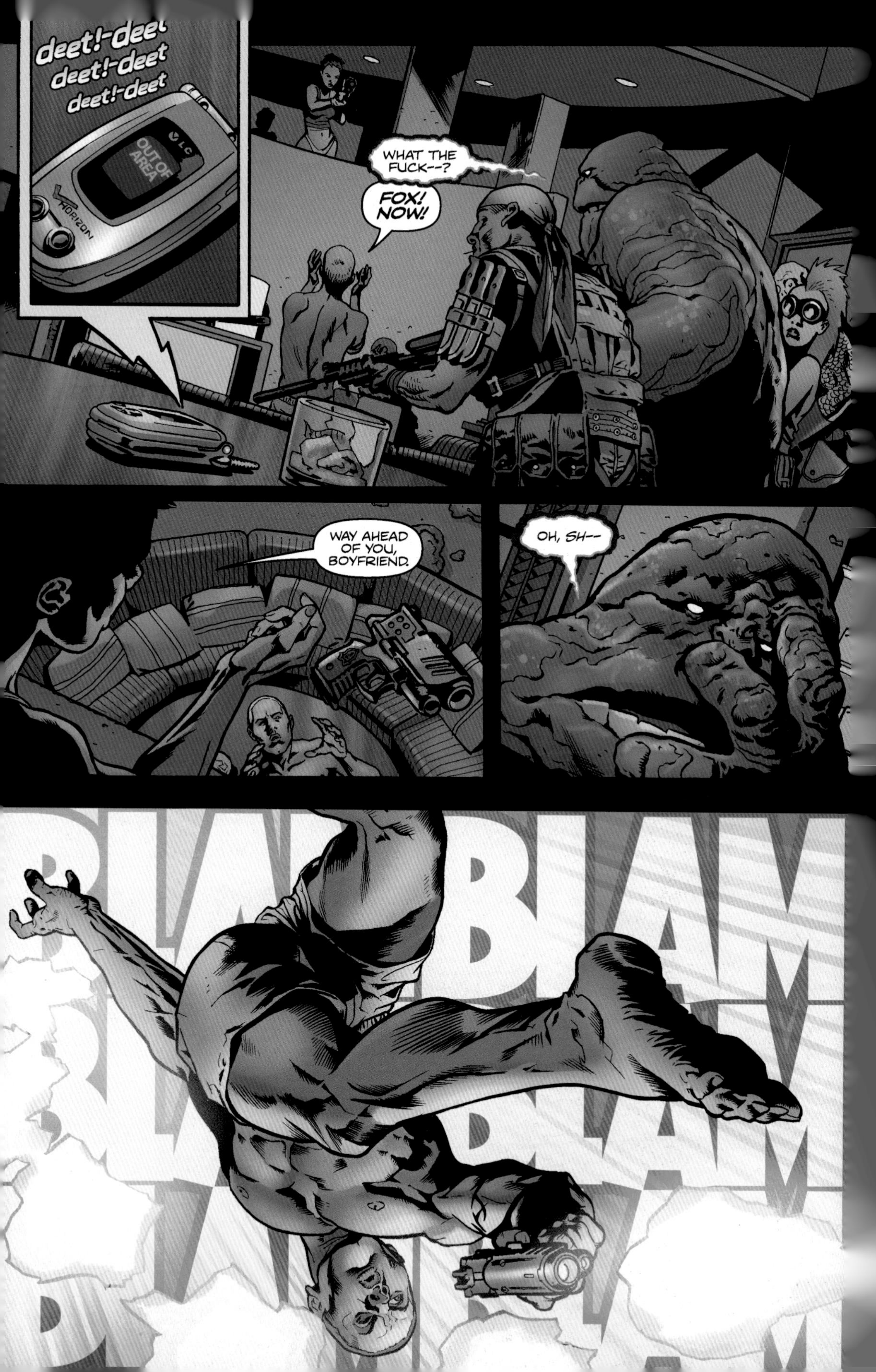
deet!-deet
deet!-deet
deet!-deet
OUT OF AREA
HORIZON
WHAT THE FUCK--?
FOX! NOW!
WAY AHEAD OF YOU, BOYFRIEND.
OH, SH--
BLAM
BLAM
BLAM
BLAM

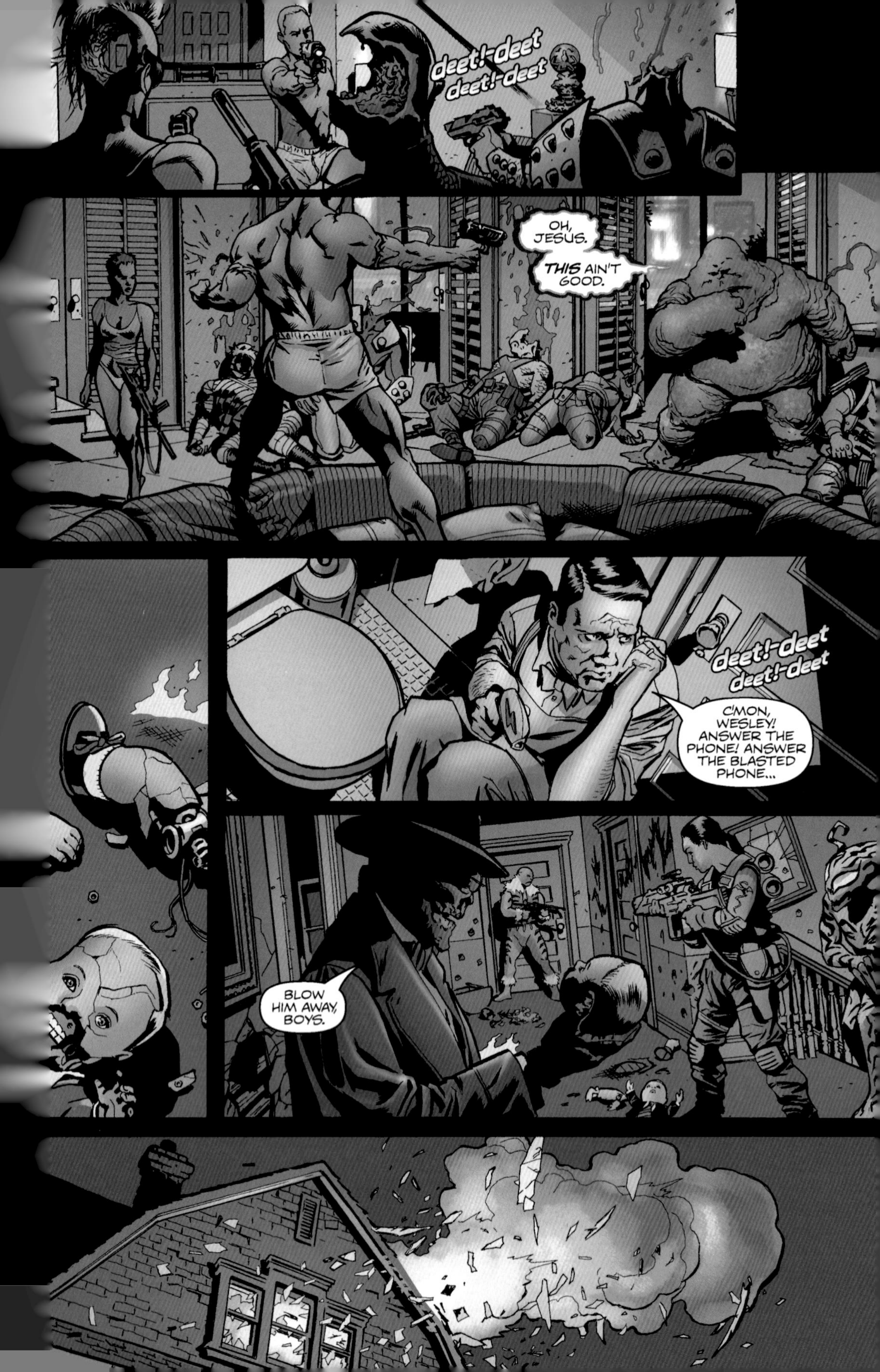
deet!-deet
deet!-deet
OH, JESUS.
THIS AIN'T GOOD.
deet!-deet
deet!-deet
C'MON, WESLEY! ANSWER THE PHONE! ANSWER THE BLASTED PHONE...
BLOW HIM AWAY, BOYS.

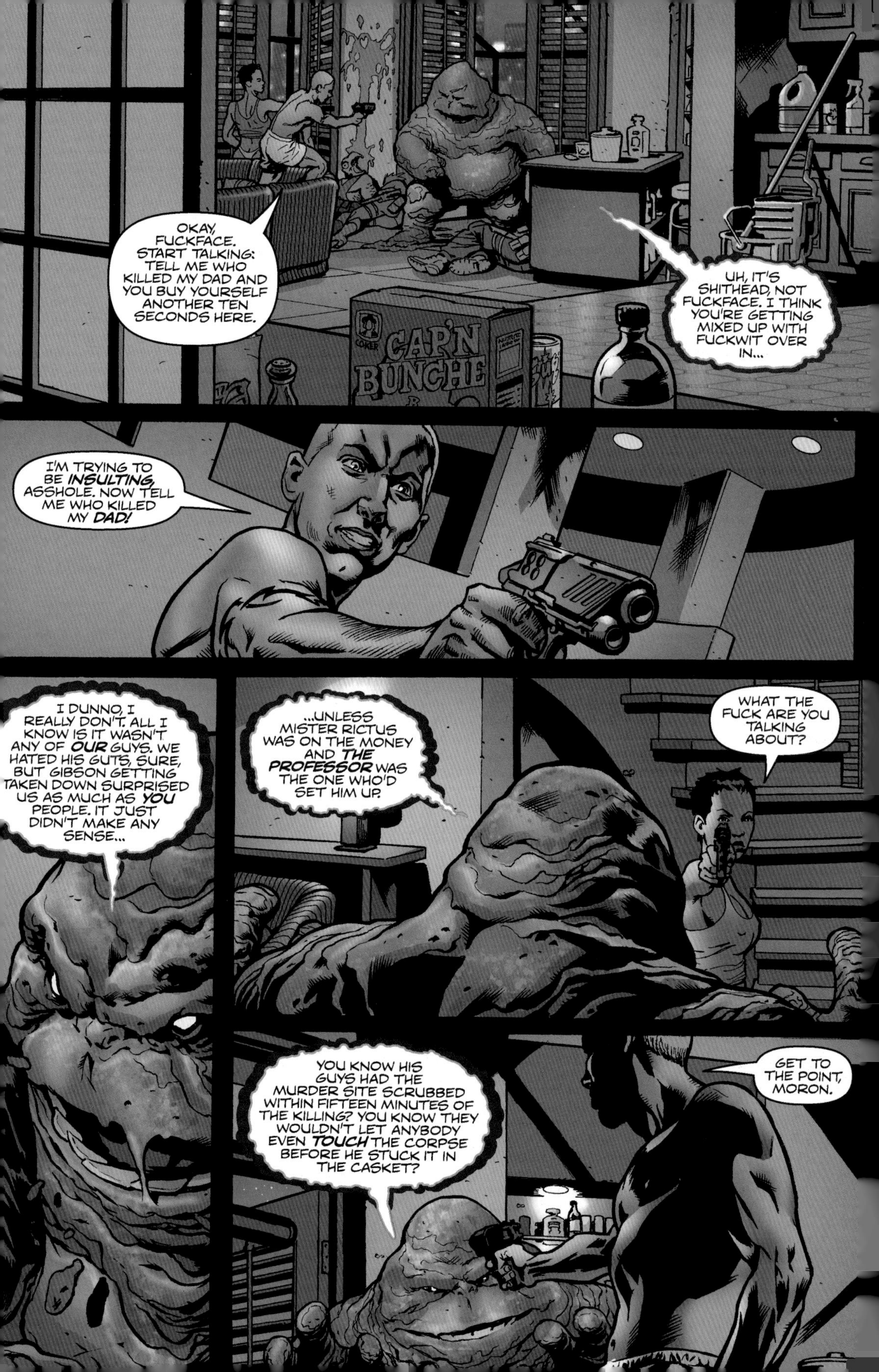
OKAY, FUCKFACE. START TALKING: TELL ME WHO KILLED MY DAD AND YOU BUY YOURSELF ANOTHER TEN SECONDS HERE.
UH, IT'S SHITHEAD, NOT FUCKFACE. I THINK YOU'RE GETTING MIXED UP WITH FUCKWIT OVER IN...
CAP'N BUNCHE
I'M TRYING TO BE INSULTING, ASSHOLE. NOW TELL ME WHO KILLED MY DAD!
I DUNNO, I REALLY DON'T. ALL I KNOW IS IT WASN'T ANY OF OUR GUYS. WE HATED HIS GUTS, SURE, BUT GIBSON GETTING TAKEN DOWN SURPRISED US AS MUCH AS YOU PEOPLE. IT JUST DIDN'T MAKE ANY SENSE...
...UNLESS MISTER RICTUS WAS ON THE MONEY AND THE PROFESSOR WAS THE ONE WHO'D SET HIM UP.
WHAT THE FUCK ARE YOU TALKING ABOUT?
YOU KNOW HIS GUYS HAD THE MURDER SITE SCRUBBED WITHIN FIFTEEN MINUTES OF THE KILLING? YOU KNOW THEY WOULDN'T LET ANYBODY EVEN TOUCH THE CORPSE BEFORE HE STUCK IT IN THE CASKET?
GET TO THE POINT, MORON.

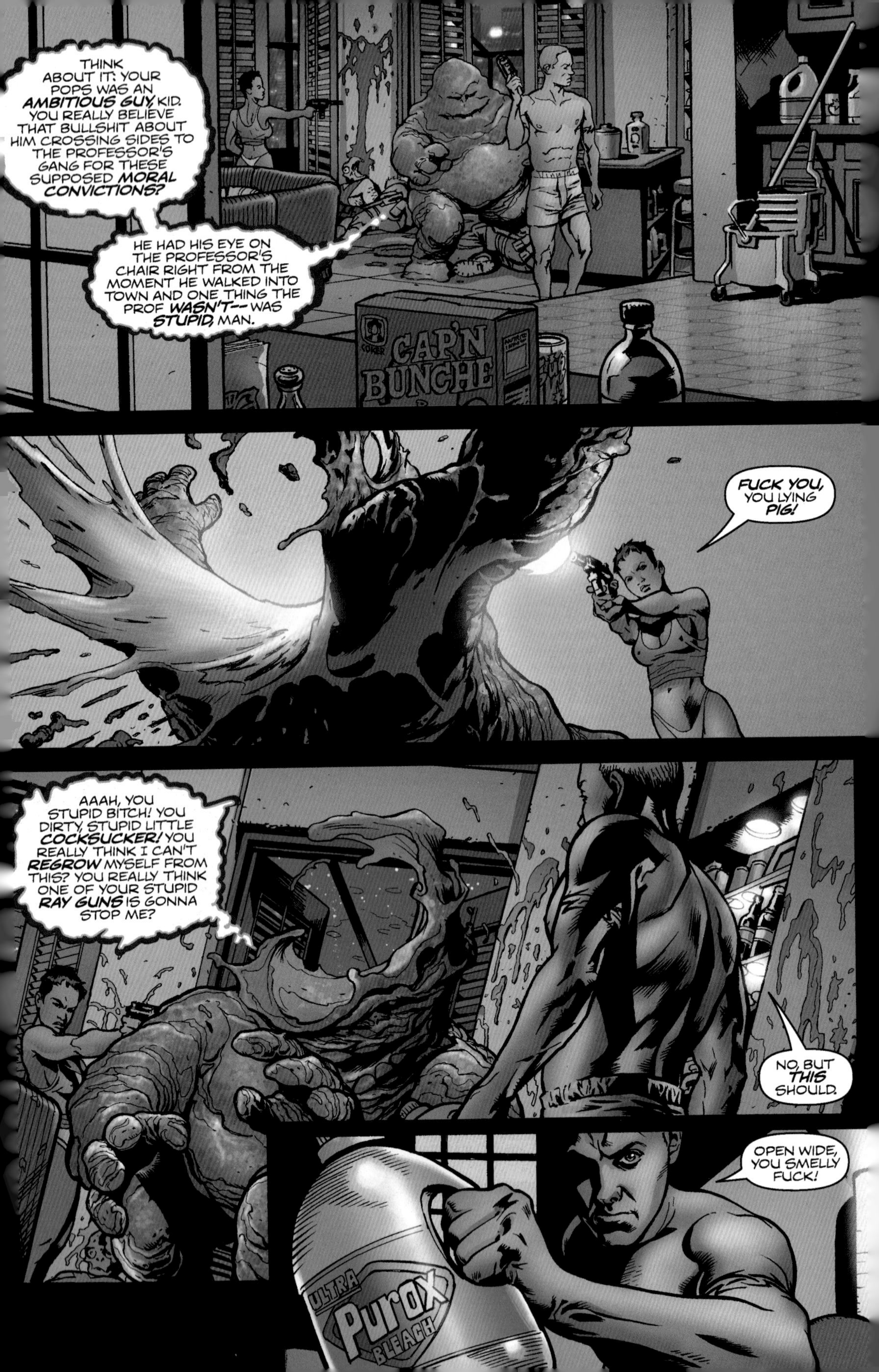
THINK ABOUT IT: YOUR POPS WAS AN AMBITIOUS GUY, KID. YOU REALLY BELIEVE THAT BULLSHIT ABOUT HIM CROSSING SIDES TO THE PROFESSOR'S GANG FOR THESE SUPPOSED MORAL CONVICTIONS?
HE HAD HIS EYE ON THE PROFESSOR'S CHAIR RIGHT FROM THE MOMENT HE WALKED INTO TOWN AND ONE THING THE PROF WASN'T-- WAS STUPID, MAN.
CAP'N BUNCHE
COKER
FUCK YOU, YOU LYING PIG!
AAAH, YOU STUPID BITCH! YOU DIRTY, STUPID LITTLE COCKSUCKER! YOU REALLY THINK I CAN'T REGROW MYSELF FROM THIS? YOU REALLY THINK ONE OF YOUR STUPID RAY GUNS IS GONNA STOP ME?
NO, BUT THIS SHOULD.
OPEN WIDE, YOU SMELLY FUCK!
ULTRA Purox BLEACH

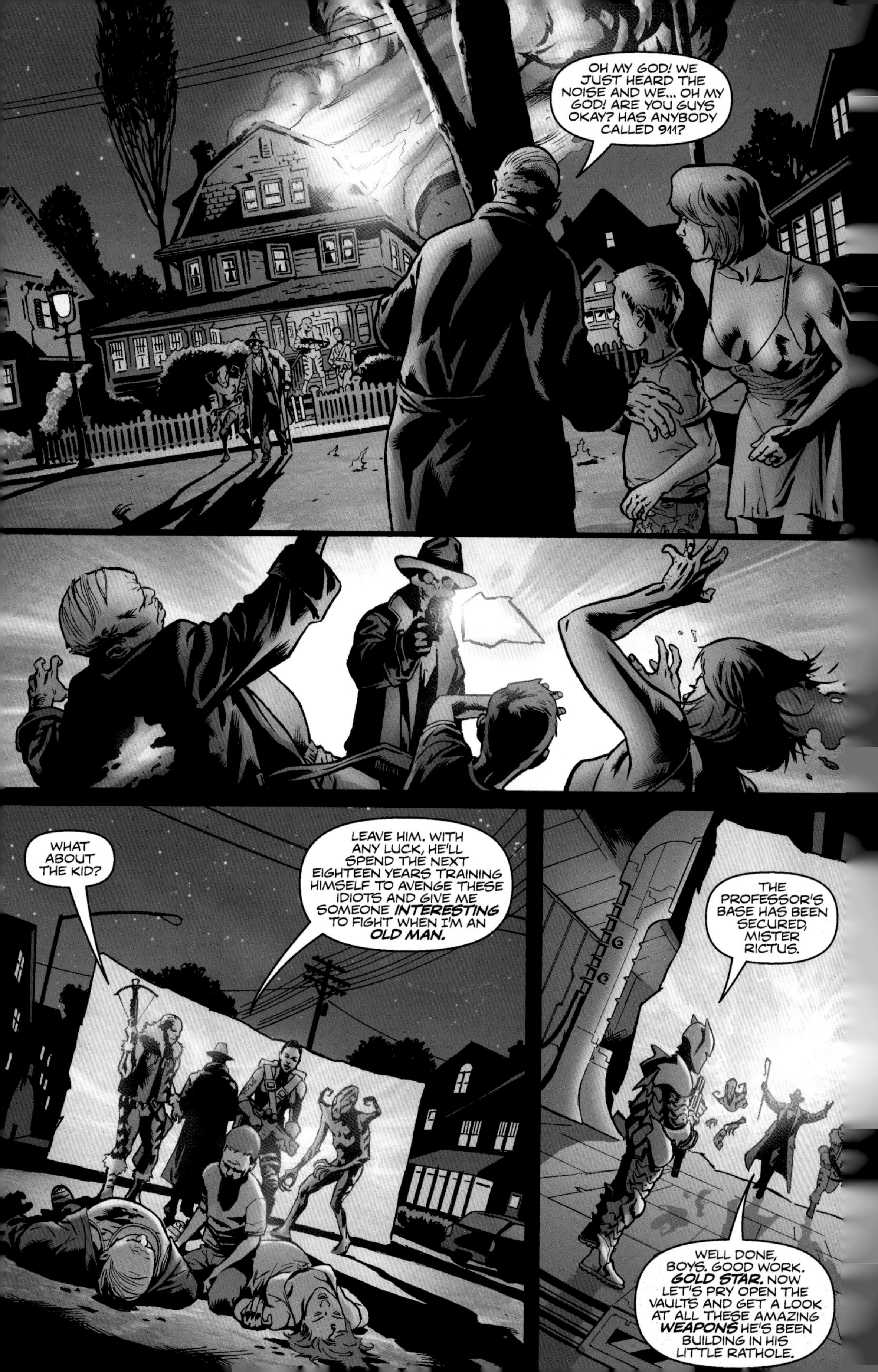
OH MY GOD! WE JUST HEARD THE NOISE AND WE... OH MY GOD! ARE YOU GUYS OKAY? HAS ANYBODY CALLED 911?
WHAT ABOUT THE KID?
LEAVE HIM. WITH ANY LUCK, HE'LL SPEND THE NEXT EIGHTEEN YEARS TRAINING HIMSELF TO AVENGE THESE IDIOTS AND GIVE ME SOMEONE INTERESTING TO FIGHT WHEN I'M AN OLD MAN.
THE PROFESSOR'S BASE HAS BEEN SECURED, MISTER RICTUS.
WELL DONE, BOYS. GOOD WORK. GOLD STAR. NOW LET'S PRY OPEN THE VAULTS AND GET A LOOK AT ALL THESE AMAZING WEAPONS HE'S BEEN BUILDING IN HIS LITTLE RATHOLE.

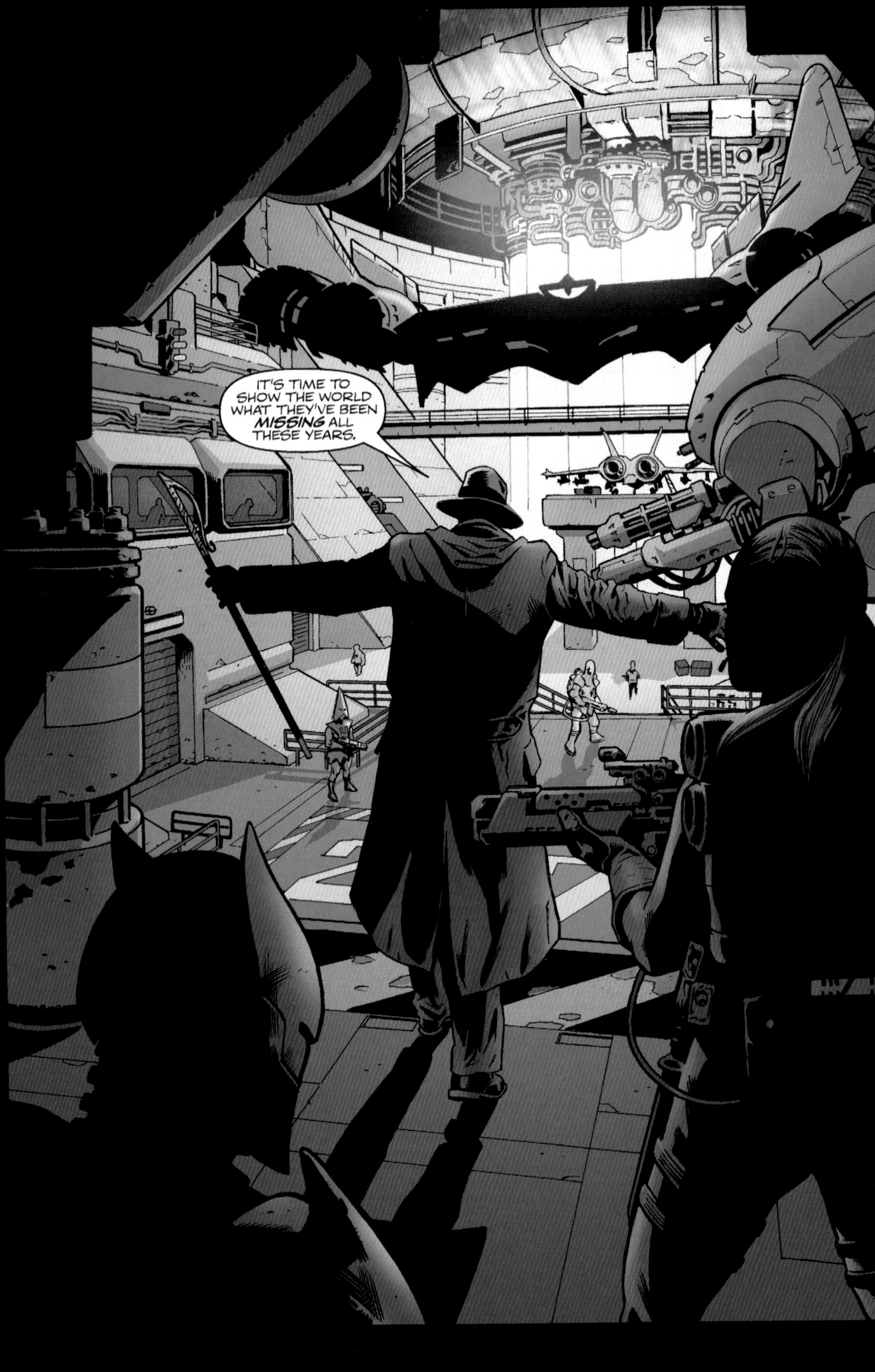
IT'S TIME TO SHOW THE WORLD WHAT THEY'VE BEEN MISSING ALL THESE YEARS.

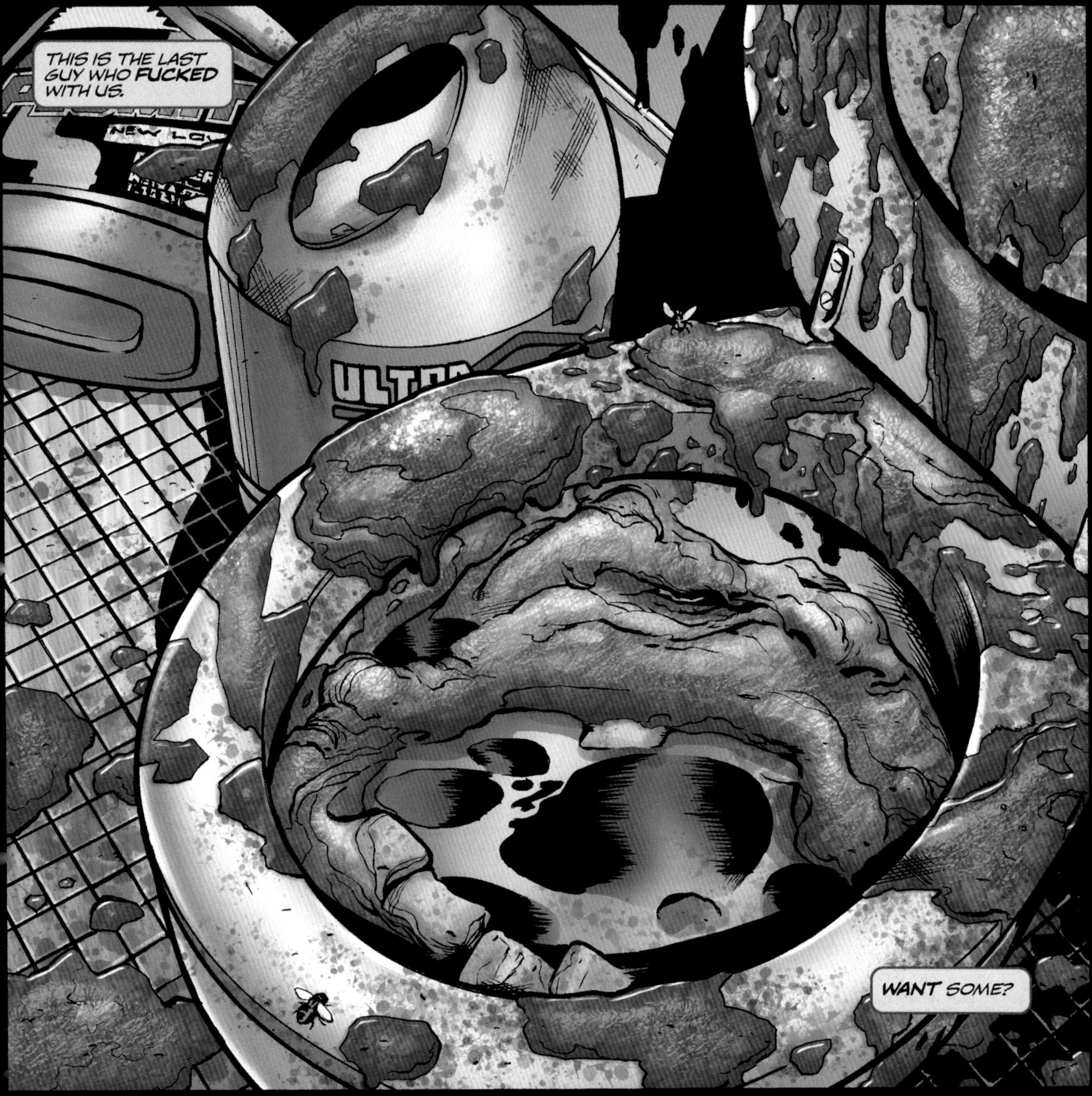
THIS IS THE LAST GUY WHO FUCKED WITH US.
WANT SOME?

THE SHIT LIST

Written by: Mark Millar

Penciled and Inked by: J.G. Jones

Colored by: Paul Mounts

Lettered by: Dreamer Design's
Robin Spehar &
Dennis Heisler

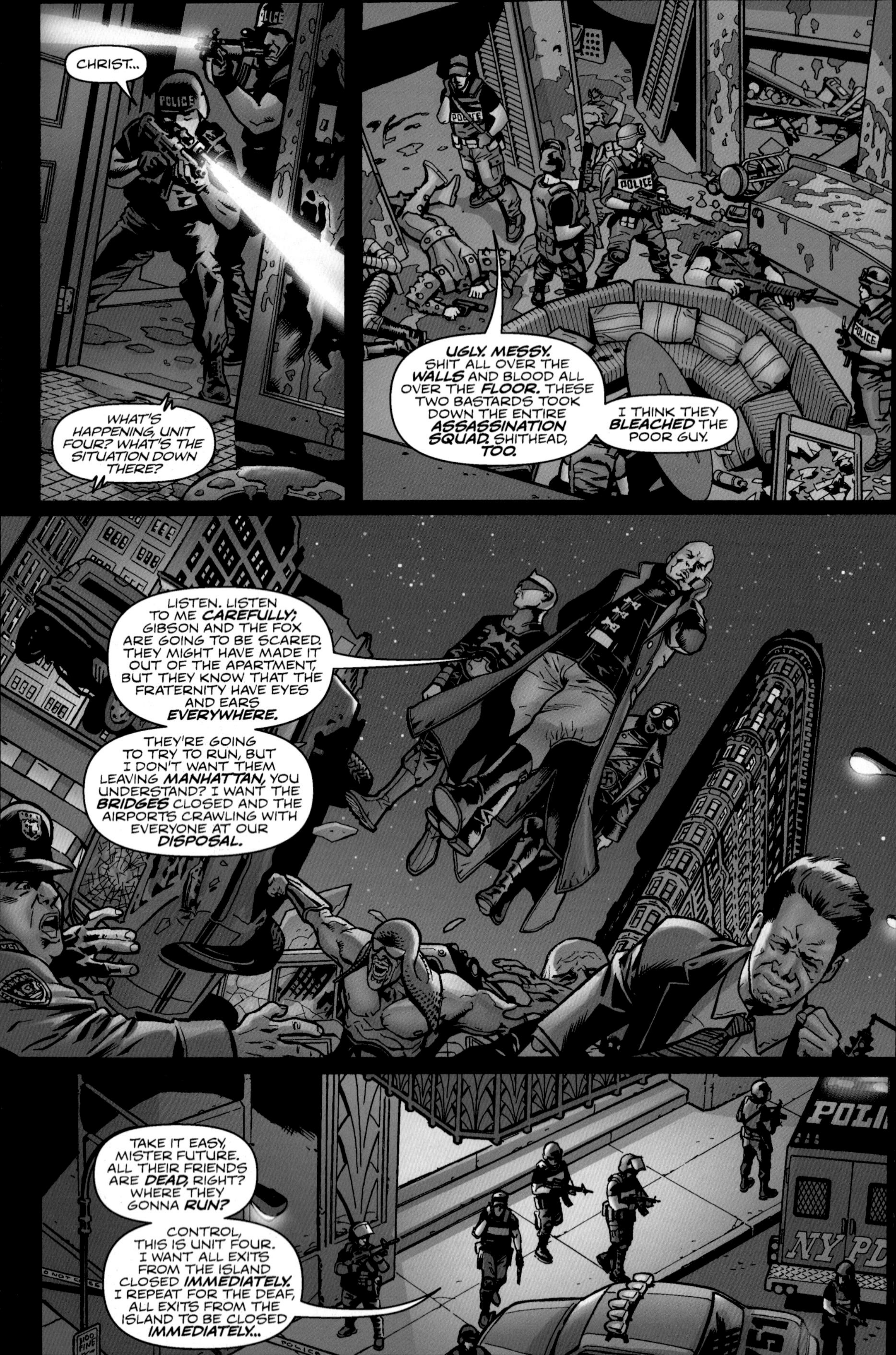
CHRIST...
WHAT'S HAPPENING, UNIT FOUR? WHAT'S THE SITUATION DOWN THERE?
UGLY. MESSY. SHIT ALL OVER THE WALLS AND BLOOD ALL OVER THE FLOOR. THESE TWO BASTARDS TOOK DOWN THE ENTIRE ASSASSINATION SQUAD. SHITHEAD, TOO.
I THINK THEY BLEACHED THE POOR GUY.
LISTEN. LISTEN TO ME CAREFULLY; GIBSON AND THE FOX ARE GOING TO BE SCARED. THEY MIGHT HAVE MADE IT OUT OF THE APARTMENT, BUT THEY KNOW THAT THE FRATERNITY HAVE EYES AND EARS EVERYWHERE.
THEY'RE GOING TO TRY TO RUN, BUT I DON'T WANT THEM LEAVING MANHATTAN, YOU UNDERSTAND? I WANT THE BRIDGES CLOSED AND THE AIRPORTS CRAWLING WITH EVERYONE AT OUR DISPOSAL.
TAKE IT EASY, MISTER FUTURE. ALL THEIR FRIENDS ARE DEAD, RIGHT? WHERE THEY GONNA RUN?
CONTROL, THIS IS UNIT FOUR. I WANT ALL EXITS FROM THE ISLAND CLOSED IMMEDIATELY. I REPEAT FOR THE DEAF, ALL EXITS FROM THE ISLAND TO BE CLOSED IMMEDIATELY...

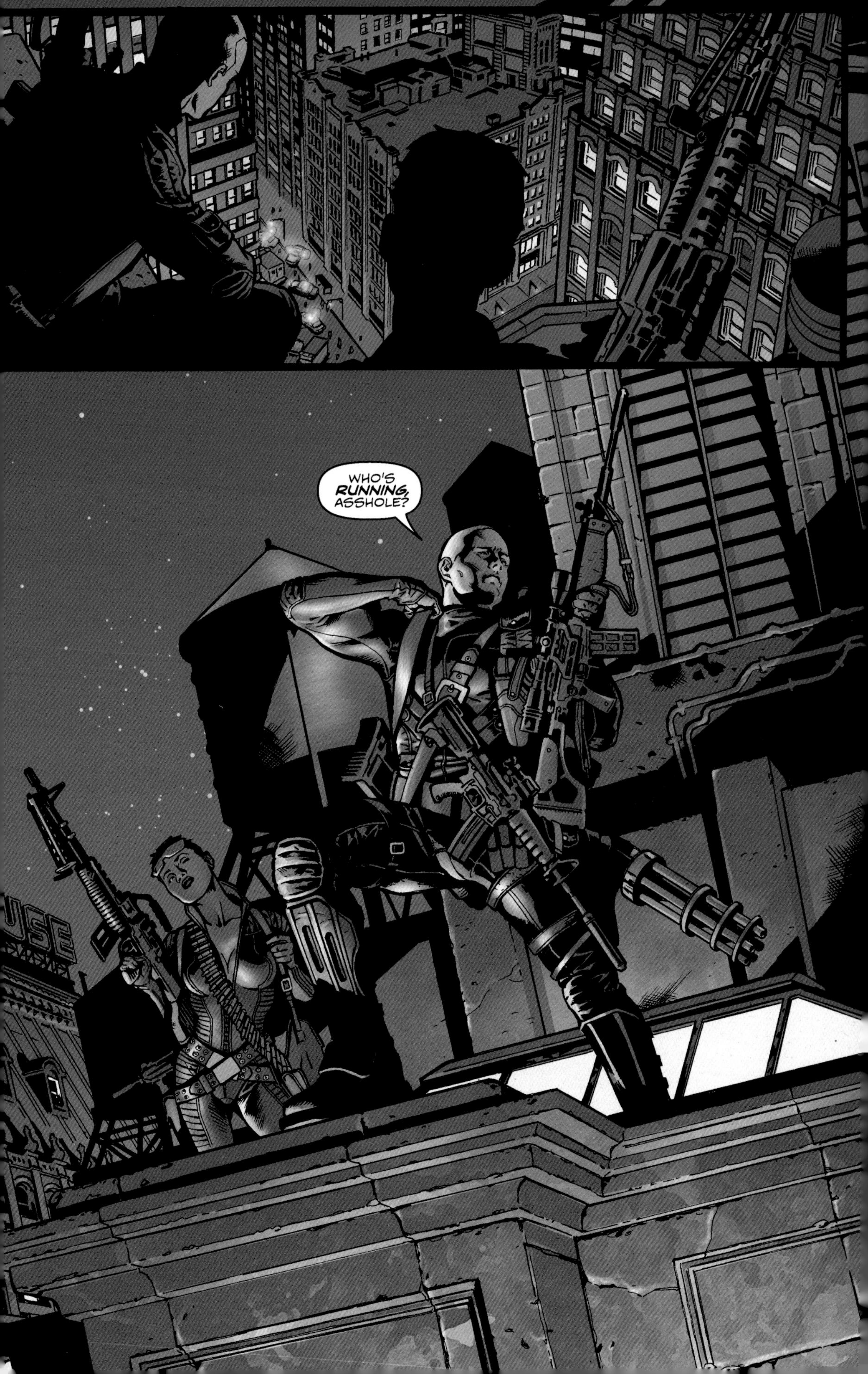
WHO'S RUNNING, ASSHOLE?

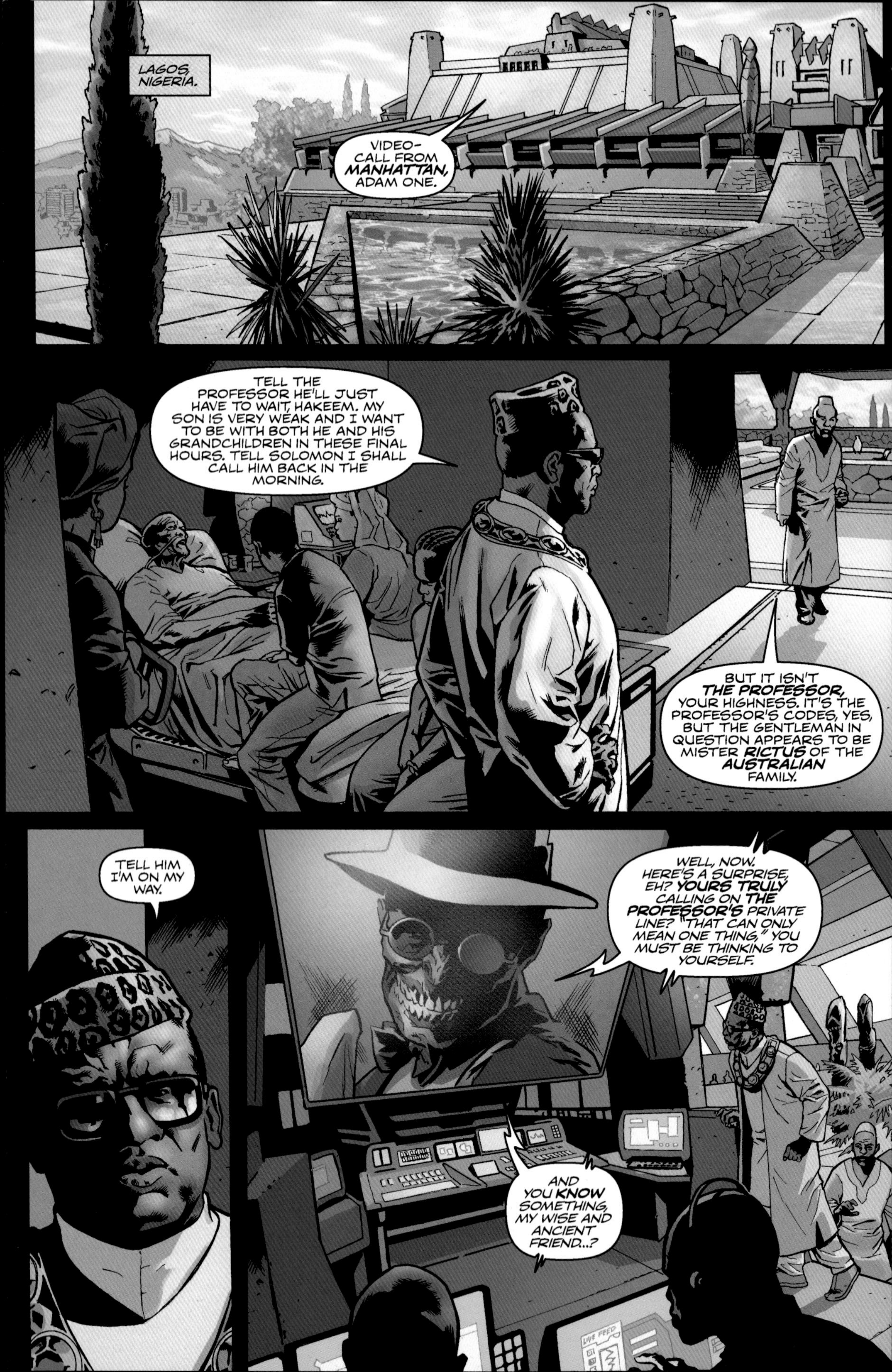
LAGOS, NIGERIA.
VIDEO-CALL FROM MANHATTAN, ADAM ONE.
TELL THE PROFESSOR HE'LL JUST HAVE TO WAIT, HAKEEM. MY SON IS VERY WEAK AND I WANT TO BE WITH BOTH HE AND HIS GRANDCHILDREN IN THESE FINAL HOURS. TELL SOLOMON I SHALL CALL HIM BACK IN THE MORNING.
BUT IT ISN'T THE PROFESSOR, YOUR HIGHNESS. IT'S THE PROFESSOR'S CODES, YES, BUT THE GENTLEMAN IN QUESTION APPEARS TO BE MISTER RICTUS OF THE AUSTRALIAN FAMILY.
TELL HIM I'M ON MY WAY.
WELL, NOW. HERE'S A SURPRISE, EH? YOURS TRULY CALLING ON THE PROFESSOR'S PRIVATE LINE? "THAT CAN ONLY MEAN ONE THING," YOU MUST BE THINKING TO YOURSELF.
AND YOU KNOW SOMETHING, MY WISE AND ANCIENT FRIEND...?
LIVE FEED

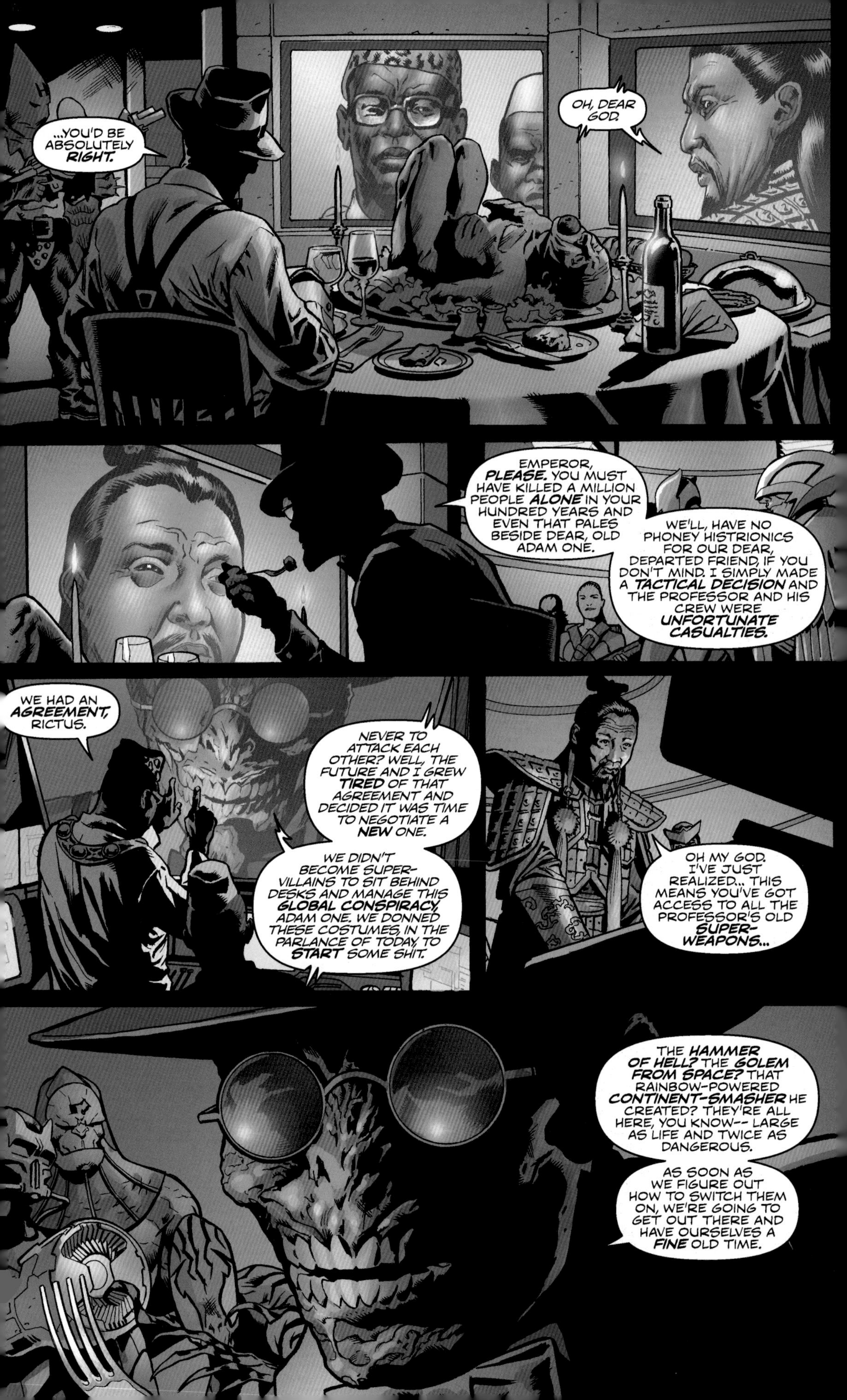
...YOU'D BE ABSOLUTELY RIGHT.
OH, DEAR GOD.
EMPEROR, PLEASE. YOU MUST HAVE KILLED A MILLION PEOPLE ALONE IN YOUR HUNDRED YEARS AND EVEN THAT PALES BESIDE DEAR, OLD ADAM ONE.
WE'LL, HAVE NO PHONEY HISTRIONICS FOR OUR DEAR, DEPARTED FRIEND, IF YOU DON'T MIND. I SIMPLY MADE A TACTICAL DECISION AND THE PROFESSOR AND HIS CREW WERE UNFORTUNATE CASUALTIES.
WE HAD AN AGREEMENT, RICTUS.
NEVER TO ATTACK EACH OTHER? WELL, THE FUTURE AND I GREW TIRED OF THAT AGREEMENT AND DECIDED IT WAS TIME TO NEGOTIATE A NEW ONE.
WE DIDN'T BECOME SUPER-VILLAINS TO SIT BEHIND DESKS AND MANAGE THIS GLOBAL CONSPIRACY, ADAM ONE. WE DONNED THESE COSTUMES, IN THE PARLANCE OF TODAY, TO START SOME SHIT.
OH MY GOD. I'VE JUST REALIZED... THIS MEANS YOU'VE GOT ACCESS TO ALL THE PROFESSOR'S OLD SUPER-WEAPONS...
THE HAMMER OF HELL? THE GOLEM FROM SPACE? THAT RAINBOW-POWERED CONTINENT-SMASHER HE CREATED? THEY'RE ALL HERE, YOU KNOW-- LARGE AS LIFE AND TWICE AS DANGEROUS.
AS SOON AS WE FIGURE OUT HOW TO SWITCH THEM ON, WE'RE GOING TO GET OUT THERE AND HAVE OURSELVES A FINE OLD TIME.

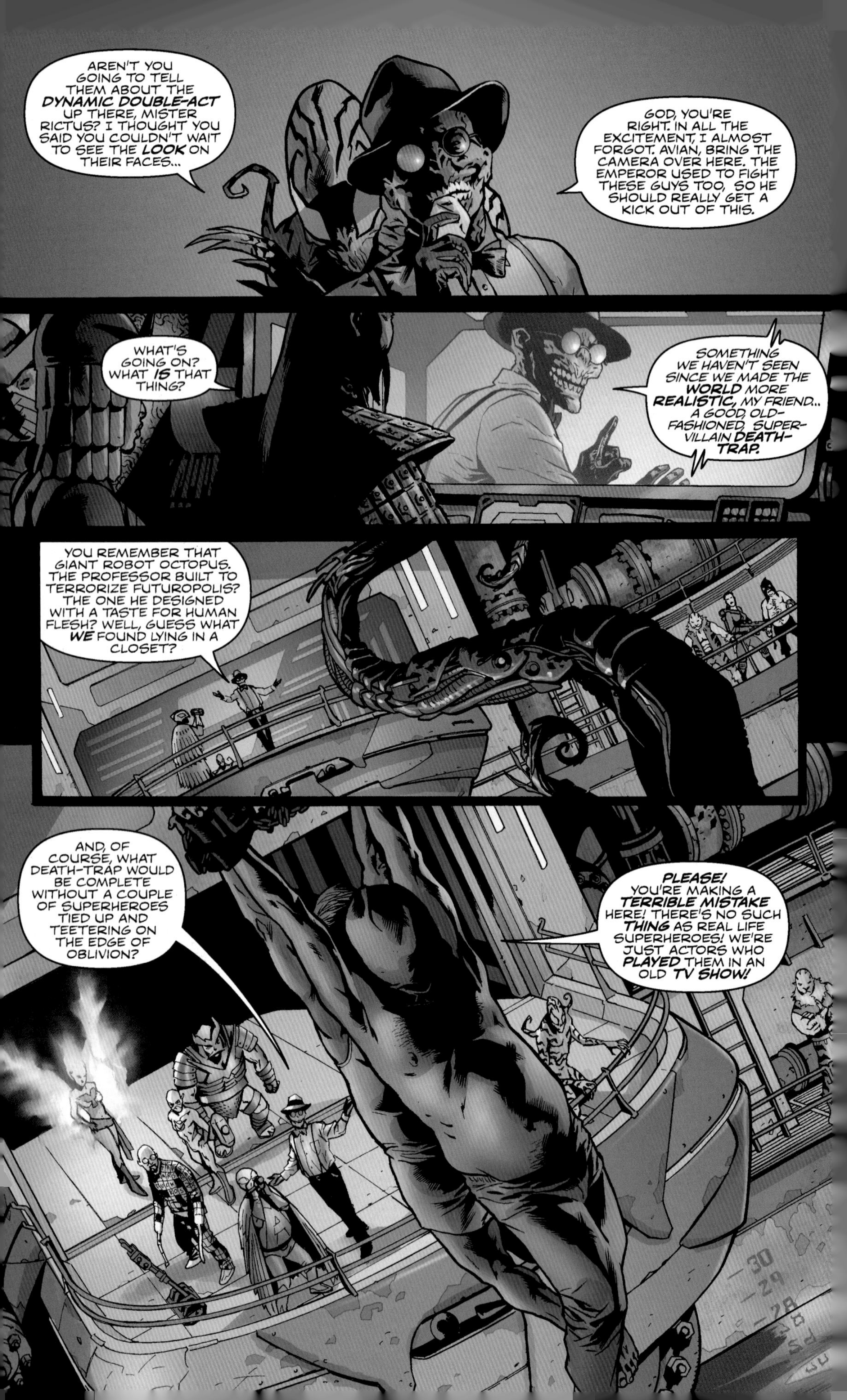
AREN'T YOU GOING TO TELL THEM ABOUT THE DYNAMIC DOUBLE-ACT UP THERE, MISTER RICTUS? I THOUGHT YOU SAID YOU COULDN'T WAIT TO SEE THE LOOK ON THEIR FACES...
GOD, YOU'RE RIGHT. IN ALL THE EXCITEMENT, I ALMOST FORGOT. AVIAN, BRING THE CAMERA OVER HERE. THE EMPEROR USED TO FIGHT THESE GUYS TOO, SO HE SHOULD REALLY GET A KICK OUT OF THIS.
WHAT'S GOING ON? WHAT IS THAT THING?
SOMETHING WE HAVEN'T SEEN SINCE WE MADE THE WORLD MORE REALISTIC, MY FRIEND... A GOOD, OLD-FASHIONED, SUPER-VILLAIN DEATH-TRAP.
YOU REMEMBER THAT GIANT ROBOT OCTOPUS. THE PROFESSOR BUILT TO TERRORIZE FUTUROPOLIS? THE ONE HE DESIGNED WITH A TASTE FOR HUMAN FLESH? WELL, GUESS WHAT WE FOUND LYING IN A CLOSET?
AND, OF COURSE, WHAT DEATH-TRAP WOULD BE COMPLETE WITHOUT A COUPLE OF SUPERHEROES TIED UP AND TEETERING ON THE EDGE OF OBLIVION?
PLEASE! YOU'RE MAKING A TERRIBLE MISTAKE HERE! THERE'S NO SUCH THING AS REAL LIFE SUPERHEROES! WE'RE JUST ACTORS WHO PLAYED THEM IN AN OLD TV SHOW!

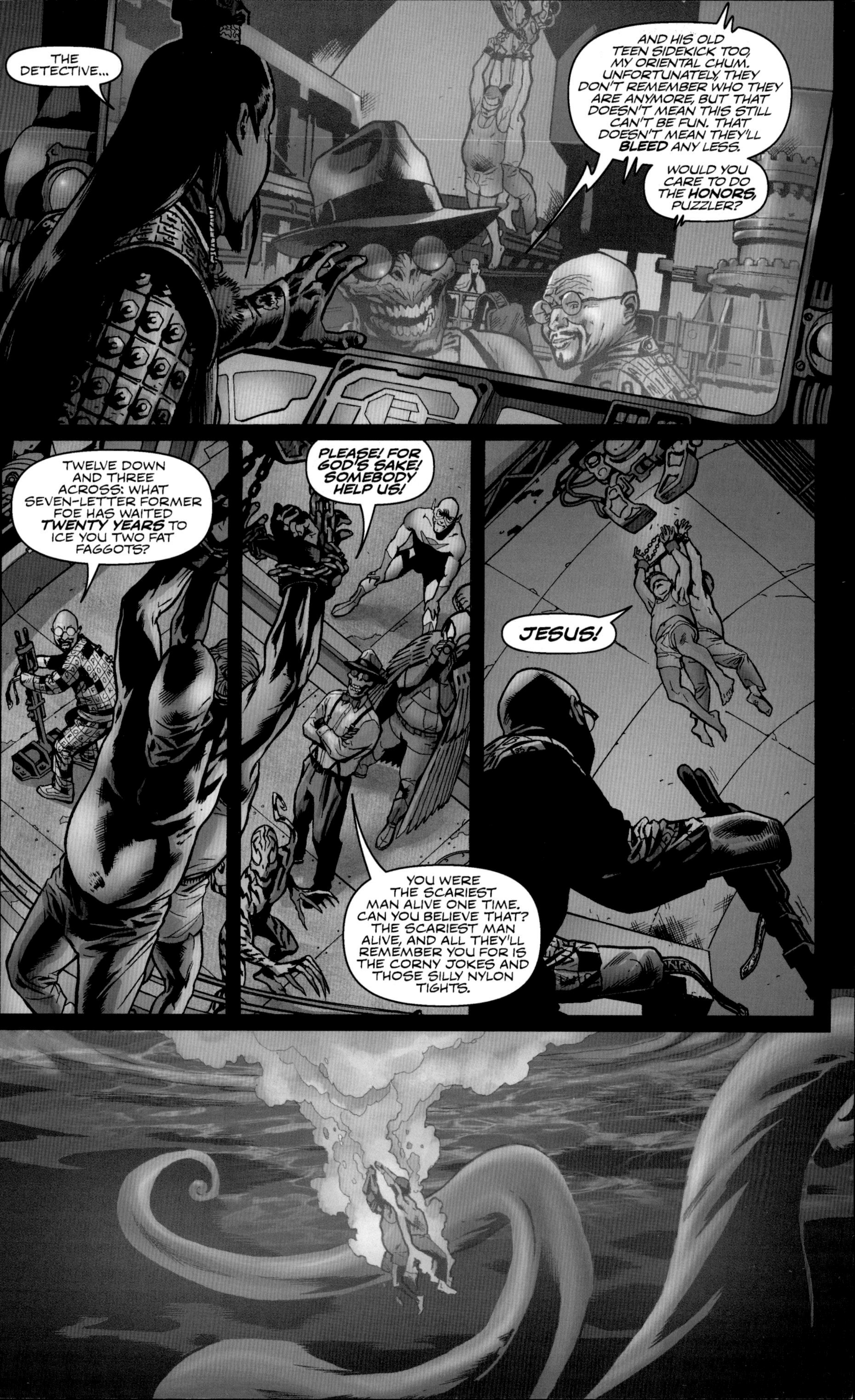
THE DETECTIVE...
AND HIS OLD TEEN SIDEKICK TOO, MY ORIENTAL CHUM. UNFORTUNATELY, THEY DON'T REMEMBER WHO THEY ARE ANYMORE, BUT THAT DOESN'T MEAN THIS STILL CAN'T BE FUN. THAT DOESN'T MEAN THEY'LL **BLEED** ANY LESS.
WOULD YOU CARE TO DO THE **HONORS,** PUZZLER?
TWELVE DOWN AND THREE ACROSS: WHAT SEVEN-LETTER FORMER FOE HAS WAITED **TWENTY YEARS** TO ICE YOU TWO FAT FAGGOTS?
PLEASE! FOR GOD'S SAKE! SOMEBODY HELP US!
YOU WERE THE SCARIEST MAN ALIVE ONE TIME. CAN YOU BELIEVE THAT? THE SCARIEST MAN ALIVE, AND ALL THEY'LL REMEMBER YOU FOR IS THE CORNY JOKES AND THOSE SILLY NYLON TIGHTS.
JESUS!

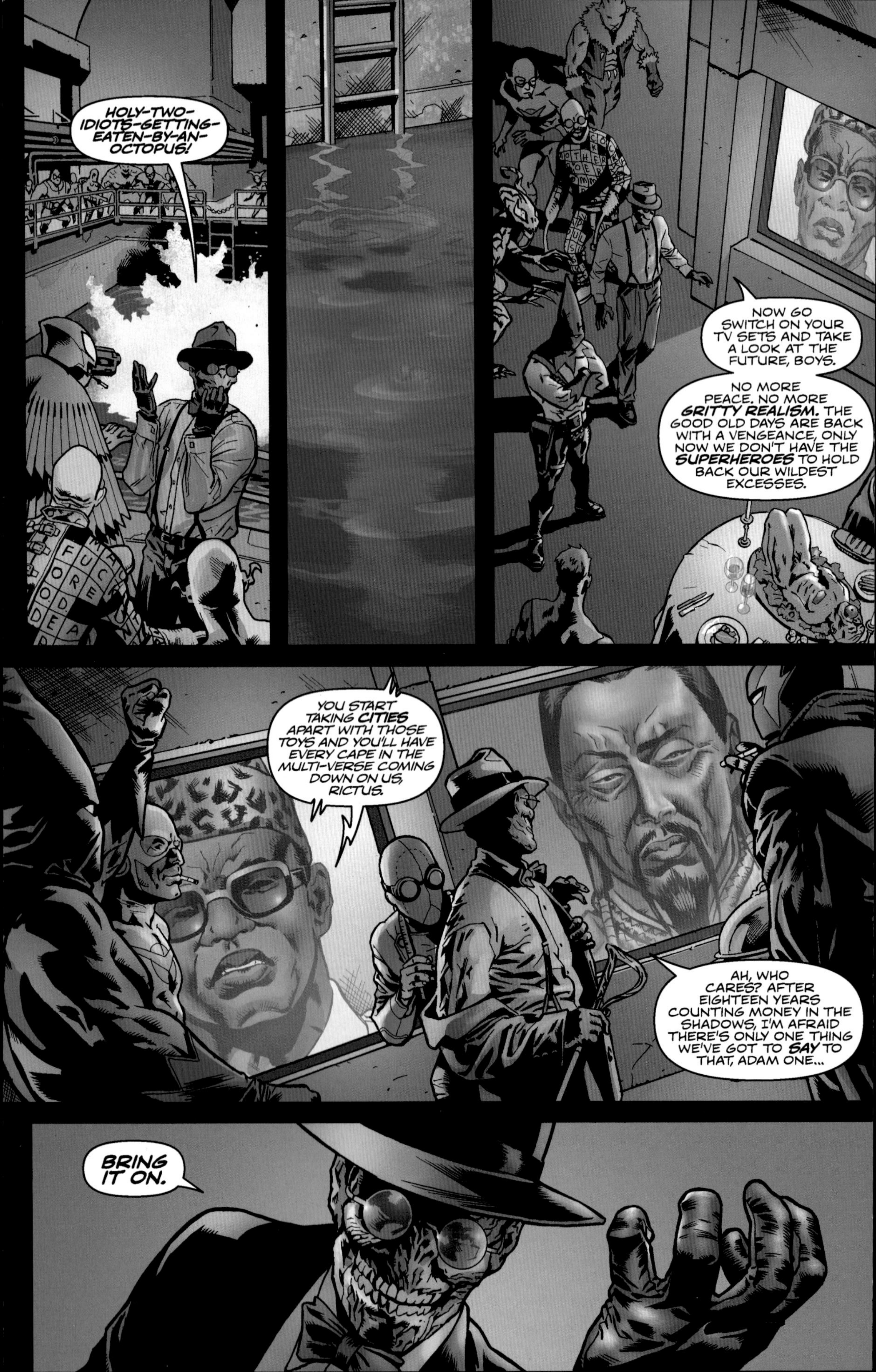
HOLY-TWO-IDIOTS-GETTING-EATEN-BY-AN-OCTOPUS!
NOW GO SWITCH ON YOUR TV SETS AND TAKE A LOOK AT THE FUTURE, BOYS.
NO MORE PEACE. NO MORE **GRITTY REALISM.** THE GOOD OLD DAYS ARE BACK WITH A VENGEANCE, ONLY NOW WE DON'T HAVE THE **SUPERHEROES** TO HOLD BACK OUR WILDEST EXCESSES.
YOU START TAKING **CITIES** APART WITH THOSE TOYS AND YOU'LL HAVE EVERY CAPE IN THE MULTI-VERSE COMING DOWN ON US, RICTUS.
AH, WHO CARES? AFTER EIGHTEEN YEARS COUNTING MONEY IN THE SHADOWS, I'M AFRAID THERE'S ONLY ONE THING WE'VE GOT TO **SAY** TO THAT, ADAM ONE...
BRING IT ON.

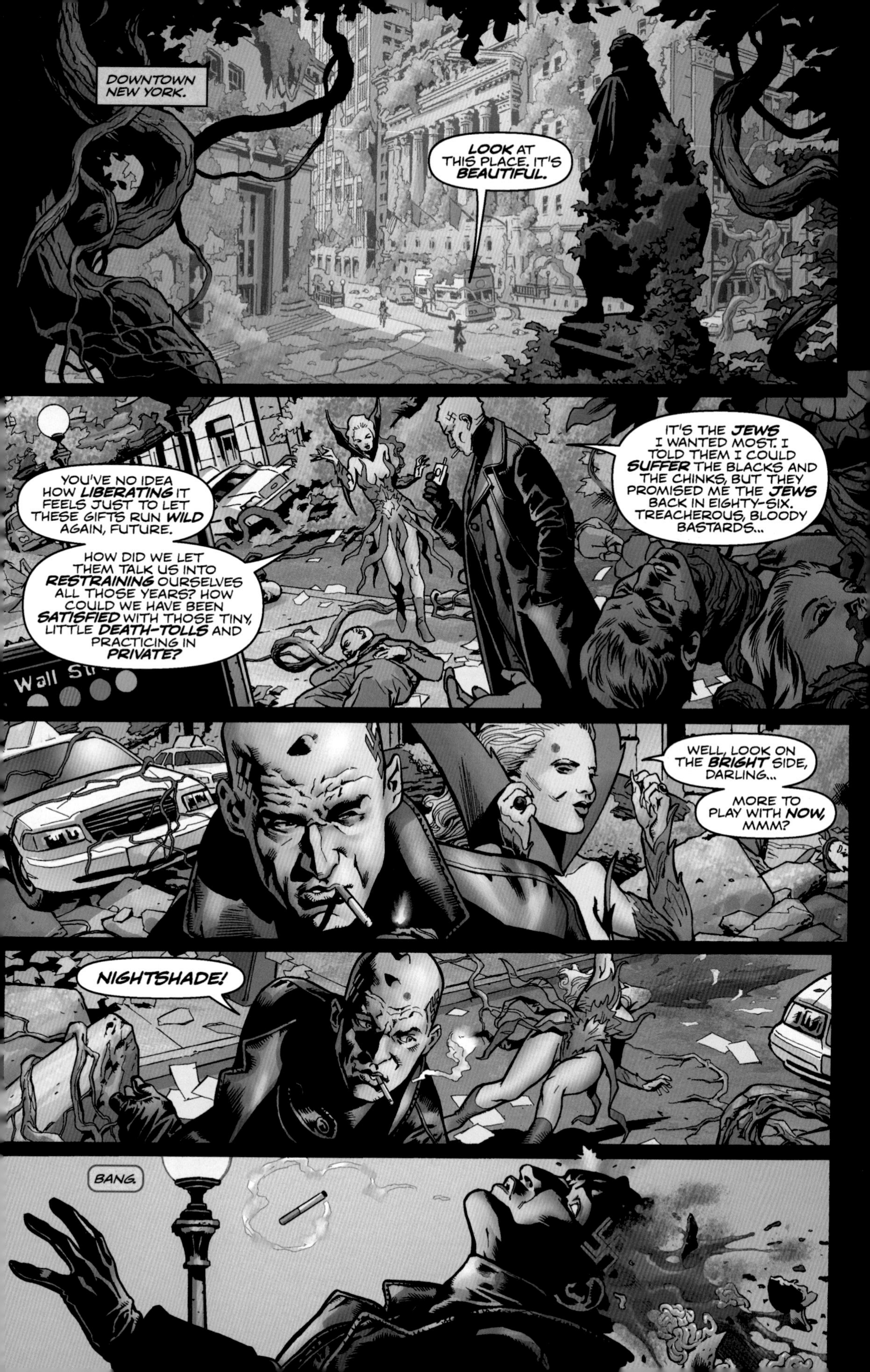
DOWNTOWN NEW YORK.
LOOK AT THIS PLACE. IT'S BEAUTIFUL.
YOU'VE NO IDEA HOW LIBERATING IT FEELS JUST TO LET THESE GIFTS RUN WILD AGAIN, FUTURE.
HOW DID WE LET THEM TALK US INTO RESTRAINING OURSELVES ALL THOSE YEARS? HOW COULD WE HAVE BEEN SATISFIED WITH THOSE TINY, LITTLE DEATH-TOLLS AND PRACTICING IN PRIVATE?
IT'S THE JEWS I WANTED MOST. I TOLD THEM I COULD SUFFER THE BLACKS AND THE CHINKS, BUT THEY PROMISED ME THE JEWS BACK IN EIGHTY-SIX. TREACHEROUS, BLOODY BASTARDS...
Wall St
WELL, LOOK ON THE BRIGHT SIDE, DARLING...
MORE TO PLAY WITH NOW, MMM?
NIGHTSHADE!
BANG.

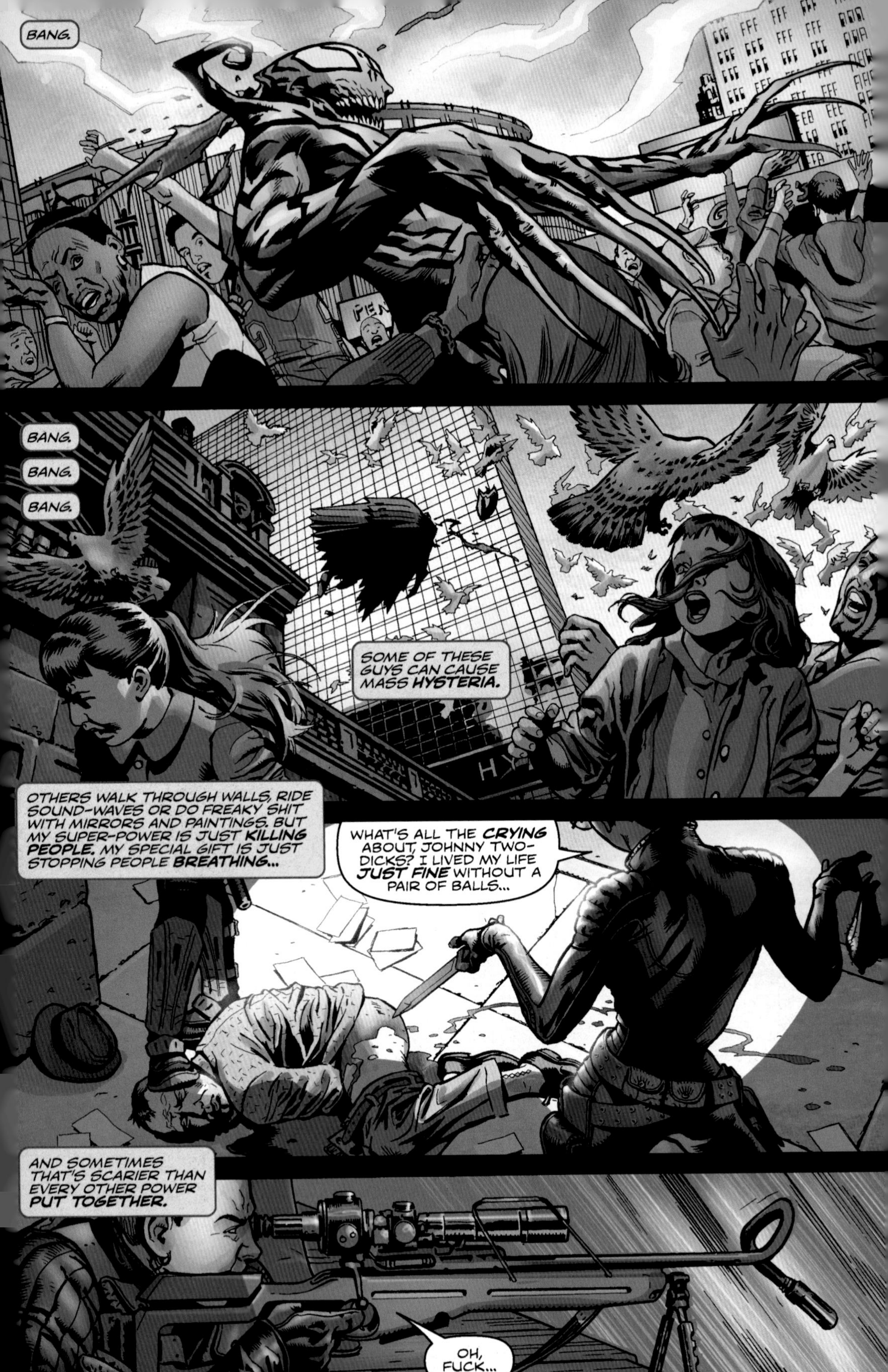
BANG.
BANG.
BANG.
BANG.
SOME OF THESE GUYS CAN CAUSE MASS HYSTERIA.
OTHERS WALK THROUGH WALLS, RIDE SOUND-WAVES OR DO FREAKY SHIT WITH MIRRORS AND PAINTINGS. BUT MY SUPER-POWER IS JUST KILLING PEOPLE. MY SPECIAL GIFT IS JUST STOPPING PEOPLE BREATHING...
WHAT'S ALL THE CRYING ABOUT, JOHNNY TWO-DICKS? I LIVED MY LIFE JUST FINE WITHOUT A PAIR OF BALLS...
AND SOMETIMES THAT'S SCARIER THAN EVERY OTHER POWER PUT TOGETHER.
OH, FUCK...

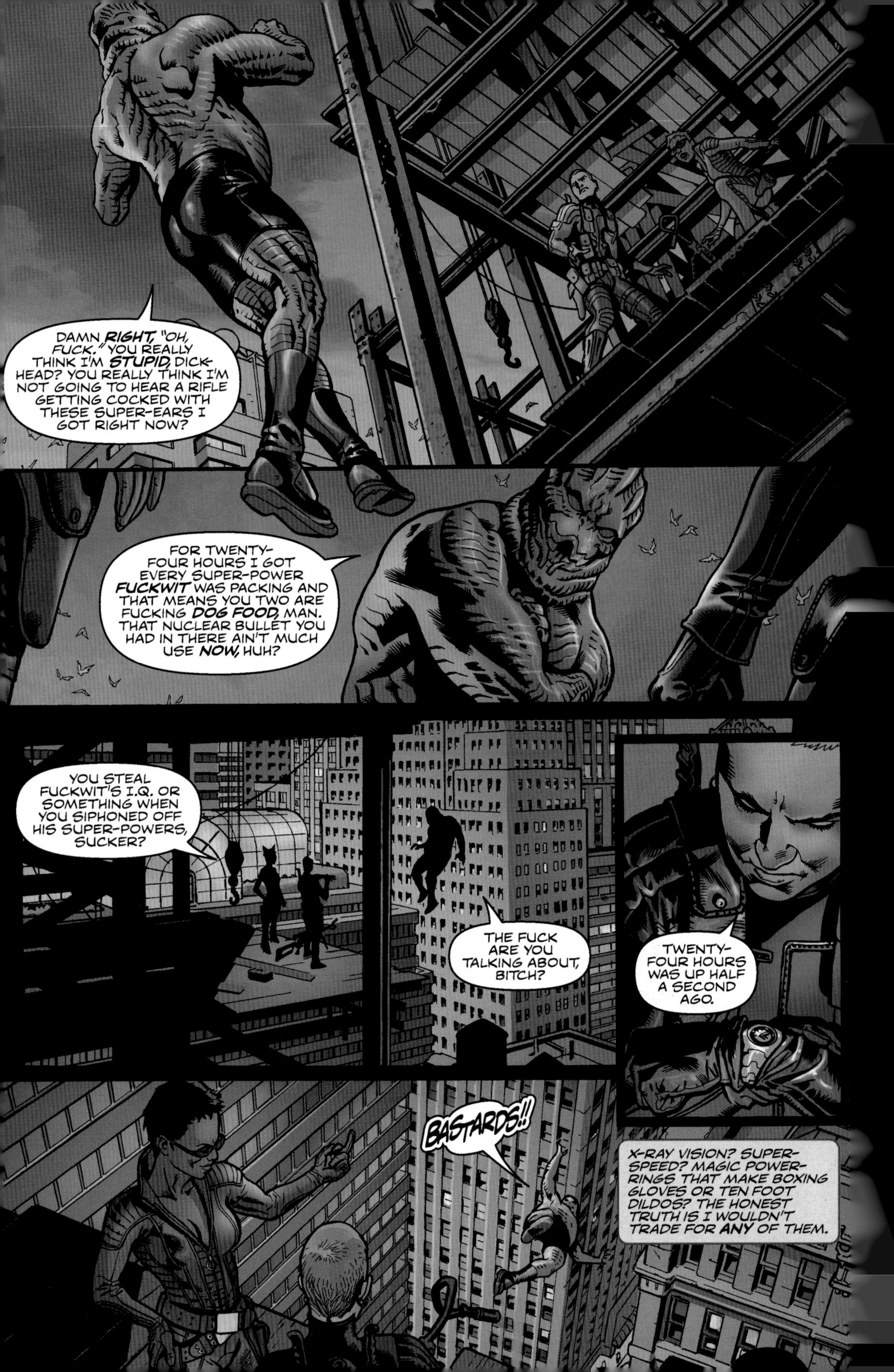
DAMN RIGHT, "OH, FUCK." YOU REALLY THINK I'M STUPID, DICK-HEAD? YOU REALLY THINK I'M NOT GOING TO HEAR A RIFLE GETTING COCKED WITH THESE SUPER-EARS I GOT RIGHT NOW?
FOR TWENTY-FOUR HOURS I GOT EVERY SUPER-POWER FUCKWIT WAS PACKING AND THAT MEANS YOU TWO ARE FUCKING DOG FOOD, MAN. THAT NUCLEAR BULLET YOU HAD IN THERE AIN'T MUCH USE NOW, HUH?
YOU STEAL FUCKWIT'S I.Q. OR SOMETHING WHEN YOU SIPHONED OFF HIS SUPER-POWERS, SUCKER?
THE FUCK ARE YOU TALKING ABOUT, BITCH?
TWENTY-FOUR HOURS WAS UP HALF A SECOND AGO.
BASTARDS!!
X-RAY VISION? SUPER-SPEED? MAGIC POWER-RINGS THAT MAKE BOXING GLOVES OR TEN FOOT DILDOS? THE HONEST TRUTH IS I WOULDN'T TRADE FOR ANY OF THEM.

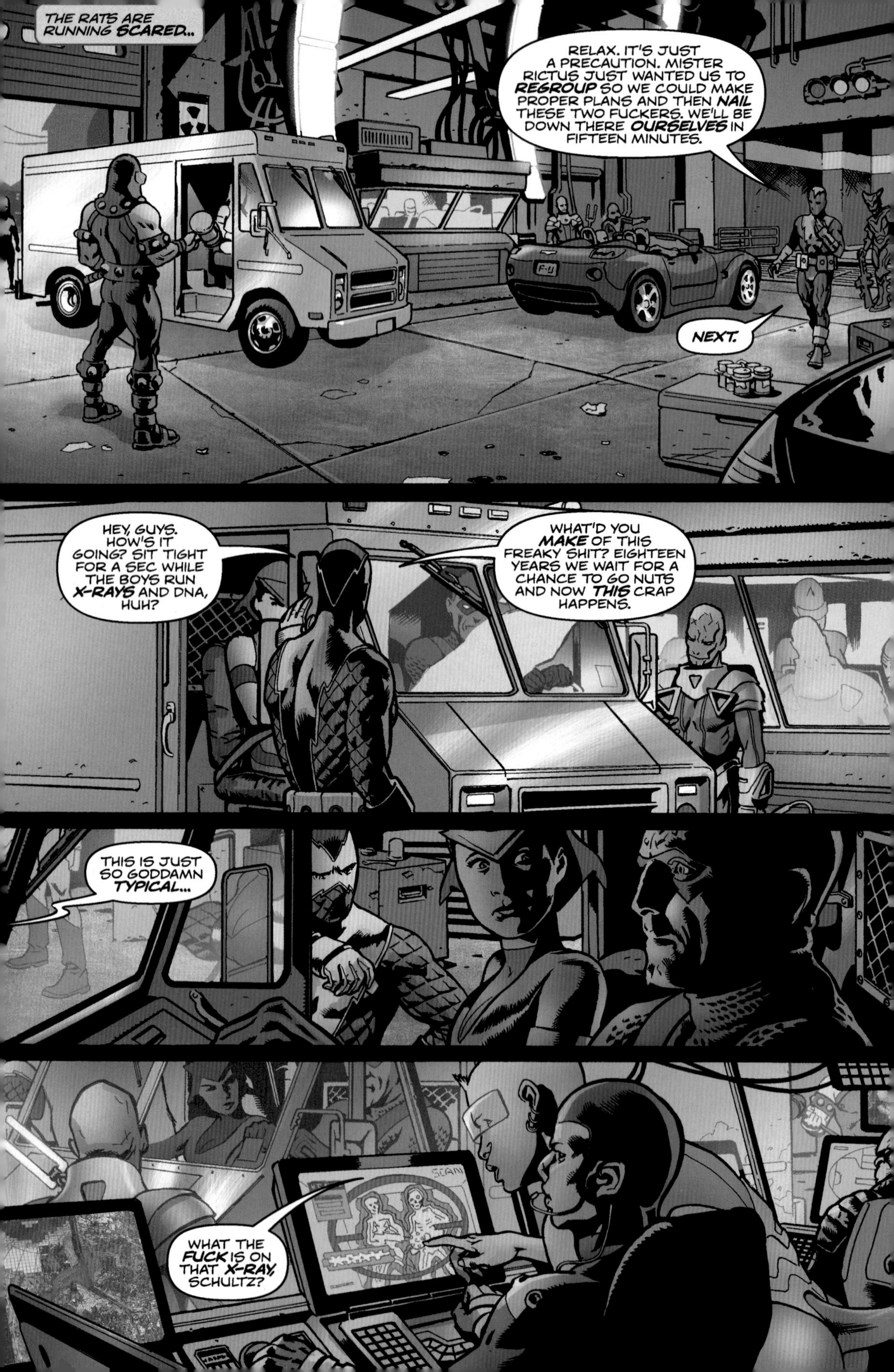
THE RATS ARE RUNNING SCARED...
RELAX. IT'S JUST A PRECAUTION. MISTER RICTUS JUST WANTED US TO REGROUP SO WE COULD MAKE PROPER PLANS AND THEN NAIL THESE TWO FUCKERS. WE'LL BE DOWN THERE OURSELVES IN FIFTEEN MINUTES.
F-U
NEXT.
HEY, GUYS. HOW'S IT GOING? SIT TIGHT FOR A SEC WHILE THE BOYS RUN X-RAYS AND DNA, HUH?
WHAT'D YOU MAKE OF THIS FREAKY SHIT? EIGHTEEN YEARS WE WAIT FOR A CHANCE TO GO NUTS AND NOW THIS CRAP HAPPENS.
THIS IS JUST SO GODDAMN TYPICAL...
SCAN
WHAT THE FUCK IS ON THAT X-RAY, SCHULTZ?

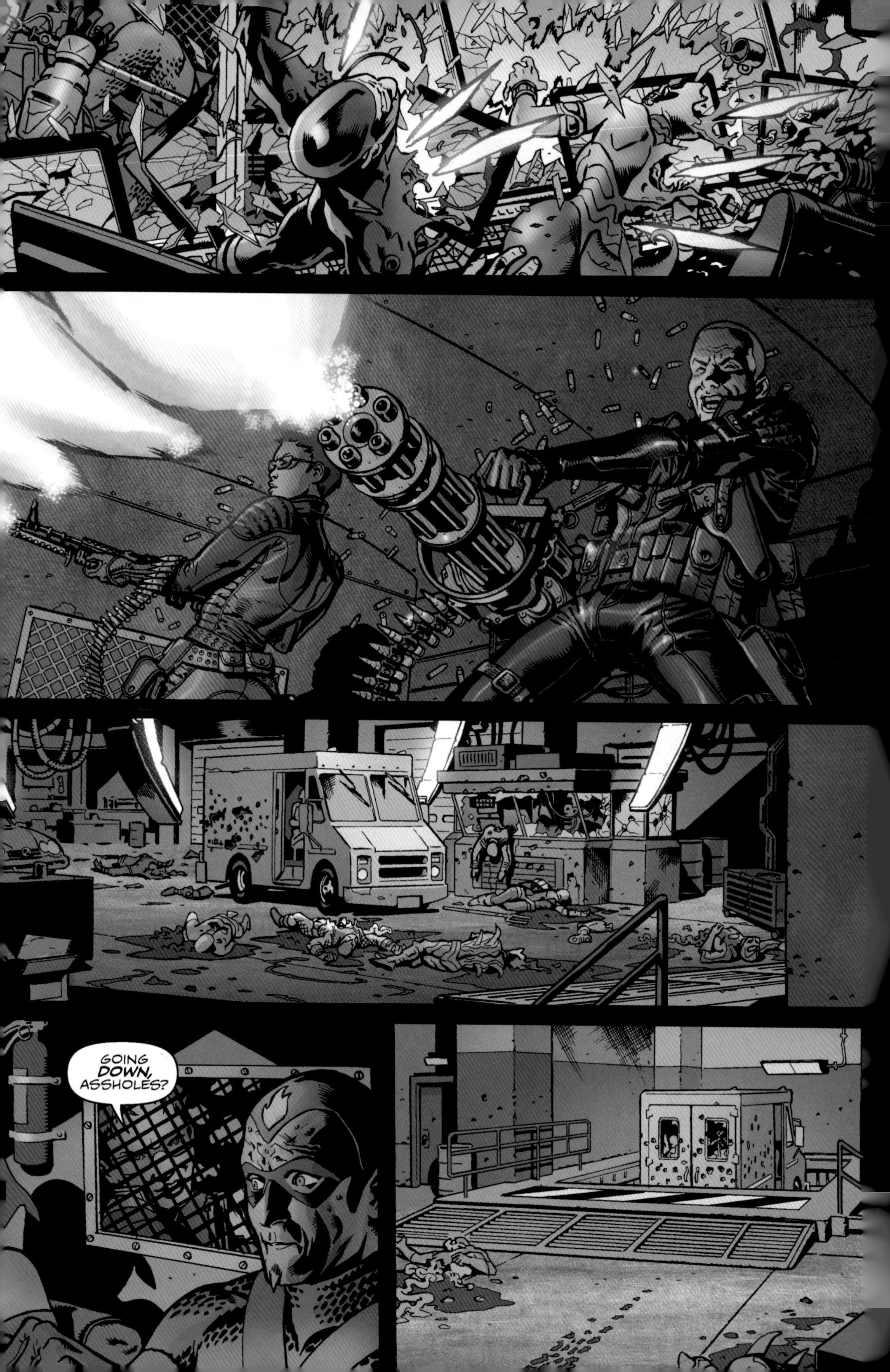
GOING DOWN, ASSHOLES?

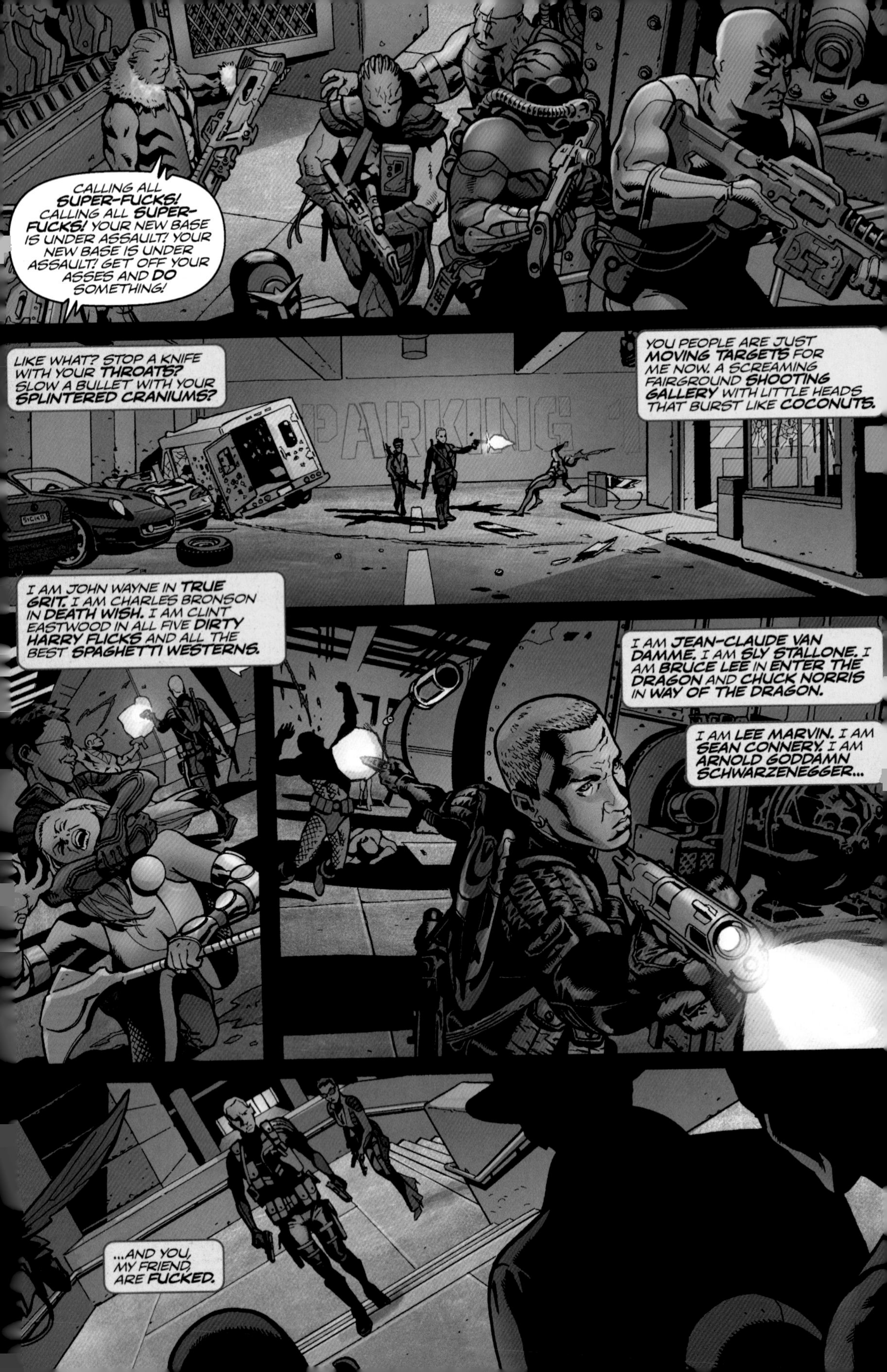
CALLING ALL SUPER-FUCKS! CALLING ALL SUPER-FUCKS! YOUR NEW BASE IS UNDER ASSAULT! YOUR NEW BASE IS UNDER ASSAULT! GET OFF YOUR ASSES AND DO SOMETHING!
LIKE WHAT? STOP A KNIFE WITH YOUR THROATS? SLOW A BULLET WITH YOUR SPLINTERED CRANIUMS?
YOU PEOPLE ARE JUST MOVING TARGETS FOR ME NOW. A SCREAMING FAIRGROUND SHOOTING GALLERY WITH LITTLE HEADS THAT BURST LIKE COCONUTS.
PARKING
I AM JOHN WAYNE IN TRUE GRIT. I AM CHARLES BRONSON IN DEATH WISH. I AM CLINT EASTWOOD IN ALL FIVE DIRTY HARRY FLICKS AND ALL THE BEST SPAGHETTI WESTERNS.
I AM JEAN-CLAUDE VAN DAMME. I AM SLY STALLONE. I AM BRUCE LEE IN ENTER THE DRAGON AND CHUCK NORRIS IN WAY OF THE DRAGON.
I AM LEE MARVIN. I AM SEAN CONNERY. I AM ARNOLD GODDAMN SCHWARZENEGGER...
...AND YOU, MY FRIEND, ARE FUCKED.

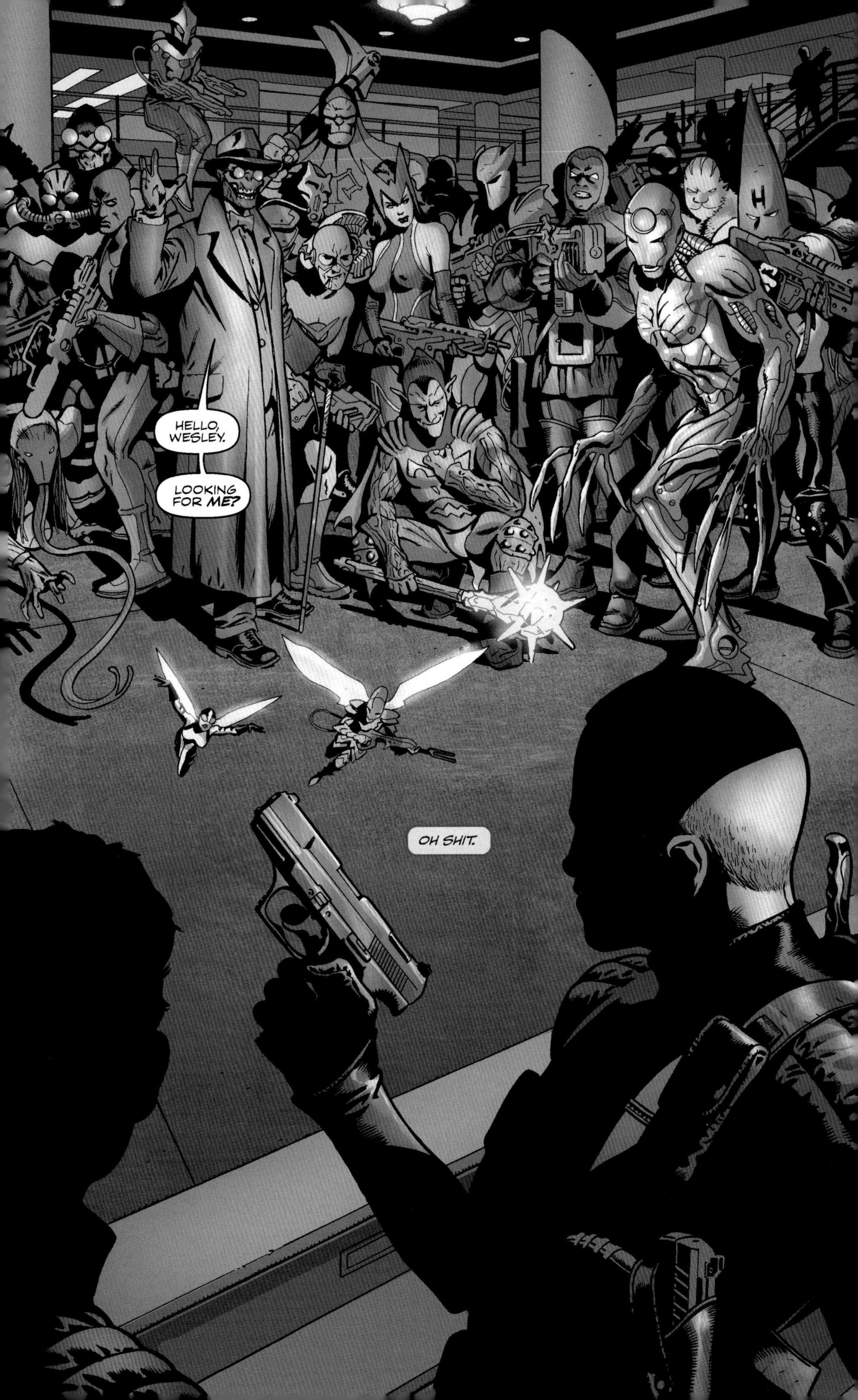
HELLO, WESLEY.
LOOKING FOR ME?
OH SHIT.

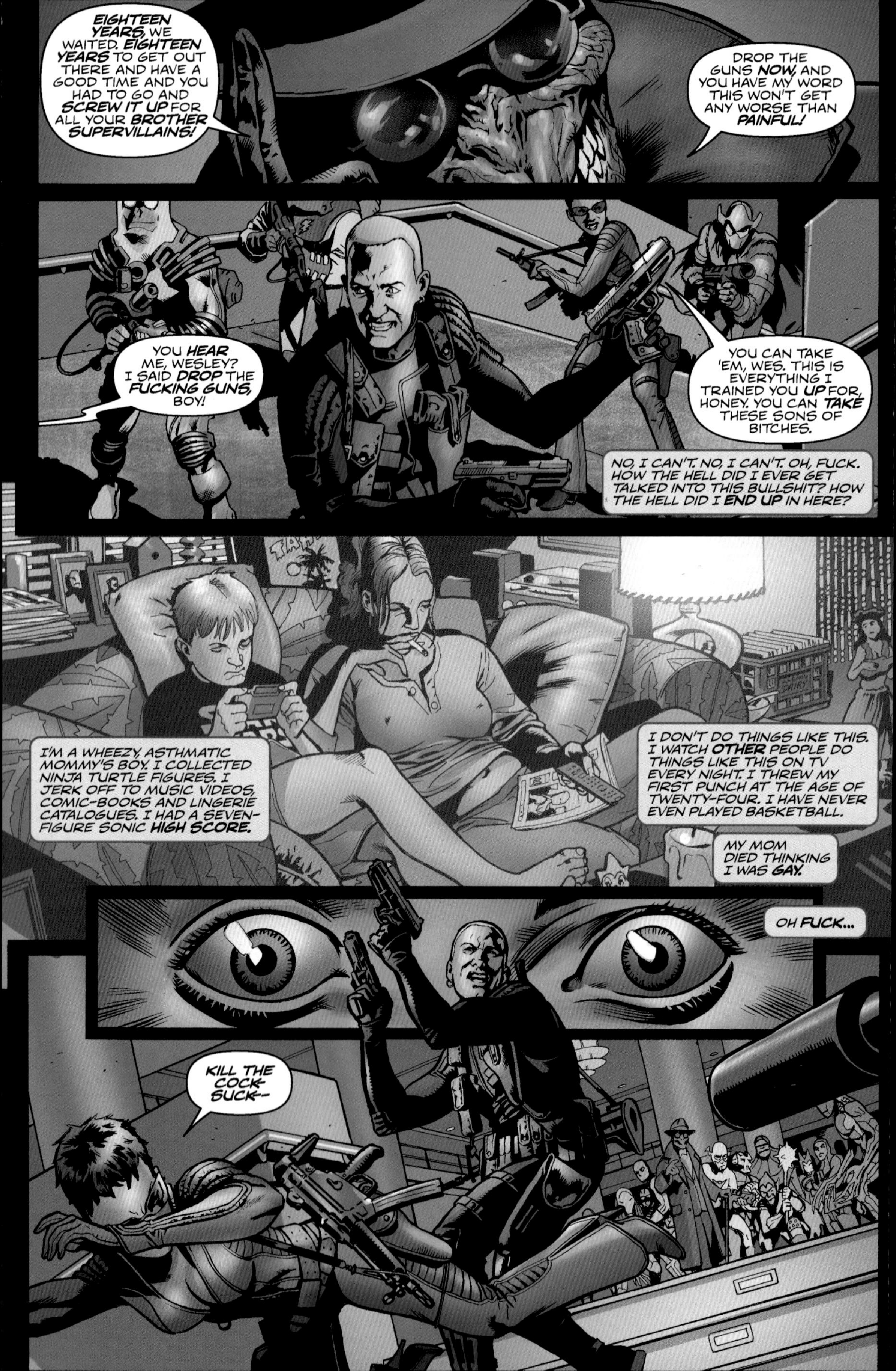
EIGHTEEN YEARS, WE WAITED. EIGHTEEN YEARS TO GET OUT THERE AND HAVE A GOOD TIME AND YOU HAD TO GO AND SCREW IT UP FOR ALL YOUR BROTHER SUPERVILLAINS!
DROP THE GUNS NOW, AND YOU HAVE MY WORD THIS WON'T GET ANY WORSE THAN PAINFUL!
YOU HEAR ME, WESLEY? I SAID DROP THE FUCKING GUNS, BOY!
YOU CAN TAKE 'EM, WES. THIS IS EVERYTHING I TRAINED YOU UP FOR, HONEY. YOU CAN TAKE THESE SONS OF BITCHES.
NO, I CAN'T. NO, I CAN'T. OH, FUCK. HOW THE HELL DID I EVER GET TALKED INTO THIS BULLSHIT? HOW THE HELL DID I END UP IN HERE?
I'M A WHEEZY, ASTHMATIC MOMMY'S BOY. I COLLECTED NINJA TURTLE FIGURES. I JERK OFF TO MUSIC VIDEOS, COMIC-BOOKS AND LINGERIE CATALOGUES. I HAD A SEVEN-FIGURE SONIC HIGH SCORE.
I DON'T DO THINGS LIKE THIS. I WATCH OTHER PEOPLE DO THINGS LIKE THIS ON TV EVERY NIGHT. I THREW MY FIRST PUNCH AT THE AGE OF TWENTY-FOUR. I HAVE NEVER EVEN PLAYED BASKETBALL.
MY MOM DIED THINKING I WAS GAY.
OH FUCK...
KILL THE COCK-SUCK--

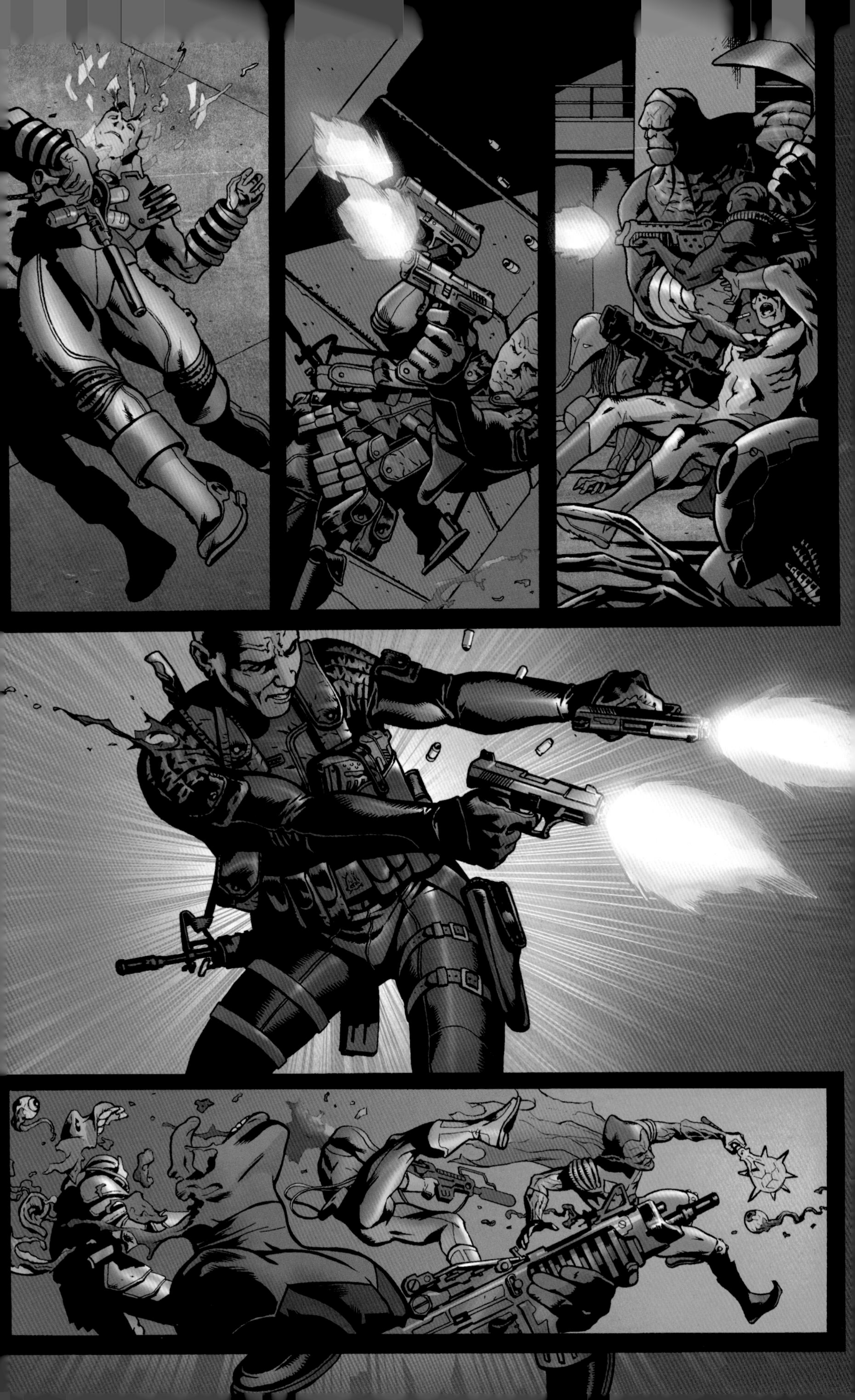

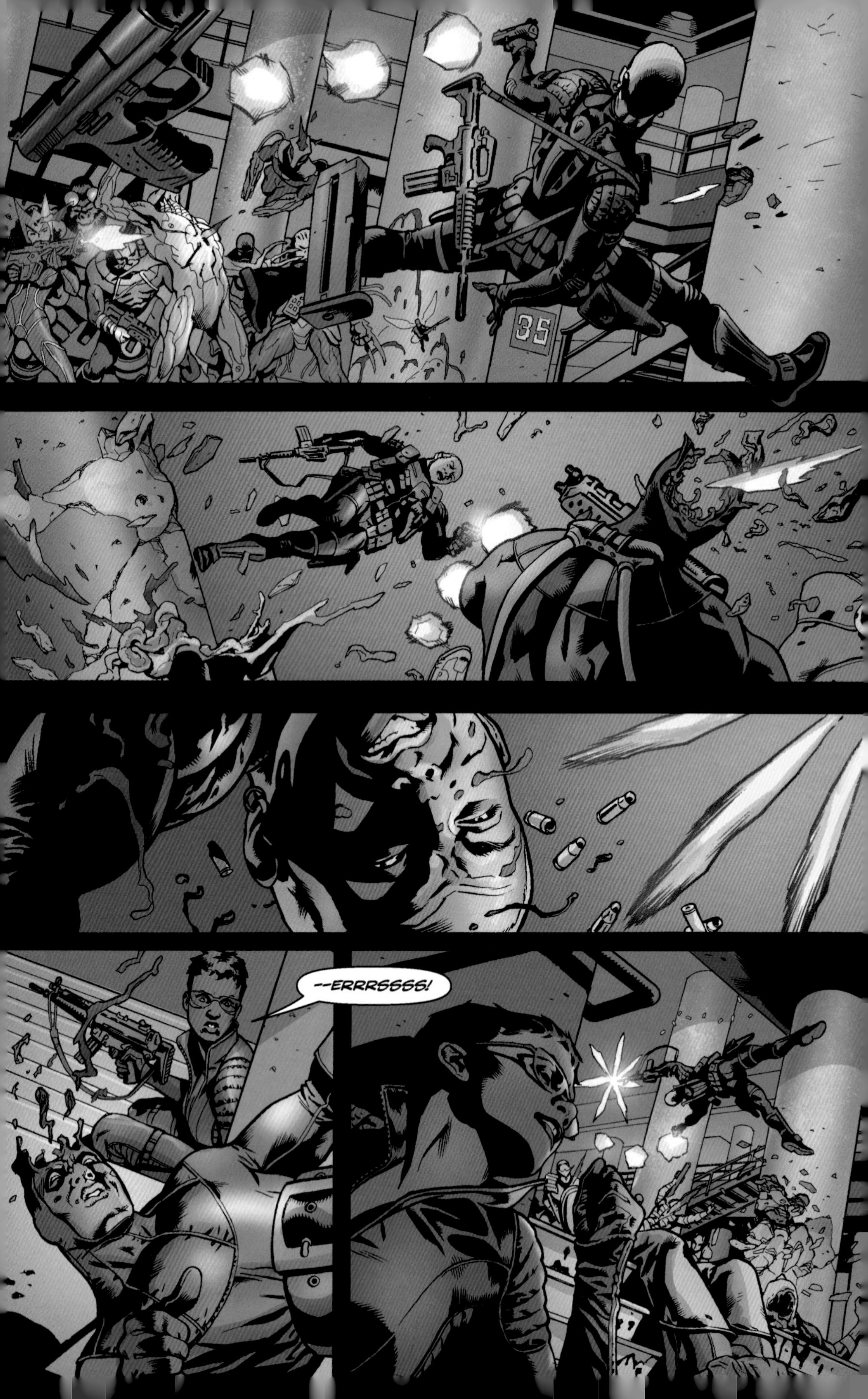
35
--ERRRSSSS!

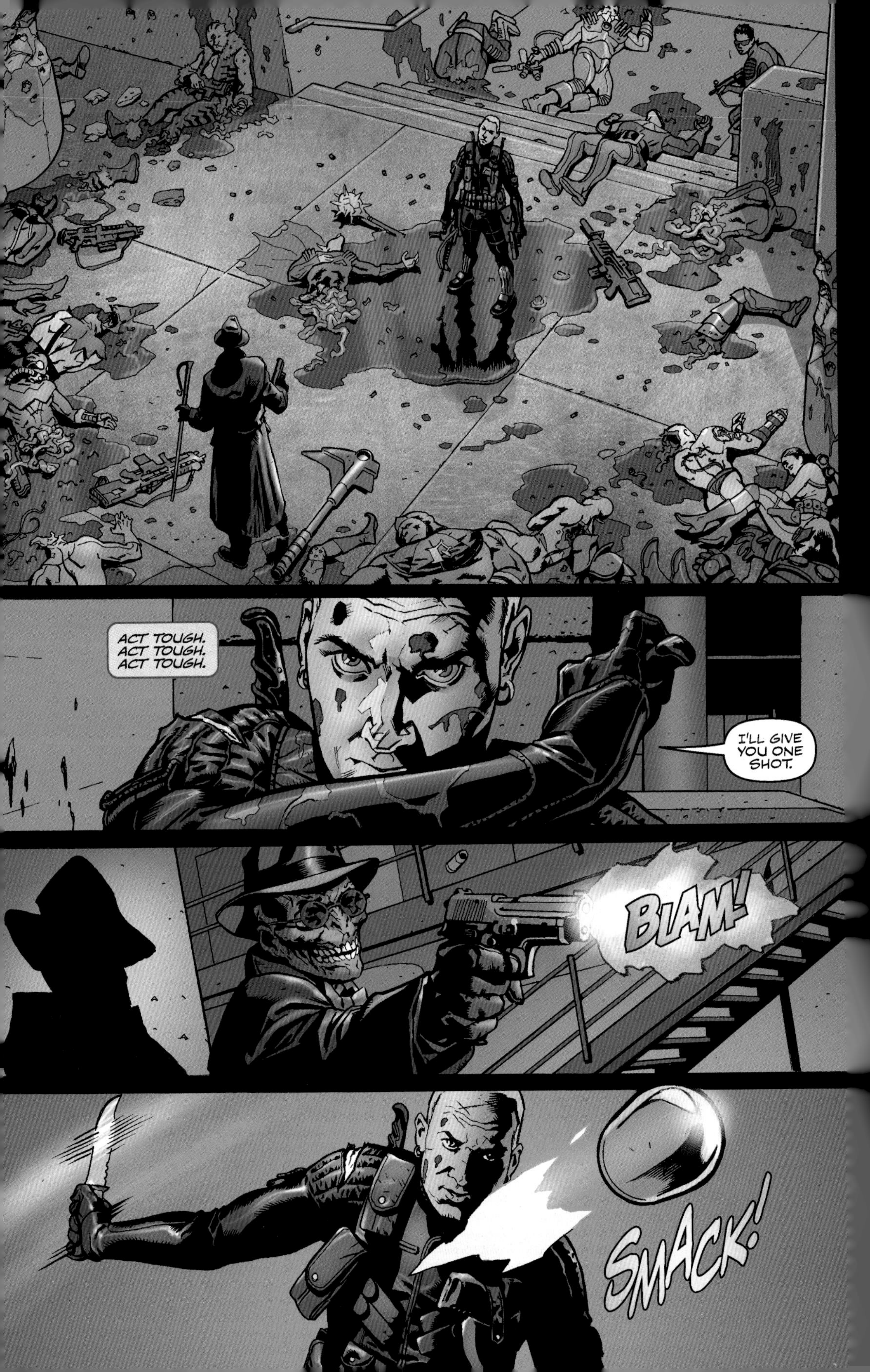
ACT TOUGH.
ACT TOUGH.
ACT TOUGH.
I'LL GIVE YOU ONE SHOT.
BLAM!
SMACK!

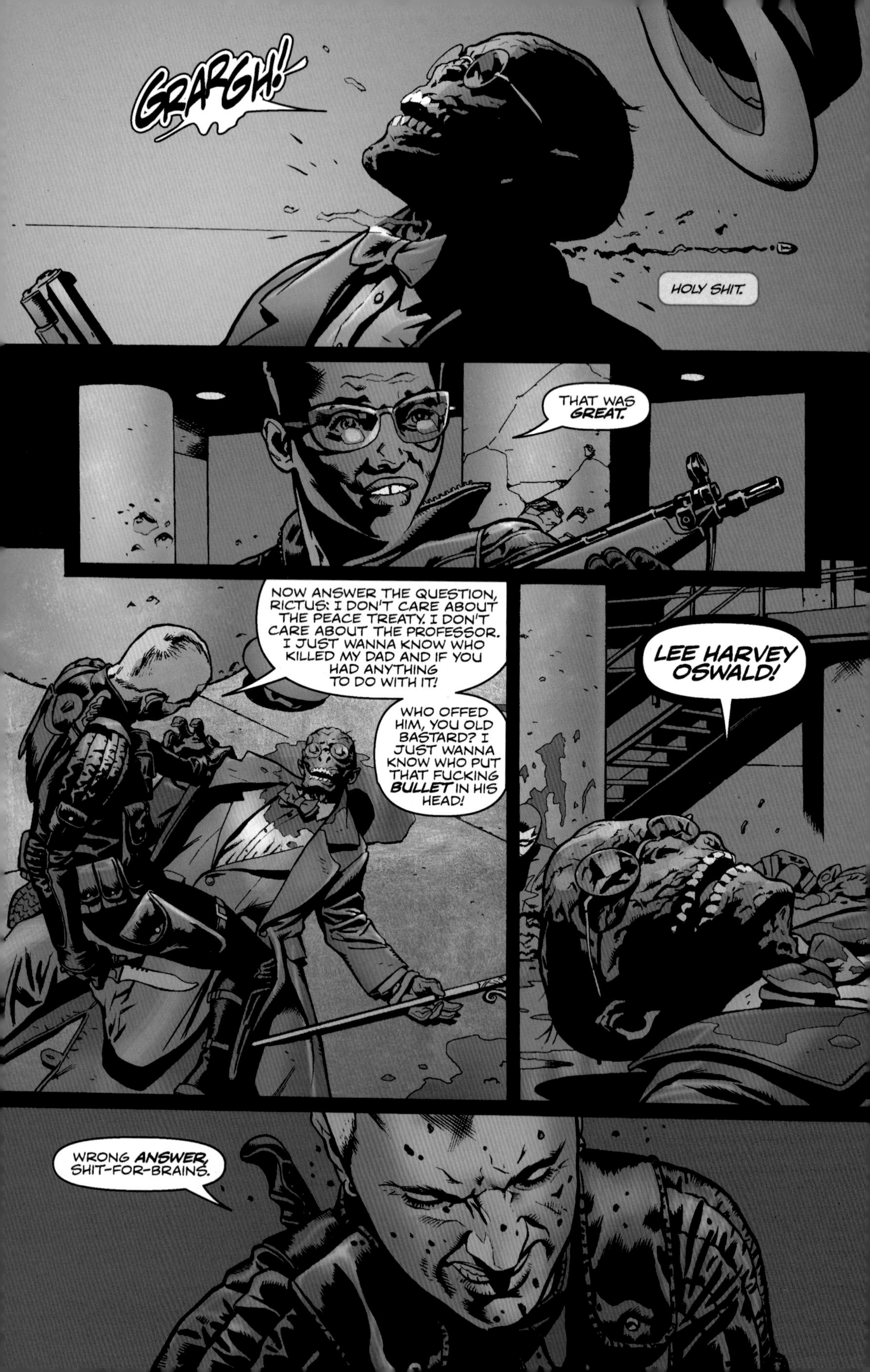
GRARGH!
HOLY SHIT.
THAT WAS GREAT.
NOW ANSWER THE QUESTION, RICTUS: I DON'T CARE ABOUT THE PEACE TREATY. I DON'T CARE ABOUT THE PROFESSOR. I JUST WANNA KNOW WHO KILLED MY DAD AND IF YOU HAD ANYTHING TO DO WITH IT!
WHO OFFED HIM, YOU OLD BASTARD? I JUST WANNA KNOW WHO PUT THAT FUCKING BULLET IN HIS HEAD!
LEE HARVEY OSWALD!
WRONG ANSWER, SHIT-FOR-BRAINS.

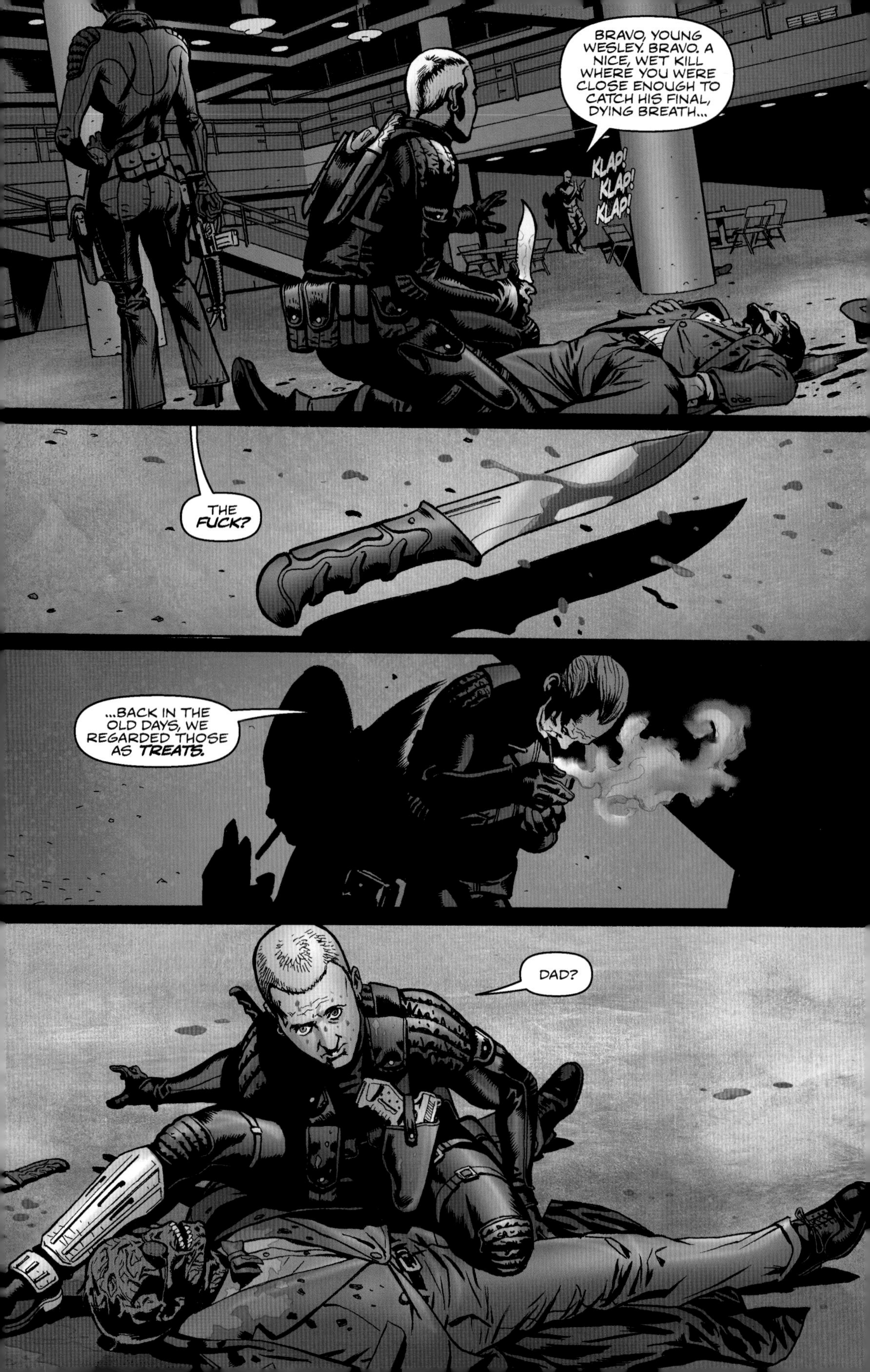
BRAVO, YOUNG WESLEY. BRAVO. A NICE, WET KILL WHERE YOU WERE CLOSE ENOUGH TO CATCH HIS FINAL, DYING BREATH...
KLAP! KLAP! KLAP!
THE *FUCK?*
...BACK IN THE OLD DAYS, WE REGARDED THOSE AS *TREATS.*
DAD?

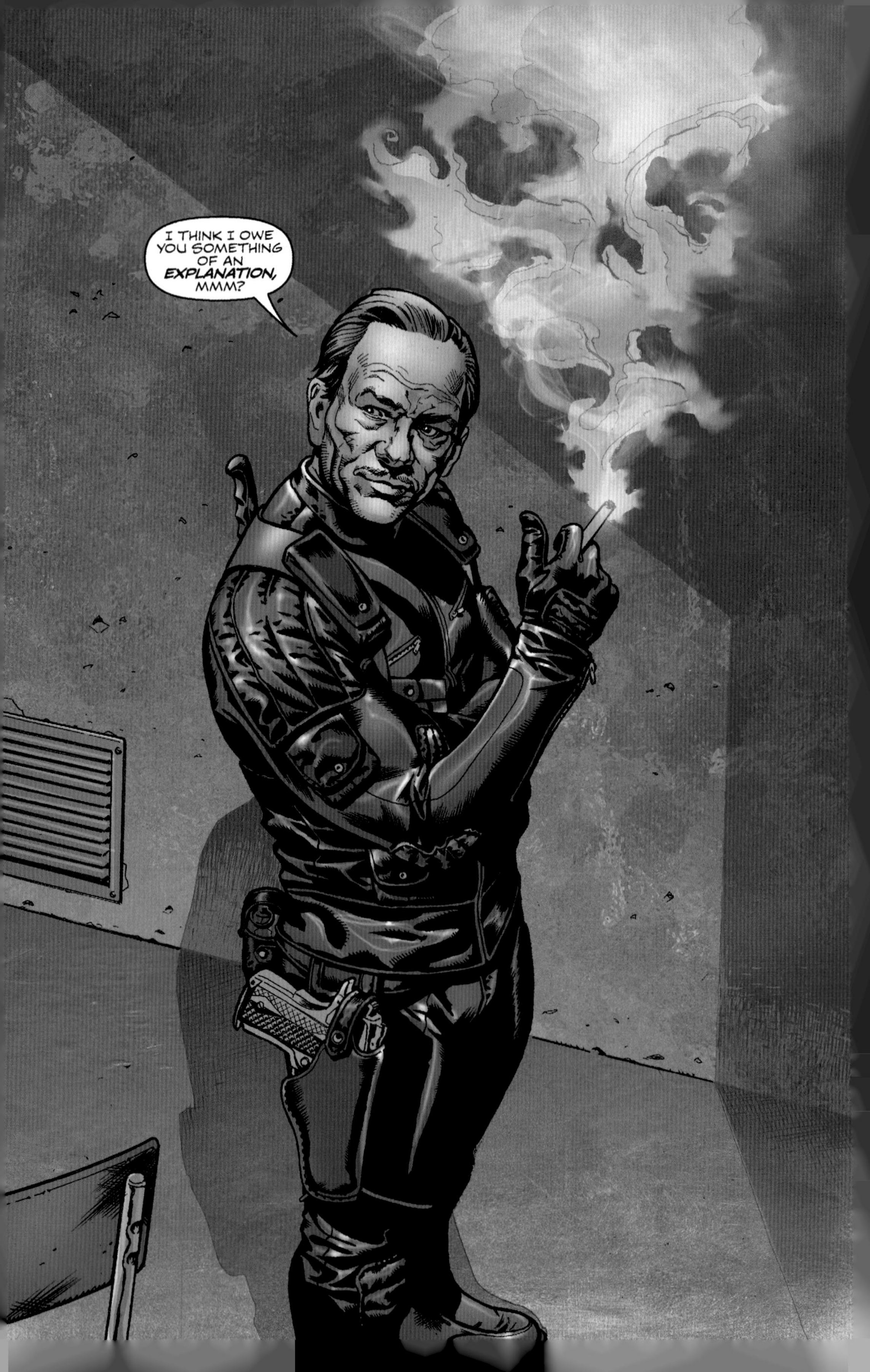
I THINK I OWE YOU SOMETHING OF AN ***EXPLANATION,*** MMM?

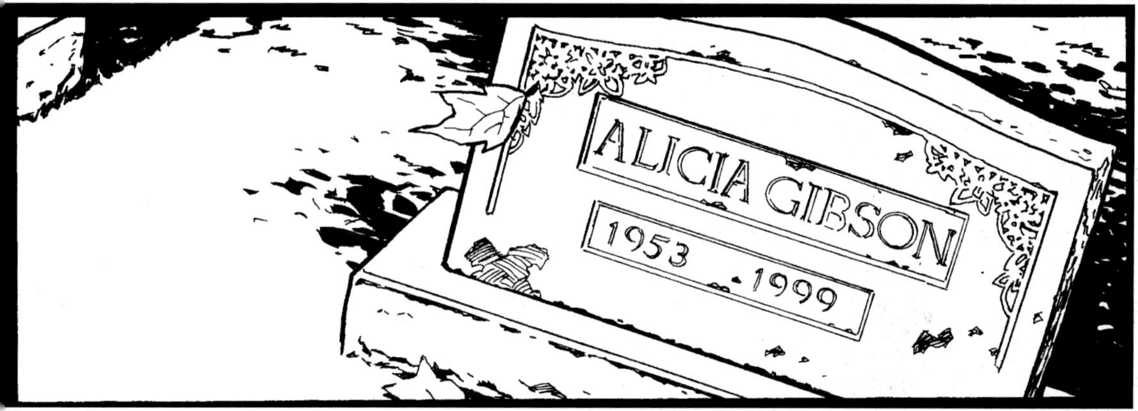
ALICIA GIBSON
1953 1999

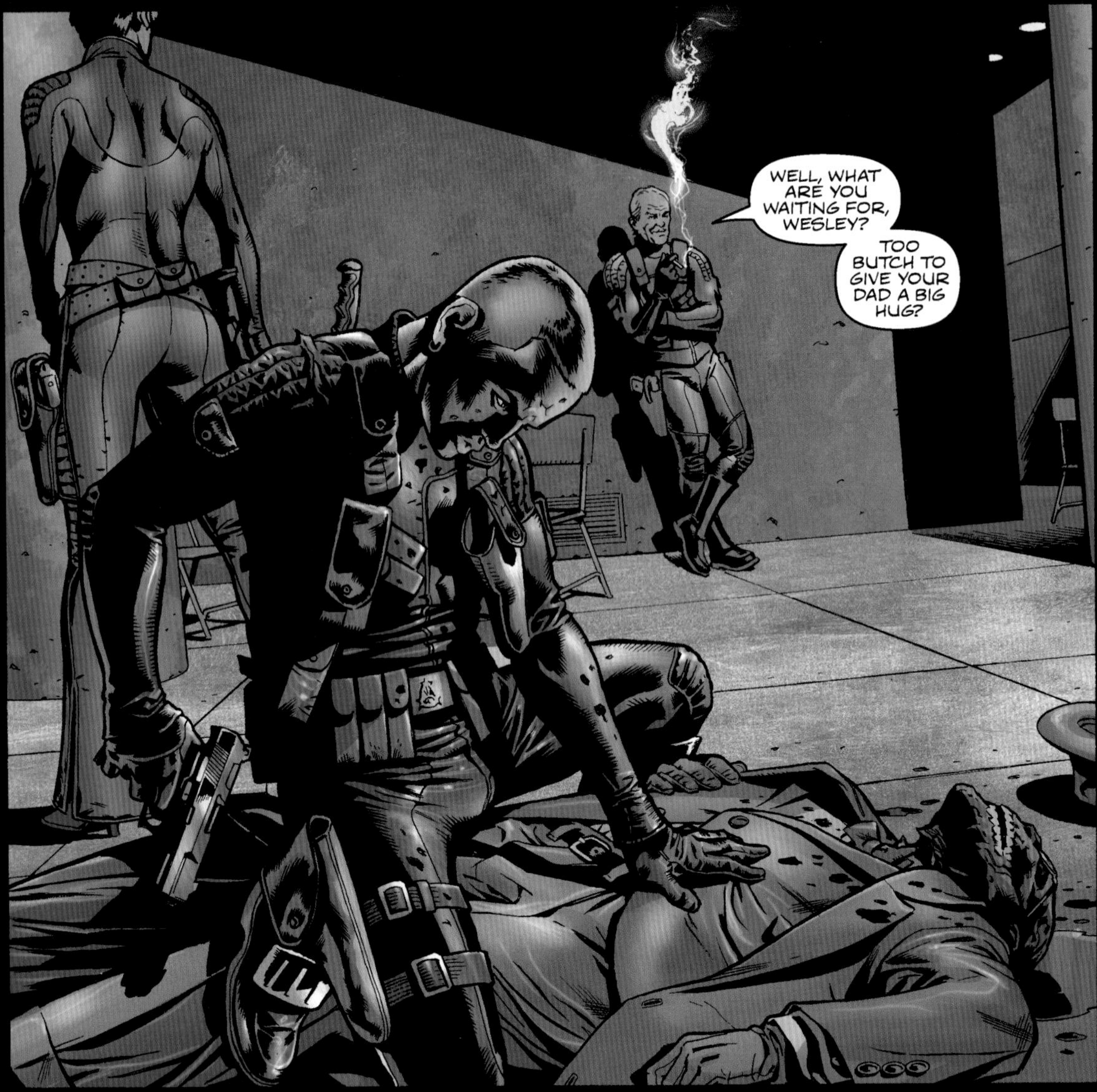
WELL, WHAT ARE YOU WAITING FOR, WESLEY?
TOO BUTCH TO GIVE YOUR DAD A BIG HUG?

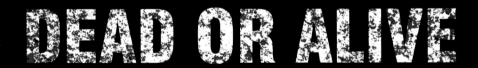

DEAD OR ALIVE

Written by: Mark Millar

Penciled and Inked by: J.G. Jones

Colored by: Paul Mounts

Flashback sequences pgs 6-10
Penciled and Inked by: Dick Giordano

Lettered by: Dreamer Design's
Robin Spehar &
Dennis Heisler

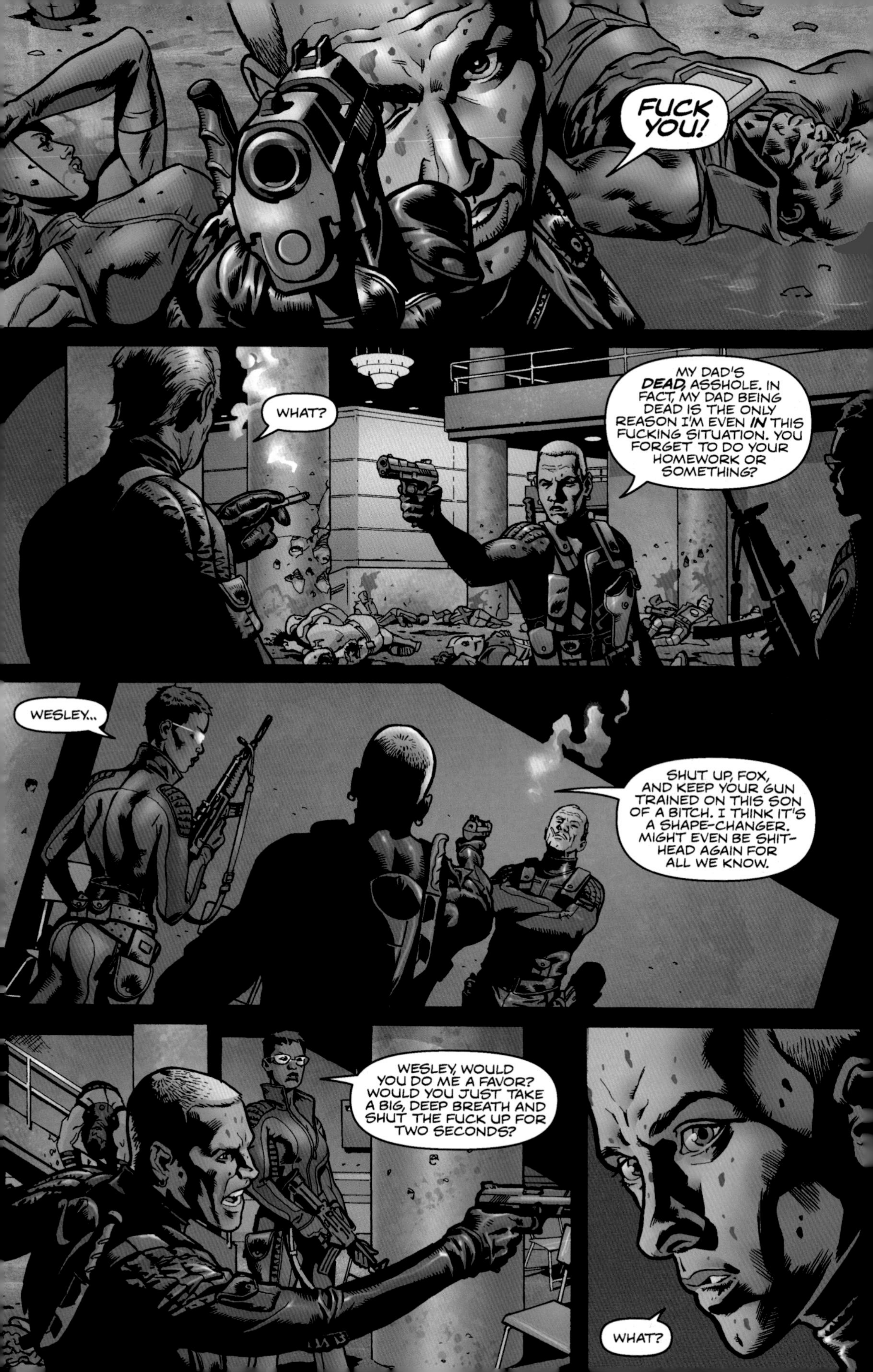
FUCK YOU!
WHAT?
MY DAD'S DEAD, ASSHOLE. IN FACT, MY DAD BEING DEAD IS THE ONLY REASON I'M EVEN IN THIS FUCKING SITUATION. YOU FORGET TO DO YOUR HOMEWORK OR SOMETHING?
WESLEY...
SHUT UP, FOX, AND KEEP YOUR GUN TRAINED ON THIS SON OF A BITCH. I THINK IT'S A SHAPE-CHANGER. MIGHT EVEN BE SHIT-HEAD AGAIN FOR ALL WE KNOW.
WESLEY, WOULD YOU DO ME A FAVOR? WOULD YOU JUST TAKE A BIG, DEEP BREATH AND SHUT THE FUCK UP FOR TWO SECONDS?
WHAT?

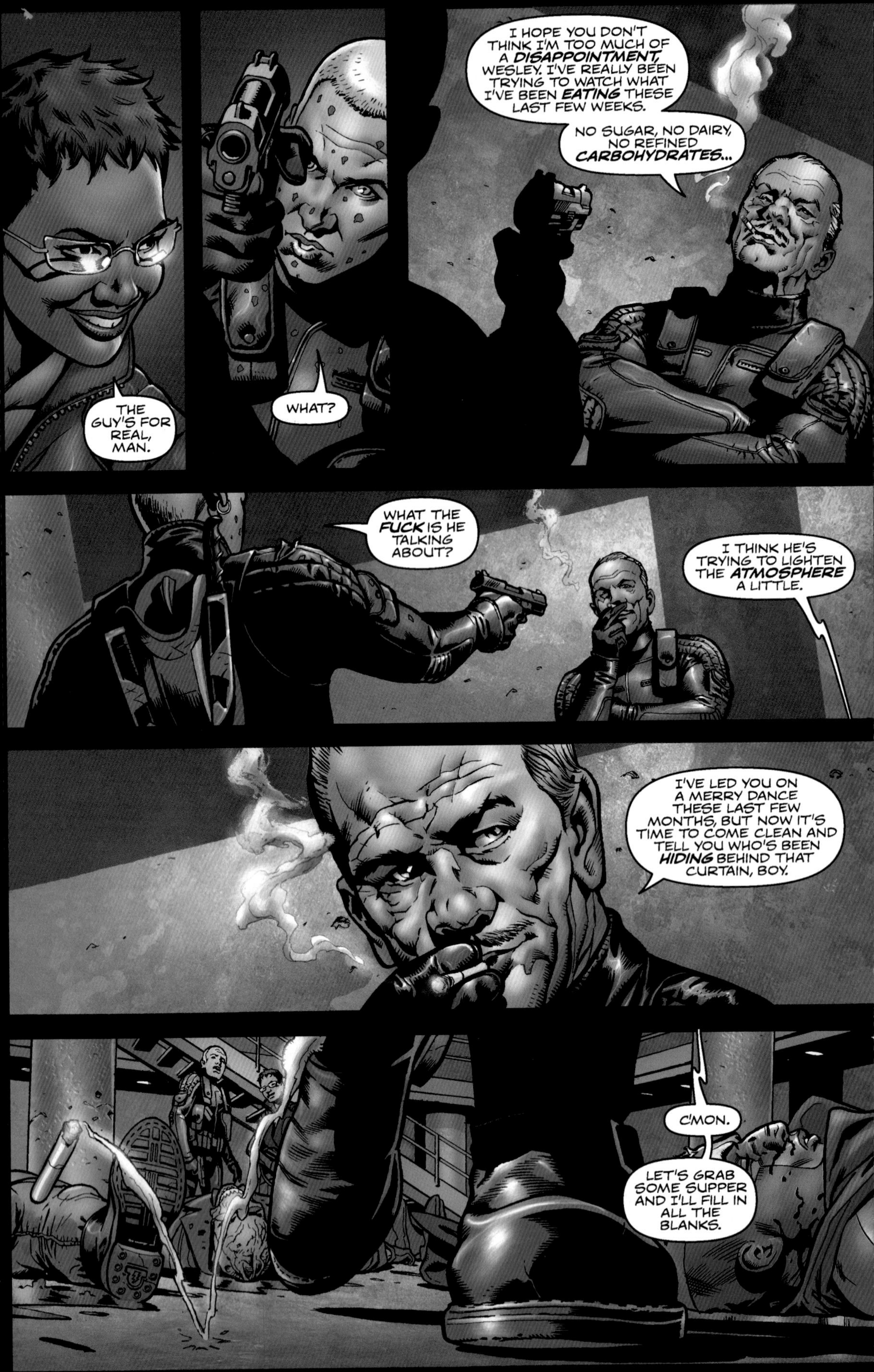
THE GUY'S FOR REAL, MAN.
WHAT?
I HOPE YOU DON'T THINK I'M TOO MUCH OF A DISAPPOINTMENT, WESLEY. I'VE REALLY BEEN TRYING TO WATCH WHAT I'VE BEEN EATING THESE LAST FEW WEEKS.
NO SUGAR, NO DAIRY, NO REFINED CARBOHYDRATES...
WHAT THE FUCK IS HE TALKING ABOUT?
I THINK HE'S TRYING TO LIGHTEN THE ATMOSPHERE A LITTLE.
I'VE LED YOU ON A MERRY DANCE THESE LAST FEW MONTHS, BUT NOW IT'S TIME TO COME CLEAN AND TELL YOU WHO'S BEEN HIDING BEHIND THAT CURTAIN, BOY.
C'MON.
LET'S GRAB SOME SUPPER AND I'LL FILL IN ALL THE BLANKS.

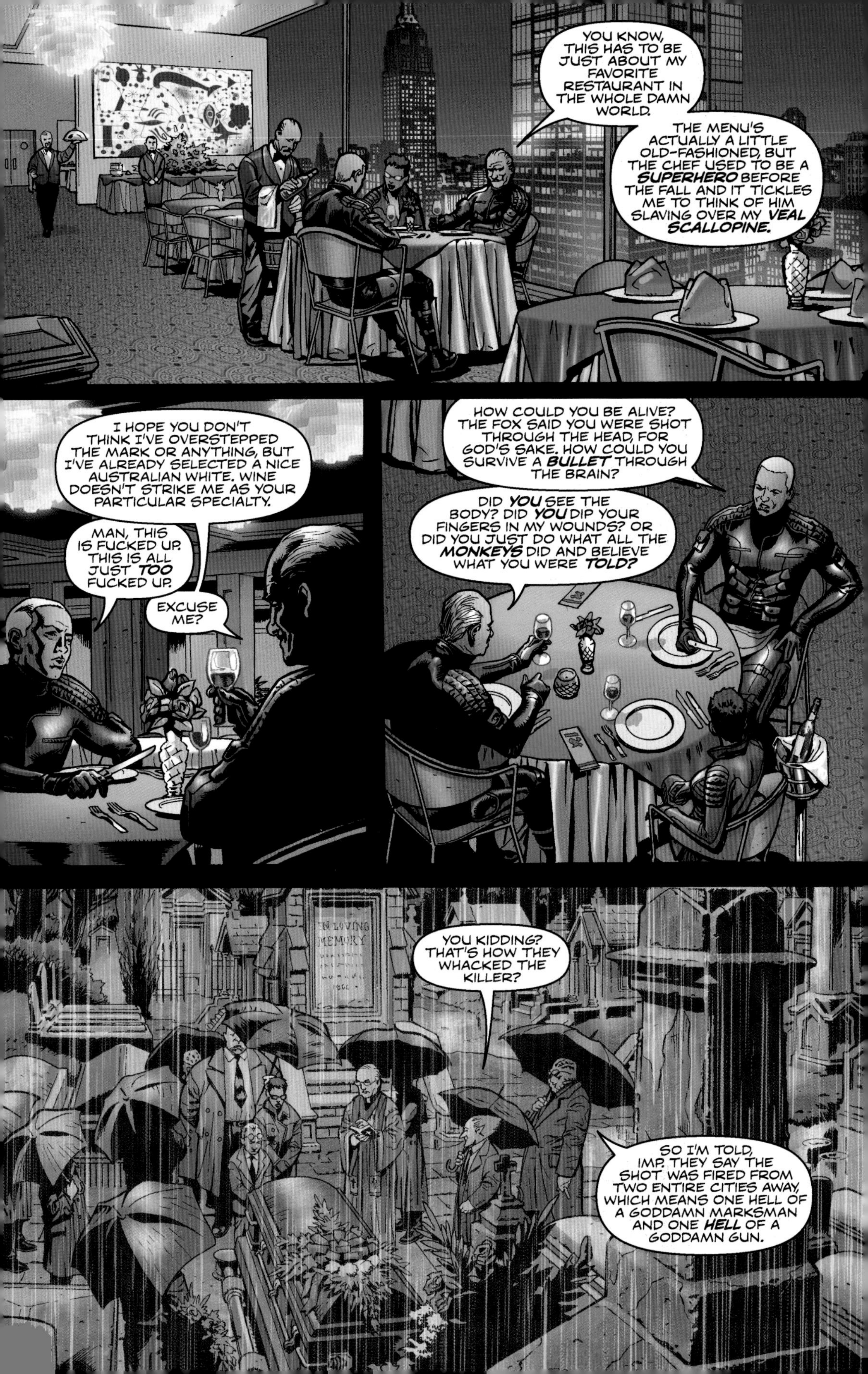

YOU KNOW, THIS HAS TO BE JUST ABOUT MY FAVORITE RESTAURANT IN THE WHOLE DAMN WORLD.
THE MENU'S ACTUALLY A LITTLE OLD-FASHIONED, BUT THE CHEF USED TO BE A SUPERHERO BEFORE THE FALL AND IT TICKLES ME TO THINK OF HIM SLAVING OVER MY VEAL SCALLOPINE.
I HOPE YOU DON'T THINK I'VE OVERSTEPPED THE MARK OR ANYTHING, BUT I'VE ALREADY SELECTED A NICE AUSTRALIAN WHITE. WINE DOESN'T STRIKE ME AS YOUR PARTICULAR SPECIALTY.
MAN, THIS IS FUCKED UP. THIS IS ALL JUST TOO FUCKED UP.
EXCUSE ME?
HOW COULD YOU BE ALIVE? THE FOX SAID YOU WERE SHOT THROUGH THE HEAD, FOR GOD'S SAKE. HOW COULD YOU SURVIVE A BULLET THROUGH THE BRAIN?
DID YOU SEE THE BODY? DID YOU DIP YOUR FINGERS IN MY WOUNDS? OR DID YOU JUST DO WHAT ALL THE MONKEYS DID AND BELIEVE WHAT YOU WERE TOLD?
IN LOVING MEMORY
YOU KIDDING? THAT'S HOW THEY WHACKED THE KILLER?
SO I'M TOLD, IMP. THEY SAY THE SHOT WAS FIRED FROM TWO ENTIRE CITIES AWAY, WHICH MEANS ONE HELL OF A GODDAMN MARKSMAN AND ONE HELL OF A GODDAMN GUN.

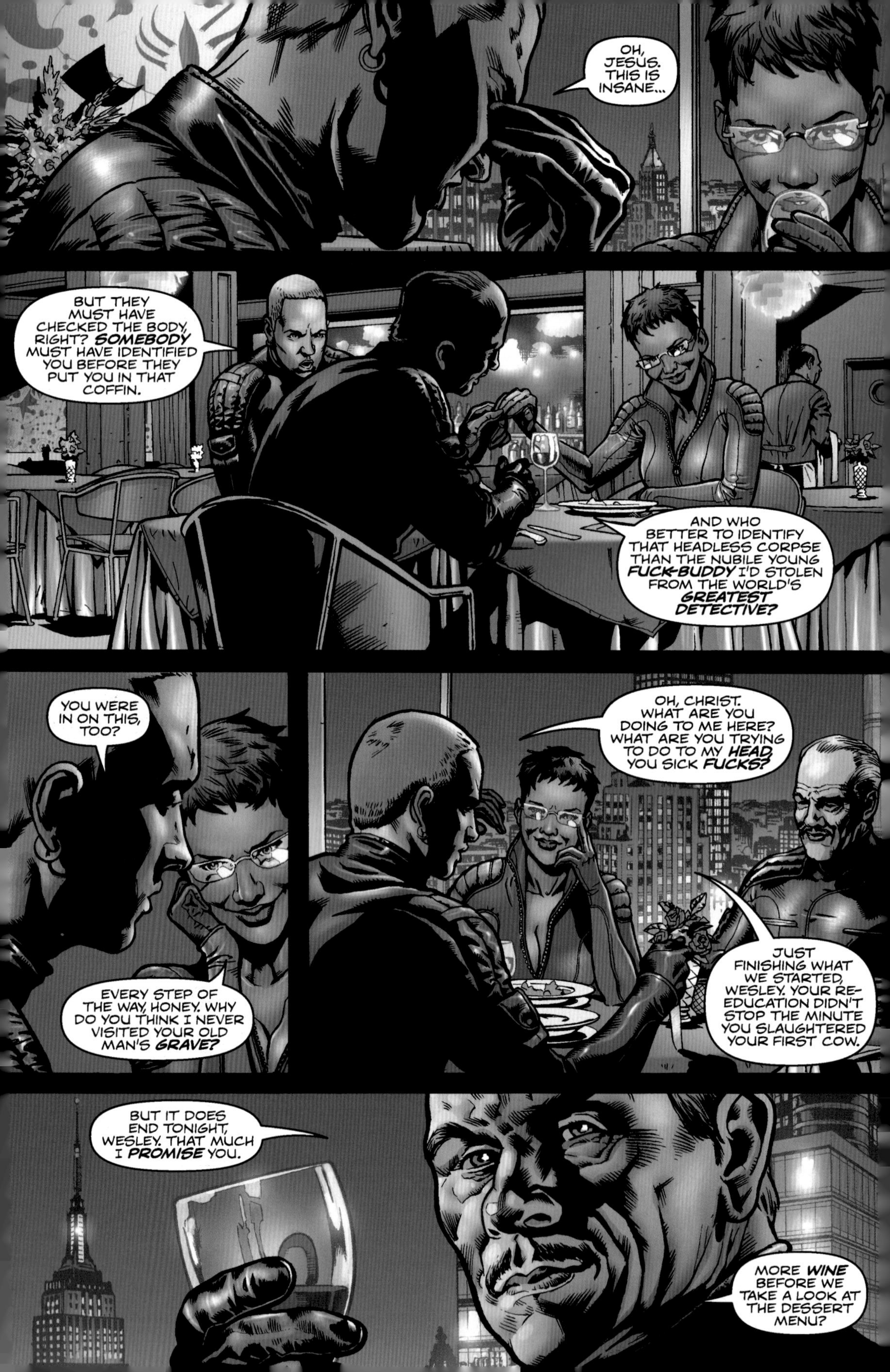
OH, JESUS. THIS IS INSANE...
BUT THEY MUST HAVE CHECKED THE BODY, RIGHT? SOMEBODY MUST HAVE IDENTIFIED YOU BEFORE THEY PUT YOU IN THAT COFFIN.
AND WHO BETTER TO IDENTIFY THAT HEADLESS CORPSE THAN THE NUBILE YOUNG FUCK-BUDDY I'D STOLEN FROM THE WORLD'S GREATEST DETECTIVE?
YOU WERE IN ON THIS, TOO?
EVERY STEP OF THE WAY, HONEY. WHY DO YOU THINK I NEVER VISITED YOUR OLD MAN'S GRAVE?
OH, CHRIST. WHAT ARE YOU DOING TO ME HERE? WHAT ARE YOU TRYING TO DO TO MY HEAD, YOU SICK FUCKS?
JUST FINISHING WHAT WE STARTED, WESLEY. YOUR RE-EDUCATION DIDN'T STOP THE MINUTE YOU SLAUGHTERED YOUR FIRST COW.
BUT IT DOES END TONIGHT, WESLEY. THAT MUCH I PROMISE YOU.
MORE WINE BEFORE WE TAKE A LOOK AT THE DESSERT MENU?

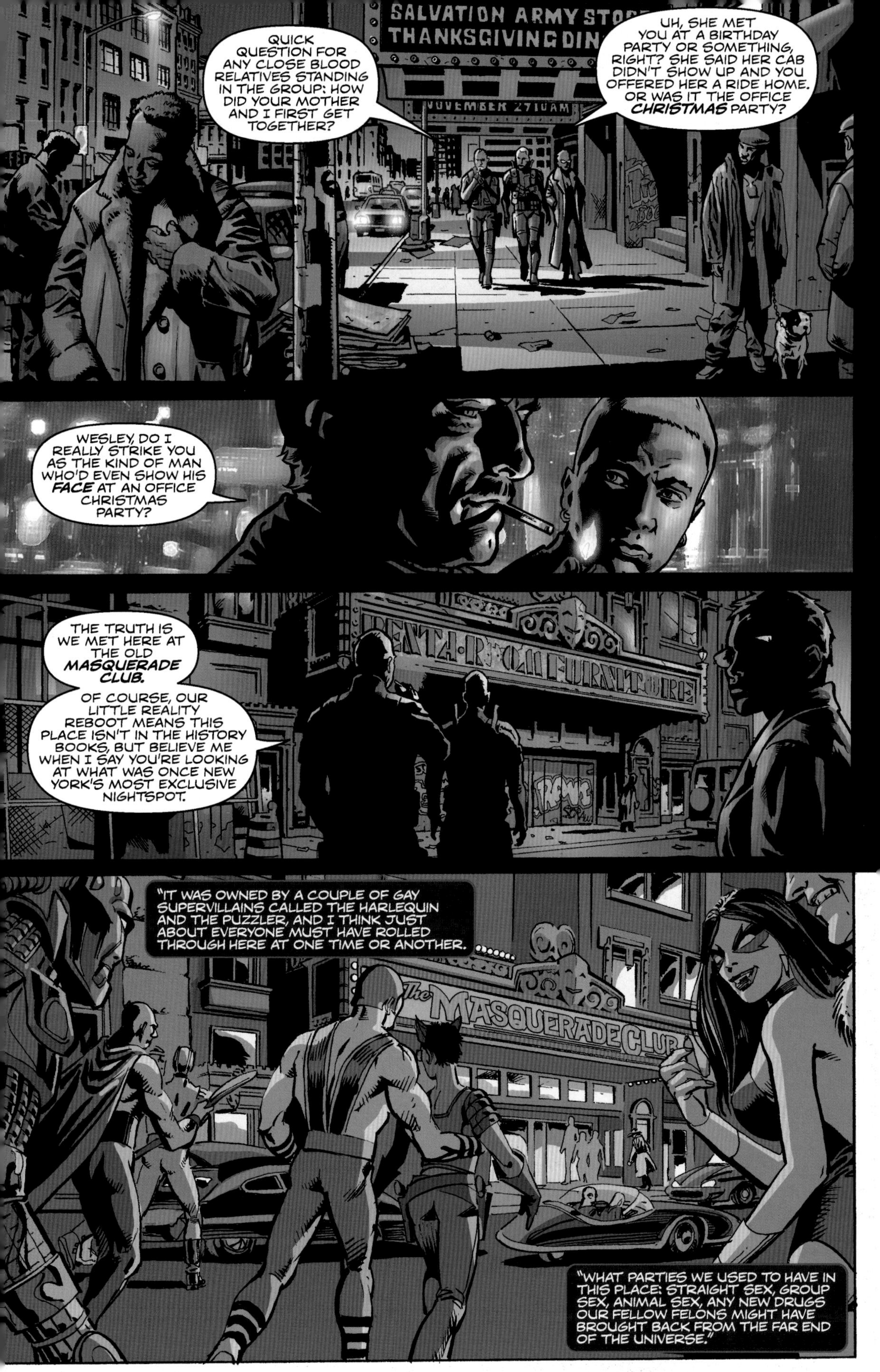
SALVATION ARMY STO
THANKSGIVING DIN
QUICK QUESTION FOR ANY CLOSE BLOOD RELATIVES STANDING IN THE GROUP: HOW DID YOUR MOTHER AND I FIRST GET TOGETHER?
UH, SHE MET YOU AT A BIRTHDAY PARTY OR SOMETHING, RIGHT? SHE SAID HER CAB DIDN'T SHOW UP AND YOU OFFERED HER A RIDE HOME. OR WAS IT THE OFFICE CHRISTMAS PARTY?
WESLEY, DO I REALLY STRIKE YOU AS THE KIND OF MAN WHO'D EVEN SHOW HIS FACE AT AN OFFICE CHRISTMAS PARTY?
THE TRUTH IS WE MET HERE AT THE OLD MASQUERADE CLUB.
OF COURSE, OUR LITTLE REALITY REBOOT MEANS THIS PLACE ISN'T IN THE HISTORY BOOKS, BUT BELIEVE ME WHEN I SAY YOU'RE LOOKING AT WHAT WAS ONCE NEW YORK'S MOST EXCLUSIVE NIGHTSPOT.
"IT WAS OWNED BY A COUPLE OF GAY SUPERVILLAINS CALLED THE HARLEQUIN AND THE PUZZLER, AND I THINK JUST ABOUT EVERYONE MUST HAVE ROLLED THROUGH HERE AT ONE TIME OR ANOTHER.
The MASQUERADE CLUB
"WHAT PARTIES WE USED TO HAVE IN THIS PLACE: STRAIGHT SEX, GROUP SEX, ANIMAL SEX, ANY NEW DRUGS OUR FELLOW FELONS MIGHT HAVE BROUGHT BACK FROM THE FAR END OF THE UNIVERSE."

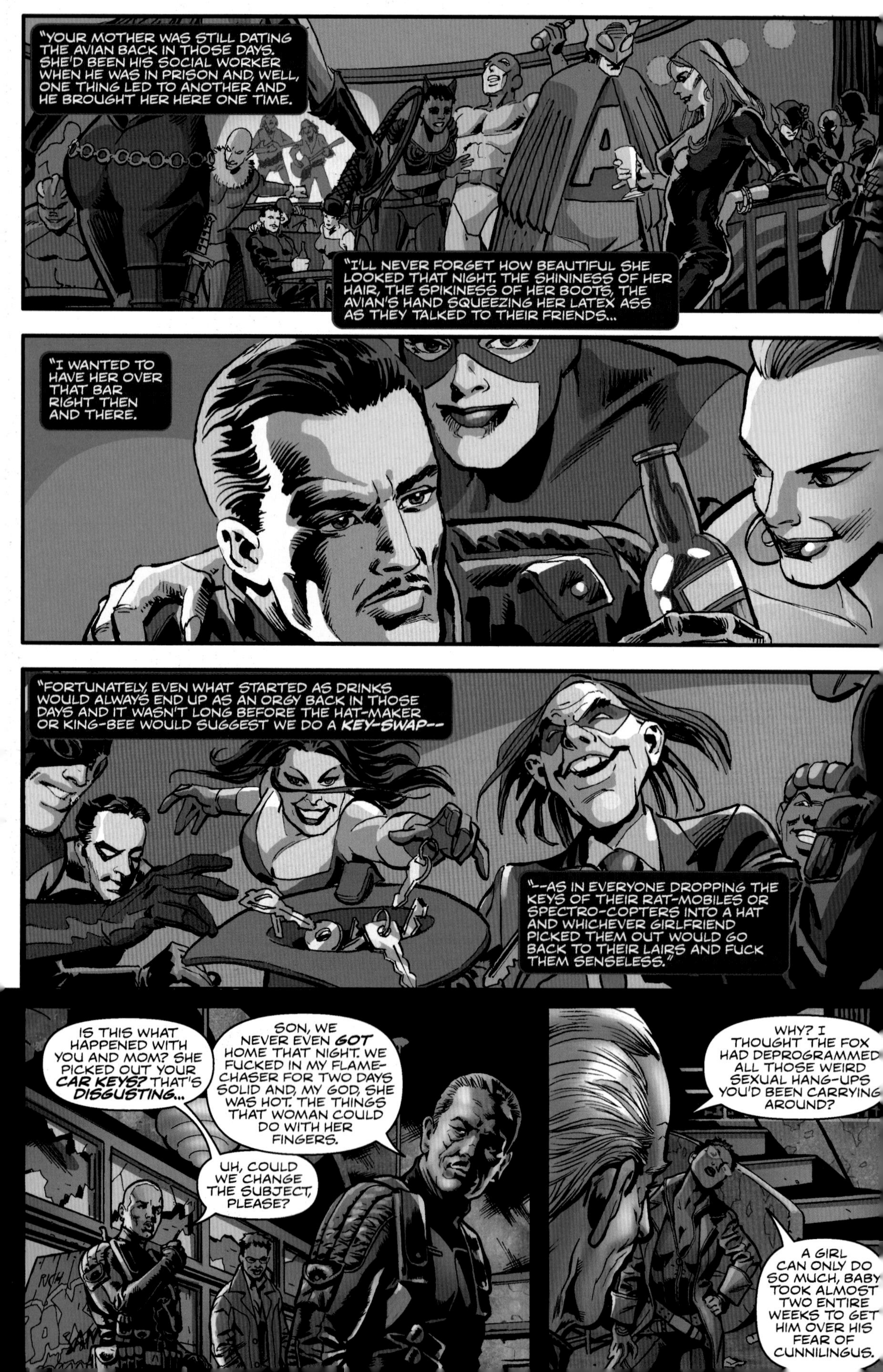
"YOUR MOTHER WAS STILL DATING THE AVIAN BACK IN THOSE DAYS. SHE'D BEEN HIS SOCIAL WORKER WHEN HE WAS IN PRISON AND, WELL, ONE THING LED TO ANOTHER AND HE BROUGHT HER HERE ONE TIME.
"I'LL NEVER FORGET HOW BEAUTIFUL SHE LOOKED THAT NIGHT. THE SHININESS OF HER HAIR, THE SPIKINESS OF HER BOOTS, THE AVIAN'S HAND SQUEEZING HER LATEX ASS AS THEY TALKED TO THEIR FRIENDS...
"I WANTED TO HAVE HER OVER THAT BAR RIGHT THEN AND THERE.
"FORTUNATELY, EVEN WHAT STARTED AS DRINKS WOULD ALWAYS END UP AS AN ORGY BACK IN THOSE DAYS AND IT WASN'T LONG BEFORE THE HAT-MAKER OR KING-BEE WOULD SUGGEST WE DO A KEY-SWAP--
"--AS IN EVERYONE DROPPING THE KEYS OF THEIR RAT-MOBILES OR SPECTRO-COPTERS INTO A HAT AND WHICHEVER GIRLFRIEND PICKED THEM OUT WOULD GO BACK TO THEIR LAIRS AND FUCK THEM SENSELESS."
IS THIS WHAT HAPPENED WITH YOU AND MOM? SHE PICKED OUT YOUR CAR KEYS? THAT'S DISGUSTING...
SON, WE NEVER EVEN GOT HOME THAT NIGHT. WE FUCKED IN MY FLAME-CHASER FOR TWO DAYS SOLID AND, MY GOD, SHE WAS HOT. THE THINGS THAT WOMAN COULD DO WITH HER FINGERS.
UH, COULD WE CHANGE THE SUBJECT, PLEASE?
WHY? I THOUGHT THE FOX HAD DEPROGRAMMED ALL THOSE WEIRD SEXUAL HANG-UPS YOU'D BEEN CARRYING AROUND?
A GIRL CAN ONLY DO SO MUCH, BABY. TOOK ALMOST TWO ENTIRE WEEKS TO GET HIM OVER HIS FEAR OF CUNNILINGUS.

COULD WE JUST GET BACK TO THE *POINT* OF THIS STORY?

THE ONLY POINT I WAS TRYING TO MAKE IS THAT YOU WERE CONCEIVED IN THE HEAT OF THE MOST INCREDIBLE PASSION, WESLEY.

NO MAN EVER WANTED A WOMAN MORE THAN I WANTED YOUR MOTHER. YOU WERE A LOVE CHILD IN EVERY SENSE OF THE WORD.

BECAUSE NOTHING LASTS FOREVER, KIDDO.

WE BOTH LIKED COOKING, WALKS IN THE PARK, AND READING *ROBERT E. HOWARD BOOKS,* BUT AFTER A WHILE ALL THE THINGS THAT ATTRACTED HER TO ME WERE ALL THE THINGS SHE WANTED ME TO STOP.

THE *SUPER-VILLAIN* STUFF?

SO WHY DID YOU WALK OUT ON US?

AFTER *YOU* WERE BORN SHE WANTED ME TO RETIRE AND LIVE OFF THE LOOT, BUT THE FRATERNITY AND I HAD *PLANS,* WESLEY. THIS SCHEME TO TAKE OVER THE WORLD HAD BEEN BREWING FOR A *LONG* TIME.

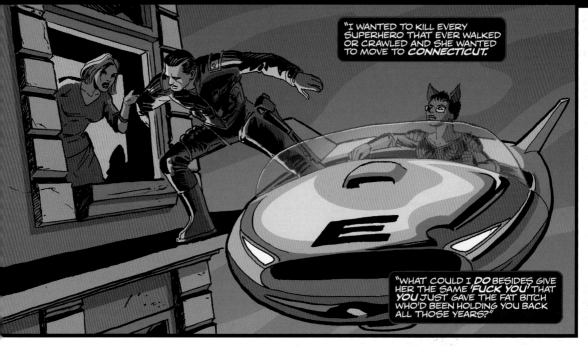

"I WANTED TO KILL EVERY SUPERHERO THAT EVER WALKED OR CRAWLED AND SHE WANTED TO MOVE TO *CONNECTICUT.*

"WHAT COULD I *DO* BESIDES GIVE HER THE SAME *'FUCK YOU'* THAT *YOU* JUST GAVE THE FAT BITCH WHO'D BEEN HOLDING YOU BACK ALL THOSE YEARS?"

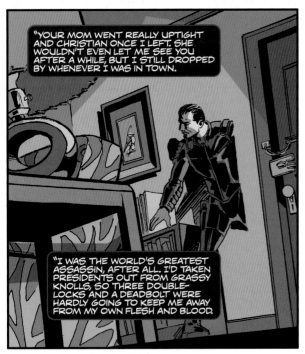

"YOUR MOM WENT REALLY UPTIGHT AND CHRISTIAN ONCE I LEFT. SHE WOULDN'T EVEN LET ME SEE YOU AFTER A WHILE, BUT I STILL DROPPED BY WHENEVER I WAS IN TOWN.

"I WAS THE WORLD'S GREATEST ASSASSIN, AFTER ALL. I'D TAKEN PRESIDENTS OUT FROM GRASSY KNOLLS, SO THREE DOUBLE-LOCKS AND A DEADBOLT WERE HARDLY GOING TO KEEP ME AWAY FROM MY OWN FLESH AND BLOOD.

"YOU WERE ALWAYS ASLEEP WHEN I APPEARED. SOMETIMES I'D LEAVE PRESENTS LIKE SOME HALF-ASSED SANTA, BUT MOSTLY I JUST SAT THERE STROKING YOUR HAIR UNTIL THE SUN CAME UP.

"THE SKY WAS SO BLUE IN THOSE DAYS, WESLEY. THE TREES WERE A DEEPER GREEN THAN YOU CAN POSSIBLY IMAGINE AND THE FOOD WAS SO RICH AND TASTY COMPARED TO THAT SHIT YOU EAT TODAY.

"THERE WAS A MOMENT WE ALMOST DIDN'T GO AHEAD WITH THAT REVOLUTION WE'D BEEN PLANNING. A MOMENT WE DIDN'T WANT TO LET THINGS GO ALL GRIM AND GRITTY...

"...BUT IT WAS ONLY FOR A MOMENT.

"SOME OF US HAD SPENT HALF OF OUR ADULT LIVES IN JAIL AND THE HEROES WERE GETTING SO GOOD AT WHAT THEY DID. WE *HAD* TO STRIKE. WHAT IF THIS WAS OUR *FINAL OPPORTUNITY?*"

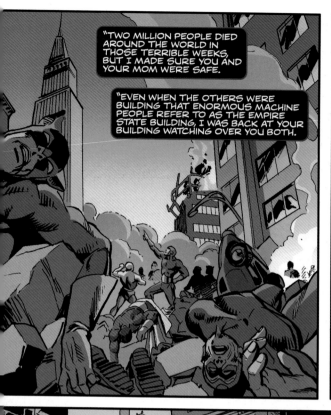

"TWO MILLION PEOPLE DIED AROUND THE WORLD IN THOSE TERRIBLE WEEKS, BUT I MADE SURE YOU AND YOUR MOM WERE SAFE.

"EVEN WHEN THE OTHERS WERE BUILDING THAT ENORMOUS MACHINE PEOPLE REFER TO AS THE EMPIRE STATE BUILDING, I WAS BACK AT YOUR BUILDING WATCHING OVER YOU BOTH.

"IT WAS THE PERFECT PLAN. WHAT BETTER WAY TO KEEP CONTROL THAN MAKING EVERYONE FORGET THERE HAD EVER *BEEN* A REVOLUTION?

"THAT MACHINE REARRANGED THE VERY ATOMS OF THE UNIVERSE THAT HOT, DAMP SUMMER IN 1986 AND THIS BEAUTIFUL LITTLE WORLD OF OURS WOULD NEVER BE THE SAME AGAIN.

"THE HEROES WERE GONE, THE VILLAINS WERE THE ONLY ONES THAT WOULD *REMEMBER* THEM AND I HELD YOUR HAND TIGHT AS THIS *NEW* EARTH FORMED ITSELF AROUND US.

"BY MORNING, ALL THE MAGIC IN THE WORLD WAS GONE AND YOUR MOTHER THOUGHT YOUR FATHER HAD BEEN AN *AIRLINE PILOT.*"

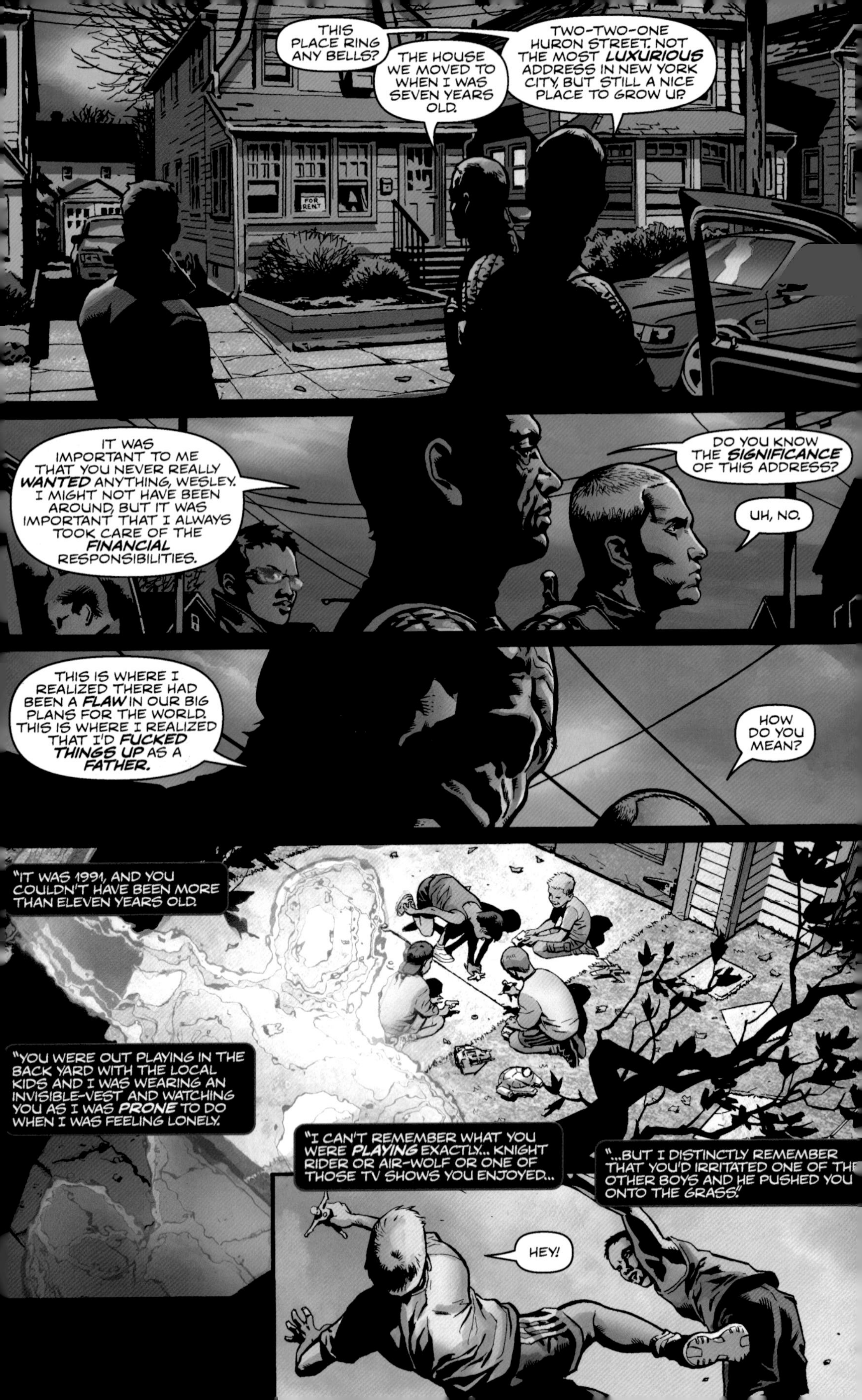
THIS PLACE RING ANY BELLS?
THE HOUSE WE MOVED TO WHEN I WAS SEVEN YEARS OLD.
TWO-TWO-ONE HURON STREET. NOT THE MOST LUXURIOUS ADDRESS IN NEW YORK CITY, BUT STILL A NICE PLACE TO GROW UP?
FOR RENT
IT WAS IMPORTANT TO ME THAT YOU NEVER REALLY WANTED ANYTHING, WESLEY. I MIGHT NOT HAVE BEEN AROUND, BUT IT WAS IMPORTANT THAT I ALWAYS TOOK CARE OF THE FINANCIAL RESPONSIBILITIES.
DO YOU KNOW THE SIGNIFICANCE OF THIS ADDRESS?
UH, NO.
THIS IS WHERE I REALIZED THERE HAD BEEN A FLAW IN OUR BIG PLANS FOR THE WORLD. THIS IS WHERE I REALIZED THAT I'D FUCKED THINGS UP AS A FATHER.
HOW DO YOU MEAN?
"IT WAS 1991, AND YOU COULDN'T HAVE BEEN MORE THAN ELEVEN YEARS OLD.
"YOU WERE OUT PLAYING IN THE BACK YARD WITH THE LOCAL KIDS AND I WAS WEARING AN INVISIBLE-VEST AND WATCHING YOU AS I WAS PRONE TO DO WHEN I WAS FEELING LONELY.
"I CAN'T REMEMBER WHAT YOU WERE PLAYING EXACTLY... KNIGHT RIDER OR AIR-WOLF OR ONE OF THOSE TV SHOWS YOU ENJOYED...
"...BUT I DISTINCTLY REMEMBER THAT YOU'D IRRITATED ONE OF THE OTHER BOYS AND HE PUSHED YOU ONTO THE GRASS."
HEY!

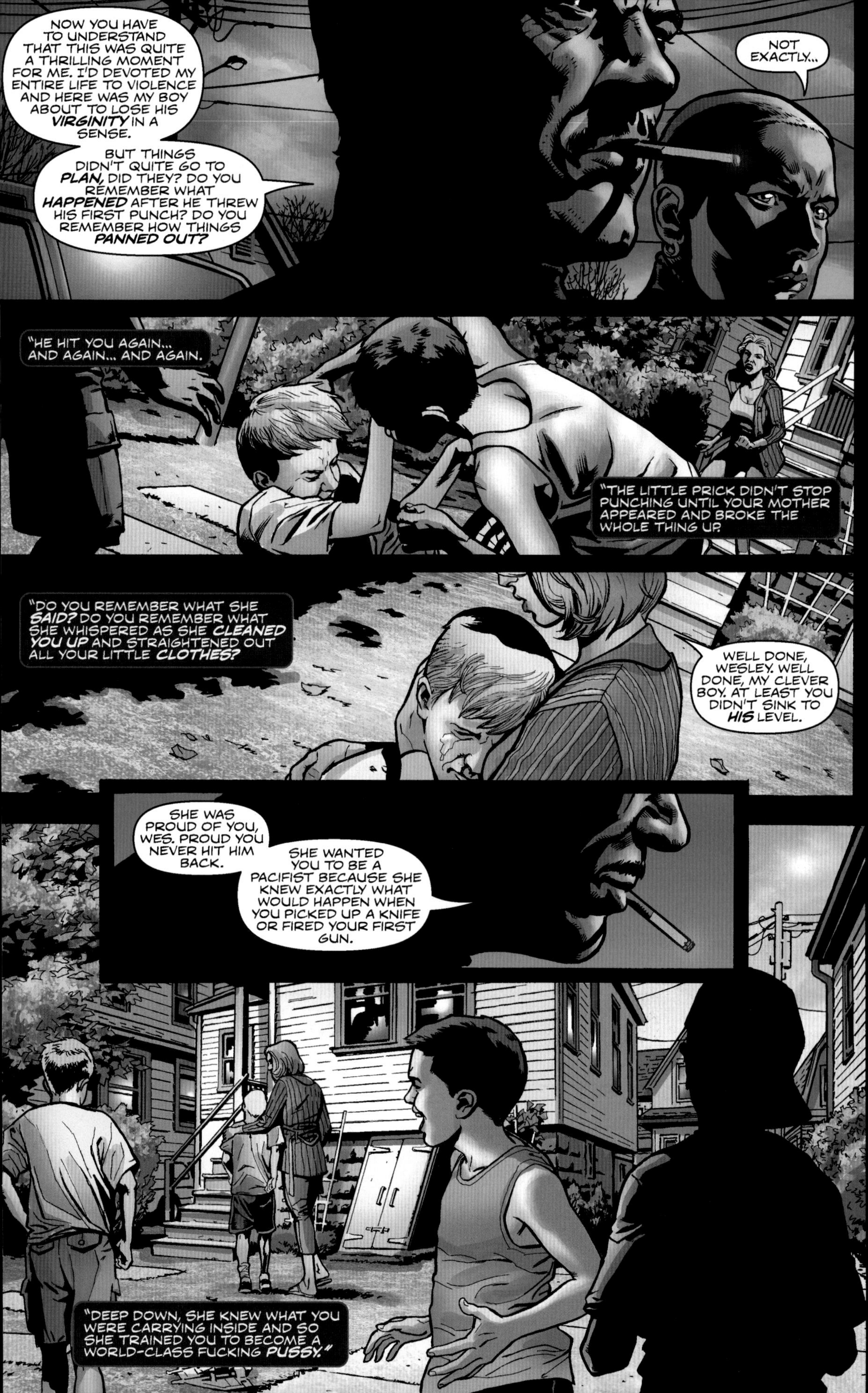
NOW YOU HAVE TO UNDERSTAND THAT THIS WAS QUITE A THRILLING MOMENT FOR ME. I'D DEVOTED MY ENTIRE LIFE TO VIOLENCE AND HERE WAS MY BOY ABOUT TO LOSE HIS VIRGINITY IN A SENSE.
BUT THINGS DIDN'T QUITE GO TO PLAN, DID THEY? DO YOU REMEMBER WHAT HAPPENED AFTER HE THREW HIS FIRST PUNCH? DO YOU REMEMBER HOW THINGS PANNED OUT?
NOT EXACTLY...
"HE HIT YOU AGAIN... AND AGAIN... AND AGAIN.
"THE LITTLE PRICK DIDN'T STOP PUNCHING UNTIL YOUR MOTHER APPEARED AND BROKE THE WHOLE THING UP.
"DO YOU REMEMBER WHAT SHE SAID? DO YOU REMEMBER WHAT SHE WHISPERED AS SHE CLEANED YOU UP AND STRAIGHTENED OUT ALL YOUR LITTLE CLOTHES?
WELL DONE, WESLEY. WELL DONE, MY CLEVER BOY. AT LEAST YOU DIDN'T SINK TO HIS LEVEL.
SHE WAS PROUD OF YOU, WES. PROUD YOU NEVER HIT HIM BACK.
SHE WANTED YOU TO BE A PACIFIST BECAUSE SHE KNEW EXACTLY WHAT WOULD HAPPEN WHEN YOU PICKED UP A KNIFE OR FIRED YOUR FIRST GUN.
"DEEP DOWN, SHE KNEW WHAT YOU WERE CARRYING INSIDE AND SO SHE TRAINED YOU TO BECOME A WORLD-CLASS FUCKING PUSSY."

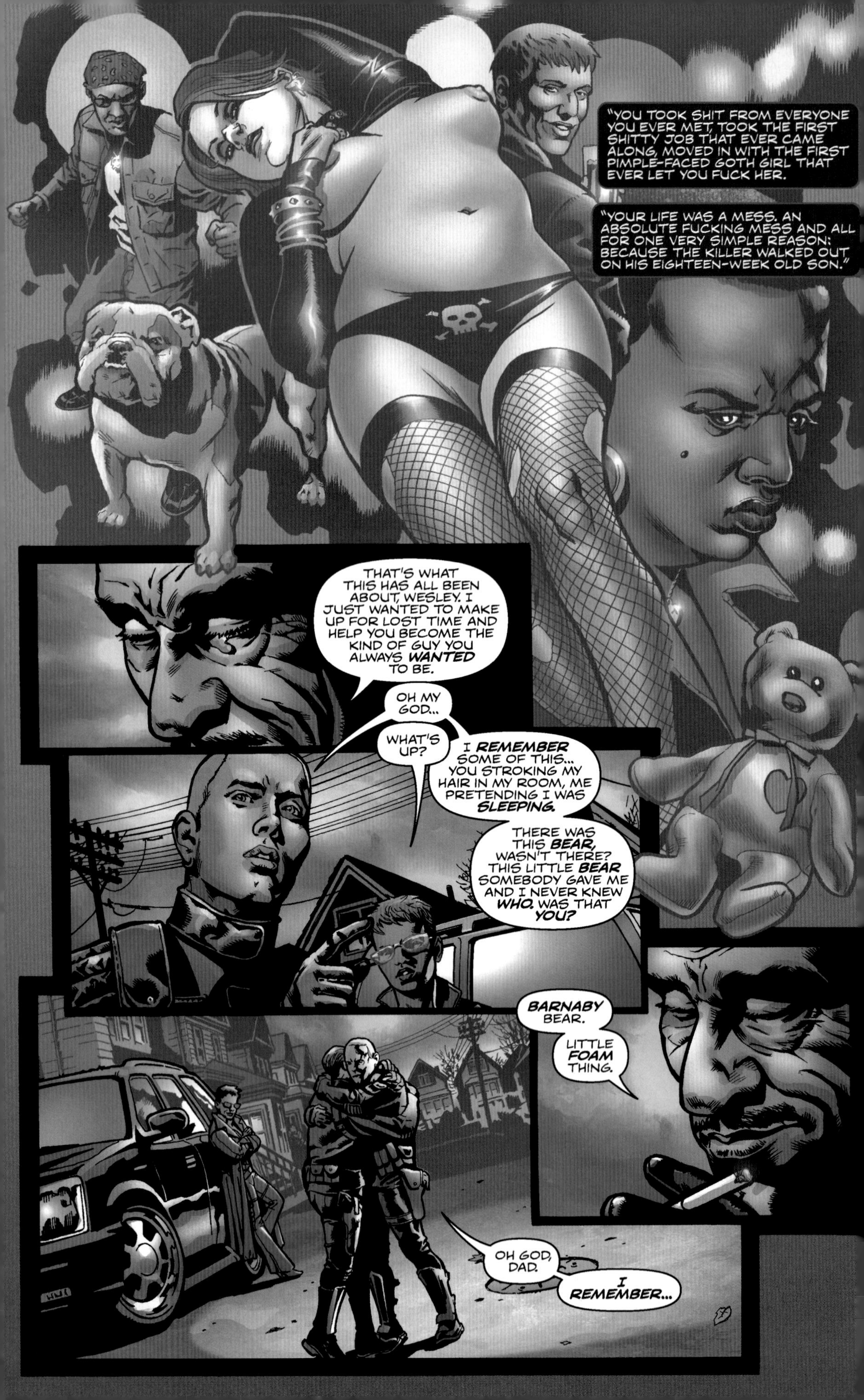
"YOU TOOK SHIT FROM EVERYONE YOU EVER MET, TOOK THE FIRST SHITTY JOB THAT EVER CAME ALONG, MOVED IN WITH THE FIRST PIMPLE-FACED GOTH GIRL THAT EVER LET YOU FUCK HER.
"YOUR LIFE WAS A MESS. AN ABSOLUTE FUCKING MESS AND ALL FOR ONE VERY SIMPLE REASON: BECAUSE THE KILLER WALKED OUT ON HIS EIGHTEEN-WEEK OLD SON."
THAT'S WHAT THIS HAS ALL BEEN ABOUT, WESLEY. I JUST WANTED TO MAKE UP FOR LOST TIME AND HELP YOU BECOME THE KIND OF GUY YOU ALWAYS WANTED TO BE.
OH MY GOD...
WHAT'S UP?
I REMEMBER SOME OF THIS... YOU STROKING MY HAIR IN MY ROOM, ME PRETENDING I WAS SLEEPING.
THERE WAS THIS BEAR, WASN'T THERE? THIS LITTLE BEAR SOMEBODY GAVE ME AND I NEVER KNEW WHO. WAS THAT YOU?
BARNABY BEAR.
LITTLE FOAM THING.
OH GOD, DAD.
I REMEMBER...

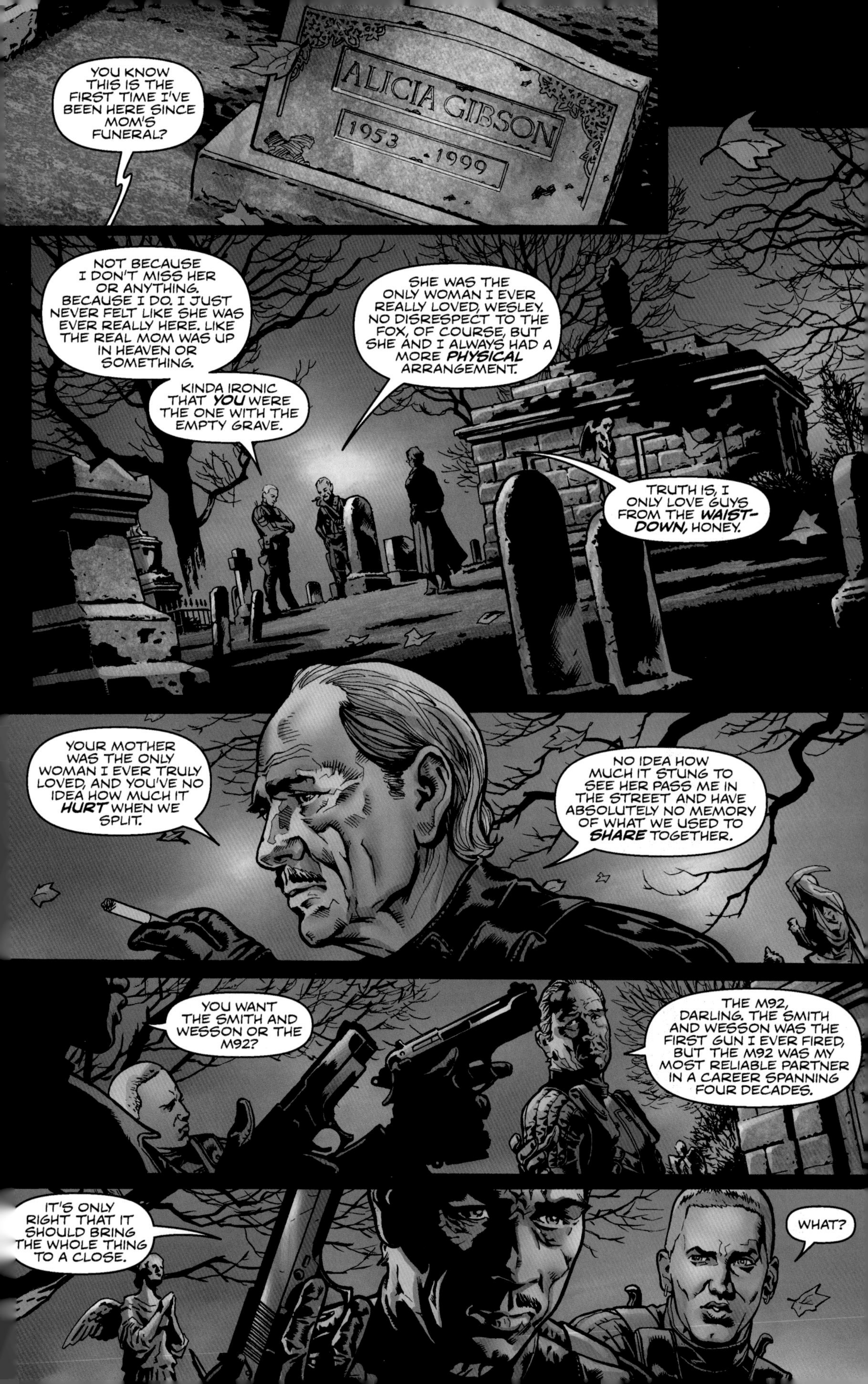
ALICIA GIBSON
1953 1999
YOU KNOW THIS IS THE FIRST TIME I'VE BEEN HERE SINCE MOM'S FUNERAL?
NOT BECAUSE I DON'T MISS HER OR ANYTHING. BECAUSE I DO. I JUST NEVER FELT LIKE SHE WAS EVER REALLY HERE. LIKE THE REAL MOM WAS UP IN HEAVEN OR SOMETHING.
KINDA IRONIC THAT YOU WERE THE ONE WITH THE EMPTY GRAVE.
SHE WAS THE ONLY WOMAN I EVER REALLY LOVED, WESLEY. NO DISRESPECT TO THE FOX, OF COURSE, BUT SHE AND I ALWAYS HAD A MORE PHYSICAL ARRANGEMENT.
TRUTH IS, I ONLY LOVE GUYS FROM THE WAIST-DOWN, HONEY.
YOUR MOTHER WAS THE ONLY WOMAN I EVER TRULY LOVED, AND YOU'VE NO IDEA HOW MUCH IT HURT WHEN WE SPLIT.
NO IDEA HOW MUCH IT STUNG TO SEE HER PASS ME IN THE STREET AND HAVE ABSOLUTELY NO MEMORY OF WHAT WE USED TO SHARE TOGETHER.
YOU WANT THE SMITH AND WESSON OR THE M92?
THE M92, DARLING. THE SMITH AND WESSON WAS THE FIRST GUN I EVER FIRED, BUT THE M92 WAS MY MOST RELIABLE PARTNER IN A CAREER SPANNING FOUR DECADES.
IT'S ONLY RIGHT THAT IT SHOULD BRING THE WHOLE THING TO A CLOSE.
WHAT?

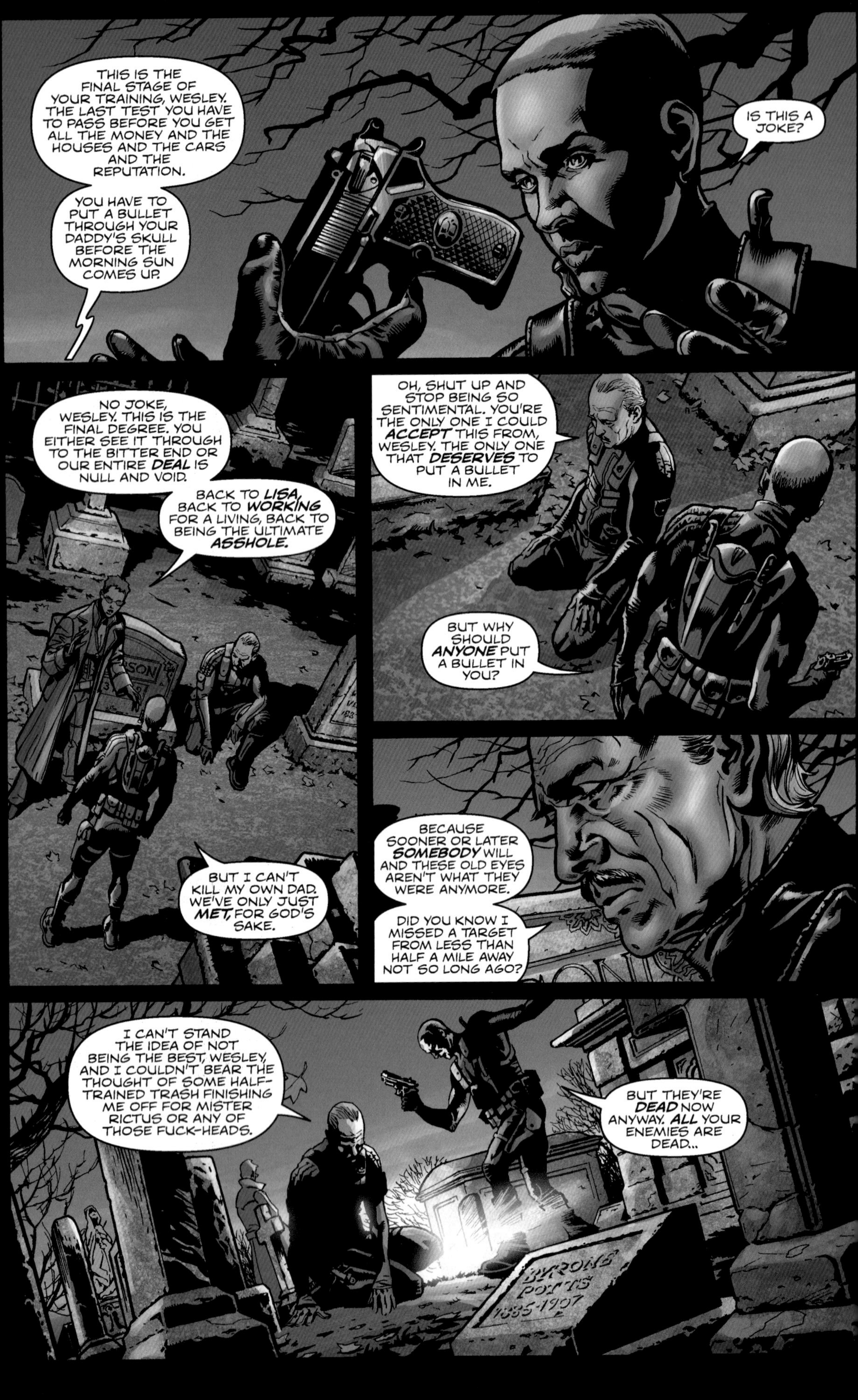
THIS IS THE FINAL STAGE OF YOUR TRAINING, WESLEY. THE LAST TEST YOU HAVE TO PASS BEFORE YOU GET ALL THE MONEY AND THE HOUSES AND THE CARS AND THE REPUTATION.
YOU HAVE TO PUT A BULLET THROUGH YOUR DADDY'S SKULL BEFORE THE MORNING SUN COMES UP.
IS THIS A JOKE?
NO JOKE, WESLEY. THIS IS THE FINAL DEGREE. YOU EITHER SEE IT THROUGH TO THE BITTER END OR OUR ENTIRE DEAL IS NULL AND VOID.
BACK TO LISA, BACK TO WORKING FOR A LIVING, BACK TO BEING THE ULTIMATE ASSHOLE.
BUT I CAN'T KILL MY OWN DAD. WE'VE ONLY JUST MET, FOR GOD'S SAKE.
OH, SHUT UP AND STOP BEING SO SENTIMENTAL. YOU'RE THE ONLY ONE I COULD ACCEPT THIS FROM, WESLEY. THE ONLY ONE THAT DESERVES TO PUT A BULLET IN ME.
BUT WHY SHOULD ANYONE PUT A BULLET IN YOU?
BECAUSE SOONER OR LATER SOMEBODY WILL AND THESE OLD EYES AREN'T WHAT THEY WERE ANYMORE.
DID YOU KNOW I MISSED A TARGET FROM LESS THAN HALF A MILE AWAY NOT SO LONG AGO?
I CAN'T STAND THE IDEA OF NOT BEING THE BEST, WESLEY, AND I COULDN'T BEAR THE THOUGHT OF SOME HALF-TRAINED TRASH FINISHING ME OFF FOR MISTER RICTUS OR ANY OF THOSE FUCK-HEADS.
BUT THEY'RE DEAD NOW ANYWAY. ALL YOUR ENEMIES ARE DEAD...
BYRON G. POTTS
1835-1907

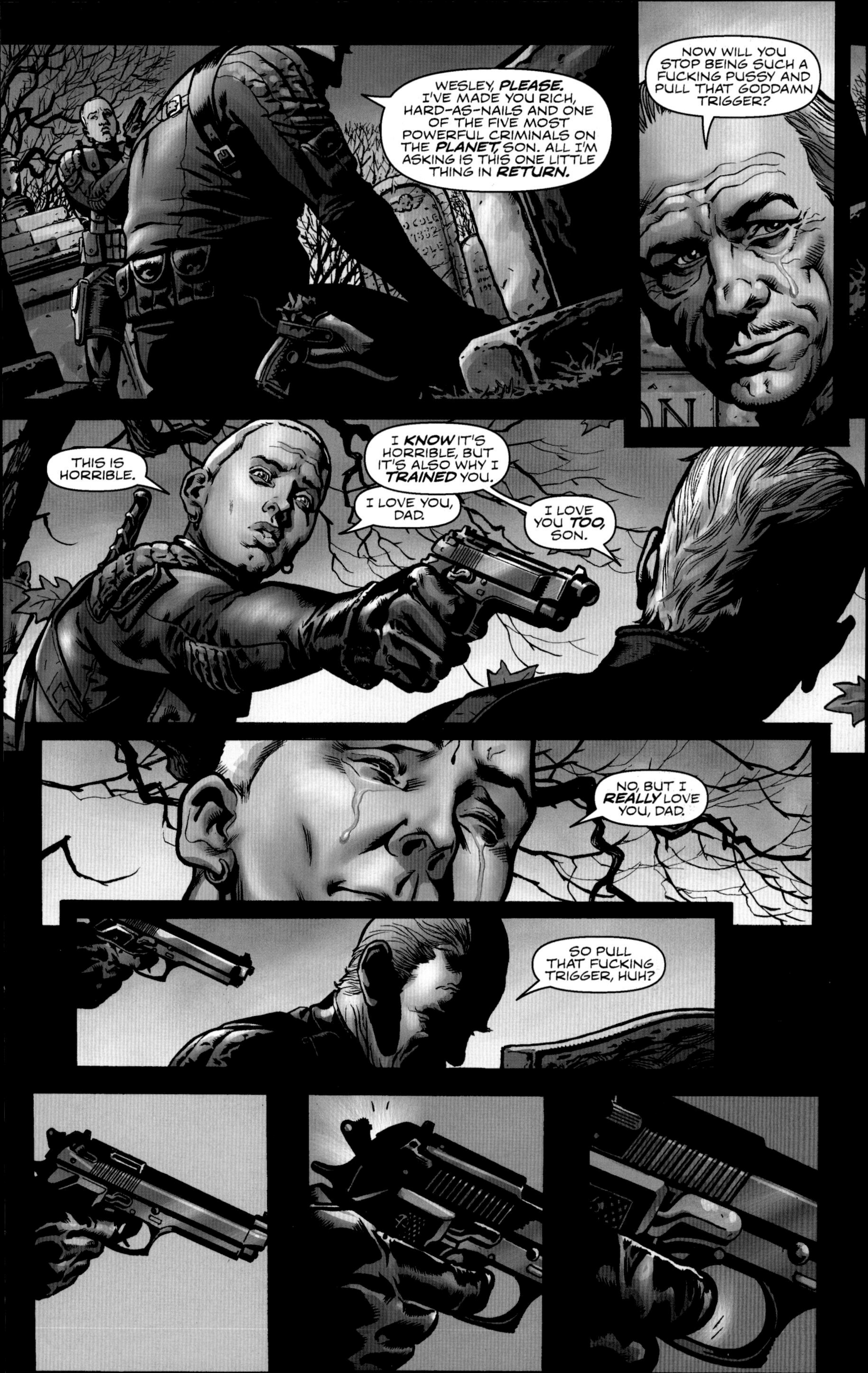
WESLEY, PLEASE. I'VE MADE YOU RICH, HARD-AS-NAILS AND ONE OF THE FIVE MOST POWERFUL CRIMINALS ON THE PLANET, SON. ALL I'M ASKING IS THIS ONE LITTLE THING IN RETURN.
NOW WILL YOU STOP BEING SUCH A FUCKING PUSSY AND PULL THAT GODDAMN TRIGGER?
THIS IS HORRIBLE.
I KNOW IT'S HORRIBLE, BUT IT'S ALSO WHY I TRAINED YOU.
I LOVE YOU, DAD.
I LOVE YOU TOO, SON.
NO, BUT I REALLY LOVE YOU, DAD.
SO PULL THAT FUCKING TRIGGER, HUH?

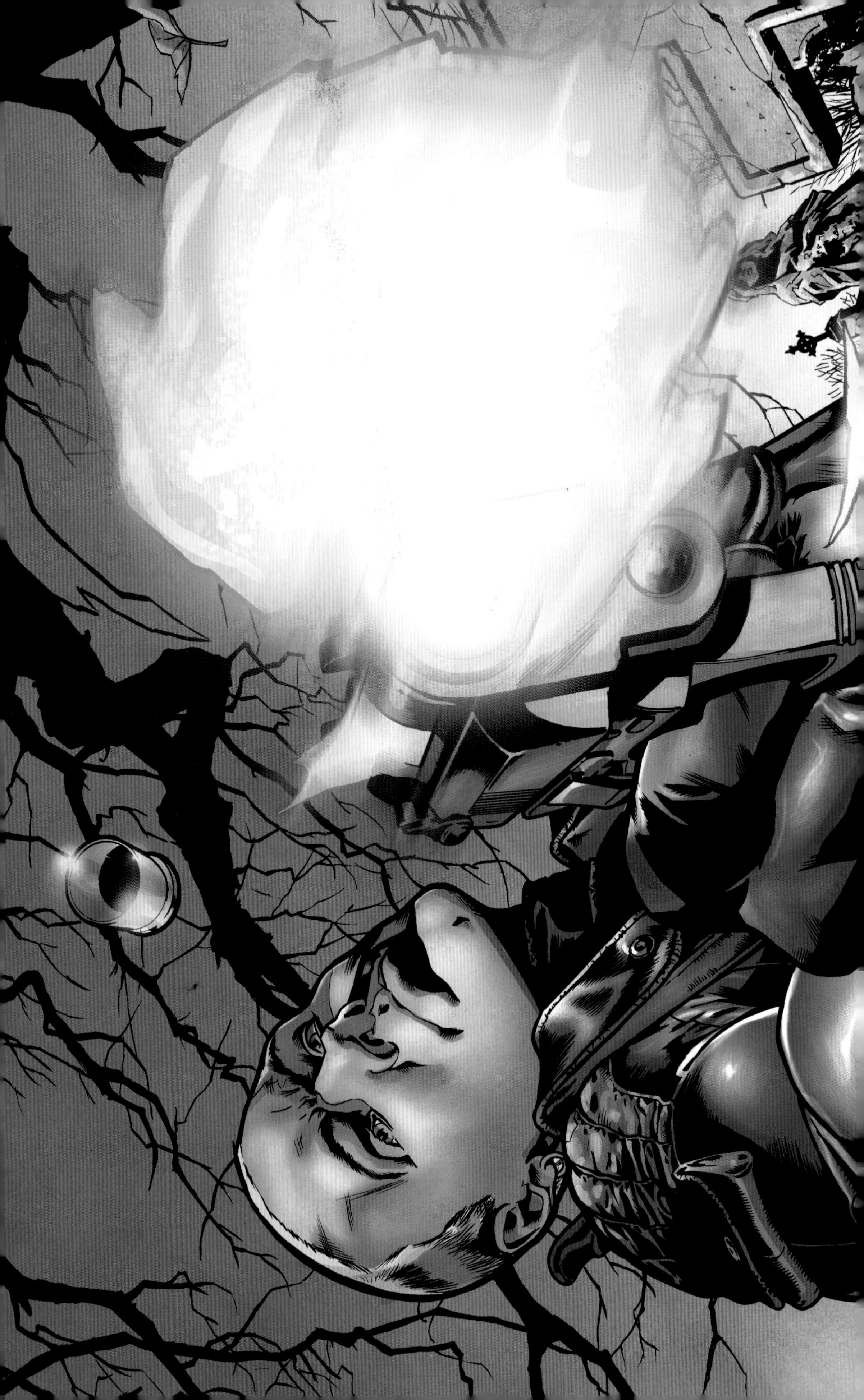

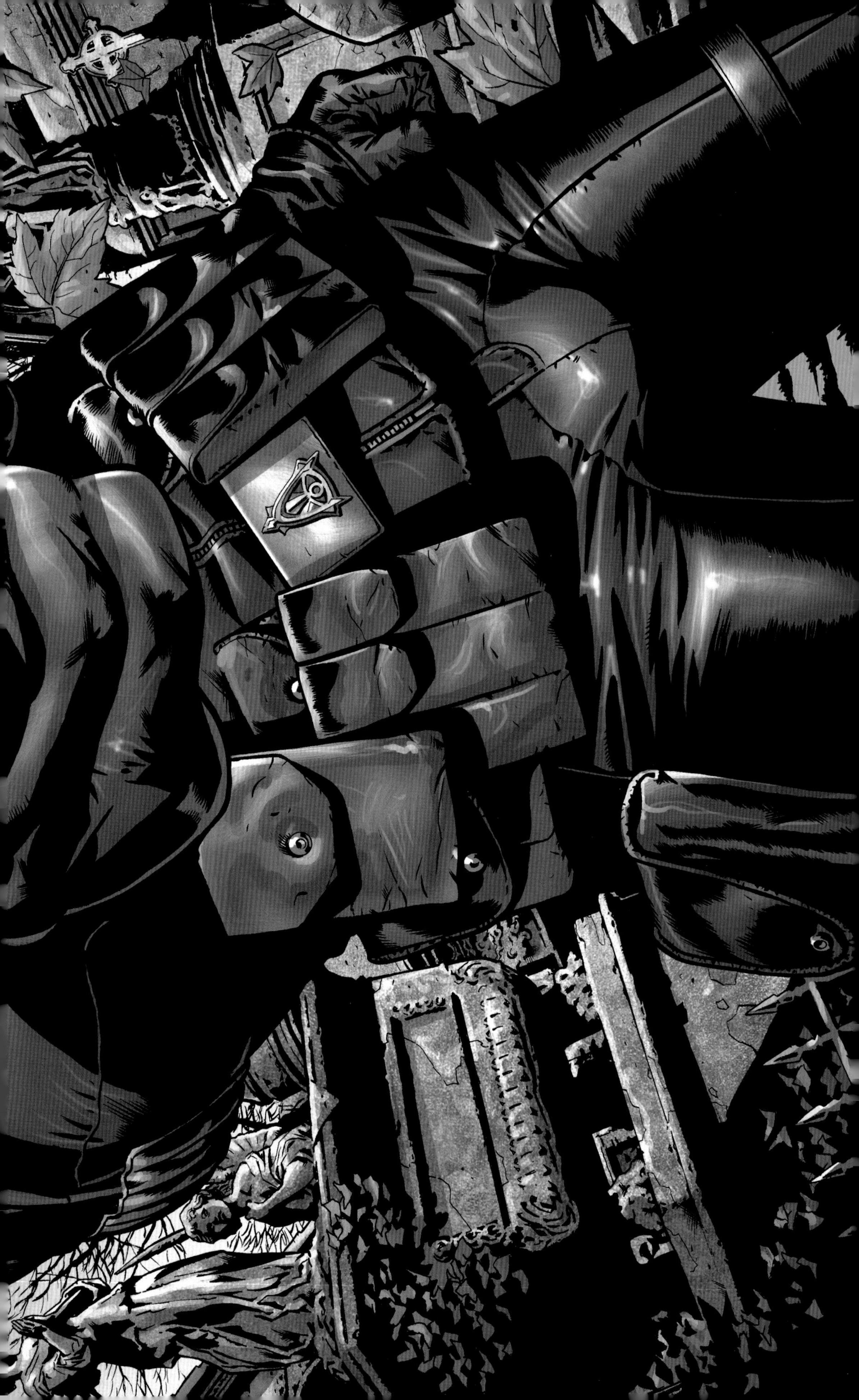

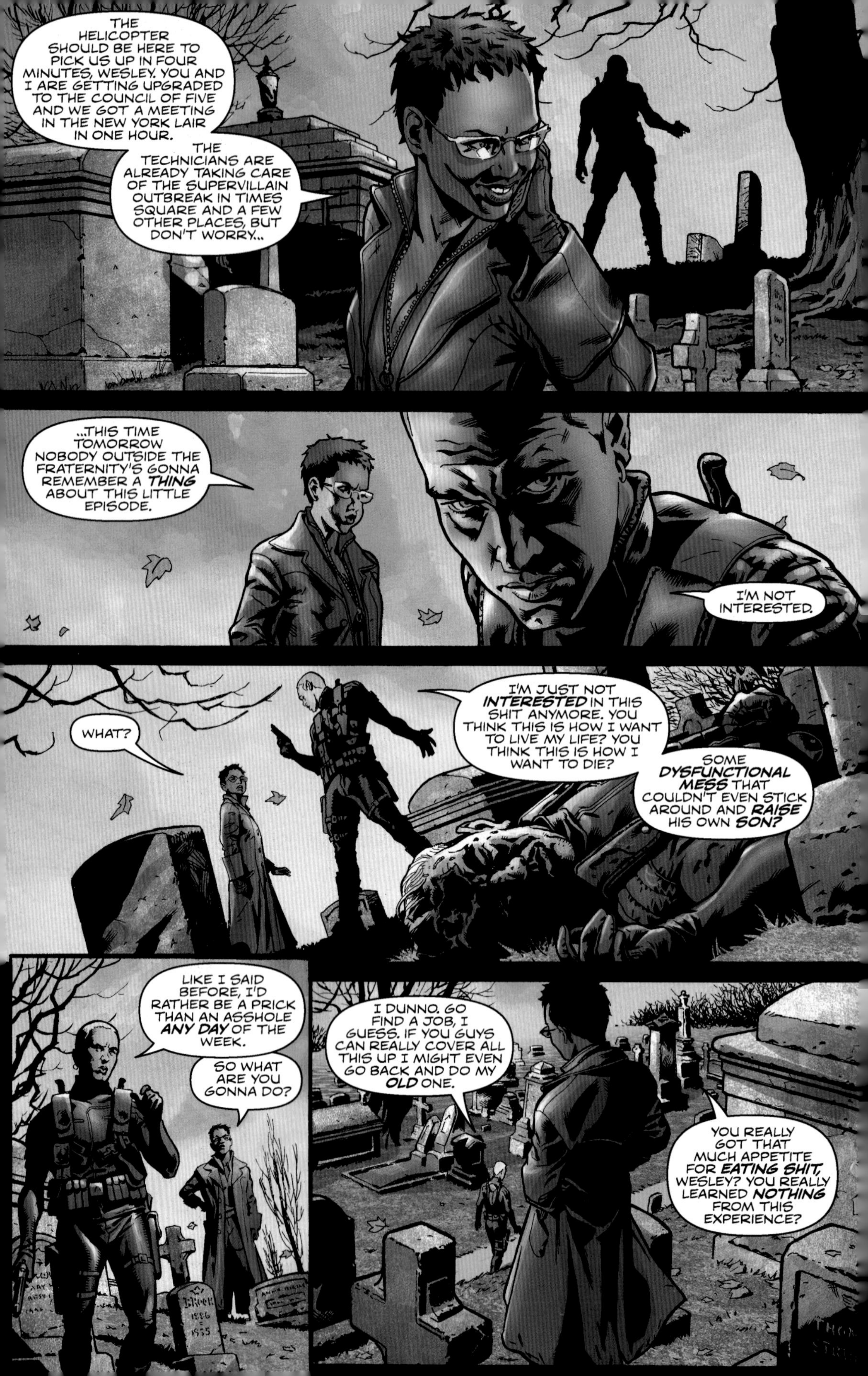
THE HELICOPTER SHOULD BE HERE TO PICK US UP IN FOUR MINUTES, WESLEY. YOU AND I ARE GETTING UPGRADED TO THE COUNCIL OF FIVE AND WE GOT A MEETING IN THE NEW YORK LAIR IN ONE HOUR.
THE TECHNICIANS ARE ALREADY TAKING CARE OF THE SUPERVILLAIN OUTBREAK IN TIMES SQUARE AND A FEW OTHER PLACES, BUT DON'T WORRY...
...THIS TIME TOMORROW NOBODY OUTSIDE THE FRATERNITY'S GONNA REMEMBER A THING ABOUT THIS LITTLE EPISODE.
I'M NOT INTERESTED.
WHAT?
I'M JUST NOT INTERESTED IN THIS SHIT ANYMORE. YOU THINK THIS IS HOW I WANT TO LIVE MY LIFE? YOU THINK THIS IS HOW I WANT TO DIE?
SOME DYSFUNCTIONAL MESS THAT COULDN'T EVEN STICK AROUND AND RAISE HIS OWN SON?
LIKE I SAID BEFORE, I'D RATHER BE A PRICK THAN AN ASSHOLE ANY DAY OF THE WEEK.
SO WHAT ARE YOU GONNA DO?
I DUNNO. GO FIND A JOB, I GUESS. IF YOU GUYS CAN REALLY COVER ALL THIS UP I MIGHT EVEN GO BACK AND DO MY OLD ONE.
YOU REALLY GOT THAT MUCH APPETITE FOR EATING SHIT, WESLEY? YOU REALLY LEARNED NOTHING FROM THIS EXPERIENCE?

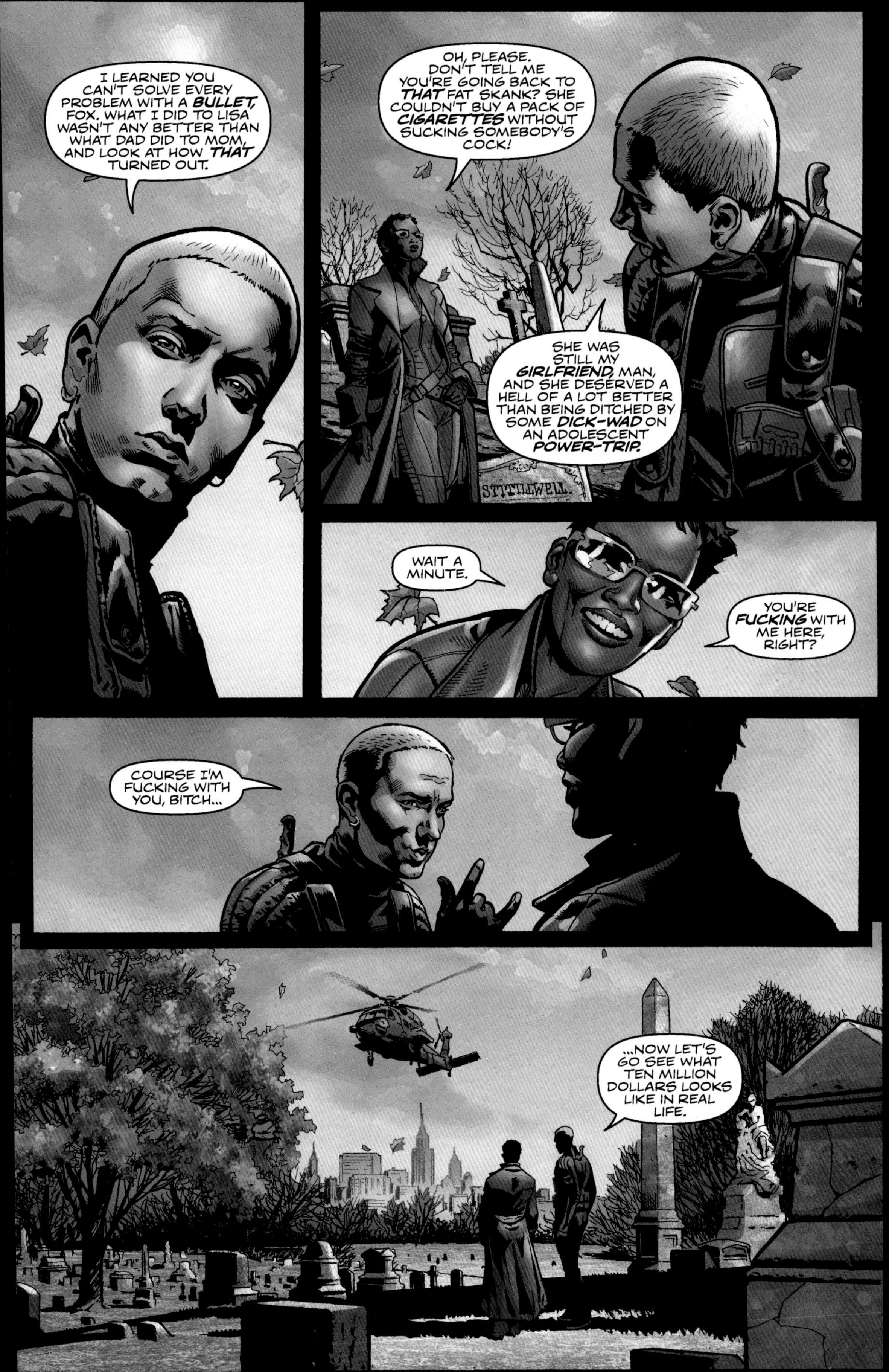
I LEARNED YOU CAN'T SOLVE EVERY PROBLEM WITH A BULLET, FOX. WHAT I DID TO LISA WASN'T ANY BETTER THAN WHAT DAD DID TO MOM, AND LOOK AT HOW THAT TURNED OUT.
OH, PLEASE. DON'T TELL ME YOU'RE GOING BACK TO THAT FAT SKANK? SHE COULDN'T BUY A PACK OF CIGARETTES WITHOUT SUCKING SOMEBODY'S COCK!
SHE WAS STILL MY GIRLFRIEND, MAN, AND SHE DESERVED A HELL OF A LOT BETTER THAN BEING DITCHED BY SOME DICK-WAD ON AN ADOLESCENT POWER-TRIP.
WAIT A MINUTE.
YOU'RE FUCKING WITH ME HERE, RIGHT?
COURSE I'M FUCKING WITH YOU, BITCH...
...NOW LET'S GO SEE WHAT TEN MILLION DOLLARS LOOKS LIKE IN REAL LIFE.

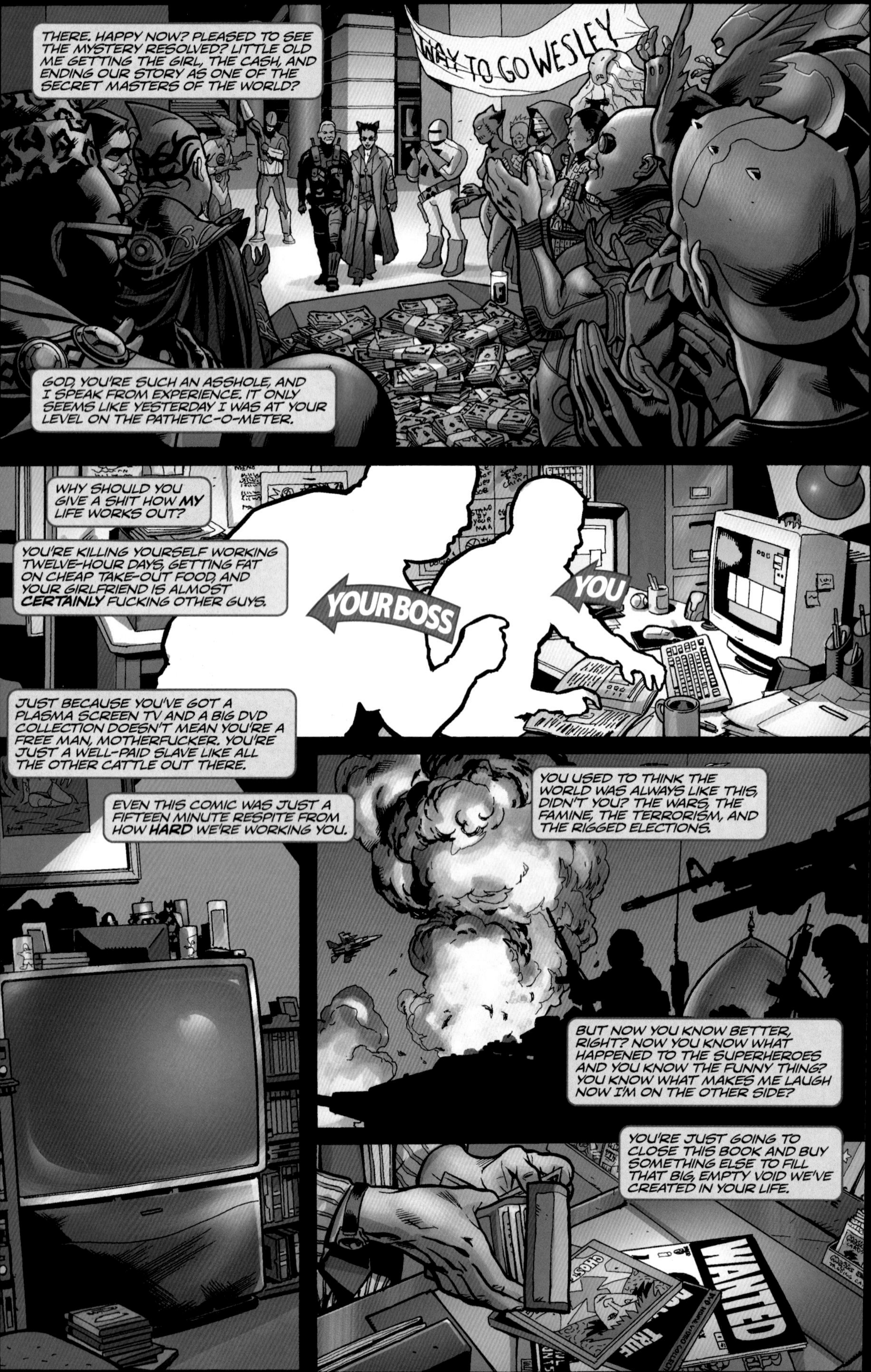
THERE. HAPPY NOW? PLEASED TO SEE THE MYSTERY RESOLVED? LITTLE OLD ME GETTING THE GIRL, THE CASH, AND ENDING OUR STORY AS ONE OF THE SECRET MASTERS OF THE WORLD?
WAY TO GO WESLEY
GOD, YOU'RE SUCH AN ASSHOLE, AND I SPEAK FROM EXPERIENCE. IT ONLY SEEMS LIKE YESTERDAY I WAS AT YOUR LEVEL ON THE PATHETIC-O-METER.
WHY SHOULD YOU GIVE A SHIT HOW MY LIFE WORKS OUT?
YOU'RE KILLING YOURSELF WORKING TWELVE-HOUR DAYS, GETTING FAT ON CHEAP TAKE-OUT FOOD, AND YOUR GIRLFRIEND IS ALMOST CERTAINLY FUCKING OTHER GUYS.
YOUR BOSS
YOU
JUST BECAUSE YOU'VE GOT A PLASMA SCREEN TV AND A BIG DVD COLLECTION DOESN'T MEAN YOU'RE A FREE MAN, MOTHERFUCKER. YOU'RE JUST A WELL-PAID SLAVE LIKE ALL THE OTHER CATTLE OUT THERE.
EVEN THIS COMIC WAS JUST A FIFTEEN MINUTE RESPITE FROM HOW HARD WE'RE WORKING YOU.
YOU USED TO THINK THE WORLD WAS ALWAYS LIKE THIS, DIDN'T YOU? THE WARS, THE FAMINE, THE TERRORISM, AND THE RIGGED ELECTIONS.
BUT NOW YOU KNOW BETTER, RIGHT? NOW YOU KNOW WHAT HAPPENED TO THE SUPERHEROES AND YOU KNOW THE FUNNY THING? YOU KNOW WHAT MAKES ME LAUGH NOW I'M ON THE OTHER SIDE?
YOU'RE JUST GOING TO CLOSE THIS BOOK AND BUY SOMETHING ELSE TO FILL THAT BIG, EMPTY VOID WE'VE CREATED IN YOUR LIFE.
WANTED

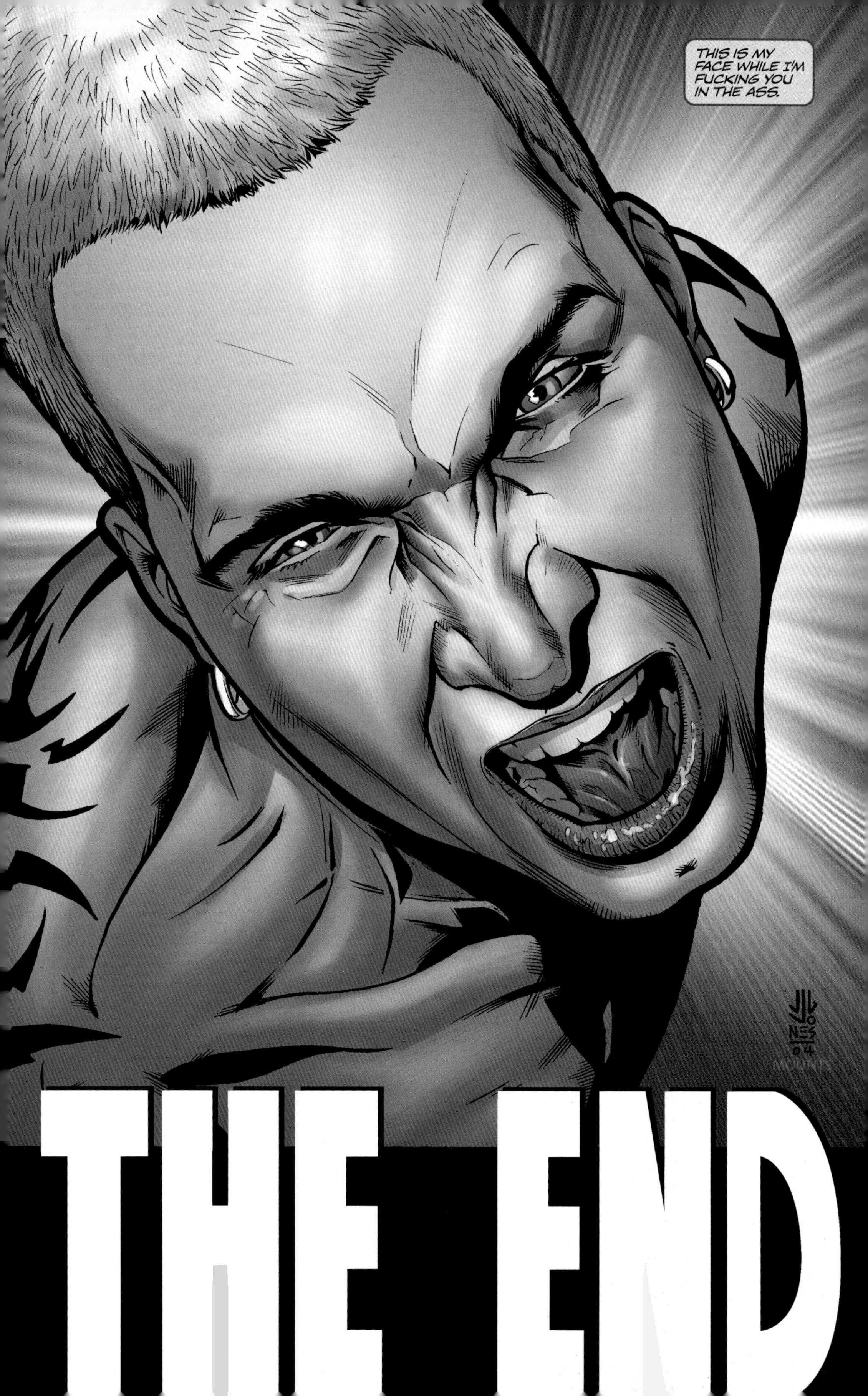
THIS IS MY FACE WHILE I'M FUCKING YOU IN THE ASS.
THE END

In some ways Wanted was the first thing I ever wrote.

I'm sitting here typing these words at the age of thirty-four, but the idea first came to me almost thirty years ago when one of my brothers pulled a great, big scam and outwitted their tiny sibling. Bear in mind that I was maybe five years old at the time and the brother in question was already halfway through a microbiology degree at university and you'll have some insight into my traumatic and often painful childhood. Anyway, here's how it happened.

When I was in what you people probably refer to as first grade, my classroom had a little library at the back where we could all sit and read some books once we'd finished our work for the day. I picked up a hardback with an image of the statue of liberty on the cover, sounded out the word "America" and thought it seemed extremely cool. When you're living in the ass-end of nowhere in one of the poorest countries in Western Europe (i.e. Scotland), America really does sound very cool indeed and thus I was drawn to all those images of hot dogs, Mount Rushmore and Jimmy Carter inside. I can remember the book in incredible detail because it all seemed so bright and glitzy and expensive compared to the low-budget, Braveheart-meets-Trainspotting kind of life going on outside and that was BEFORE I even saw that picture of the real-life Superman standing there with a gangster pointing a gun at his chest.

This wasn't a comic. This wasn't Superman as channeled by Curt Swan and Tex Blaisdell with dialogue by Cary Bates and Curt Swan. This was the real thing. I looked at the picture and read the caption over and over again and all it said was "Superman: The Great American Hero." To me, this was as big and as life changing as Moses getting a call from that burning bush when he was on the way to Wherever-The-Hell in the desert (comics always seemed much more interesting than the Old Testament). This was Superman and he was as real as Jimmy Carter, Mount Rushmore or any of those hot dogs. Just as I was starting to have my doubts about Santa Claus, here was a whole new preposterous character to think about and I couldn't bear to part with this crappy book. I wanted to tell the world what I'd found and so I did something I've never done before or since; I slipped it into my bag and sneaked it home to pore over the picture at some considerable length.

An important thing to realize is that we didn't have cable TV in the UK back in those days. We had a mere three channels and,

quite interestingly, one of the lowest obesity rates in the western world (think there might be a connection, fan-boy?). We paid a LICENSE for our television sets every year and the notion of paying money for re-runs was decidedly un-British. Sure, Superman appeared here in the late fifties when it first aired in the States, but it had never been shown again after cancellation and I didn't even know the show had existed. George Reeves was as unknown to me as Linda Lovelace when I was six years old. When I saw this picture of that middle-aged, slightly dumpy-looking Superman standing there it was Curt Swan's art incarnate. This was Superman and the one thing I dearly wanted to know was what the fuck had happened to him.

I can remember the scene with absolute clarity. I was sitting in my shared bedroom (there were eight of us in the house) re-reading the book again and again by the glow from by two-bar electric fire and I asked my brother Bobby what had happened to Superman. Why were there plane crashes on the news? Why were there earthquakes? Why didn't Superman help people in real life like he did in the comics if he was this great American hero? Bobby grinned the same grin he pulled when he told me my Dad killed Hitler during the war, that he could read my mind and that I'd inherit superhuman powers on my seventh birthday. "What happened to Superman? Didn't you hear?" he asked. "Superman disappeared during a big war with all the super-villains. Superman, Batman, Spider-Man, Captain America; they all disappeared during this enormous battle and they've never been seen again."

Gutted, I sloped off to bed. The greatest man in human history was gone forever and, with him, my hopes of becoming some kind of wisecracking boy sidekick. All my training had been for nothing. Superman was dead, the other heroes were dead and, as Bobby explained, the villains had made us forget they even existed. All we had in their place were comic books. Crude, four-color approximations of their adventures by stoned, slightly crazy misfits who could somehow half-remember their adventures and get them down on the printed page. But who even read comics anymore? And what happened to the villains?

Read on.

Mark Millar,
18th March 2004
The Ass-End of nowhere
Excerpted from the WANTED: Dossier May 2004

AFTER

WANTED: DOSSIER

The **WANTED: Dossier** was a printed supplement to the **WANTED** Series. In it, the heroes and villains of Wesley Gibson's world were illustrated by some of comics' brightest stars. The following characters were illustrated by the artists listed below, turn the page to see their unique visions of Mark Millar's characters from **WANTED**.

THE KILLER
Pencils: **John Romita Jr.**
Inks: **Scott Hanna**
Colors: **Paul Mounts**

FOX
Pencils: **Marc Silvestri**
Inks: **Joe Weems V**
Colors: **Steve Firchow**

PROFESSOR SOLOMON SELTZER
Pencils, inks and colors:
Dave Johnson

ORIGINAL KILLER
Pencils and Inks: **Tim Bradstreet**
Colors: **Paul Mounts**

THE COUNCIL OF FIVE
Pencils, inks and tones: **Ashley Wood**
Colors: **Paul Mounts**

THE HEROES
Pencils, inks and colors:
Ty Templeton

DOLL-MASTER
Pencils and inks: **Brian Michael Bendis**
Colors: **Paul Mounts**

IMP and DEADLY NIGHTSHADE
Pencils, inks and colors:
Chris Bachalo

SHIT-HEAD
Pencils and inks: **Bill Sienkiewicz**
Colors: **Paul Mounts**

FUCKWIT
Pencils and Inks: **Frank Quitely**
Colors: **Paul Mounts**

SUCKER
Pencils: **Joe Quesada**
Inks: **Mark Millar**
Colors: **Paul Mounts**

MISTER RICTUS
Pencils and inks: **Jae Lee**
Colors: **June Chung**

The Killer

Wesley Gibson's life spun out of control one deadly day in a wash of blood and a hail of gunfire. Or did it finally spin into control?

Gibson had been leading the life of quiet desperation—boring girlfriend, dead-end job, surfing for Internet porn on a daily basis. But when the Fox plucked him out of his humdrum existence, she showed him possibilities unimagined: He was The Killer, heir to a vast fortune and superpowers he didn't even know he had.

The scales finally dropped from Wesley Gibson's eyes, and he saw the hidden clockwork of the real power behind the throne. A vast supervillain Fraternity was running the world, and had been since 1986, when they teamed up to destroy all the superheroes.

Wesley was taken under the wing of The Fox and Professor Solomon Seltzer, and embraced his life as the new Killer. He could steal, kill, or fuck whoever he wanted, all without repercussion. He was born again, baptized in blood and fire, as The Killer.

Pencils: John Romita Jr.
Inks: Scott Hanna
Colors: Paul Mounts

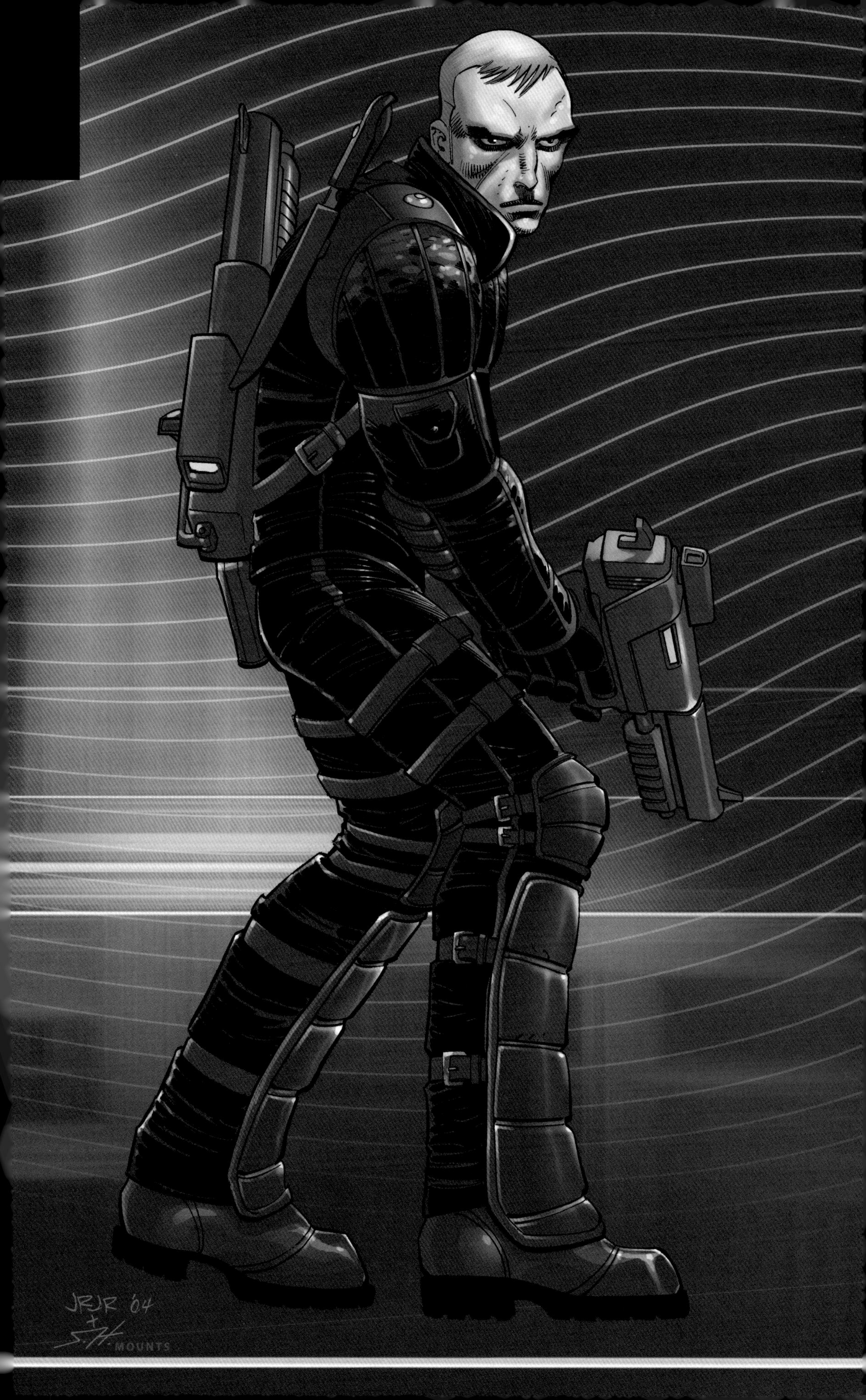
JRJR '04
+
MOUNTS

FOX

She shoots from the hip—and what hips they are.

The woman who would become The Fox grew up poor, in the kind of neighborhood where the only ways up and out are sports, hip-hop, or crime.

Guess what? She can't rap and she can't dunk a basketball.

The Fox used her natural gifts of agility and strength, and combined them with a crass disdain of humanity to become one of the deadliest killers the world has ever seen. She kills, because she does not care. Stopping someone else's breathing is as natural as breathing to her.

The Fox has never forgotten where she came from. She may lack formal education, but she has street smarts in spades—and she knows how to hitch her wagon to the right star. She unleashed her insatiable appetite for sex on the original Killer, becoming his consort, and cementing her position in the supervillain Fraternity. When The Killer died, she turned her vulva on his son—Wesley Gibson, the new Killer.

What's she want? Money? Sex? Power? All of the above. And Wesley Gibson just might be nothing more than the latest tool in her arsenal.

Pencils: Marc Silvestri
Inks: Joe Weems V
Colors: Steve Firchow

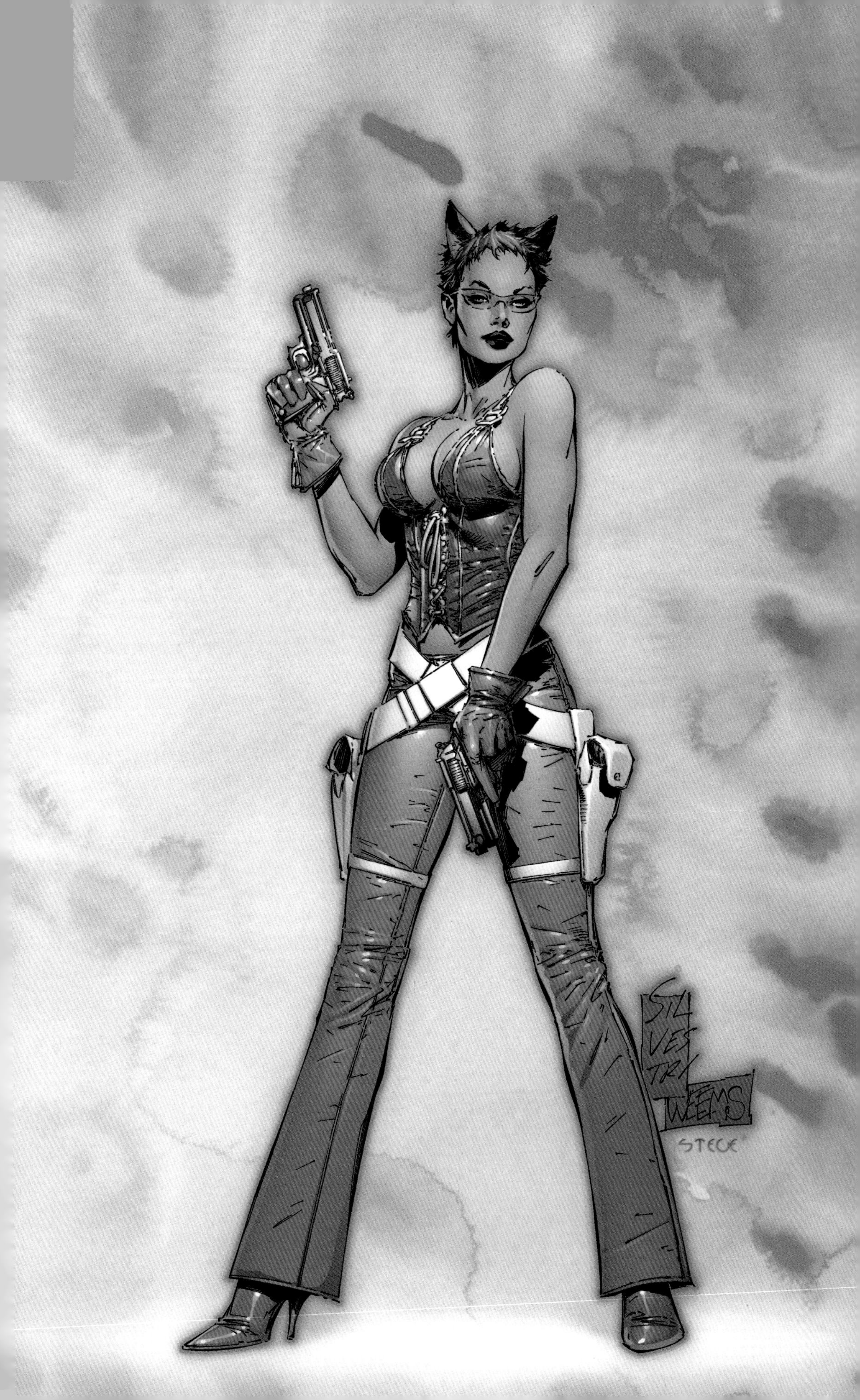

Professor Solomon Seltzer

Professor Solomon Seltzer is a schemer who maps the human soul...and fucks 18-year-old prostitutes.

He started talking when he was still in the womb, was reading and solving math problems before he could walk, and had graduated *magna cum laude* with a bio-mechanics degree before his friends had reached kindergarten.

The Professor is the smartest man who's ever lived, a billionaire by ten years old. Rumor has it—and there's not much doubt—that this Level Nine intelligence put together the plan to vanquish all the superheroes in 1986. The villainous Mister Rictus likes to take credit for that act, but he knows in his blackest of hearts that he can't. Rictus is insanely jealous of The Professor for his vast intelligence, and the two are adversaries of the highest order.

Pencils, inks, and colors: Dave Johnson

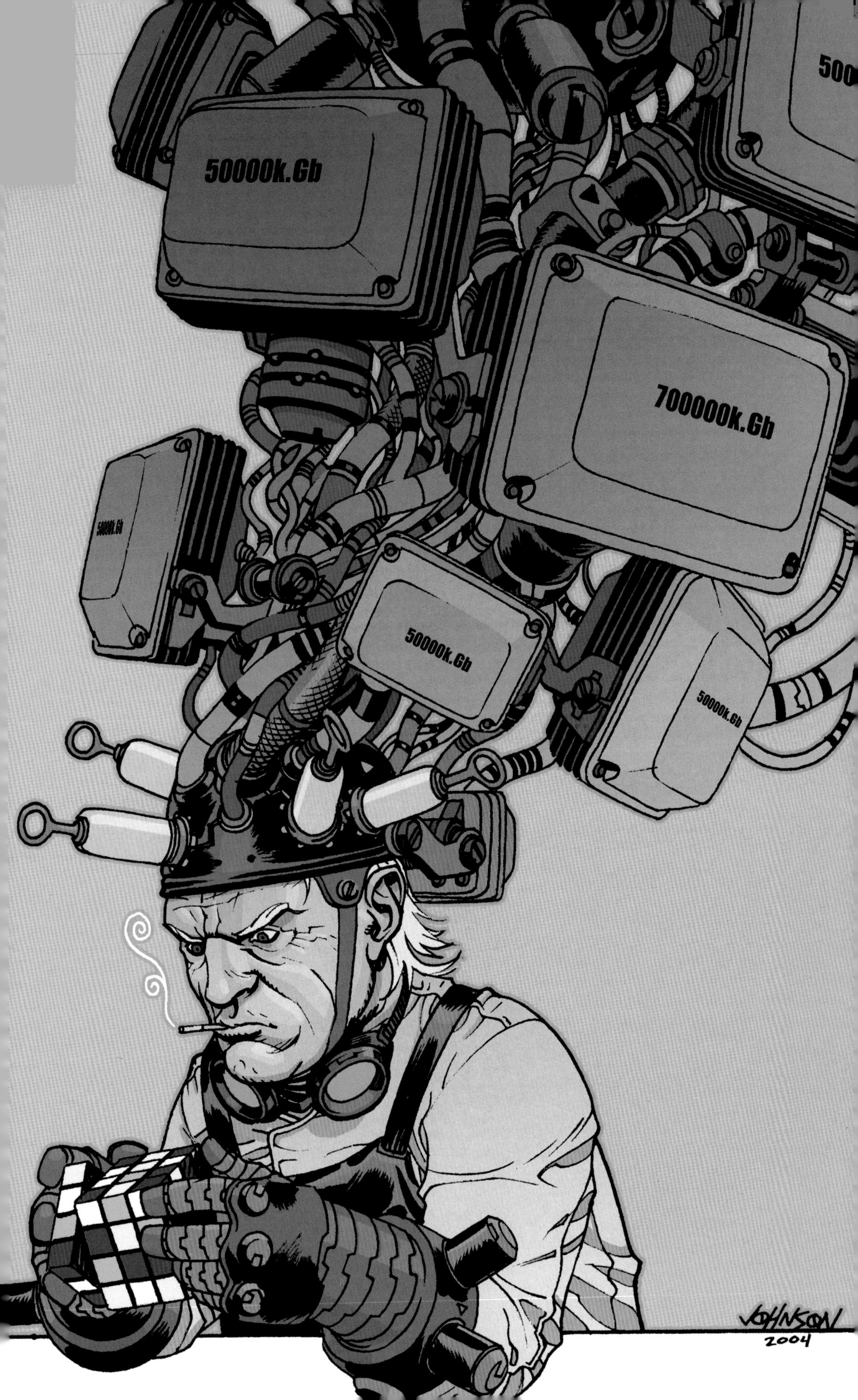
50000k.Gb
700000k.Gb
50000k.Gb
50000k.Gb
JOHNSON
2004

Original Killer

The world's deadliest assassin is dead, the victim of assassination himself. But while he was alive, The Killer lived up to his name—frequently, and without remorse.

The Killer killed for money, for sport, to advance his own cause. He killed for fun. The riches he gained bought him the Epicurean lifestyle he so greatly desired. He bathed in the finest champagne. He devoured the finest caviar. He bedded the finest women—and sometimes, the finest men.

So dangerous a foe was he, that when The Killer met his end, he was shot through the head with a gun from two cities away. No one would dare get closer. But The Killer passed on his legacy—and his unerring aim and killer instinct—to his illegitimate son, Wesley Gibson.

Pencils and inks: Tim Bradstreet
Colors: Paul Mounts

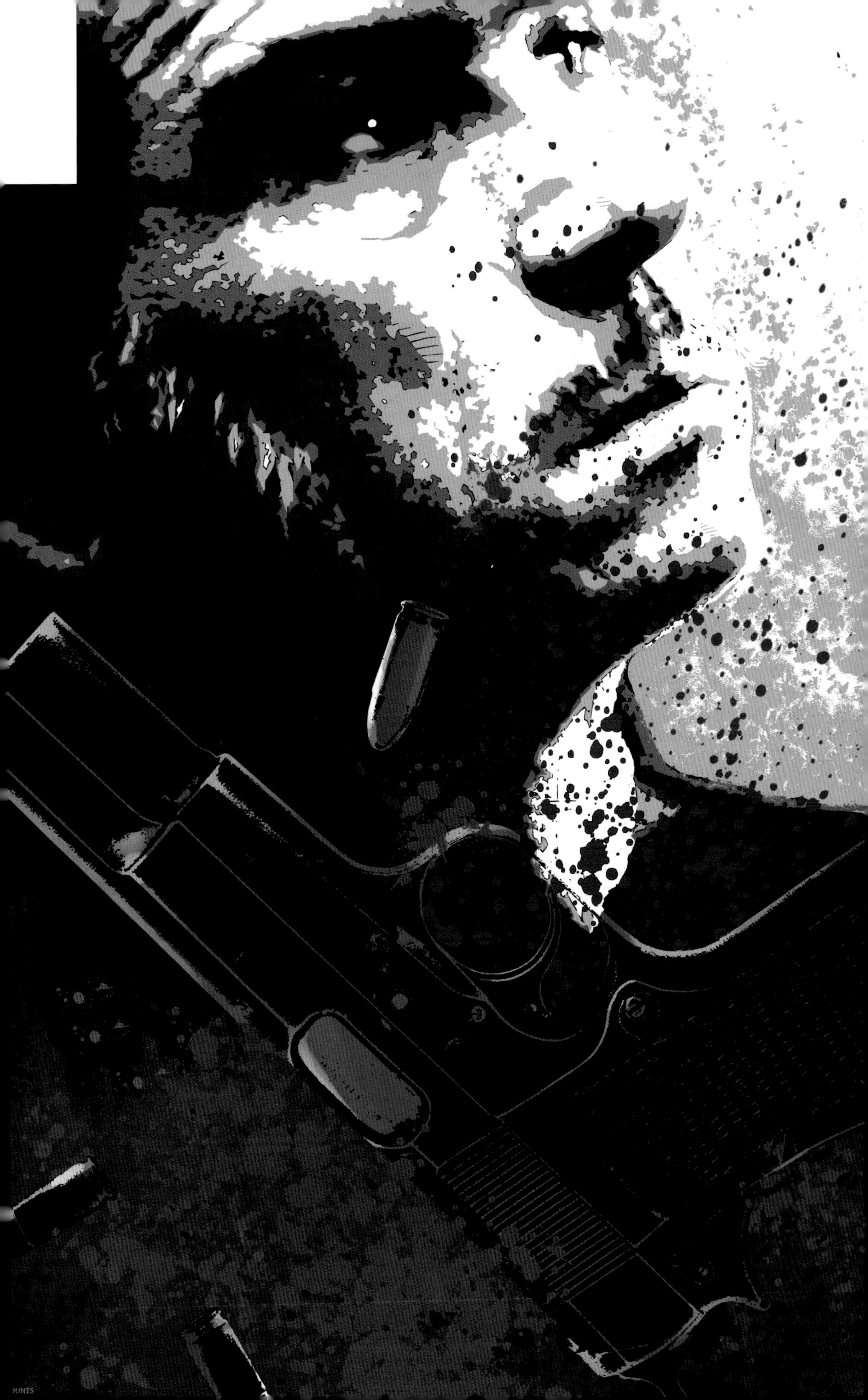

The Council of Five

The Illuminati is real—and God help us, they have superpowers.

When the supervillains finally destroyed all the heroes in 1986, they carved the world up five ways.

Five "heads" of the supervillain families hold sway over their territories:

• Professor Solomon Seltzer got North and South America

• Adam-One, the world's oldest man, took Africa

• The Future, a savage Nazi bastard, got Europe

• The Emperor, a Chinese crimelord, took control of Asia

• Mister Rictus got stuck with Australia

From behind a veil of secrecy, the Council of Five act as the real clockwork of the world, pulling the strings of global society. Not a legbreaking gets done, not an illegal act takes place, without their knowledge and consent.

But that veil of secrecy has been called into question. The Professor and Adam-One like things to remain behind the scenes—when the underworld stays underground, there's more loot for everyone to divvy up.

The Future and Rictus, on the other hand, tire of remaining in shadow. They want the world to piss its pants when it hears the mere letters in their names.

The Emperor? He's the swing vote, constantly in play. Meetings of the Council of Five have taken on the air of an armed camp. Daggers are drawn, searching for a back to be planted in.

The Illuminati is real—and God help them, they may turn against each other.

Pencils, inks and tones: Ashley Wood
Colors: Paul Mounts

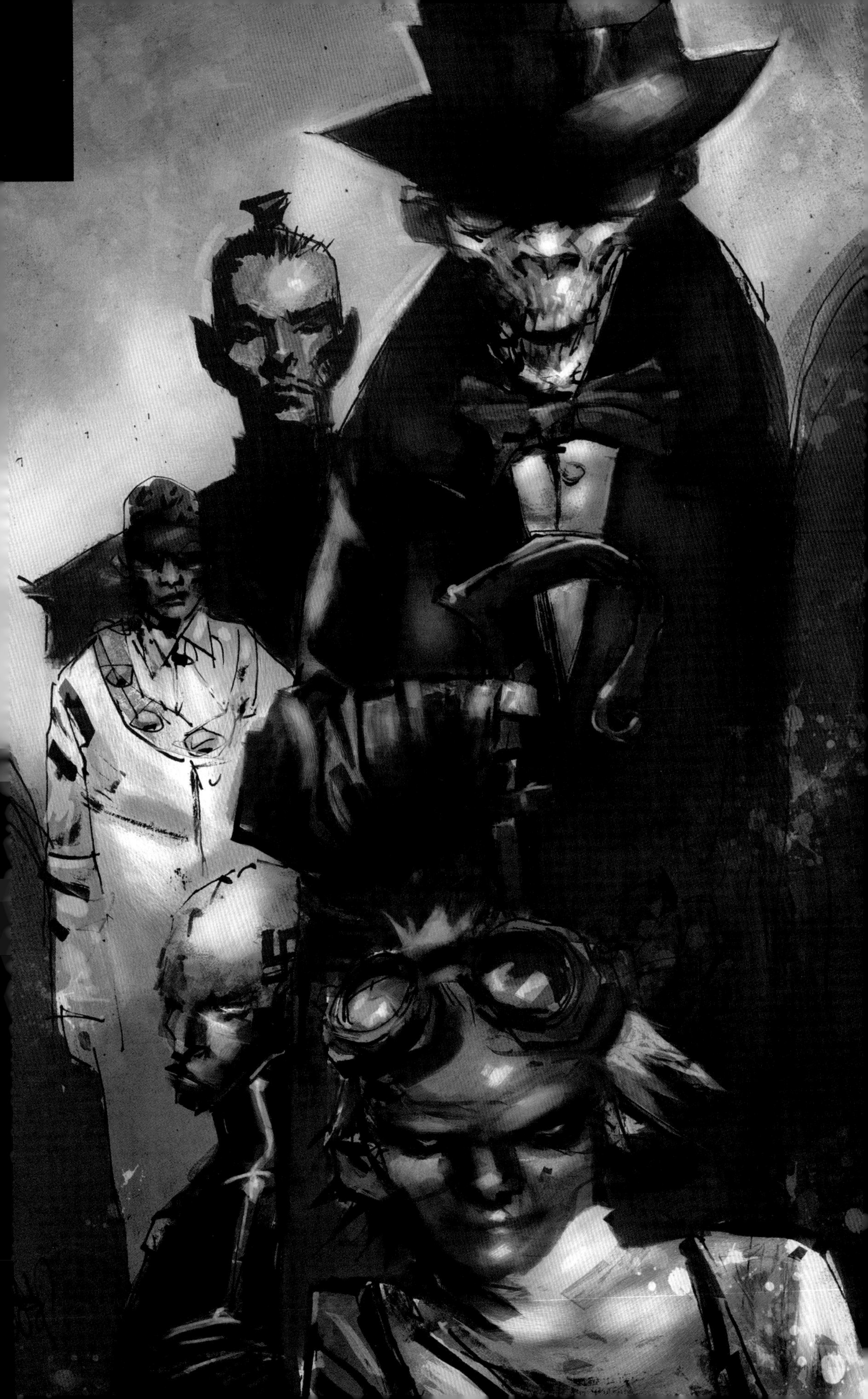

The Heroes

The bad guys won. Led by Professor Solomon Seltzer,
ALL the supervillains finally teamed up and destroyed
all the superheroes in a cataclysmic battle back in
1986.

But it wasn't enough just to kill them—they had to
destroy them MORE completely. Reality was folded
and unfolded by the Fraternity's cognoscenti, seven-
dimensional imps, and alien super-computers. All
vestiges that the heroes had ever existed were
destroyed. We were left with a world where humanity,
at best, has vague, Alzheimer's-esque memories of
superheroes. That, and the comic books.

But who reads comic books anymore?

Pencils, inks and colors: Ty Templeton

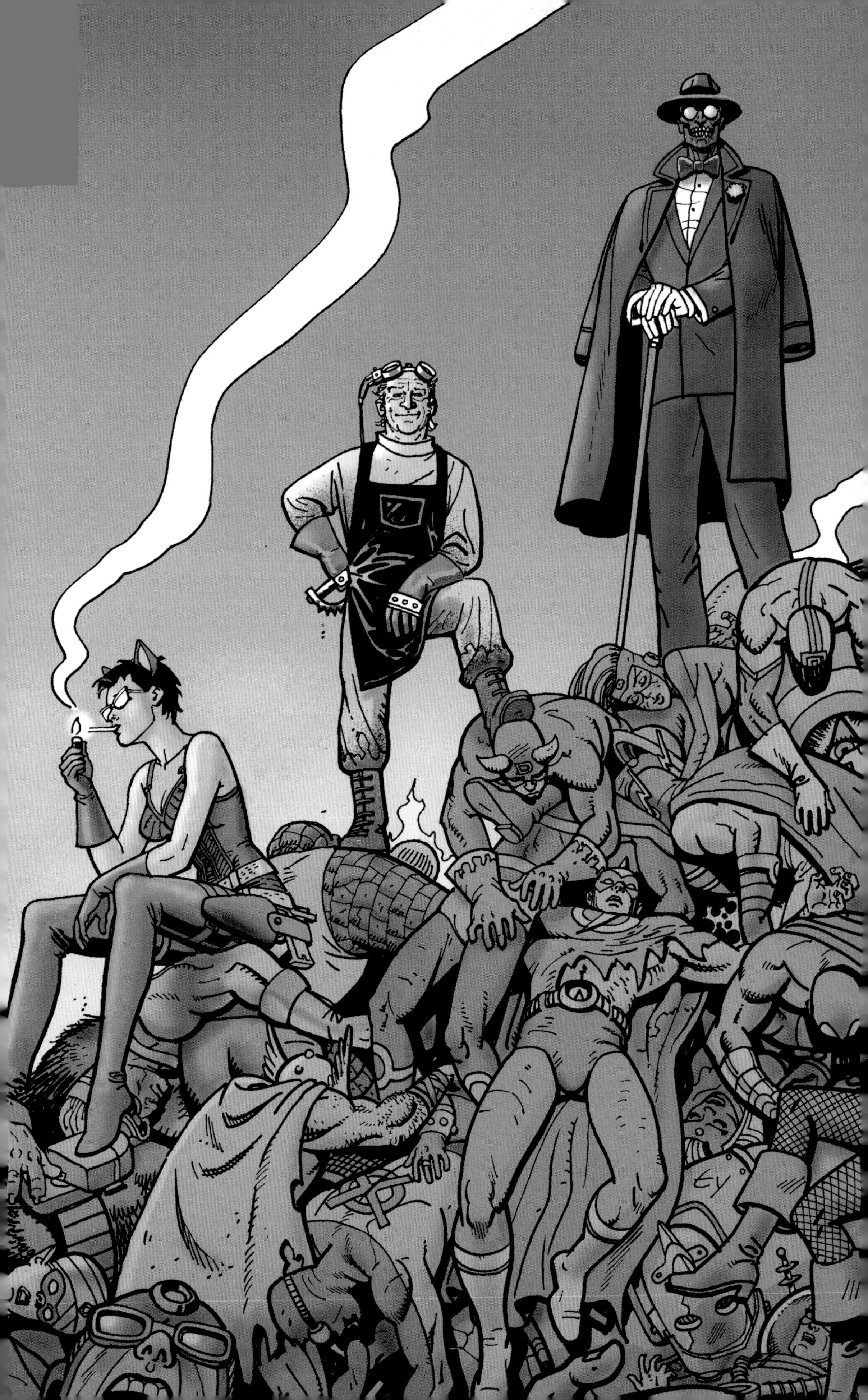

Doll-Master

He has a wife, two beautiful young daughters, a house in the suburbs, and wears a bow tie. He's the most docile, kind-hearted, well-spoken gentleman you're likely to meet. You'd be proud to have him as your neighbor. Too bad he's also one of the most nefarious super-criminals the world has ever seen.

The Doll-Master combines an uncanny knack for micro-mechanics with a Gepetto-like love for his "babies" that's definitely three steps over the line of creepy, and borders on the insane. His smile is halfway between "kindly old uncle" and "pedophile." He is indeed the master of his doll-like automatons...but these babies are killing machines that can rend the flesh from your bones.

He'll order his dolls to fillet a man, but he never swears in front of children. He'll blow up a bank, killing dozens...but always leaves the toilet seat down for his wife. And if so much as a tiny tear appears in his dolls' suits, he'll lovingly stitch it up himself. He is the master of his puppets...but they pull the strings of his heart.

Pencils and inks: Brian Michael Bendis
Colors: Paul Mounts

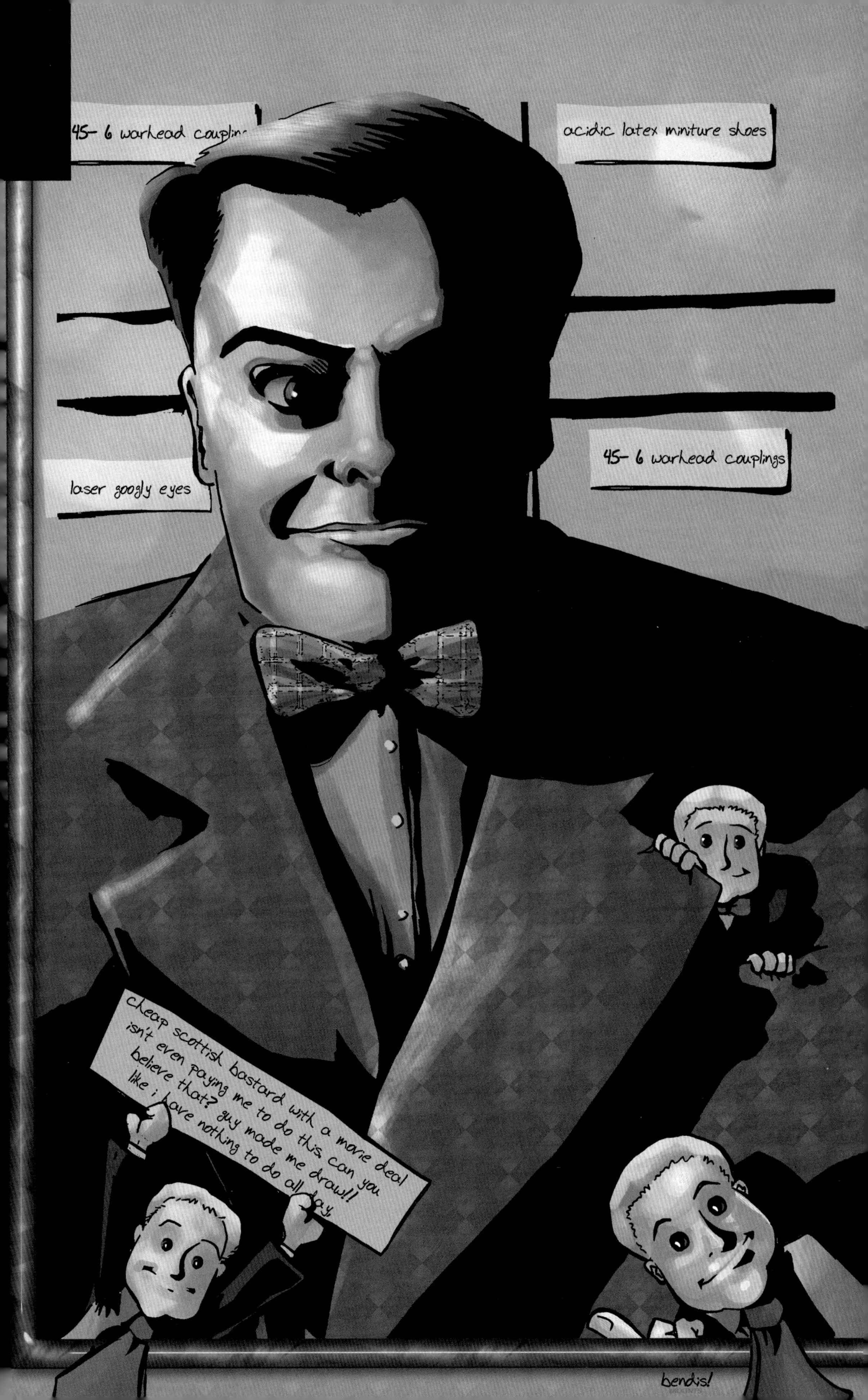

45- 6 warhead couplin
acidic latex miniture shoes
45- 6 warhead couplings
laser googly eyes
cheap scottish bastard with a movie deal isn't even paying me to do this can you believe that? guy made me draw!! like i have nothing to do all day.
bendis!

IMP

The power to fold and unfold reality is in the hands of a child.

Despite the fact that he's thousands of years old, Imp is considered an infant in the seven-dimensional reality from which he hails. He visits us when his parents aren't looking. What we see when we look at him is just the three-dimensional aspect—but there are four more levels you and I can't even dream of.

With his higher consciousness, Imp has the power to shape reality in our dimension as easily as an artist can shape a world with a pencil and eraser. He's limited only by his imagination. In the past, he turned America into a marshmallow-land for 12 hours. He made buildings come alive and slug it out with buildings from other major cities. He turned his greatest super-foe into ice cream on a lark. Part of the Professor's crew, he has been convinced to tone things down a tad when he visits our realm, as he is so powerful, he could accidentally unmake reality.

Deadly Nightshade

She is the deadliest of blossoms. She can envelop you in her petals, and give you the most exquisite of deaths as her pollens fill your lungs, choking the life out of you.

Deadly Nightshade is an assassin in Rictus' crew with a secret. She's so enamored of living on the edge, that she's having an affair with Imp. The cross-camp romance is the most dangerous of games, as tensions between Rictus and the Professor always threaten to boil over. Couple that with the fact that she knows Imp could unmake reality in an orgasm-induced loss of control, and Deadly Nightshade takes all of our lives into her petals every time she slips between the sheets.

Pencils, inks and colors: Chris Bachalo

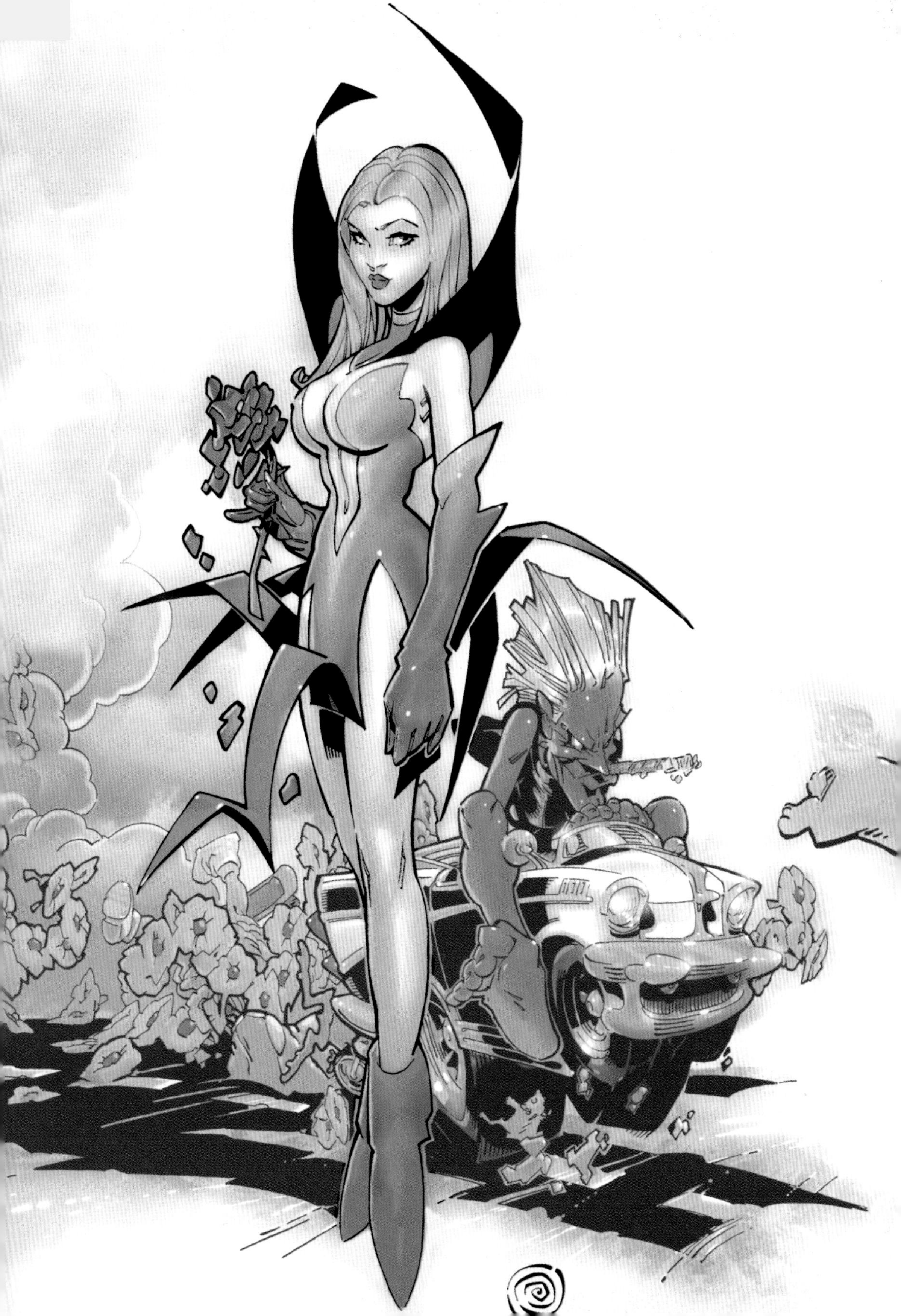

SHIT-HEAD

The collected feces of the 666 most evil beings ever to walk the earth have taken on sentience. There's a little Hitler in there, a touch of Ed Gein, half a pound of Jeffrey Dahmer.

No one knows how this walking, steaming shit-pile came to life. Many say it formed in the world's sewers, the result of a mystic spell, or perhaps science gone horribly awry. Suffice it to say that Shit-Head is part of Mister Rictus' army, perhaps the most vile creature among a horrifically vile crew.

Shit-Head is a mere footsoldier in Rictus' crew, used as muscle. He can make his body diarrhea-soft, bloody constipation-hard, or any consistency in-between. As such, he can pound an enemy with the force of a freight train, then slip away, liquid-smooth, through a sewer grate.

Shit happens. Just pray he never happens to you.

Pencils and inks: Bill Sienkiewicz
Colors: Paul Mounts

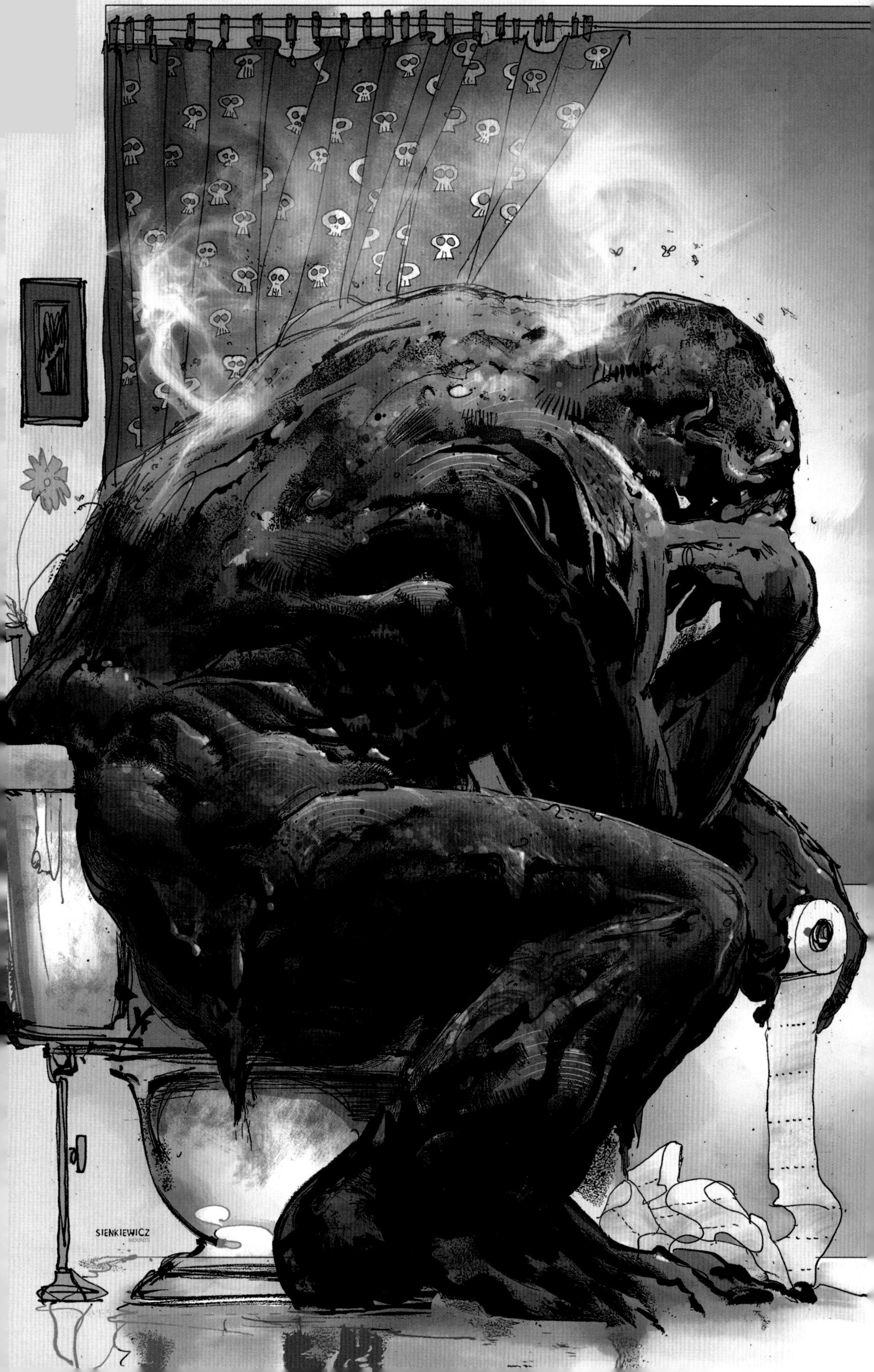
SIENKIEWICZ
MOUNTS

FUCKWIT

Meet the Down's Syndrome copy of the world's (former) greatest hero.

Fuckwit is the product of an experiment to create a superman. Part of the experiment worked: The body is there. The brain...not so much so.

Fuckwit is massively powered, but dumb as a bag of hammers. He is the concept of the child with the gun, writ large. He'll yank your arm off trying to shake your hand, and not even realize he's done anything wrong...or was that right?

Fuckwit has all the endearing qualities of a new puppy—he's friendly, loyal, and loves you unconditionally. Unfortunately, he also has all the toilet training of a new puppy.

What if the most powerful man in the universe had brain damage? He'd be a Fuckwit, now wouldn't he?

Pencils and inks: Frank Quitely
Colors: Paul Mounts

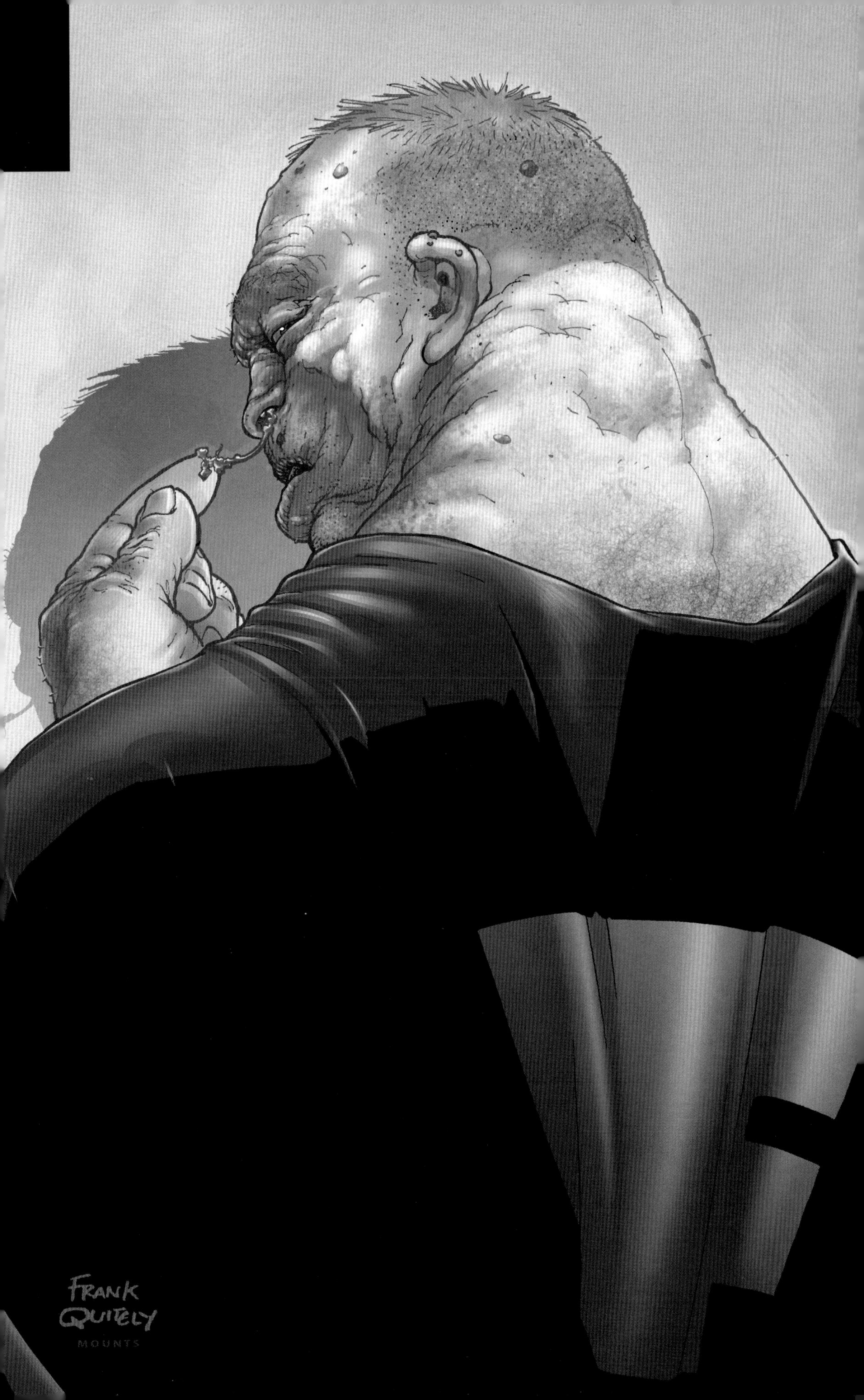
FRANK QUITELY
MOUNTS

SUCKER

Sucker came to Earth thousands of years ago, a parasitical alien organism. He forms a symbiotic bond with a host and, to stay alive, has to feed it with the life-force of other living creatures. The second he stops delivering, the host dies, and Sucker moves on to a new one.

This is especially effective when Sucker drains the life-force of a superpowered being—Sucker has access to the powers himself, and a superpowered pawn to put into play.

Sucker enjoys a good cigar—Cubans, of course. He leaves those like he leaves his parasitical victims—drained, dead, and dusty.

Pencils: Joe Quesada
Inks: Mark Millar
Colors: Paul Mounts

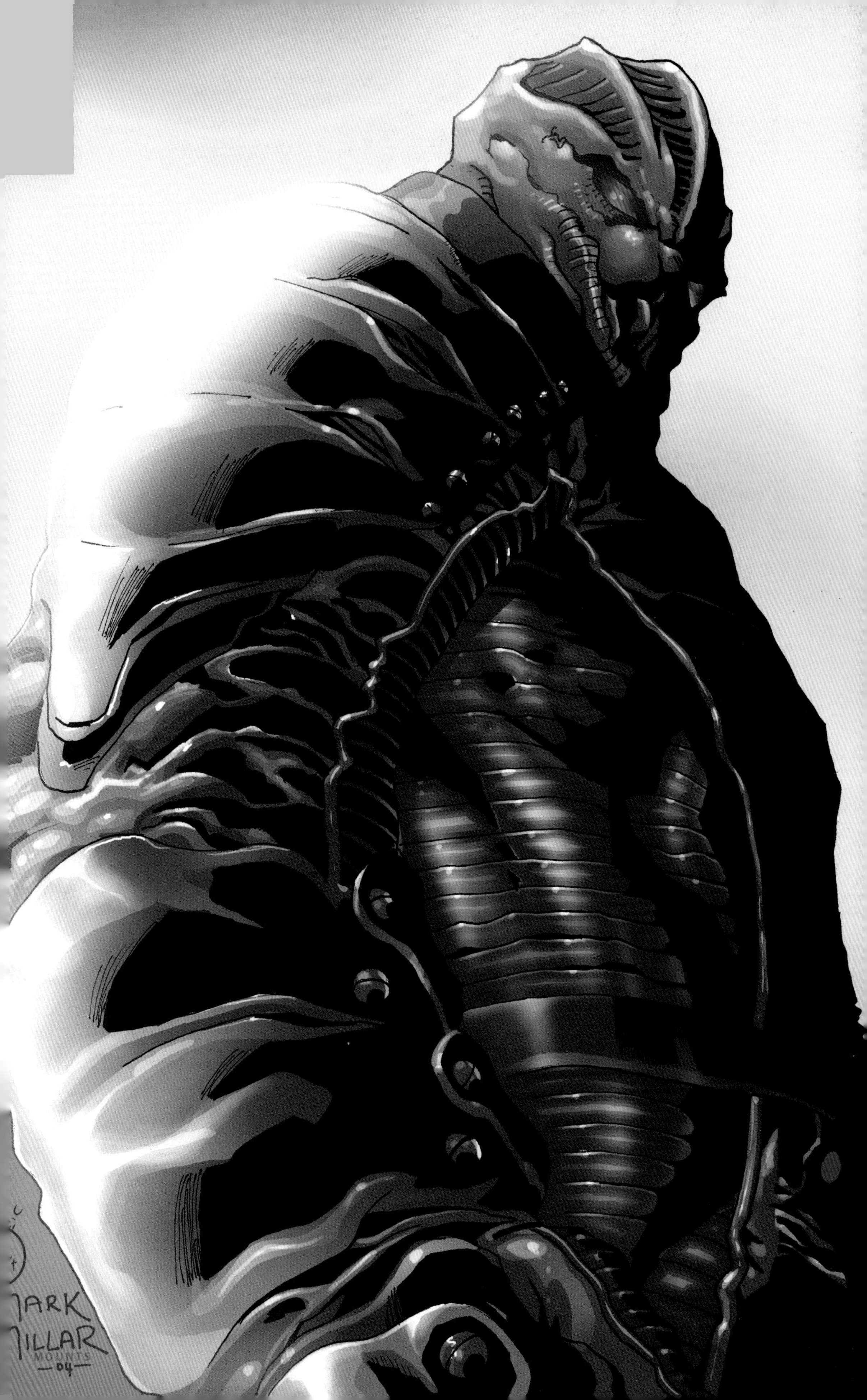
ARK
ILLAR
MOUNTS
—04—

Mister Rictus

Once, he saved souls. Now he damns them.
The man who would become Mister Rictus was once a devout Christian, the most pious of men. But he died briefly on the operating table after a horrible accident. He expected Heaven, but found...
Nothing.
No God. No Heaven. No afterlife. None of what he had been promised for living his devout life. Just a void. And the void left a void in his heart.
The incident created a man without a conscience. Rictus now lives completely without moral compass. He knows there is no eternal consequence to his action. He lives for the day, and that is all.
Rictus does everything you've ever thought about in your darkest moments. Every whim he comes up with, he caters to. And his whims tend toward the dark end of the spectrum.
If he wants to eat, fuck, or kill something, he does it, without thought. He is the creature of pure id. Rictus spent years embracing the light, a light that was never there. Now, there is only darkness.

Pencils and inks: Jae Lee
Colors: June Chung

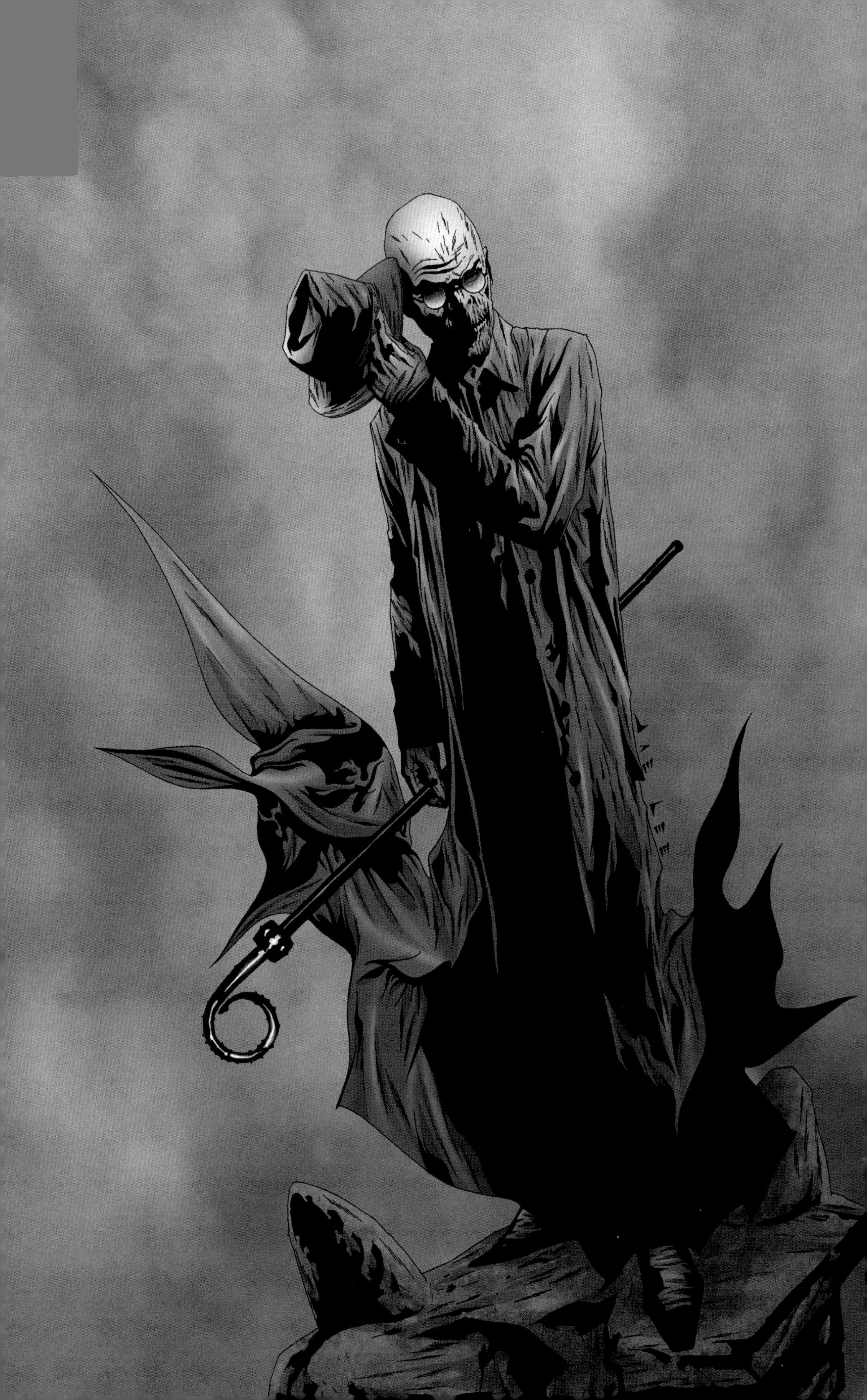

COVER GALLERY

“Now get in the car while I still got this Little Miss Patient smile on my face, asshole!”

—THE FOX

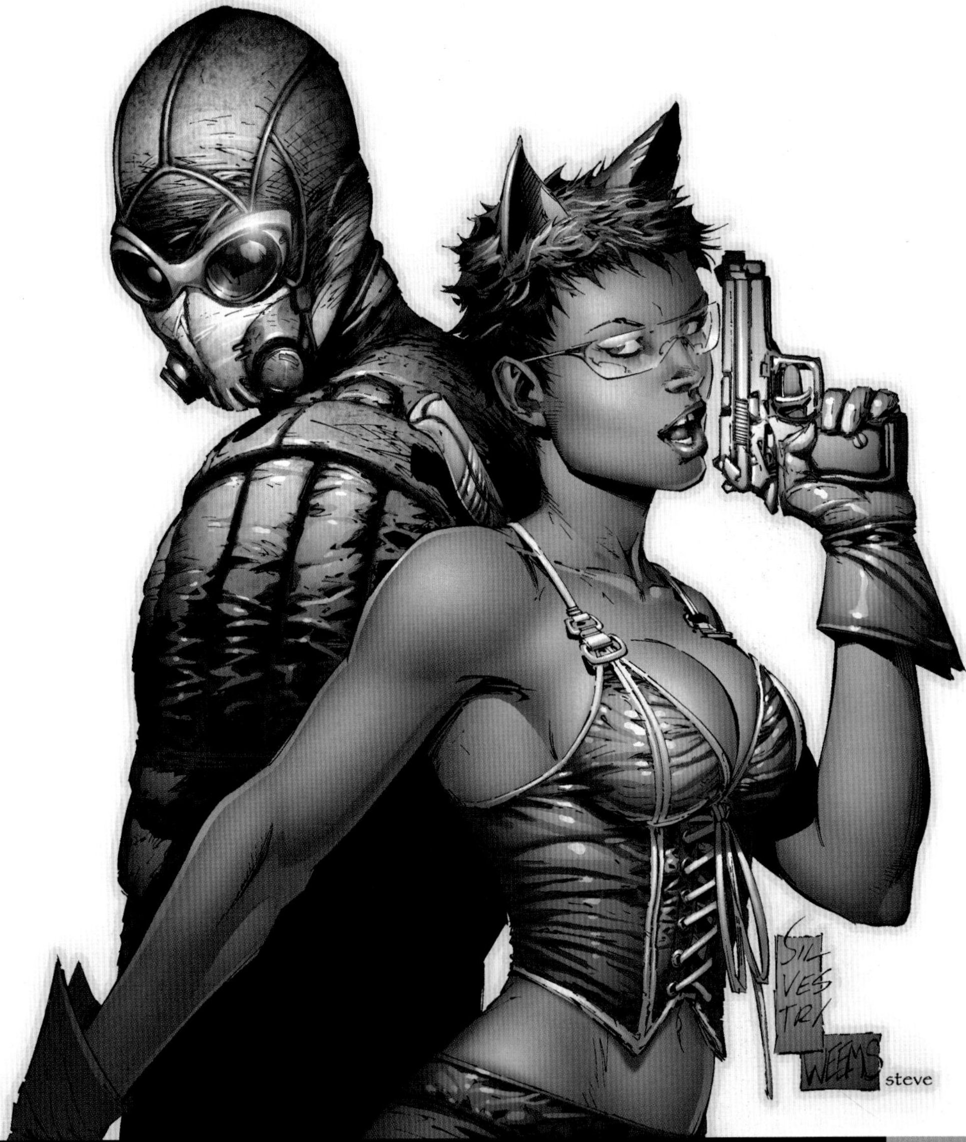
SIL
VES
TRI
WEEMS
steve

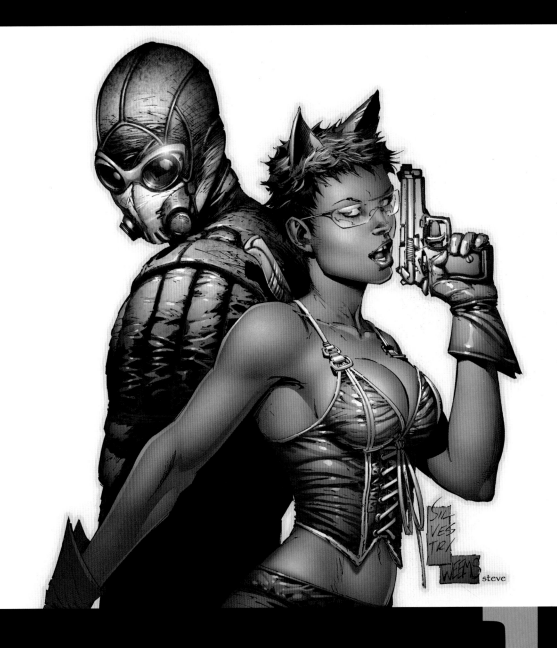

"I'm the scariest super-fuck who ever walked the earth..."

—THE KILLER

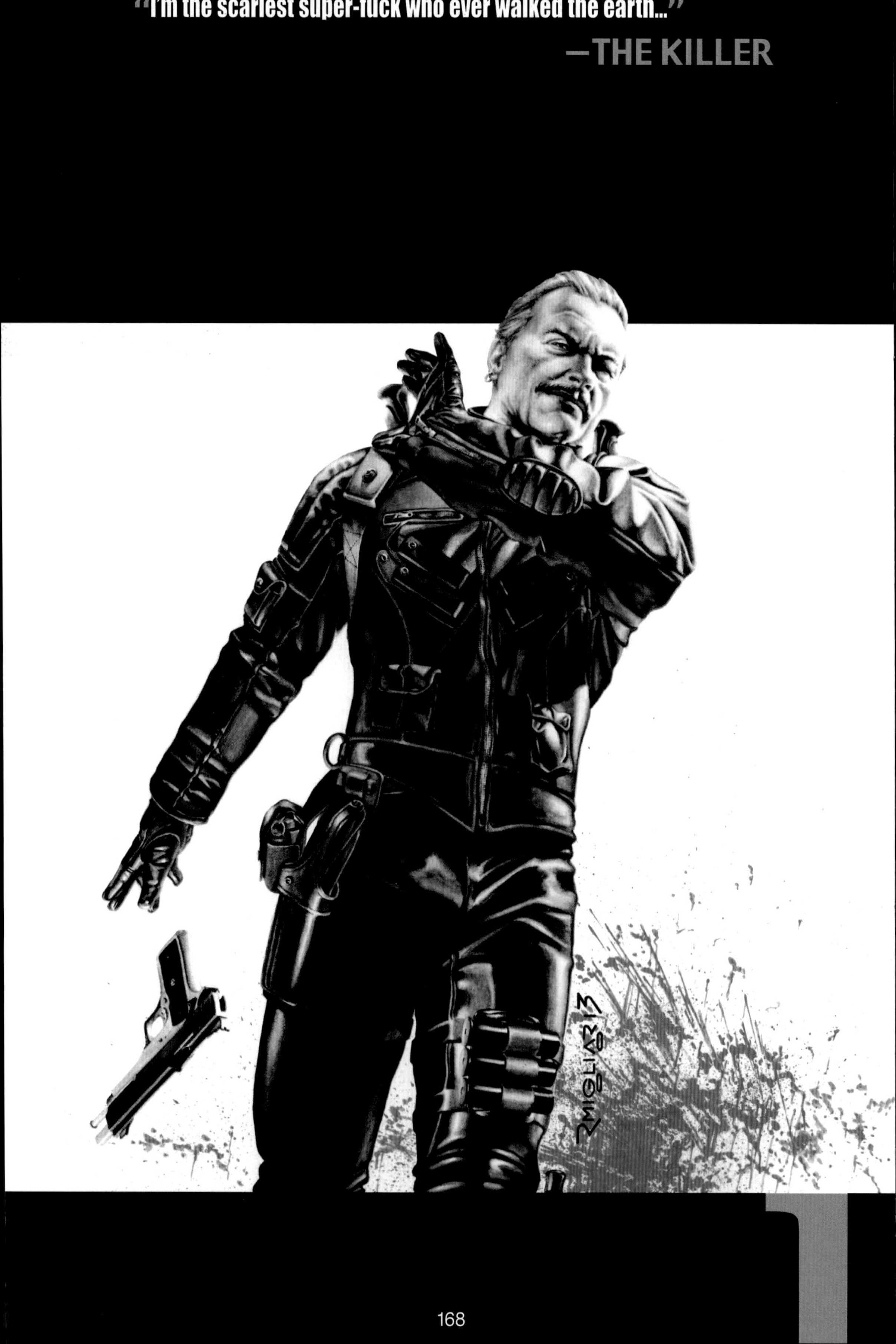

"If I was chocolate, I swear I'd eat myself right now."

—WESLEY GIBSON

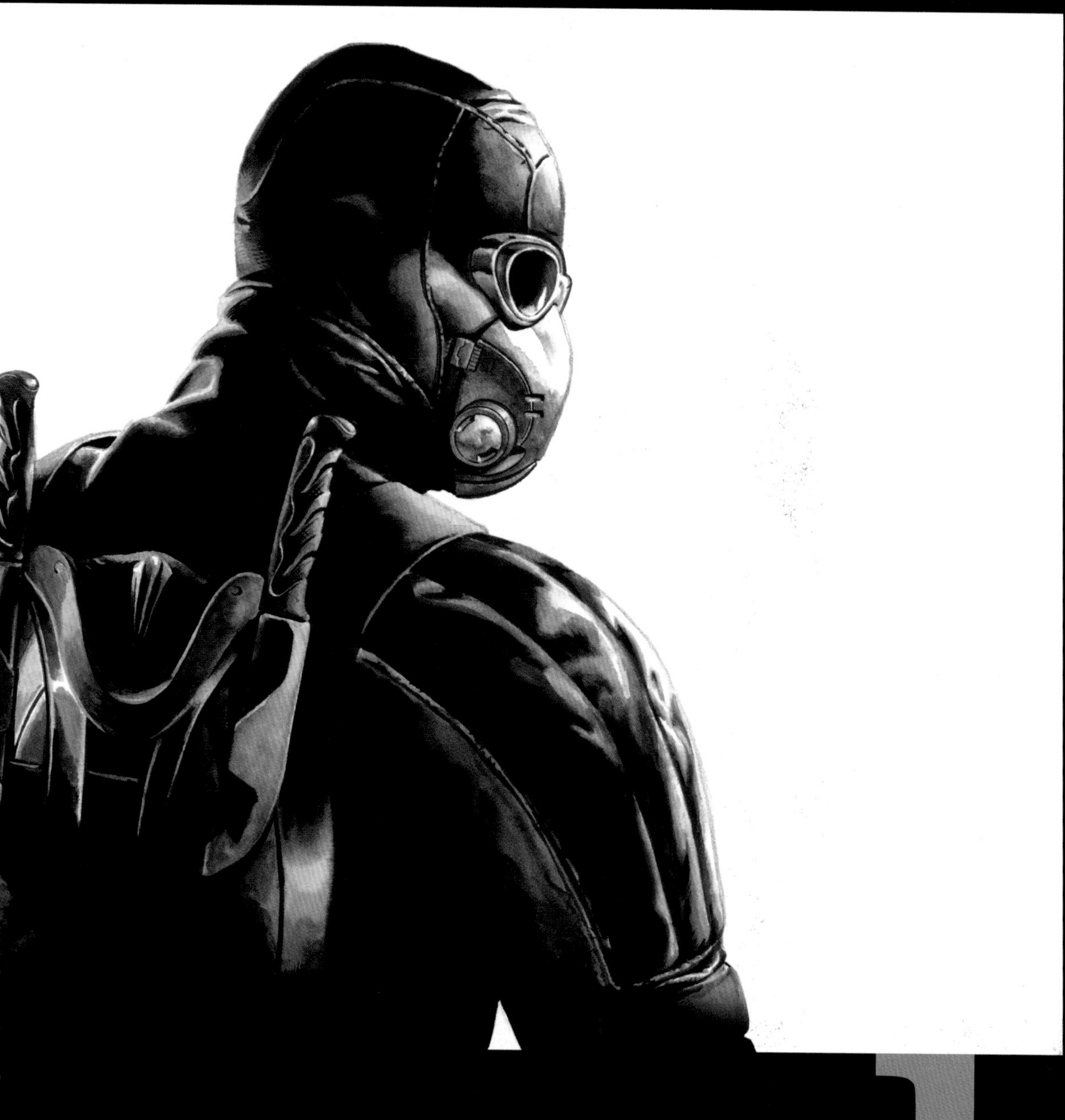

"Only difference between a dream and a nightmare is how big your balls are, bitch."

—THE FOX

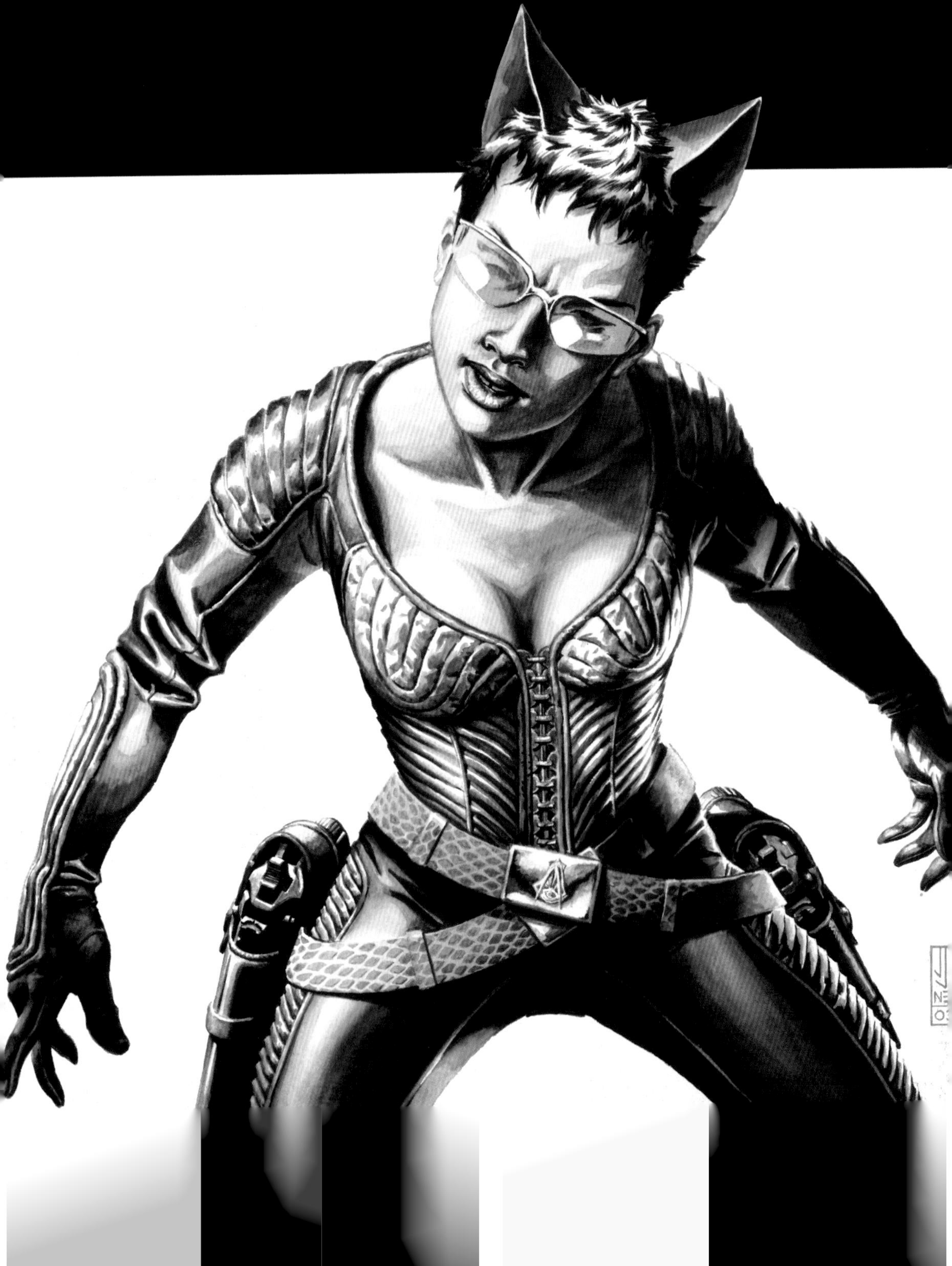

"That's exactly what you think it is. My own little 'fuck you' to the world."

—PROFESSOR SOLOMON SELTZER

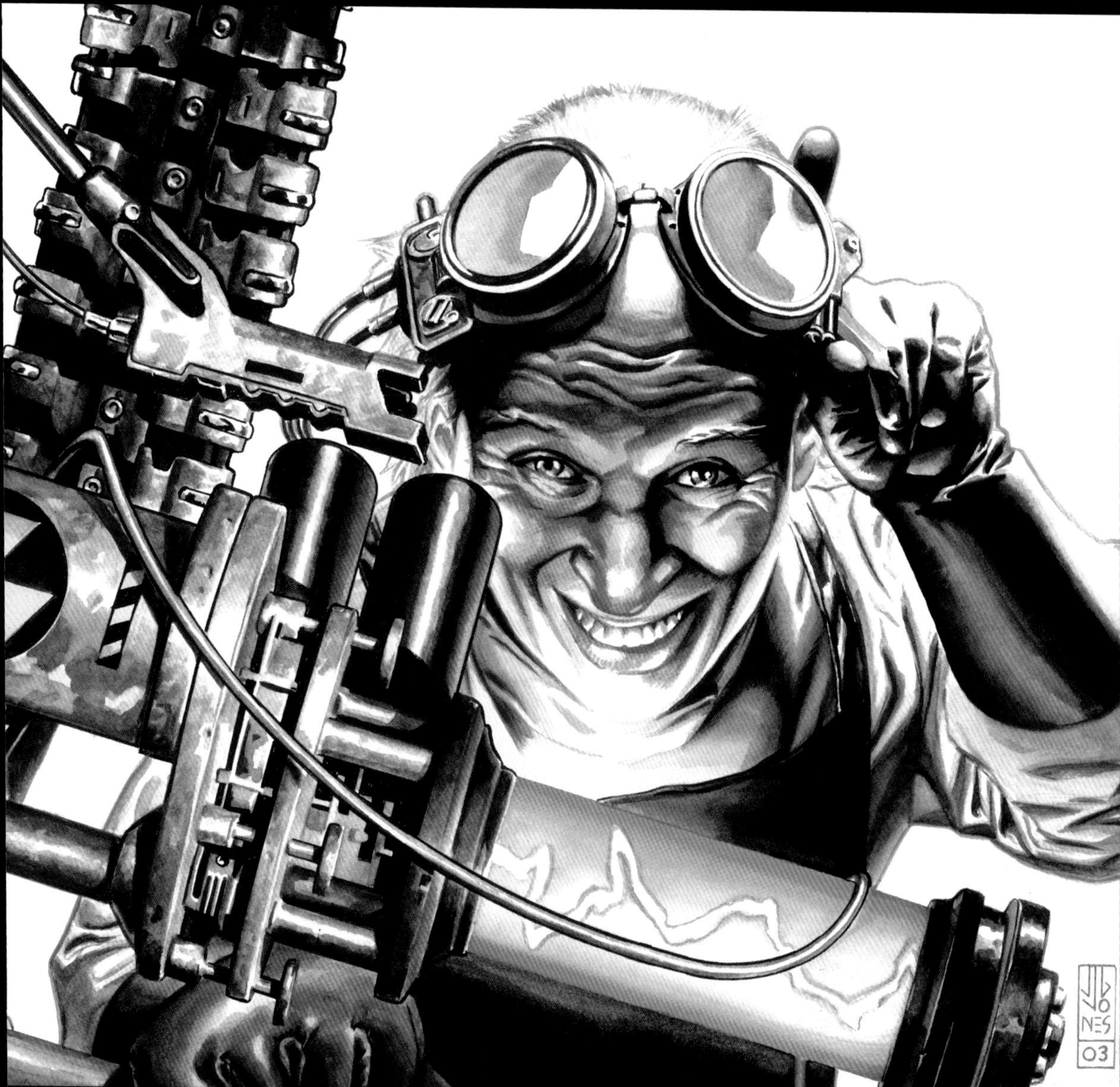

JG JONES 03

3

"Boys, I want you to kill these motherfuckers..."

—DOLL-MASTER

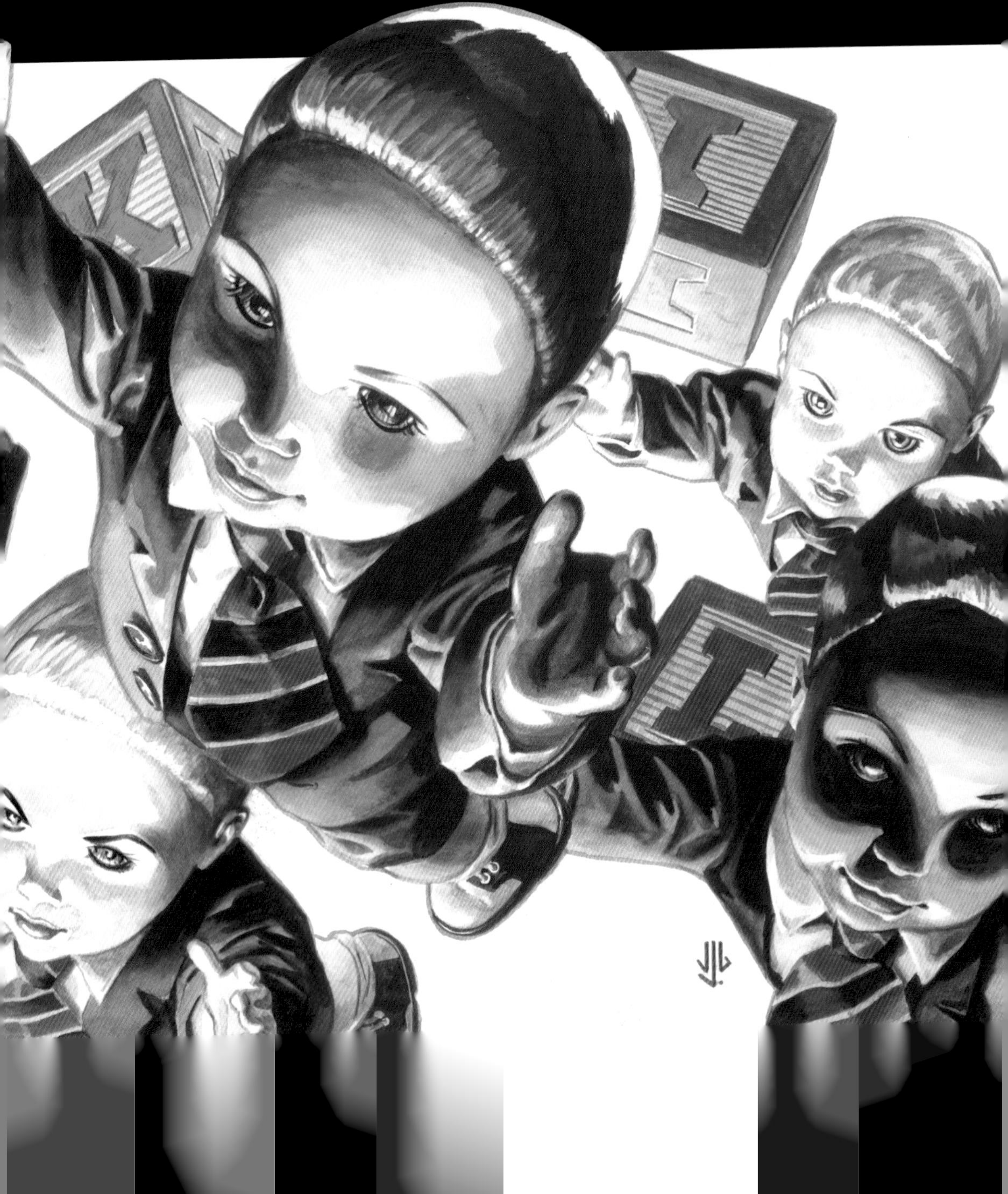

"I don't fuck goats, Mister Gibson. I make love to them."

—MISTER RICTUS

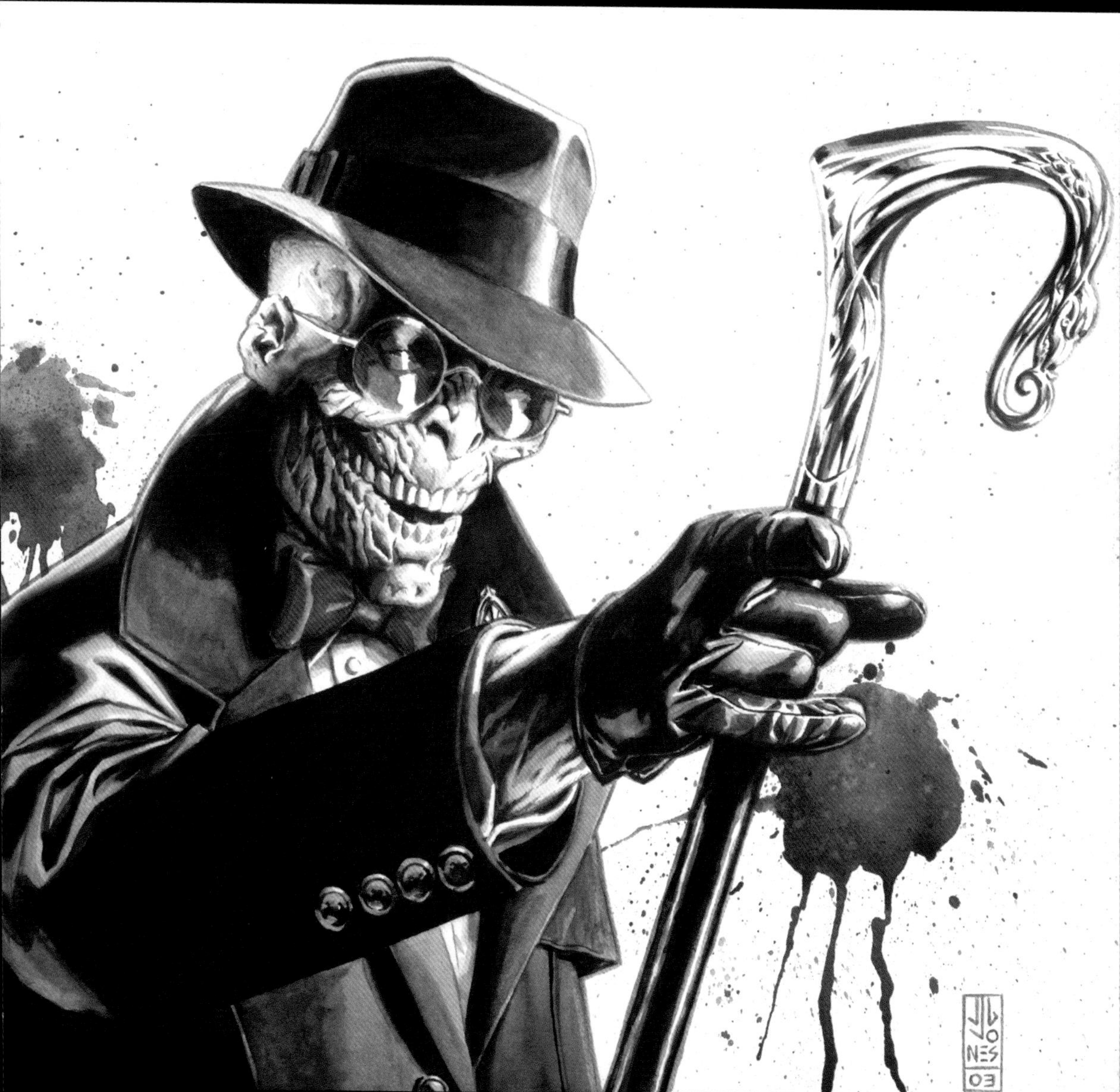

JG JONES 03

5

"I'm a wheezy, asthmatic mommy's boy. I collected Ninja Turtles figures. I jerk offto music videos, comic-books and lingerie catalogues. I had a seven-figure Sonic high score. I don't do things like this."

—WESLEY GIBSON

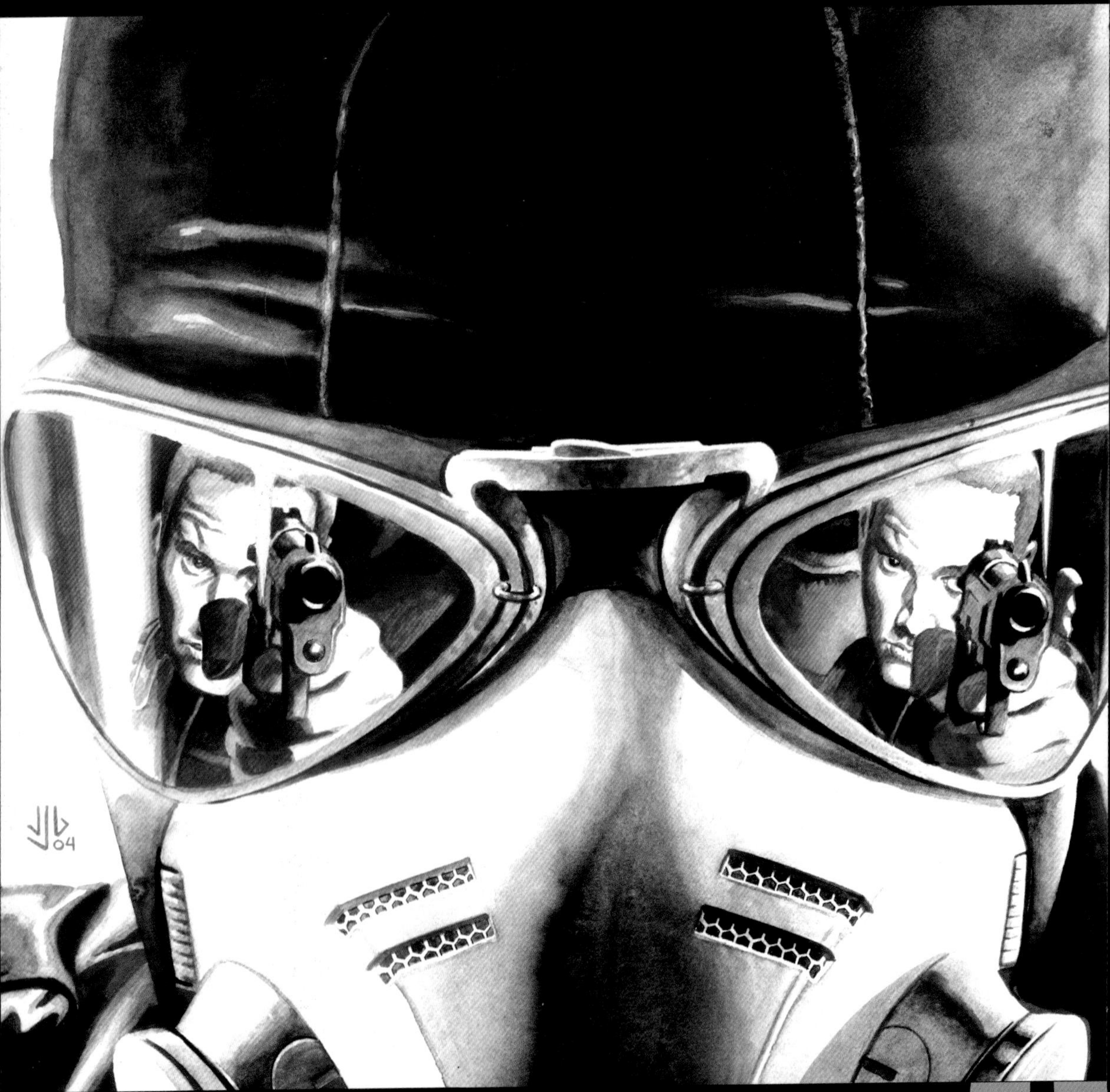

6

"Didn't you hear? (He) disappeared during a big war with all the super-villains ...they all disappeared during this enormous battle and they've never been seen again."

—BOBBY MILLAR

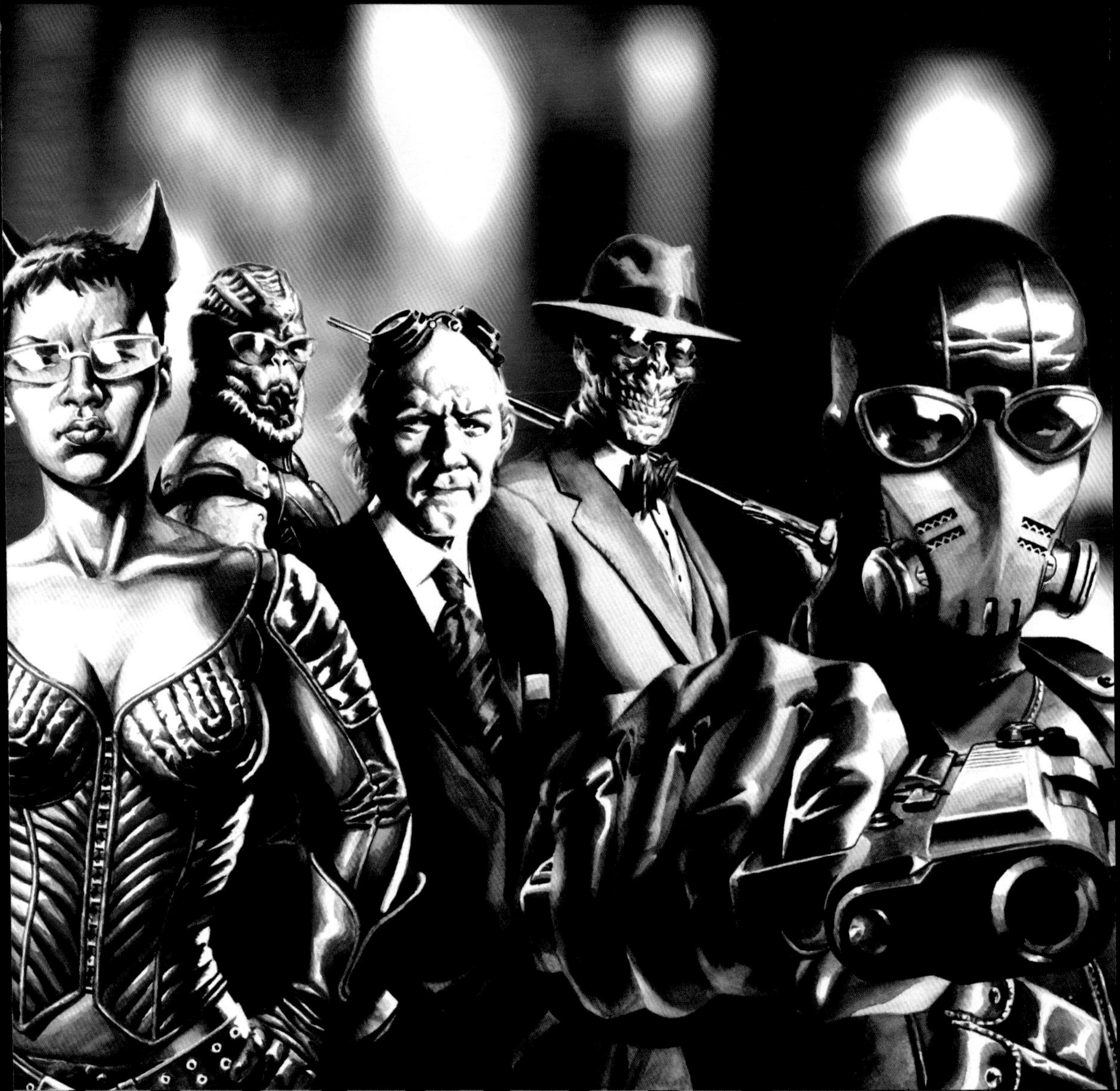

DOSSIER

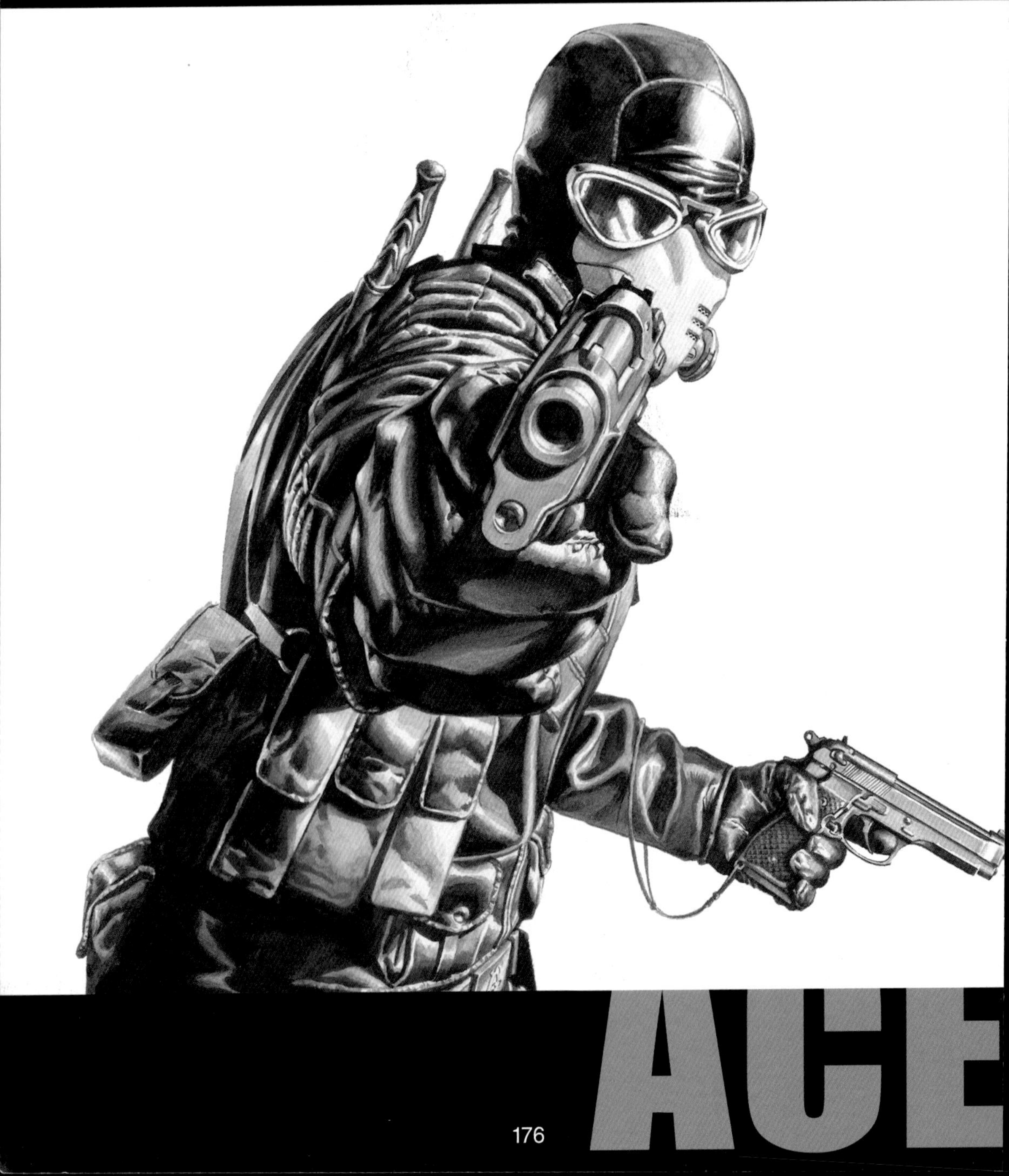

ACE

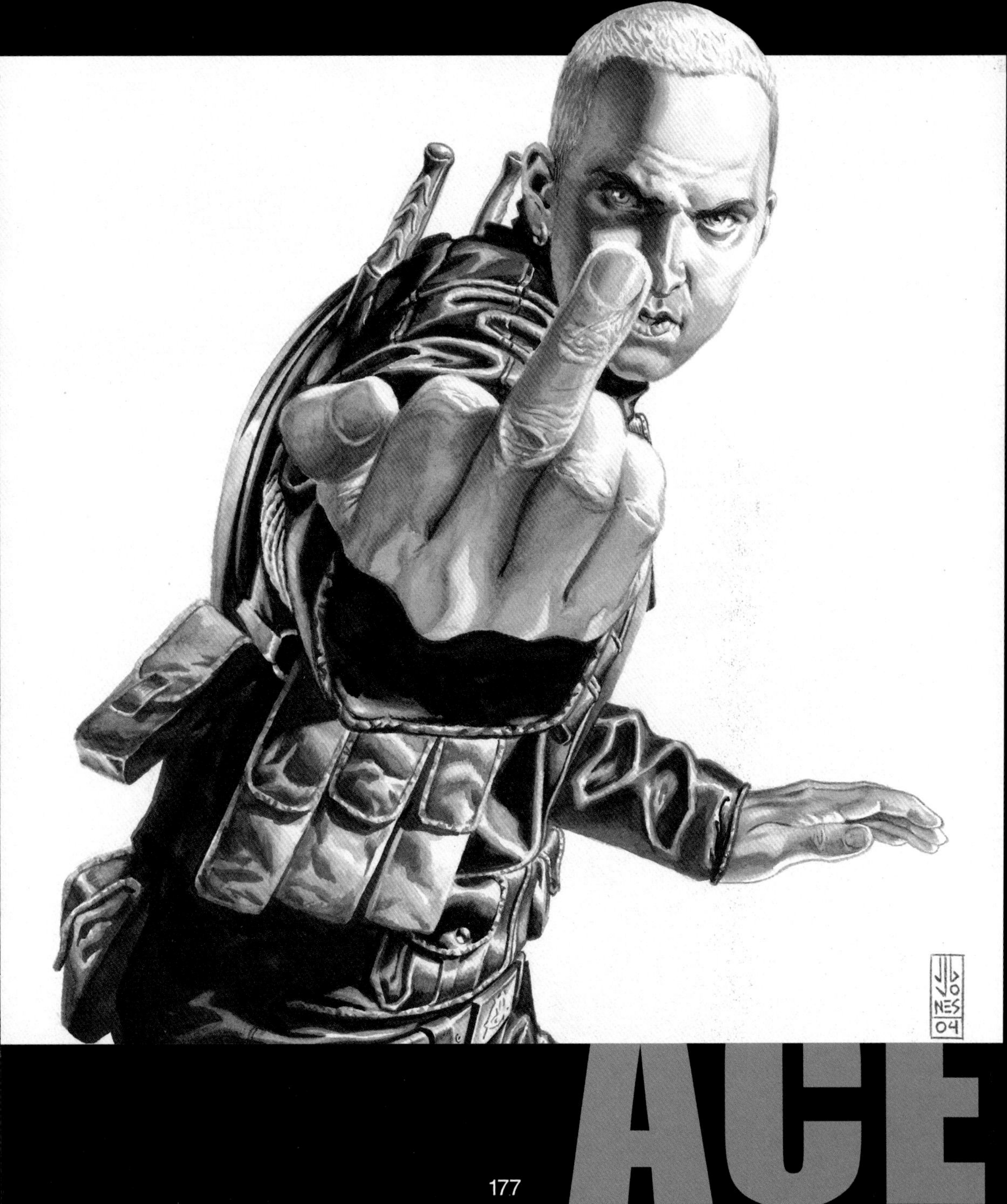

ACE

WANTED DEATH ROW EDITIONS

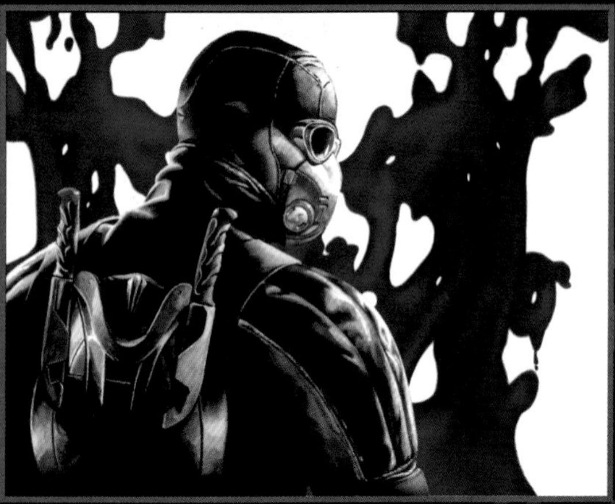

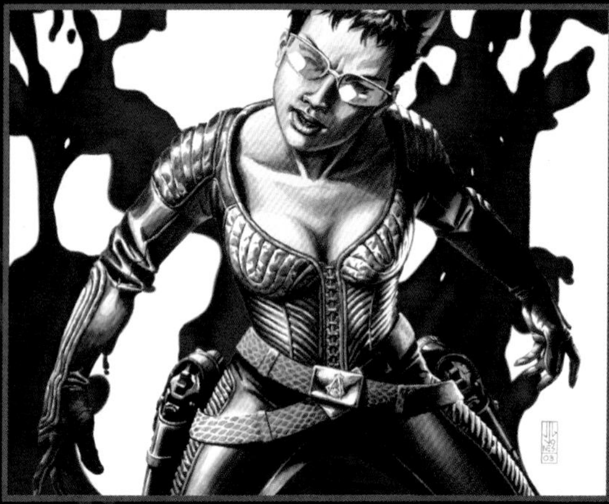

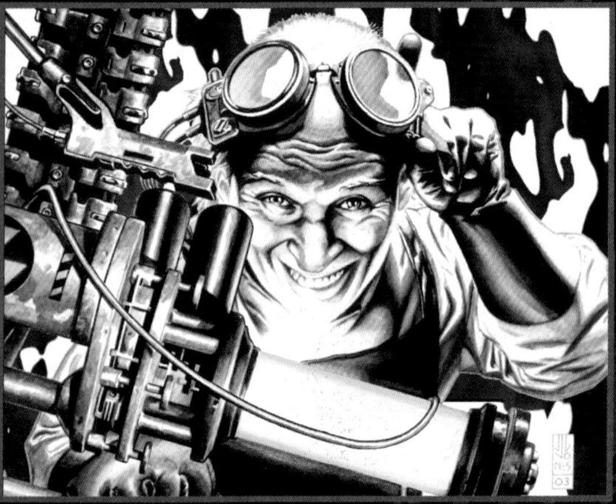

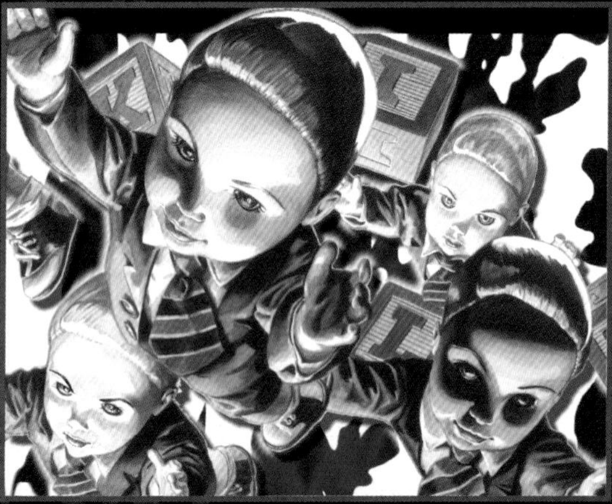

The Death Row editions were second printings with variant covers and contained bonus materials which are included in this trade.

WANTED CONVENTION VARIANTS

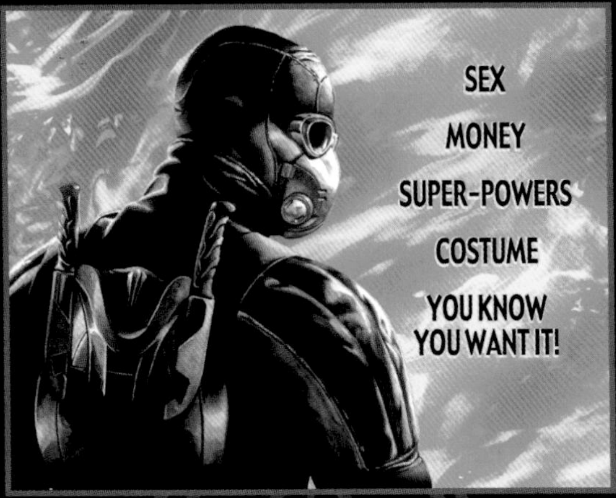
SEX
MONEY
SUPER-POWERS
COSTUME
YOU KNOW YOU WANT IT!

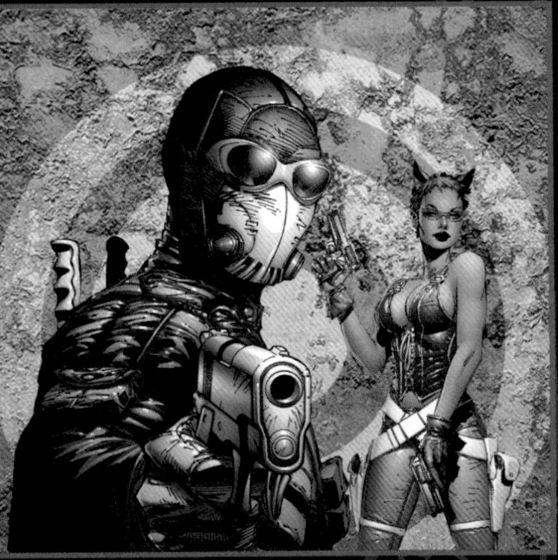

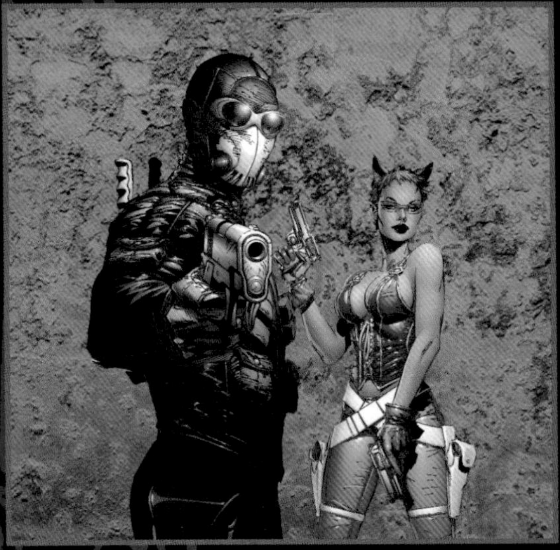

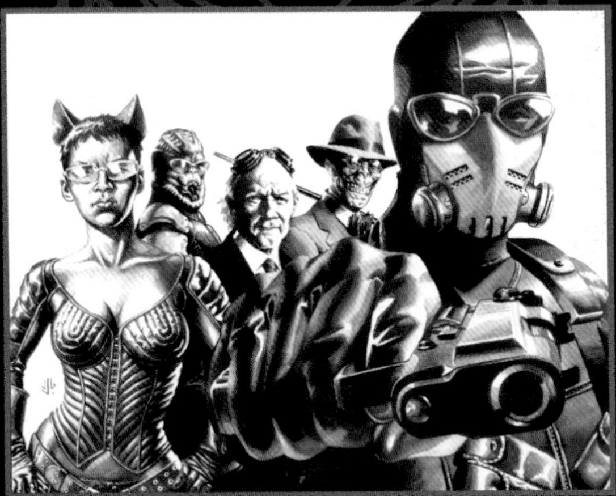

WANTED #6 VARIANTS

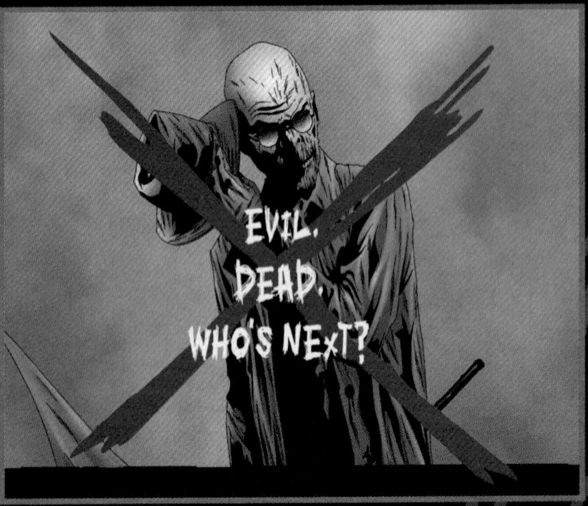
EVIL.
DEAD.
WHO'S NEXT?

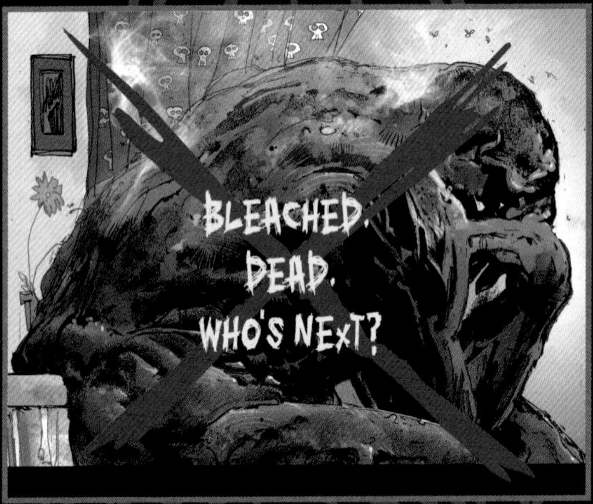
BLEACHED.
DEAD.
WHO'S NEXT?

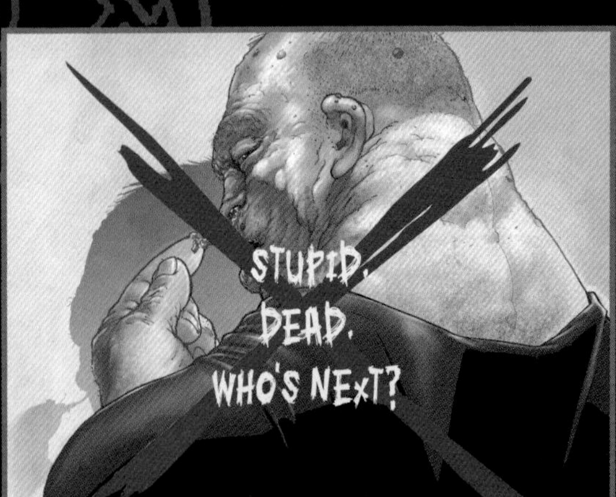
STUPID.
DEAD.
WHO'S NEXT?

WANTED
BEHIND THE SCENES, CHARACTER DESIGNS AND DELETED SCENES

Take a look behind the scenes of Wanted with these initial character designs from artist extraordinaire **J.G. Jones.**

CHARACTER DESIGN_
THE KILLER, A.K.A. WESLEY GIBSON

J.G. Jones nailed the design of Wesley Gibson in the "Killer" garb pretty much right out of the box. The costume is very "world outside your window," all real-world stuff that the stylish killer–on–the–go wouldn't be caught dead without.

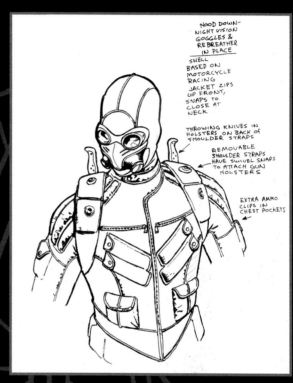

HOOD DOWN—
NIGHT VISION
GOGGLES &
REBREATHER
IN PLACE

SHELL
BASED ON
MOTORCYCLE
RACING

JACKET ZIPS
UP FRONT,
SNAPS TO
CLOSE AT
NECK

THROWING KNIVES IN
HOLSTERS ON BACK OF
SHOULDER STRAPS

REMOUABLE
SHOULDER STRAPS
HAUE SWIVEL SNAPS
TO ATTACH GUN
HOLSTERS

EXTRA AMMO
CLIPS IN
CHEST POCKETS

CHARACTER DESIGN_
IMP

The Imp gets his in Wanted #4. But before he could die, he had to come to life in the design of J.G. Jones. J.G.'s design was pretty much spot-on, and no real changes were made from the initial take. "I was sorry to see Imp go." said Jones. "He and Sucker were two of my favorite characters, both to design and to draw."

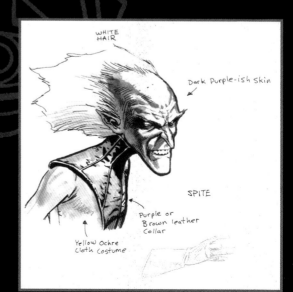

WHITE
HAIR

Dark Purple-ish Skin

SPITE

Purple or
Brown leather
collar

Yellow Ochre
cloth costume

CHARACTER DESIGN
THE ORIGINAL KILLER

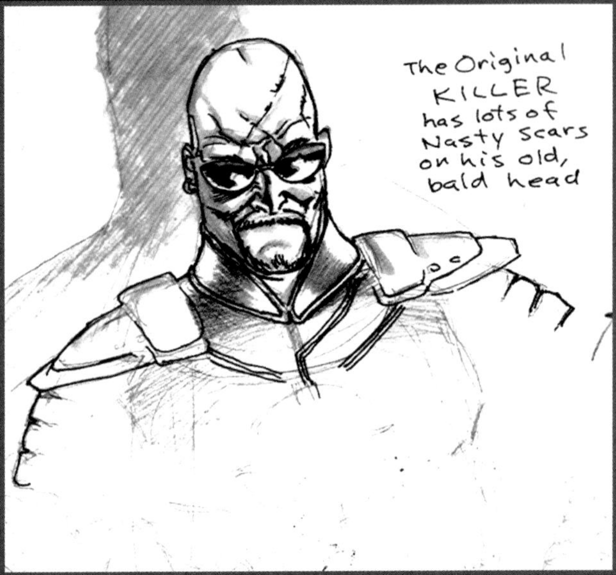
The Original KILLER has lots of Nasty Scars on his old, bald head

Wesley's papa, on the other hand, went through a bit of revision. The original guy seemed a bit too chunky for a man of such power. The revised Original Killer was sleek and sophisticated.

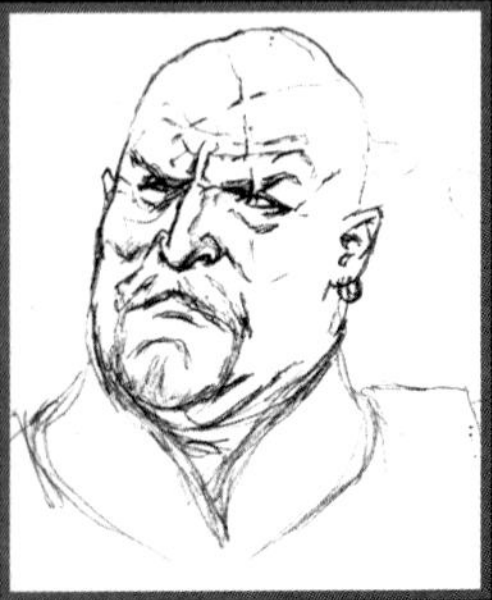

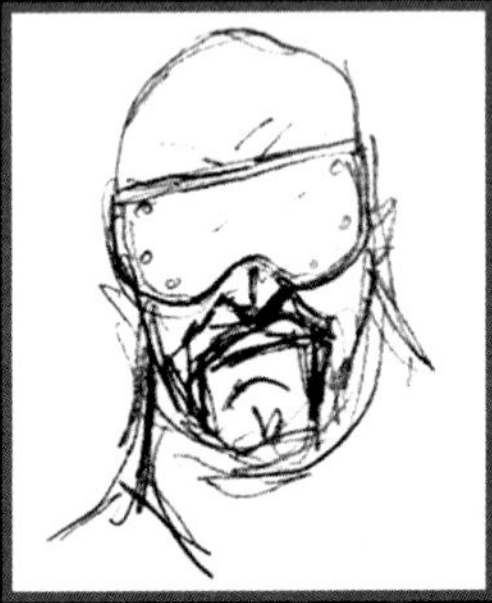

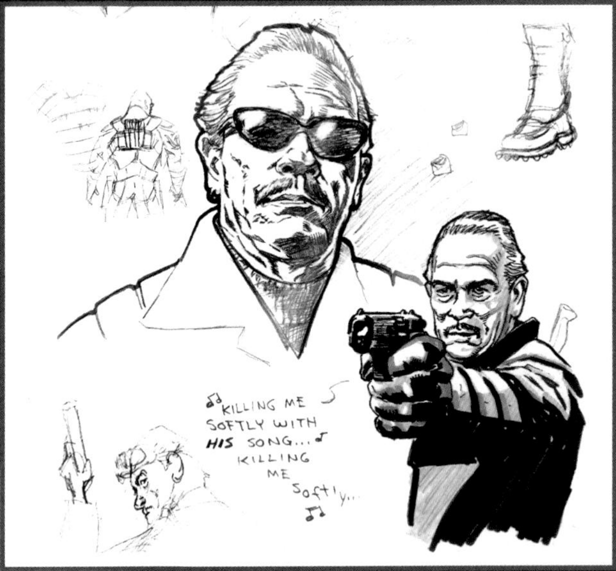
KILLING ME SOFTLY WITH HIS SONG... KILLING ME Softly...

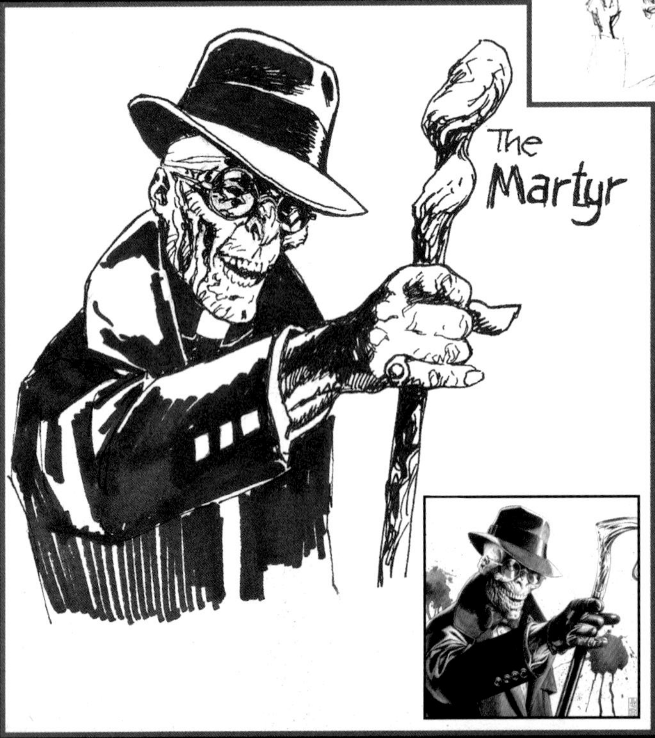
The Martyr

CHARACTER DESIGN
MISTER RICTUS

The haunting presence of Mister Rictus first appears in WANTED #2. Different names were bandied about and at one point the character was going to be called *The Martyr.*

J.G.'s original character design was eventually the basis for the WANTED #5 cover.

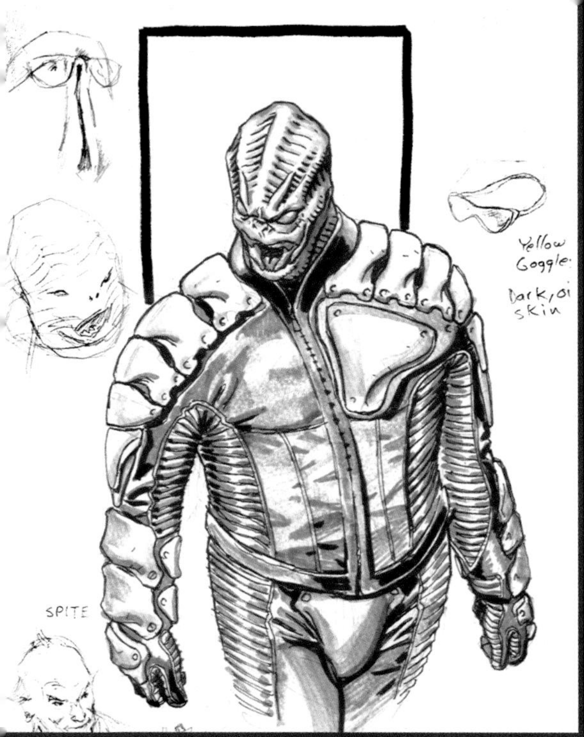
Yellow Goggle
Dark, oi skin
SPITE

CHARACTER DESIGN__
SUCKER

Like most of the villains, Sucker shows up for the firs time in costume in WANTED #2. J.G. Jones' first tr at Sucker's look and costume was the only try needec The design was perfect right off the bat!

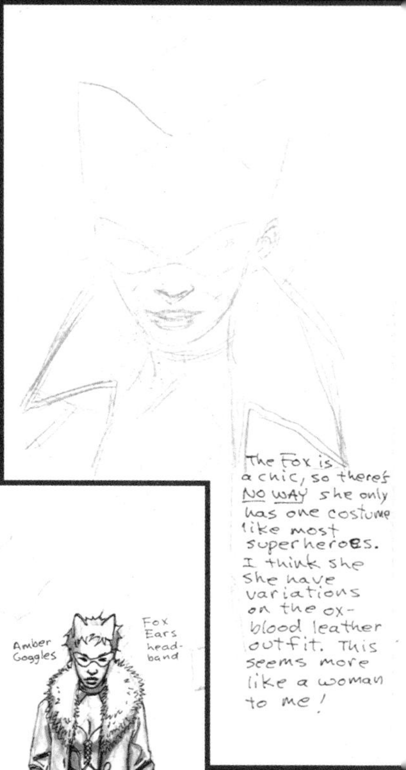
The Fox is a chic, so theres NO WAY she only has one costume like most superheroes. I think she She have variations on the ox-blood leather outfit. This seems more like a woman to me!

CHARACTER DESIGN__
FOX

lot a single accessory went overlooked in J.G. Jones' design for the Fox! Cuffs, collar, and even the cut of her pants are all addressed, along with provision for costume changes.

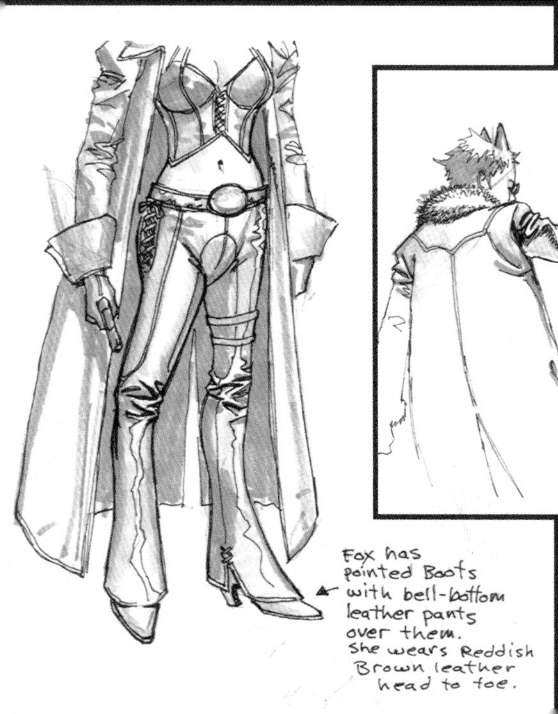
Fox has pointed Boots with bell-bottom leather pants over them. She wears Reddish Brown leather head to toe.

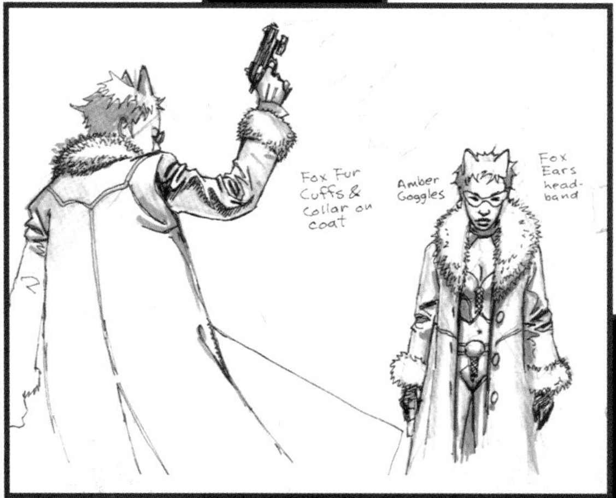
Fox Fur Cuffs & Collar on coat
Amber Goggles
Fox Ears head-band

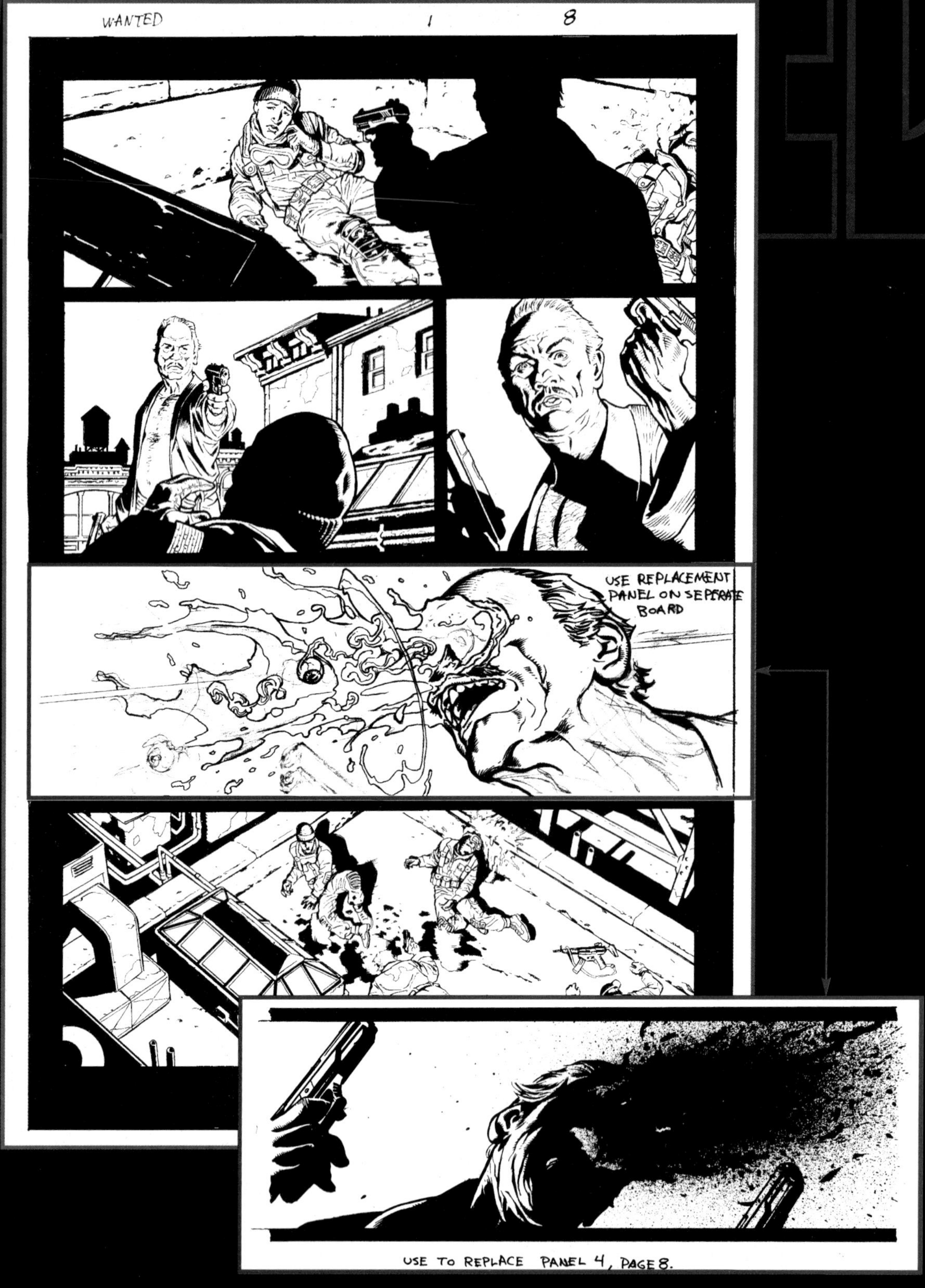
WANTED 1 8
USE REPLACEMENT PANEL ON SEPERATE BOARD
USE TO REPLACE PANEL 4, PAGE 8.

WANTED #1_PG. 8

Man that he is, artist J.G. Jones hoes to the end of the row! J.G. did two distinct versions of The Killer getting his head blown up, and went with the "giant hole" version. "Drawing all the bits of the brain made it look a little slow and fussed over," J.G. says. "I wanted to go with something that had the impact of a bullet through the head."

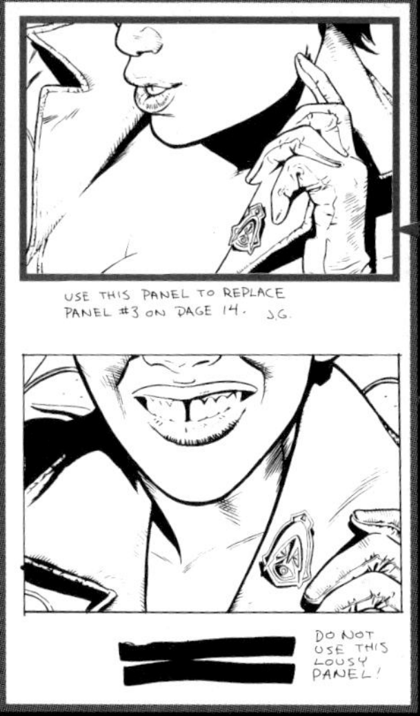

USE THIS PANEL TO REPLACE PANEL #3 ON PAGE 14. J.G.
DO NOT USE THIS LOUSY PANEL!

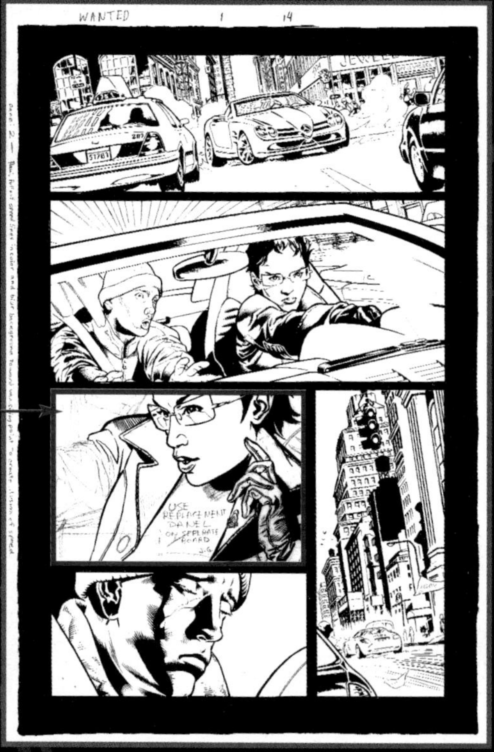

WANTED 1 14
USE REPLACEMENT PANEL ON SEPARATE BOARD J.G.

WANTED #1_PG. 14

The all important pin that symbolizes The Fraternity went through three separate takes before J.G. settled on winner. "I was just monkeying around with Masonic-type symbols. *The Man Who Would Be King* is one of my favorite movies after all," says J.G.

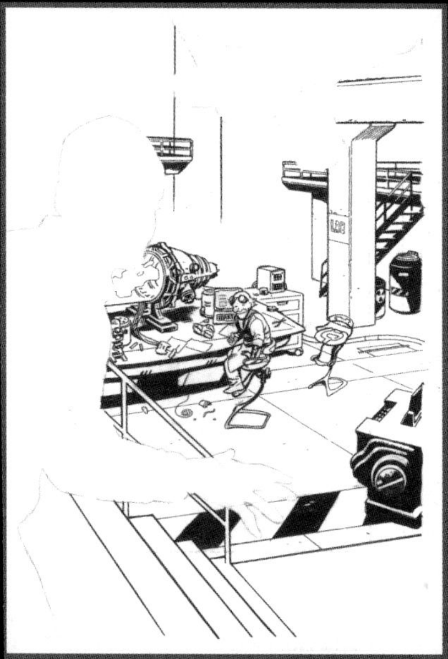

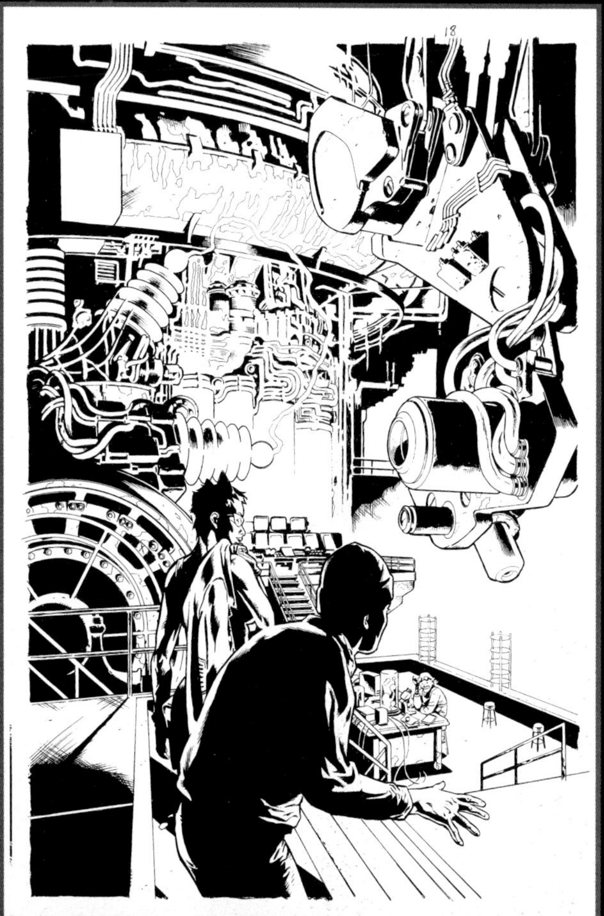

18

WANTED #1_PG. 18

As if this massive splash page could get any more elaborate, J.G. added additional backgrounds and cosmic goo-gob to page 18. "I drew this page early on so that we could have a teaser to release online. After drawing the rest of the book, the lab didn't match what I needed for the rest of the scene, so I changed part of the page to make the whole thing work," says J.G.

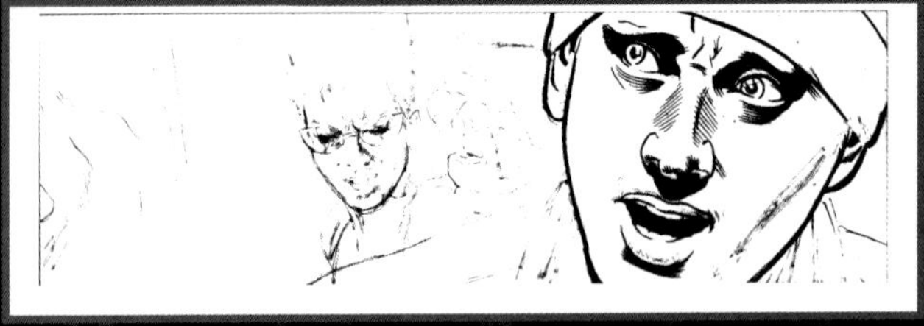

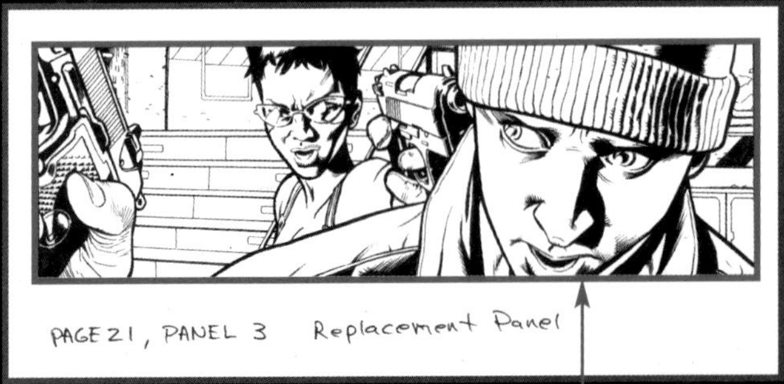
PAGE 21, PANEL 3 Replacement Panel

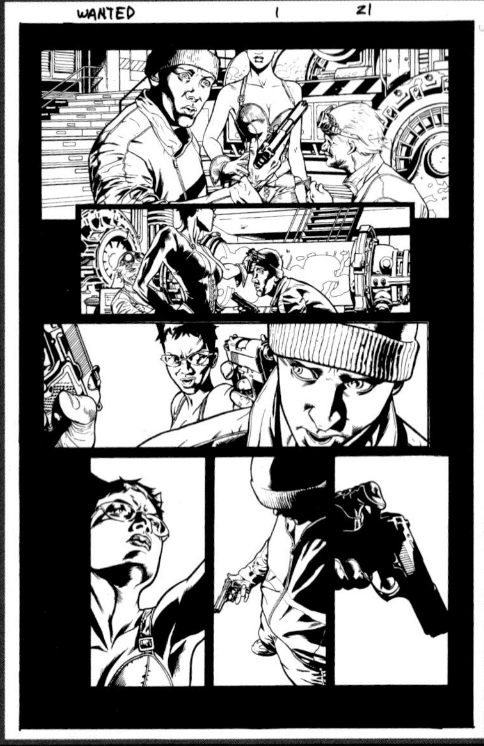
WANTED 1 21

WANTED #1_PG. 21

The scared to death expression of Wesley on page 21 went under the knife before J.G. settled on the final version. "I had to get the face just right to show Wesley starting to freak out," says J.G.

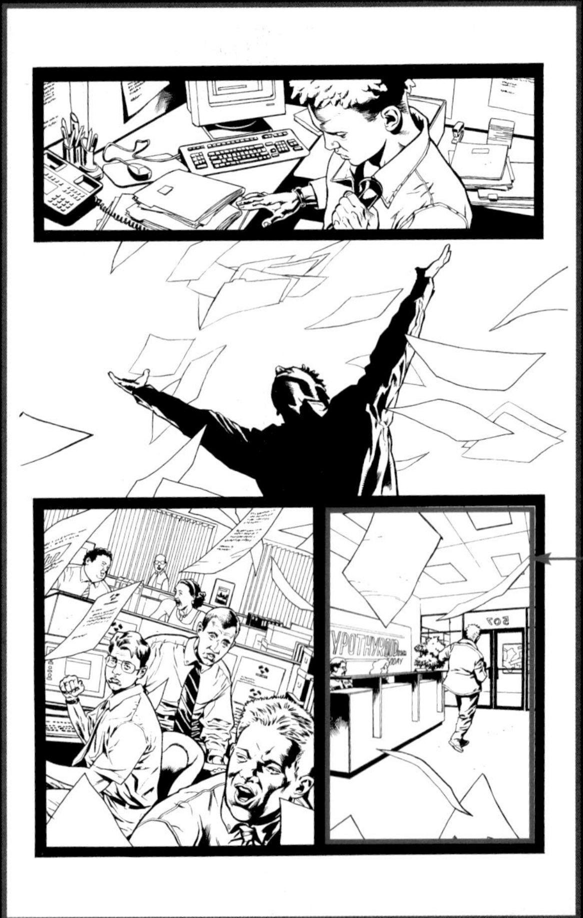

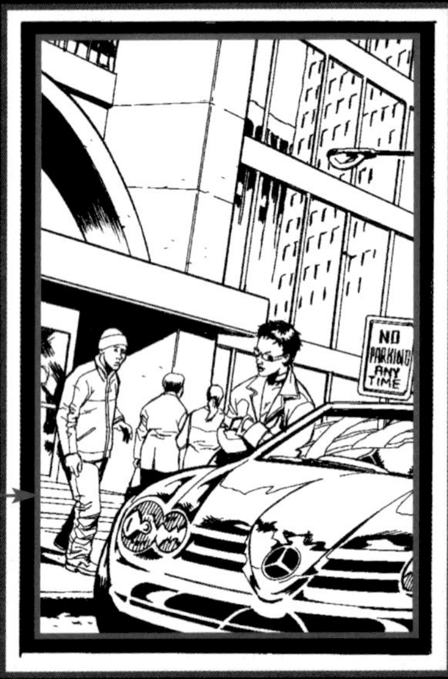
NO PARKING ANY TIME

WANTED #2_PG. 4

Writer Mark Millar changed the pace of the story just a tad on pages 4 and 5. Millar felt that having the "Wesley quits" scene extended over two pages didn't set up the next scene well enough. Millar offered to pay artist J.G. Jones out of his own pocket to make the changes to tighten up the "Wesley quits scene to end on pg. 4. *(And cheap Scotsman that he is, Millar is yet to pay*

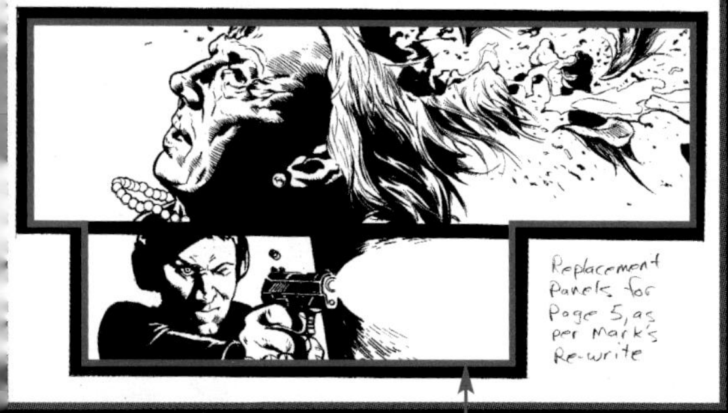
Replacement Panels for Page 5, as per Mark's Re-write

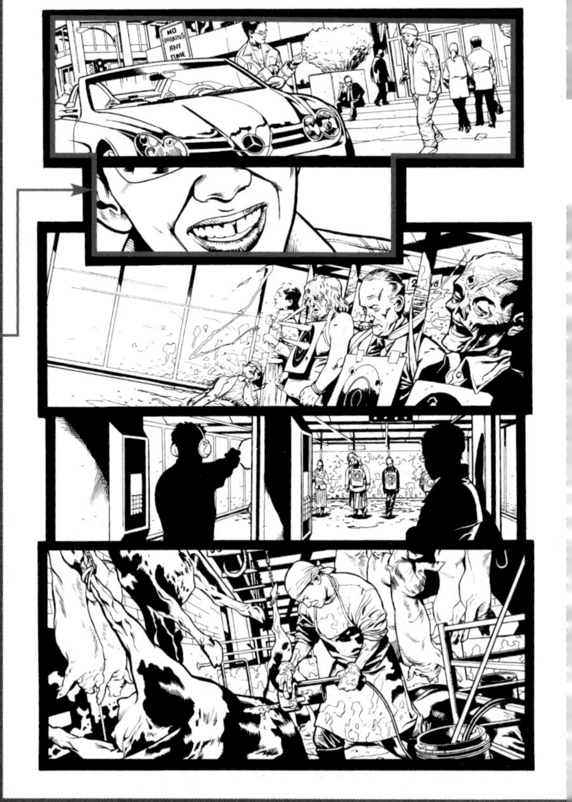
NO PARKING ANY TIME

WANTED #2_PG. 5

Similarly a rewrite on page 5 led to a redraw of page 5. J.G. Jones worked like a demon to get the revisions done, finishing on Christmas Eve, then retiring for the holidays with a tumbler of Scotch. "It was Macallan," Jones says. "A single malt, rich and smoky, with a good dose of that peat-y flavor."

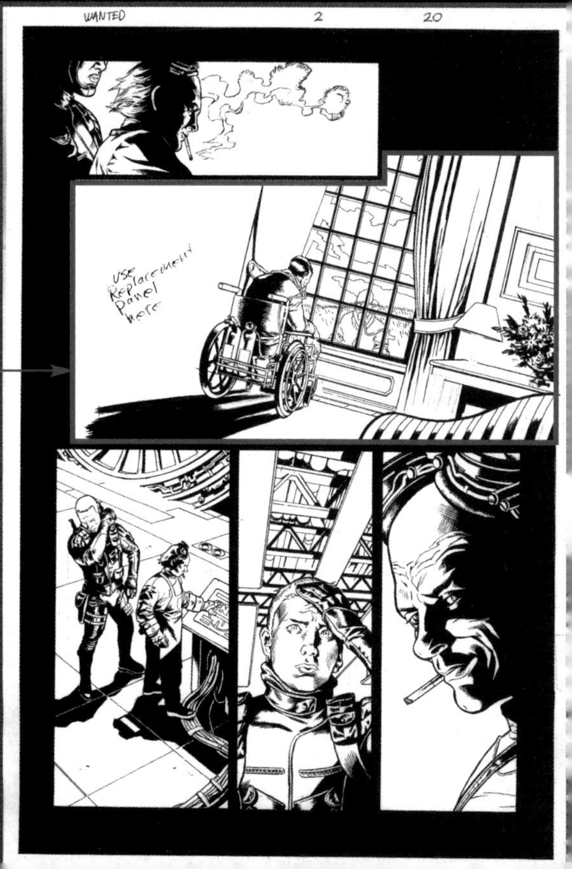
WANTED
2
20
Use Replacement Panel here

WANTED #2_PG. 20

Artist J.G. Jones was moved to re-draw a panel on page 20 when he really "got" the impact of what was meant here. "I think you'll note a pasing resemblance to a certain well-known strange visitor," Jones notes. "But only a passing resemblance. We'd never venture into the arena of identity theft."

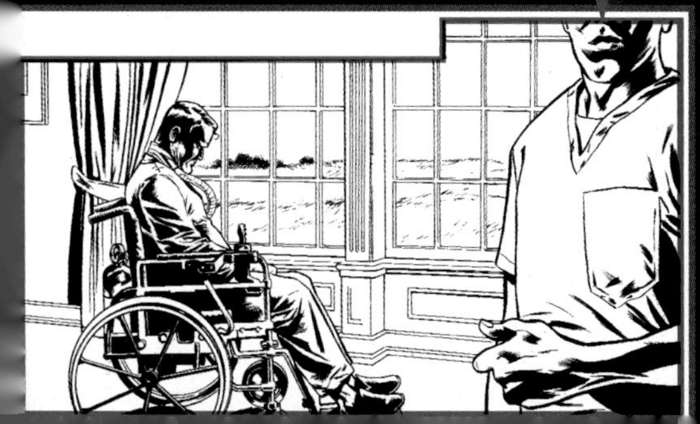

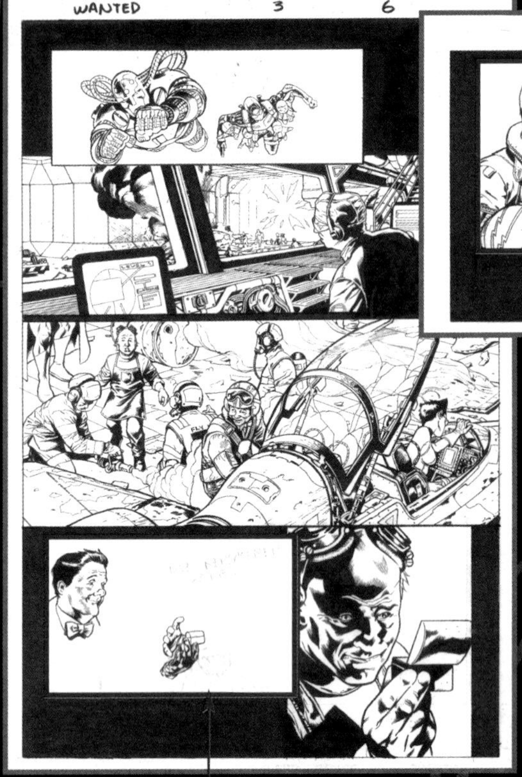
WANTED 3 6

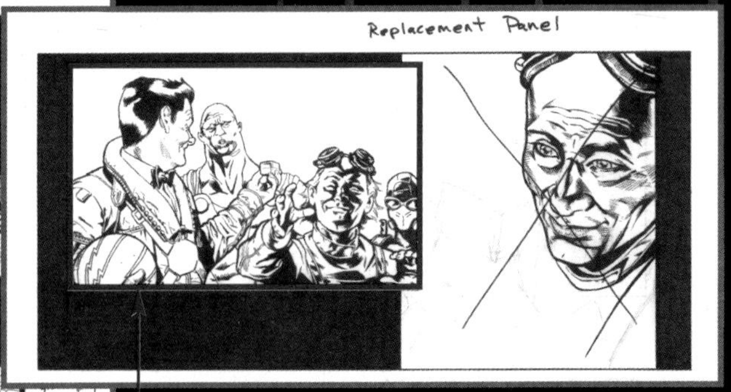
Replacement Panel

WANTED #3_PG. 6

Artist J.G. Jones realized he was running into an angle problem on page 6, the handoff of the radioactive condom from Doll Master to the professor. He redrew the shot for a better reveal, and even a nice warm glow from the radiation on the Prof's face.

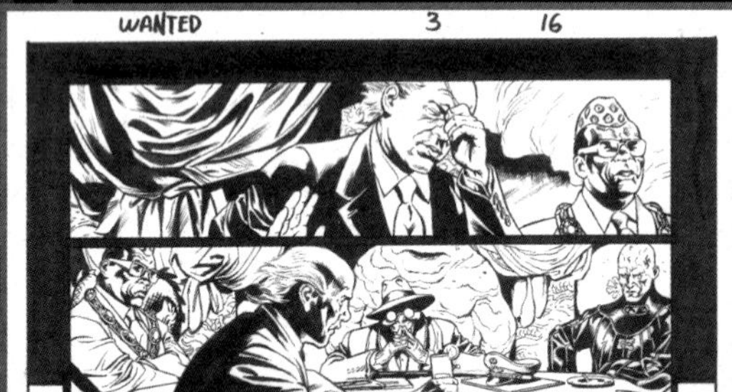
WANTED 3 16

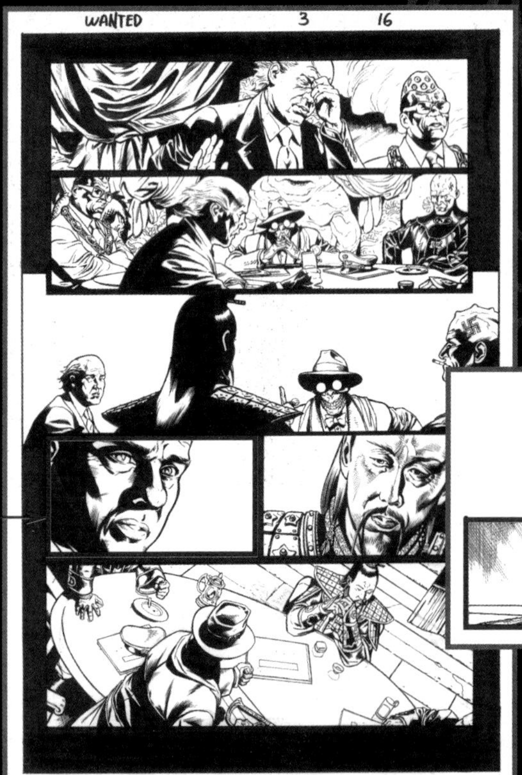
WANTED 3 16

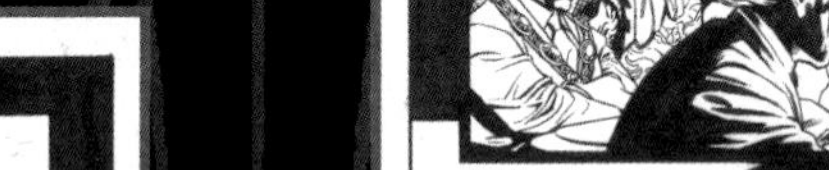
Issue 3
Page 16
Panel 4
Replacemt Panel

WANTED #3_PG. 16

Foreshadowing! Your key to quality funnybook entertainment!

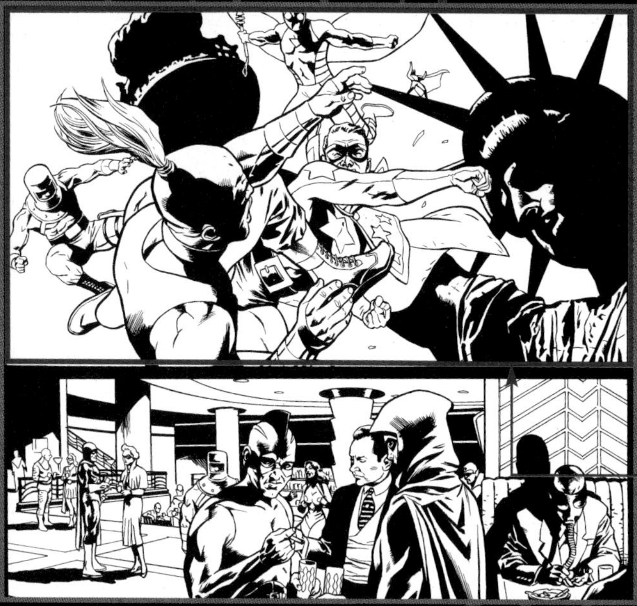

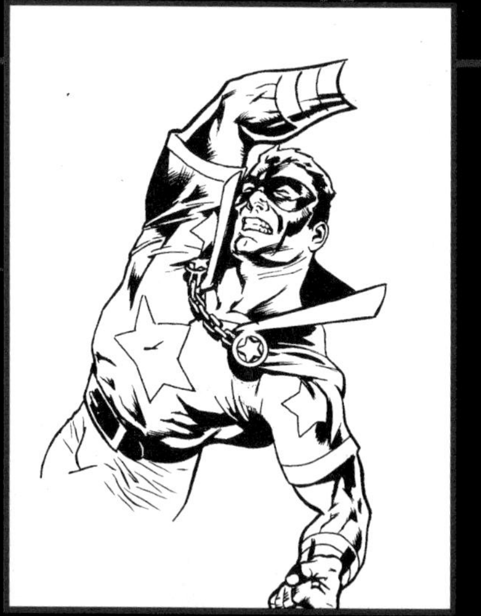

WANTED #4_PG. 6

Artist J.G. Jones did a bit of a flip-flop on "generic patriot good guy" on page 3, panel 1. "The figure looked a little flat to me, so I went for something with more energy and impact."

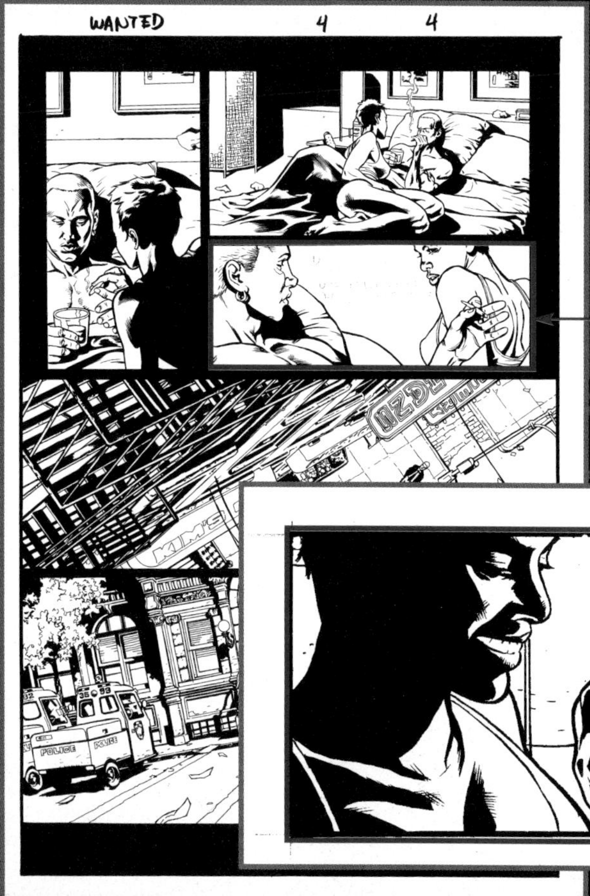

WANTED
4
4
POLICE
POLICE

WANTED #4_PG. 4

Similarly, the Fox and Wesley were reversed on page 4, panel 3. "Here I wanted to emphasize the dim, moody lighting, so I switched to a shot that would backlight the figures and give me more shadows."

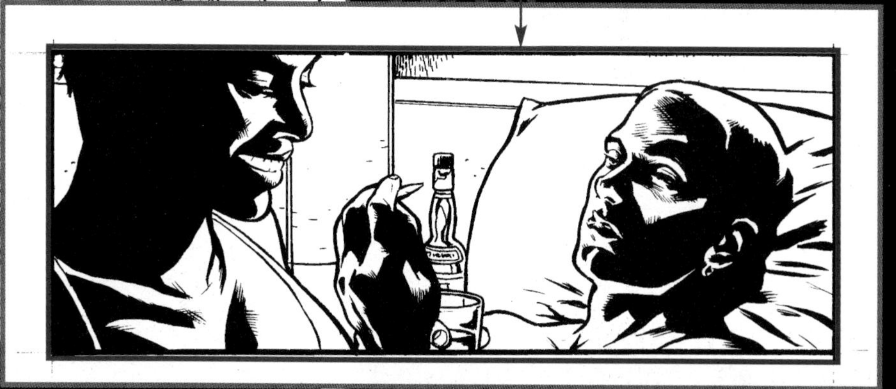

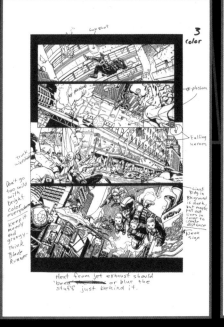

Gun shot
3
color
ex-plosion
Falling heroes
Truck windshield
Don't go too wild with bright color everywhere
Keep it moody and grungy- Think Blade Runner
Giant Bldg in Bkground is dark, but maybe put out lines in color to create distance
Neon Sign
Heat from jet exhaust should 'bend or blur the stuff just behind it.

4
color
Plasma wall
Dim lighting inside Control Booth
These little wings are on his costume
This is the same building
Hilight on glass canopy
Dark Blue Choppers w/ white lettering
Missle fired from chopper
Dark, Smokey Glass

COLOR NOTES_

WANTED #3_PGS. 3 AND 4

Perfectionist that he is, Dr. Jones supplies copius color notes to huemaster Paul Mounts. J.G.'s notes include tone and feel ("Keep it moody and grungy-think Blade Runner"), specific color direction ("Dark blue choppers w/white lettering"), and even head off questions ("This is the same building").

21
Color

WANTED
4
21
2
3
4
5

COLOR NOTES_

WANTED #4_PG. 21

J.G. also supplies balloon placements to the letterer, so as to not cover important elements of the art. Compare this sample to the actual page 21, and you'll see that letterer Robin Spehar follows these placements…to the letter.

WANTED
NEW BONUS MATERIAL, FROM SCRIPT TO PRESS

Here is a quick look at the evolution of writer Mark Millar's story from the original script to the finished page, using the classic final fight scenes between Mr. Rictus and Wesley from *Wanted* #5 pages 19 and 20.

Page Nineteen

1/ Pull back and the most astonishing, Kill Bill-kinda overhead where we see the smallish figure of Wesley standing here with the circle of dead bodies around him. Rictus is standing here alone and is very obviously the next target. Wesley stands here with his head down and a smoking gun in each hand, The Fox still down on the ground and surrounding by all these bloodied corpses.

NO DIALOGUE

2/ Close on Wesley as we go all John Woo and have him raise his head and look right into our eyes with an I'm-gonna-fuck-you-up intensity. He's covered in blood and dripping with intense, but restrained emotion here as he takes out his knife.

1 WESLEY CAPTION : Act tough. Act tough. Act tough.
2 WESLEY GIBSON : I'll give you one shot.

3/ Mister Rictus reacts by firing off a shot towards us, slightly panicked looking. He's a dangerous mother-fucker, but even HE knows his time is up.

3 SOUND F/X : BLAM!

4/ Super-cool shot as the intense Wesley just smacks (yes, smacks) the bullet aside with the blade of his knife like he's playing ping-pong.

4 SOUND F/X : SMACK!

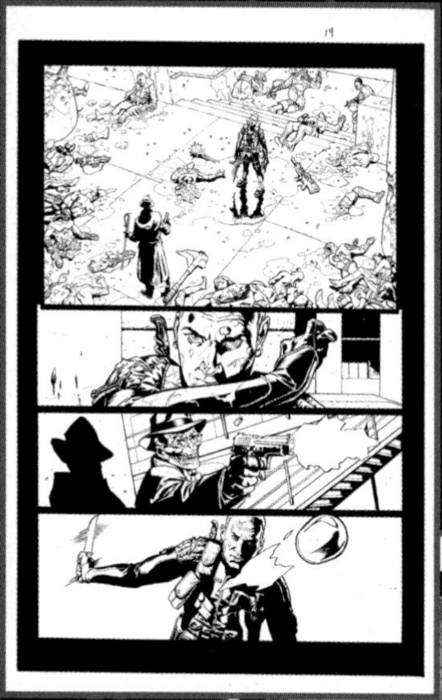
19

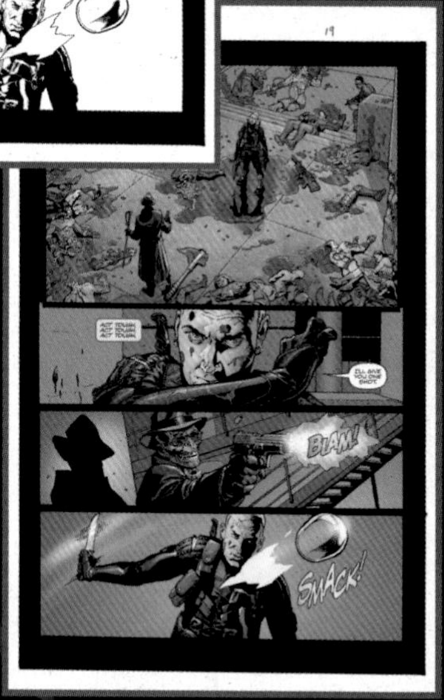
19
BLAM!
SMACK!

Page Twenty

1/ Reaction shot as this bullet fires back towards it's intended target and just shoots Mister Rictus right through the throat, coming out the back off his neck. His hat comes off for the first time and we're quite surprised by the suddenness of all this.

1 RICTUS (big) : GRARGH!
2 WESLEY CAPTION : Holy shit.

2/ Reaction shot from The Fox and even SHE'S surprised by the suddenness of all this, hardly able to take in just how good this off-panel kid has become.

3 THE FOX : That was GREAT.

3/ Wesley squats over the wounded body of Mister Rictus as he lies here bleeding on the floor. He's got his hunting knife out and looks cold and menacing as he basically says goodbye. The Fox is watching the whole thing with some interest.

4 WESLEY GIBSON : Now answer the question, Rictus: I don't care about the peace treaty. I don't care about Goddamn The Professor. I just wanna know who killed my Dad and if you had anything to do with it!
5 WESLEY GIBSON : Who killed him, you old bastard? I just wanna know who put that fucking BULLET in his head!

4/ Close on Mister Rictus as he lies back here, the bullet-wound in his throat, as he coughs through blood to hiss his defiant last words.

6 RICTUS (huge) : HOW THE FUCK SHOULD I KNOW?

5/ Reaction shot from Wesley as he grits his teeth and looks quite feral. Off-panel, he's clearly plunging the knife in here and we get a big spurt of blood right across his face.

7 WESLEY GIBSON : Wrong ANSWER, cock-sucker.

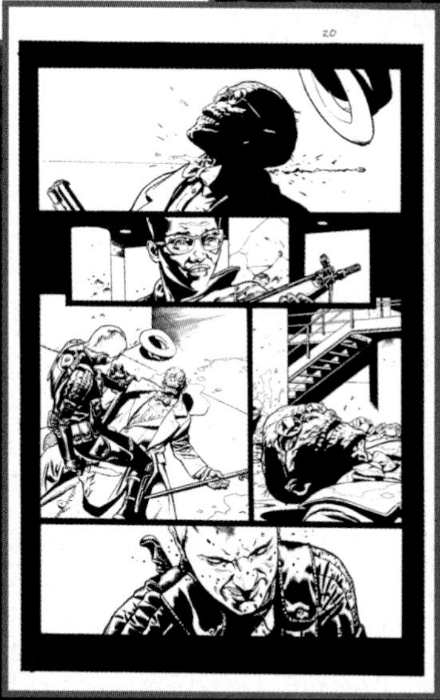
20

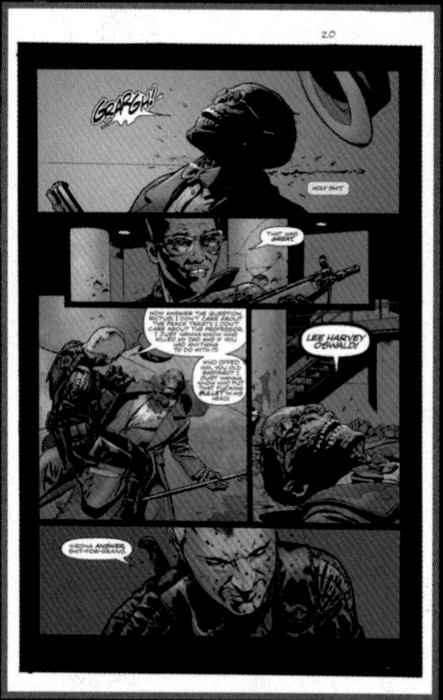
20
GRARGH!
HOLY SHIT!
LEE HARVEY OSWALD!

Also available from Titan Books